THE
FEATHERS AND PLUMAGE
OF BIRDS

BIOLOGY SERIES

GENERAL EDITOR: R. Phillips Dales

*Reader in Zoology in the University of London
at Bedford College*

A HUNDRED YEARS OF EVOLUTION
G. S. Carter

THE BIOLOGY OF THE SEA-SHORE
F. S. Flattely and C. L. Watson

VERTEBRATE ZOOLOGY
G. R. de Beer, F.R.S.

ANIMAL EVOLUTION
G. S. Carter

A GENERAL ZOOLOGY OF THE INVERTEBRATES
G. S. Carter

PARASITISM AND SYMBIOSIS
Maurice Caullery

ANIMAL ECOLOGY
Charles Elton, F.R.S.

THE NATURE OF ANIMAL COLOURS
H. Munro Fox, F.R.S. and H. G. Vevers

In preparation:

EARLY VERTEBRATE EVOLUTION
G. S. Carter

BIOLOGICAL OCEANOGRAPHY
A. J. Southward

PRINCIPLES OF HISTOCHEMISTRY
W. G. Bruce Casselman

THE BIOLOGY OF ESTUARINE ANIMALS
J. Green

RADIOBIOLOGICAL TECHNIQUES IN BIOLOGY
G. Parry Howells

DEVELOPMENTAL GENETICS AND ANIMAL
PATTERNS
K. C. Sondhi

The
Feathers and Plumage
of Birds

A. A. VOITKEVICH

LONDON

UNIVERSITY OF WASHINGTON PRESS

SEATTLE

Originally published in Russian under the title
Pero Ptitsy

Translated by Scripta-Technica

This edition published 1966
© Sidgwick and Jackson 1966

Printed in Great Britain by
William Clowes and Sons, Ltd
London and Beccles
for Sidgwick and Jackson Ltd
1 Tavistock Chambers, Bloomsbury Way
London, W.C.1

CONTENTS

LIST OF ILLUSTRATIONS

LIST OF TABLES

INTRODUCTION

THE birds are pre-eminent among vertebrates by virtue of
their highly differentiated vestiture with its astonishing variety
of structure and colour. The feathers have a complicated structure and development compared with the epidermal derivatives of other vertebrates. The follicles can form feathers of
different types for each skin area, and their arrangement is
precisely determined, the whole pattern forming a coherent
plumage and imparting a range of features indicating the age,
sex, and way of life of the individual.

There are several reasons for the increasing interest shown
by biologists in the development and regeneration of plumage
in birds: above all that of poultry-farming practice. The productivity, rearing, and feeding of farm poultry can be carried
out better with a thorough understanding of the processes of
plumage formation and moulting. This question is important
also in carrier-pigeon breeding, since there is a close correlation between plumage formation and flight capacity. The
natural nesting time of birds, their seasonal migration, and
long-distance flights are correlated with the condition of their
plumage.

Research on plumage formation also has wider implications
in general biology. The plumage of birds plays an important
rôle in thermoregulation, it protects the body against mechanical injury, and is an adaptation for flight. In many species the
seasonal change of plumage during moult leads to replacement by feathers of another type, such as the nuptial plumage
which plays an important rôle in reproduction. Changes in
plumage are accompanied by regeneration of other products
of the epidermis, in particular of the beak and the claws.
Periodic regeneration of the vestiture is a common phenomenon in all vertebrates, and one which has passed through a
long process of evolution. Elucidation of the nature of the

development and periodic regeneration of skin derivatives in vertebrates is therefore of some importance.

The subject to which this book is devoted has a long history. In his *History of Animals* Aristotle described the regeneration of the vestiture in animals and particularly emphasised the seasonal character of moult in birds. The work of Wolff on chick embryos was a starting-point for extensive research on embryonal stages (see Gaisinovich, 1961). The egg of the bird is a convenient object for experiment by the embryologist and has also led to the publication of some morphological studies on plumage.

Detailed investigations on the structure, colouring, development, and replacement of the feathers were carried out in the last century. In addition to numerous purely descriptive reports, these studies included some attempts to analyse experimentally the process of plumage formation. Bogdanov (1858, a, b) provided the first rational explanation for variations in the colouring of birds. L'vov (1887) published a histological study on the basic structure and development of various parts of the feather. These studies, as well as related investigations by Samuel (1870), Studer (1873), Davis (1889), Strong (1902, a, b) and others, led to a generally accepted scheme of plumage development. They studied the specific formation of various structural elements in feathers of different types and established those features which distinguished plumage formation in birds of different species. Subsequent papers provided additional and more detailed data on plumage formation, and clarified some debatable problems of the origin and development of the structural elements of the feather.

Rul'e (1855) collected numerous facts to show the dependence of the colouring of the vestiture in vertebrates, and bird plumage in particular, on environmental conditions. Severtsov (1856) published an unsurpassed survey of the complex dependence on environmental conditions of various periodical phenomena (including moult) in birds and other animals.

Bogdanov wrote the following on the scientific importance of the studies carried out by Severtsov. 'Had this work been published in a language easily accessible to European scientists, whose knowledge of it was based on short abstracts only, it would have made a greater contribution to European orni-thology than a dozen expeditions, however splendid.'

Subsequently, morphological and physiological studies extended and deepened our knowledge of the laws governing the development and periodic renewal (moult) of bird plum-age. The influence of the thyroid hormone, (Zavadovskii, 1923-1927), as well as other hormonal influences, leading to sexual dimorphism in the structure and appearance of the plumage, upon the growth, pigmentation, and regeneration of feathers have been demonstrated experimentally (Goodale, 1914-1918; Pezard, 1912-1928; Zavadovskii, 1922). Larionov and co-workers (1934-55) studied natural moult and regenera-tion of the plumage in various species of domestic and wild birds; their findings provided a basis for the regulation of plumage regeneration. Investigations over the past two decades have led to the differential analysis of the hormonal influences which govern the formation of the finest structures within the feathers and their pigmentation (Juhn, 1933-1958; Lillie, 1931-1956; Willier, 1941-1953).

This book does not aim to cover all the known facts regard-ing plumage formation. Study of the literature and our own experimental investigations have led us to the conclusion that three basic factors emerge from the whole complex of condi-tions and factors influencing feather formation. These are: the *feather-forming tissue,* with its local features, different for each pteryle and even for each individual feather follicle: this morphological aspect with its local physiological features is functionally dependent on regulating factors whose influ-ence extends over the whole animal body; these include, in particular, *neuro-humoral factors,* in the absence of which the feather-forming tissue is unable to fulfill its specific mor-phogenetic function, and in the light of the latest experiments the feather papillae are regarded as special 'receptors' with a selective response to hormones; finally, neuro-humoral regula-tion of the plumage formation process is closely linked with the *environmental factors.*

The character and time of the moult in various species reflect their adaptation to specific living conditions. These processes induced by seasonal changes in the environment have become permanently rhythmic.

Considerable material has been gathered over the past few years on the importance of the nervous system and the hormones secreted by the endocrine glands in various biological processes. In analysis of the rôle played by the nervous system in morphogenesis, the nervous system's importance as a co-ordinating factor ensuring the unity of the organism must be evaluated, as must the system's influence on the function of the endocrine glands and on local physiological processes in the feather-forming tissue itself.

I dedicate this work to the
memory of my friend, the gifted
research worker and experimentor
Evgenii Svetozarov
killed near Voronezh in the war
against the Germans.

A. A. Voitkevich

CHAPTER I

THE STRUCTURE, PIGMENTATION, DEVELOPMENT AND RENEWAL OF PLUMAGE

THE structure of the feather and its variations in different species of birds have been thoroughly investigated in numerous morphological studies by various authors. There are certain laws in the development of feathers with topographical and functional peculiarities. The nature of various plumage colours has been established and the main mechanisms of pigmentation determined. Detailed data have been obtained on the age and seasonal changes in plumage, as well as moulting in birds of different toxonomical position in relation to their ecology. The most recent observations and experiments have consolidated the data on the development of feather structure in connection with the formation of the adaptational pattern of the garb. There have already been numerous reviews by our predecessors in the field which concerns us, including those by N. A. Kholodkovskii and A. A. Silant'ev (1901), M. A. Menzbir (1909), Biedermann (1926-28), Stresemann (1927), Gröbels (1932-36), A. Ya. Tugarinov (1932-41), S. A. Buturlin and G. P. Dement'ev (1934), Vilter (1935), L. M. Shul'pin (1940), G. P. Dement'ev (1940 b), Lillie (1942), V. F. Larionov (1945), O. Heinroth (1947), Willier (1953), Juhre (1959), and Stefanescu, Balasescu and Severin (1961).

Our studies were made predominantly on the contour feathers which form the final (definitive) garb of the bird. It was therefore considered essential to give a preliminary account of the morphology of contour plumage, preceded by a brief description of the primary garb (embryonic down) whose primitive structure has a number of features in common with the definitive plumage. Embryonic down is a peculiar, simplified 'study' for the more complex structure of the definitive feather of an adult bird.

THE PRIMARY FEATHER

The embryonic, otherwise juvenile, down or the primary feather (neoptile), which forms the juvenile garb (neosoptiles) is the bird's first covering which often develops during embryonic life within the egg. There is a correlation between the degree of development of juvenile down and the general differentiation of the bird at the time of hatching (Riddle, 1908a; Rand, 1954; Wetherbee, 1957; Nikitina, 1955; Denisova, 1958; Priklonskii, 1958). The young of the so-called nidicolae group of birds hatch naked or with only sparse down. The differences in the extent of down covering in the nidicolae depend on the ecological conditions: the young of Passeriformes, who nest in the open, have a better developed downy habit than those of birds who nest under cover. The young of the so-called nidifugae group of birds hatch with a well-developed downy garb. Embryonic down is not, as a rule, an independent formation, but represents a modified upper part of the first contour feathers. The feather follicle in the initial phase of development forms the primary down feather; during the following phase it forms the contour feather.

The base of the primary feather is formed by a small cylindrical barrel from which several (8-12) primary barbs branch out, carrying softer secondary barbs. In many waterfowl the barbs are attached to a primitive shaft which brings this structure close to the organisation of some definitive feathers. The primary barbs of embryonic down have common structural features with the barbs of the definitive feather (especially in its downy part); they consist of two types of cells which form the inner and the outer parts of the barb. The cells which form the secondary radii (barbs) are arranged in a single row, their dimensions decreasing gradually as they become more distal to the primary barb. There are slight thickenings at the points of cell junction. The embryonic down is pigmented in some birds; in some nidifugae the uneven distribution of pigmentation leads to a primitive plumage pattern. Pigmentation of embryonic feathers also occurs in birds whose definitive plumage lacks the corresponding pigment (white pelicans).

During early development (varying from species to species, but usually on the fourth to seventh day of embryonic life) the germ of the embryonic feather resembles the germ of reptilian scales (L'vov, 1887); Gadow, 1891; Riddle, 1908 a, b; Vilter, 1935). It consists of a small aggregate of mesenchymal cells covered by a thin layer of epidermis. The epidermal cells divide intensively and form an envelope over the rapidly enlarging mesenchymal papilla. The subsequent growth of such a feather germ combines with the gradual sinking of the germ and the tissues adjacent to it into the deeper layers of the skin. The two processes directed in opposite senses (the sinking of the germ within the skin and its progressive growth) result in the formation of the feather follicle whose walls are formed by areas of epidermis which are directly continuous with the envelope of the germ. The young feather quill increases in size principally through the multiplication of the cells which constitute the base of the epithelial cylinder, in its generative zone. The progressive growth of the quill occurs in association with the progressive differentiation of its apical part. The formation of the structural elements of the feather takes place at the expense of epithelial cells whose behaviour is different at different sites. The superficial cell layer, which corresponds to the stratum corneum, becomes very flattened and gradually cornifies, carrying with it part of the cellular material from the deeper layers, to form a thin transparent feather integument; the latter then separates from the deep layers of the stratum germinativum, whose cells differentiate relatively slowly and form the basic structural elements of the feather.

The main distinctive feature of the organisation of the primary feather in many birds is the radial laying down of the barbs. The barbs of the embryonic feather are formed from epithelial cells. These cells are unequal in size, the largest one lying closest to the papilla. The common feature in the organisation of primary epithelial folds—ridges, is the graduated size of their constituent cells, which decrease from the centre towards the periphery. In each primary epithelial fold the central part is occupied by larger cells which later form the primary barb. The cells which are arranged in regular rows along the periphery of the fold form the second-ary barbs, which are attached in a definite sequence and with strict geometrical orientation with respect to the primary barb. Later both categories of cells undergo elongation com-bined with progressive cornification (keratinisation); both these processes first involve the apical part of the feather quill —the upper parts of the barbs, i.e. the areas which had been laid down earlier in time.

Cornification is preceded by vacuolation of the cytoplasm and mutual compression of the cells which are directly con-cerned in the formation of each barb. The process of keratini-sation fixes, as it were, the permanent structure of an ex-tremely dynamic formation, whose cells had acquired a multi-faceted shape by mutual compression. The rate of growth of the different radially arranged areas of the epithelial part of the feather quill is not uniform. It is highest in the peripheral parts (in the region of the outer feather integument) and relatively insignificant in those parts which are directly adja-cent to the papilla. The apices of the primary barbs being formed are attached to the inner surface of the integument and this explains their intensive elongation and curvature during growth. The general direction of cornification in the feather quill represents, as it were, the resultant of two vec-tors: from the distal parts of the feather which arise early on to the proximal ones (apical—basal direction) and at the same time, from the peripheral to the central parts of the epidermal integument.

When cornification has reached the base of the barbs a short barrel begins to be formed gradually, the bases of the barbs being attached to its upper portion. The formation of a primary feather does not in all cases terminate with the forma-tion of a small barrel, but frequently, as already mentioned by Menzbir (1909), the downy barbs continue directly into the vane barbs or the shaft of the next contour feather. This link between two generations proves to be so close that the primary down is pushed out by the growing contour feathers, remaining for some time attached to the ends of the definitive feather barbs. In some birds the embryonic down is anchored directly in the skin. In these cases the completion of the development and growth of embryonic feathers coincides with the laying down of the feather germs of the nestling (juvenile) plumage.

The replacement of the primary down by the juvenile plumage occurs at different times in different birds. In some, for example water-fowl, the primary down is retained for a very long time during post-embryonic life, whilst in others, for example Megapadius freycinnti, it is lost still within the egg, so that the young hatch in contour plumage.

THE PERMANENT (DEFINITIVE) FEATHER

Structure

The organisation and microscopic structure of the definitive feather have been thoroughly investigated (Clement, 1876; Strong, 1902, a, b; Riddle, 1907, 1908, b; Miller, 1937; Sick, 1937; Auber and Appleyard, 1955).

The permanent feathers (teleoptiles) which form the definitive vestiture of birds can be divided into three groups: The contour feathers (*pennae*), the down feathers (*plumae*) and the hairlike filoplumes (*filoplumae*). We should also mention the special tactile bristles (*vibrissae*) which grow on the skin of the head. Ornithologists distinguish an intermediate group, the so-called half-down feathers (*semiplumae*) in the vestiture of some birds, particularly nocturnal ones.

The contour feathers (for example, the large feathers on the wings and the tail—the flight or helm feathers) have a central shaft (*scapus*) which has finer branches on either side. These form a solid elastic vane or web (*vexillum*), or more precisely two symmetrically arranged halves, the outer and inner vanes. The proximal part of the shaft, the so-called barrel (*calamus*) is a hollow cylinder with an indentation (*umbilicus inferior*) at its base. This indentation contains the quiescent anlage of the feather for the next generation. The shaft tapers distally to form the rachis, which has a rectangular cross-section, unlike the calamus, which is circular or oval in cross-section. Where the calamus passes into the rachis there is a further indentation on the lower surface of the rachis. This is the upper navel (*umbilicus superior*), from which a furrow runs to the tip of the rachis. The inner surface of the upper navel sometimes contains the aftershaft (*hypo-rachis*) of an accessory feather; in the cassowaries these are the same size as the main rachis. The external surface of the rachis as well as that of the whole feather is convex along its short and long axes.

From the superior umbilicus, nearer the outer surface, the sides of the rachis carry the first-order barbs (*rami*). These are arranged symmetrically, and consecutively form the silky (proximal), the fluffy (middle), and the contour (upper or distal part) of the vane (Fig. 1). There is much variation in the extent of the contour and of the fluffy parts, according to the site and functional destination of the feather. Generally speaking, the fluffy feathers on a bird's body are covered by the contour parts of adjacent feathers.

In the permanent feathers the first-order barbs carry the second-order barbs (radii), symmetrically arranged, which in turn carry the third-order barbs (hamulae) or elongated hair-like processes (cilia).

The rudimentary condition of the second-order barbs is typical for the proximal silky part of the vane. In the fluffy part of the vane the first-order barbs have well-developed radii; these, however, lack the third order barbs, the cilia or hamuli. The presence of third-order barbs is typical for the contour part of the vane. The contour part is formed by first-order elastic barbs which gradually become thinner and lie symmetrically on the rachis. They carry second-order barbs. The upper row of these have the hamuli mentioned above. These hamuli cover the adjacent barbs of the next radius, which has no hamuli, and ensure coherence of the parallel-barbs system and hence coherence of the vane as a whole. The structure and number of the hamuli is constant for each bird species; many ornithologists regard them as species-specific features.

The cells which form the rachis of the feather and the first-order barbs are of three types, arranged in clearly discernible layers. These are: (1) the surface layer (*cuticula*); (2) the

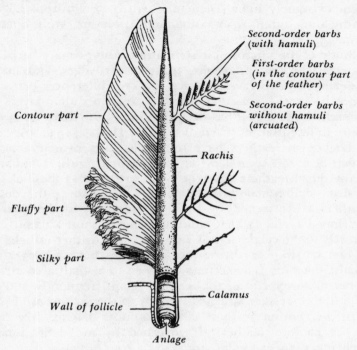

Second-order barbs
(with hamuli)

First-order barbs
(in the contour part
of the feather)

Second-order barbs
without hamuli
(arcuated)

Contour part

Rachis

Fluffy part

Silky part

Calamus

Wall of follicle

Anlage

Fig. 1. Schematic structure of a contour feather

cortical layer (*substantia fibrosa*); and (3) the medullar layer
(*substantia medullaris*). Klein (1949), Kelso (1952), Driesen
(1955), and Bruge (1956) have studied these layers, using
phase-contrast, ultraviolet, and ordinary microscopes, and discovered a wide range of cytological variations for each of the
three types of keratinised cell.

The cuticula is formed by keratinised squamous epithelium and surrounds the cortical layer beneath it as a thin
transparent membrane. It is well developed on the calamus
and on the outer surface of the rachis in the contour feathers.

The cortical layer consists of densely packed fusiform or
strongly flattened cells (Auber, 1955).

The medullar layer is formed by multiangular cells of
varying size, which have air filled cavities. This feature endows
the feathers with great resilience and at the same time makes

them extremely light (Dement'ev, 1940, b; Philipp, Lagermann, and Graten, 1950; Auber and Appleyard, 1951; Shestakova, 1953).

Study of the microscopic structure of the primary barbs in pigeons, chicken, pheasants, turkeys, partridges, and many passeriform birds revealed such marked differences between the cells in the cuticular, cortical, and medullar layers of different birds that it has been possible to use them for systematic differentiation (Chandler, 1916; Hosker, 1936, b).

The down feathers have numerous long primary barbs, which bear soft secondary barbs without hamuli. The barbs of the down feathers have the same structure as those of the primary embryonal down feather. The barbs of the down feathers are attached by their bases either to the poorly-developed rachis, which continues into a short calamus, or directly to the calamus sunk into the small feather follicle.

The hairlike or threadlike filoplumes have a very thin rachis; the vane is sometimes confined to a small area at the upper or lower end of the feather, but is frequently absent. The filoplumes are attached directly to the skin or are fused with the contour feathers. The filoplume placing, like that of the contour feathers, is governed by well-defined laws (Fehringer, 1912; Pfeffer, 1952).

There are other epidermal formations homologous to the common feathers but of more limited importance. These include the brushlike feathers in the region surrounding the coccygeal gland, which perform the function of wicks, becoming abundantly impregnated with the oily or waxy secretions of the gland. It is interesting that in birds without coccygeal glands, such as goatsuckers and herons the protection of the plumage against moisture has been taken over by modified feathers which, together, form the so-called 'powder puff'. They are confined to certain areas—the chest or the region above the tail. When the bird's beak presses on them they disintegrate into fine particles and are then transferred to the surface of the plumage.

Before describing the development of the permanent contour feathers some problems of terminology require discussion since some authors refer to different formations by the same name.

When using the term 'feather-forming tissue' we refer to the system of all the morphological elements in the skin which contribute towards formation of new feathers, as well as to the sum of their physiological features, particularly those which emerge in response to neuro-hormonal influences.

The 'feather follicle" is a part of the feather-forming tissue, including the preformed anlage of the feather, the feather bag, and the adjacent parts of the dermal connective tissue.

The feather 'anlage' (referred to by some authors as 'feather embryo') is a complex formation consisting of a mesenchymal (connective tissue) papilla covered by an epithelial sheath; the anlage is initially formed during the period of embryonal development.

As soon as the growth of a feather is completed, the anlage of a new feather is formed within a spherical indentation at the base of the calamus, the *umbilicus inferior*.

The 'feather papilla', i.e. the mesenchymal connective-tissue part of the anlage, is richly vascularised and undergoes intensive growth during the development of the young feather. Some authors call this papilla, together with the covering epithelial sheath, the 'blastema' of the feather, trying to draw a parallel between the renewal of the plumage and the reparative regeneration process. In our opinion this is not justified, as there are important differences between the development of the feather and the phenomena of reparative regeneration. These differences are particularly clear in that the development of a new feather usually begins from a preformed anlage which has been in a state of rest for a prolonged period. The regenerative blastema which develops on amputation surfaces represents a transitory dynamic formation in the morphogenetic process, and its morphological organisation persists for only a limited period. One can hardly equate a formation which develops immediately after the amputation of an organ with a preformed resting anlage of a new feather which subsequently develops into a feather of predetermined shape and structure.

We shall show below that after the removal of an immature feather the development of a new feather is preceded by the formation of a feather anlage. We are here justified in drawing an analogy with the reparative regeneration process, as in this case the injured area had not been previously 'prepared' for the formation of a regenerate despite possessing a regenerative potential.

'The germinative or generative zone'—the matrix—consists of an area at the base of the feather anlage (later at the base of the feather shaft) which is formed by a complex of ring-placed epithelial cells capable of intensive multiplication.

The 'feather shaft' is a formation which develops from the anlage and persists from the first phase of growth until the development of the distal vane; it is richly vascularised and hyperaemic. From the moment the vane has opened we no longer speak of a 'feather shaft' but of a young or immature feather.

The 'feather sheath' is a layer of flattened squamous keratinised epidermal cells which covers the shaft and is later destroyed in the distal area when the vane begins to develop.

The 'feather bag' is formed by a thin layer of epidermis (sometimes referred to as the 'wall of the feather follicle') which penetrates deeply into the corium during embryonal development. The epithelial borders of the bag are well defined, but the outlines of the connective tissue part are less distinct.

The 'regeneration of the feather' refers to the development of a new feather after removal or destruction of the immature preceding feather. This term is somewhat unfortunate but convenient for the discussion, as opposed to the development of new feathers from a preformed anlage during the natural moult. The term regeneration, i.e. restoration or removal, should not be used for the development of a feather from a preformed anlage, as this represents only continued development.

Development

As we have said above, the development of the permanent feather is preceded by the formation of the feather anlage. The latter lies in a groove at the base of the calamus of its predecessor and remains in a resting state until activated naturally at the time of moult, or artificially by removal of the preceding feather.

The first generation of permanent feathers develops from feather rudiments arising from the calami of the embryonal down feathers. Their time of formation and rate of development varies considerably from one species to another. The development of the permanent feathers from the pteriles begins in chickens during the embryonal period, in pigeons several days after hatching, and in ducks not until they are a few weeks old.

Let us now deal with the morphology of the feather anlage and the development of the contour feather. A number of histological studies have been published in this field and the reader may be referred to the descriptive and experimental papers by Studer (1873, 1878), Klee (1886), L'vov (1887), Davis (1899), Biedermann (1926-28), Rakhmanov and Voznaya (1932), Lillie (1932-44), Wilter (1935), Frieling (1936 a, b), Peredel'skii (1941), Troitskii (1948), as well as to our own observations (Voitkevich, 1947).

As already mentioned, the feather anlage consists of a connective-tissue papilla (*pulpa*) and an epithelial sheath which is a protrusion from the bottom of the feather bag. The epithelial cells in the anlage are of varying size and structure; they are arranged in several layers in which the flattened cells of the outer layer show signs of incipient keratinisation. The cells of the connective-tissue papilla are arranged in two zones, an upper zone with loosely arranged flattened cells, and a lower zone (the site of which corresponds to that of the matrix) with more densely grouped round cells.

When a mature feather is plucked the underlying feather anlage may be injured. In this case the formation of a new anlage will be different from the development observed during a natural moult. Plucking mature feathers generally leads to injuries to the resting anlage in the period preceding the moult or during the actual moult (particularly in ducks), when the rudimentary feathers begin to grow before the old feathers have fallen out. We have never observed damage to the anlage when birds are plucked in any other season. The anlage is protected against mechanical injury during the falling-out of the old feathers by its own elasticity and by a covering of several layers of keratinised cells.

In the early stages of development considerable changes

take place in the anlage and in the surrounding tissues. Proliferation may be observed within a few hours of activation of the anlage. At this stage there are changes in the growth of the cellular material of the basal part of the anlage, particularly in the germinative zone. Early stages of development see intensive proliferation of the connective-tissue papilla (*pulpa*), increased blood supply, and progressive growth. At the peak of development the weight of the vascularised papilla is on the average three times that of the fully developed feather. The total weight of the pulpas in all feathers subject to moult is a quarter of the bird's total body weight (Lillie, 1940). In the pulpa of the feather shaft an extremely fast rate of growth may be observed in the extensive sinusoid capillary network, which forms a regular geometrical pattern in the peripheral parts of the pulpa and is frequently in contact with the epithelial substrate of the developing feather. Goff (1949) studied the vascular system in the connective tissue components of the feather anlage and of the feather shafts in whole body preparations by means of micro-injections of Neutral red. The rapid development of the network of peripheral blood vessels, which lie at the periphery of the papilla and come together as a common central vessel at its apex, keeps pace with the growth of the anlage. Because the capillaries do not enter the epithelial cylinder of the feather shaft, it follows that all parts of the developing feather receive their nutrients by means of diffusion (Peska, 1927; Saunders, 1950). The increase in vascularisation is matched by the formation of new nerve fibres which grow into the feather papilla. It should here be mentioned that in addition to the subepithelial nerve plexus, which spreads out under the epithelium, there are special nerves which wind round the feather pocket and branch directly into the papilla of the developing feather (Rakhmanov and Voznaya, 1932).

The structure and development of the embryonal down plumage and the permanent contour feathers have many features in common, but also some important differences. The sequence of vestitures during the individual development of birds partly reflects the common phylogenetic rule of transition from a radial to a bilaterally symmetrical arrangement of the component structures. Radial symmetry is typical of the structure of embryonal down plumage and bilateral symmetry of the structure of the permanent contour feather. A peculiar 'polarisation' may be observed in the initial stages of development of the contour feathers, and this applies to the activation of pulpa cells as well as to changes in the epithelial components of the anlage. The component structures of the feather grow more rapidly in the dorsal part of the feather shaft where the calamus is formed. Growth is less active in the ventral part of the shaft, and this explains the formation of bilateral contour feathers.

The developing feather shaft is a cylinder which thins towards its distal end and grows rapidly both in length and thickness. In step with the growth of the shaft, the upper layer of the epidermis thickens, owing to the intensive multiplication of flattened keratinised surface cells which form the external keratinised sheath. The upper part of this keratinised sheath of the feather shaft is usually destroyed simultaneously with the formation of the vane. Local denervation interferes with both processes, and so do some avitaminoses and hereditary disorders. Hutt and Long (1950) studied mutations of this type.

The layer of keratinised cells which usually covers the feather anlage and the wall of the feather follicle, gradually becomes desquamated, thus ensuring the free sliding of the soft shaft between the elastic walls of the follicle. Later the shaft pushes the mass of keratinised cells out of the follicle.

Even before the apex of the shaft appears on the skin surface, clear signs of morphological differentiation may be observed in histological preparations, this process culminating in the keratinisation of the tips of the barbs in the apical part of the shaft.

Microscopically the following three zones can be discerned in a young shaft where the apex grew beyond the opening of the follicles. (1) An undifferentiated or germinative zone or matrix, in the lower part of which intensive proliferation and growth may be observed, and above which there is (2) a zone of differentiation in which the cells acquire a number of new features and are arranged in a corresponding order, and (3) the zone of keratinisation which extends over the remaining

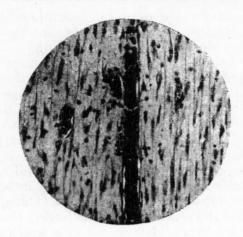

Fig. 2. The structure of the upper part of a feather papilla: elongated fibroblastlike cells with numerous processes; well developed network of blood vessels (× 280).

upper part of the shaft. In the lower part of this zone the epithelial cells are thickened, and the pulpa cells are vacuolised; in the upper part, the epidermal cells are fully keratinised and the connective-tissue cells undergo necrosis (Fig. 2).

The development of the contour feathers passes through a number of stages. Soon after the anlage has begun to grow, and before the cells of the external feather sheath show the first signs of keratinisation, the initial rearrangement of epithelial cells (preceded by numerous cell divisions) can be seen in the upper part of the epidermal cylinder. Initially the cells are arranged in radial folds or crests similar to the process described for the embryonal-down plumage. In each of these primary folds the cells are further divided into three layers: a central layer and two marginal layers.

In addition to the marginal layers, further rows of cells form within each of these folds; these cells subsequently form the second-order barbs. The formation of the barbs begins in a plane which lies perpendicular to the main longitudinal axis of the shaft. Later, the outer ends of the barbs begin to bend upwards. The external feather sheath plays a special rôle in the simultaneous processes of bending and elongation of the barbs. The growth of the sheath outstrips that of all other epidermal parts in the young shaft. The first-order barbs do not form simultaneously; their full development is preceded by the differentiation of the second-order barbs from cells which lie in the central area of the primary epithelial fold. As a result of their multiplication and subsequent differentiation the cells form a column to which the bases of the second-order barbs are attached. The cells of the first-order barbs become differentiated in two ways during development. They form two different layers: an external cortical one with very flat, massive, elongated cells, and an internal medullar layer formed by large cells which become multi-angular owing to mutual compression during keratinisation.

The peak of the young stub appears above the skin surface before formation of the shaft. The upper and other parts of the shaft form differently. In the upper part of the stub the initial differentiation somewhat resembles the development of the embryonal feather: in both cases the cells are arranged radially. The formation of the shaft differs from that of any of the barbs. It originates from a large number of cells in two symmetrically arranged zones on the dorsal surface of the young stub.

The formation of the shaft is closely connected with the development of the first-order barbs. Initially, the first-order barbs appear as epithelial folds or crests, but only in the dorsal part of the young stub. Later, they begin to form on both sides of the ventral side of the shaft and finally also on it. A cross-section at any level above the matrix reveals evenly distributed epithelial crests surrounding the stub. The formation of the first-order barbs and their gradual change in position are connected with shaft development. A cross-section through the developing stub, slightly below the level where the bases of the barbs are formed, shows the arrangement of the material destined to form the future shaft. Its formation and the primary differentiation of the cells destined to form the barbs begin at the same level, in a plane perpendicular to the longitudinal axis of the feather stub. The shaft which forms on the dorsal side of the stub, by the coalescence of two formerly separate folds, carries some of the cells which are a common source of origin for the shaft and the barb bases. Together with the movement of the epithelial cells to the dorsal surface. the peaks of an increasing number of new barbs form in the

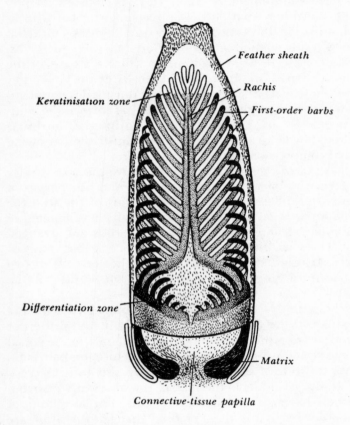

Fig. 3. Development of the feather shaft (partly from data by Vil'ter)

ventral region of the shaft. Fig. 3 seeks to convey a spatial conception of this sequence of events.

If the dorsal and ventral halves of the anlage of different feathers are joined by autotransplantation, the results will vary according to the source of the material used. Lillie and Wang (1944) have shown that the transplantation of a fragment from the dorsal part of the anlage into the ventral region of another anlage leads to the development of a double feather with a common stem. The same can be achieved by a longitudinal incision into the dorsal region, i.e. the tissue destined to form the rachis. Transplantation of the ventral half did not lead to similar results but produced, in some cases, an increase in the size of the vane in the recipient.

The continuous and rapid growth of the shaft helps one to gain a more precise conception of the dynamic character of the structural development of the feather. As soon as the structural elements in the upper part of the shaft become differentiated (where the anlage of the rachis is of the same size as that of the barbs), an annular differentiation zone appears among the epithelial cells in the lower parts of the shaft. In the dorsal region, the cellular ring becomes elongated upwards, its walls joining at an angle to form the rachis. A cross-section through the young shaft shows how, at various distances from the rachis, the different parts of the barbs become consecutively differentiated. The peaks of the barbs are formed furthest from the rachis (ventral region); the more proximal parts of the barbs are formed nearest the rachis. Consequently, any cross-section through a young shaft shows different parts of the primary barbs in a specific order.

The barbs and the rachis develop in a very similar manner. The cells differentiate into two layers, different in location and structure (medullar and cortical layers). The arrangement and shape of the cells in the cortical layer vary according to the part of the feather: on the dorsal side the cells are smaller, flattened, and show a more compact arrangement than on the ventral side. The medullar layer is formed by large inflated cells with thick walls. Keratin granules fill the intercellular space.

The development of the lower part of the feather—the fluffy part of the calamus—differs from that of the upper part, the vane. As soon as the development of the vane is complete, the feather grows much more slowly. This can perhaps be explained by the special histogenesis of the lower part of the feather. The epithelial folds in this region (anlage of the down barbs) are typically arranged strictly parallel to the longitudinal axis of the shaft. This is similar to the formation of barbs in the stiff part of the vane. Development is very similar to that of the anlage and to the further development of the embryonal down-feathers. The number of cells in the anlage of the down-feather barbs can be almost three times as great as the number of cells in the contour part of the same feather. The epithelial cells which form the down-feather barbs reach the keratinisation zone with some delay, as the feather grows more slowly at this stage. Also typical of the development of the fluffy part is the elongation of the cells within the barbs (5-10 and more times the original length). As each barb becomes longer, its diameter becomes less, owing to the elongation of the constituent cells. The fully developed barb is several times longer than its original anlage.

During the formation of the rachis base and of the vane, the relative proportion of material participating in the formation of the quill and of the barbs respectively changes increasingly in favour of the quill. In the preceding period two folds form on the ventral surface of the growing rachis and penetrate deeper and deeper into the connective tissue of the shaft papilla. Later, at the point of transition into the quill, the epithelial folds unite and divide the papilla obliquely into upper and lower parts. The lower part is preserved and continues to function as long as the feather continues to grow. Degeneration begins only when growth is complete. The upper part of the papilla, however, atrophies from progressive ischaemia, dries up, and finally is shed completely. This action coincides in time with the end of barb formation. There is also a marked decrease in the number of peripheral blood vessels in the pulpa of the young feather (Goff, 1949). Later again, the remnant of the totally degenerate and desiccated papilla falls off, together with the horny sheath. The point where the two epithelial folds unite remains visible on the fully developed feather as a small indentation at the vane base (upper navel or *umbilicus superior*).

Changes in the differentiation of the cellular material forming the quill are brought about by separation of the lower part of the papilla by the epithelial folds. The quill is formed only of cortical-layer cells. The keratinization of the cells in the quill, which here too moves from the peripheral to the inner layers and from the upper to the lower parts, is followed by the gradual descent of the papilla and its epithelial cover. As the upper parts of the papilla become necrotic, the inner epithelial sheath changes correspondingly: the cells of its external layer become more closely packed and finally change into keratinised flakes. The 'retreat' of the papilla, combined with the desiccation of the upper parts, takes place stepwise. This leads to the formation of a series of transparent and mutually connected cylinders known as the pith of the quill. The intermittent character of this regressive process leads to the formation of a number of isolated chambers which protect the live parts of the papilla against any injury affecting the developed parts of the feather. Its development completed, the feather loses all vascular and nervous connections and becomes physiologically isolated from the rest of the body. The process of differentiation which leads to keratinisation begins from the peripheral and upper parts of the shaft and progresses towards the centre and base of the feather. The proliferating cellular material grows in the opposite direction—from the central parts towards the periphery and from the base upwards, resulting in the continuous growth of the shaft. The formation of the different parts of the feather takes place consecutively. In every part of the feather, but particularly in the annular zone of intensive growth and initial differentiation, the secondary barbs are formed first, then the primary barbs and finally the rachis. Thus it appears that there are marked differences between the development of the upper and lower parts of the definitive feather. The upper part of the vane, which phylogenetically is the oldest structure in the vesture of birds, develops like the primary embryonal-down feathers. The formation of the phylogenetically younger upper part of the feather (the firm part of the vane) obeys different laws, and would be described as an 'anabolic' phenomenon by Severtsov (1939).

The full development of the quill, the degeneration of the connective-tissue papilla and the formation of the pith all coincide in time with the formation of the anlage of a feather of the next generation. It is assumed that the new anlage is formed from the lower and inner parts of the epithelial and connective-tissue elements of the old feather. We have shown, however, that the anlage develops from new elements which accumulate at the base of the feather follicle when the lower parts of the quill become keratinised and the old papilla necrotic (Voitkevich, 1936, d, 1938, a).

All authors are agreed on the origin of the connective-tissue papilla (pulpa) of the new feather anlage. The growth of the base parts of the pulpa and the simultaneous reduction of the apical parts ensures a constant size for the pulpa throughout development of the feather (Lillie, 1940). Study of histological sections shows that degeneration of the old primary papilla begins with phagocytosis and ends with complete atrophy. The peak of the new papilla is in contact with the epithelial cap. The wall of this cap thickens and forms the matrix. The horny membrane which forms the upper navel of the quill tightly encloses the new feather anlage, separating it from the developed feather and preventing its further growth by mechanical restriction.

Whenever the growth of a feather is completed, over many generations of feathers which develop in the lifetime of a bird, a new anlage is immediately formed.

In every feather anlage the structural elements develop from its epithelial part. The connective-tissue papilla, which ensures supply of nutrients for the developing feather, lessens in size as the feather grows. When growth is complete, a new anlage is formed. Different feathers of the definitive vesti-ture show appreciable variations in the relative size of the contour (stiff) and fluffy parts of the vane. Two types of feather can be distinguished: some with a well-developed fluffy section and others with it poorly developed or completely absent.

The qualities of a feather are determined by a number of properties. These include the elasticity, the loose texture of the fluffy part, the small relative density—features which vary from one species to another. In this respect the trunk feathers of aquatic birds such as geese and ducks have the best properties. Goose feathers are the fluffiest and have the smallest relative density, since the medullar layer has the most porous texture, the cortical layer being rather dense. This ensures a greater elasticity (Svetozarov and Straikh, 1939). The same bird has different types of feathers: the juvenile feather is less well developed than those of the definitive plumage. In those species which moult twice a year the winter vestiture is of higher quality than the summer vestiture.

PIGMENTS

Pigments play an important part in the formation of vestiture patterns in birds; they are found not only in the feathers but also in the skin, in the spur scales, in the beak, and in various appendages on the head. Pigments also occur in the membranes surrounding various organs and tissues, such as the periosteum, the epimysium, and the perimysium of Dungan (Turkestan) hens, and in the testicular membrane in some passeriform birds. Pigment is found in the secretions of various glands; it is excreted, for example, by the glandular wall of the oviduct (eggshell) in females of many species.

The presence of pigment, its quantity, and its shade do not represent constant features for either the plumage or other skin derivatives subject to certain seasonal changes (Witschi and Woods, 1936; Tucker, 1949; Jaap, 1955).

The presence of pigment in the skin does not necessarily coincide with its occurrence in the internal organs; various and even completely opposed combinations may be observed. Pigment may occur in the skin and in the internal organs (Hustman, Jerome, and Snyder, 1959), or only in the skin, or, conversely, in various organs, combined with an albino plumage. The latter case is typical for the race of Dungan hens (Vudzhi) mentioned above.

There are wide variations in plumage colour. No other vertebrates have the enormous range of vestiture colours and shades that birds have in their plumage. The colouring differences not only help us to distinguish various species but are also typical of various parts of the vestiture of an individual bird—such as feathers belonging to different pterylae—or even for various parts of the vane on the same feather. Nevertheless, this colour variety is the result of various combinations of a relatively small number of pigments and of changes in the surface structure of the cortical layers in different feathers.

The first to study bird-plumage pigmentation in detail was the zoologist Bogdanov (1856, 1858, a, b). His studies are still important today. Bogdanov opposed the previously firmly-

established view that plumage colouring depended only on
the structure of the feather. He showed that the plumage
colour depended on the presence of pigments in the feather.
In *The Colouring of the Bird's Feather* he described the chemical and physical properties of various pigments, and their biological importance, and put forward the first classification.

Similar studies were later carried out by Fatio (1866),
Gadow (1882), Aerby (1855), Suermann (1889), Post (1894),
and Rabl (1894). These authors showed that the colouring of
the plumage depends on the distribution of the pigment and
described the changes in the colouring associated with feather
development. Pigmentation development was later studied in
greater detail by Strong (1902a, 1915, 1917), Spöttel (1914),
Schultz (1916), Giersberg (1923), Görnitz (1923), Glasewald
(1926), Greite (1931), Kawamura (1933), Caridroit and Regnier (1934), Sarasin (1934), Dorst (1950, 1951), and Rawles
(1955).

The pigments differ in their origin, in the colour they provide, and in their distribution within the feather (Kölliker,
1887; Haecker, 1890; Götz, 1925). The most important pigment (and phylogenetically the oldest*) is melanin, which is
present in the cytoplasm of special stellate chromatophores
or melanophores (melanocytes). These cells are highly active
during feather development, and deposit pigment as spheroid
or bacilliform granules into the keratinised substrate of
the feather. It should be said here that the presence of a
chromatophore in a developing feather is not always accompanied by the formation and deposition of pigment granules.
The pigment cells are frequently regarded as an independent
third structural element of the feather anlage (in addition to
the epithelial cap and the mesenchyma of the pulpa).

The second type of pigment, the lipochromes, are characterised by their diffuse distribution within the cell. The physical
and chemical properties of both types of pigment have been
described in detail in the publications by Bogdanov mentioned above and also in papers by Kniesche (1914), Götz
(1925), Steinbacher (1931), Völker (1937-51), and Driesen
(1953).

---

* i.e. predominating in most primitive birds.—*Ed.*

Melanin pigments

The melanins are present in various parts of the vane and the barrel, and give the feather a black, reddish-brown, brown, or yellow colour, the shade of which is determined by the character and partly by the number of granules (Khvatova, 1948). It should be emphasized that a bright yellow or ochre colour is more frequently produced by lipochromes than by melanin. Oxidation of the same substance, a propigment, leads to development of different variations of melanin (Mason, 1948). Pigment intensity depends on the activity of the oxidative processes within the bird's body (Groody and Groody, 1942; Smyth, Porter, and Bohren, 1951). Melanin within the feather occurs in two closely related forms, as eumelanin and phaeomelanin, two varients of the same propigment. Both types of melanin develop, always as granules, in the cytoplasm of special pigment cells, the melanophores, and may occur in all structural elements of the feather. Eumelanin granules are usually rod-shaped (0.5-1.2μ) and when present in large quantities produce a dark colour. Phaeomelanin occurs in the shape of spheroid or ovoid granules of smaller size than those of eumelanin, and produce a colouring which varies from rusty brown to pale yellow when the granules are smallest. Dorris (1938) has shown that the process of melanin synthesis begins with the formation of small yellow granules, which become larger and simultaneously dark brown or black. This author assumes that the intensity of the colour depends on the stage at which oxidation of tyrosin ends.

Eumelanin most frequently predominates in the upper part of the barbs, phaeomelanin in the lower. Phaeomelanin is soluble in alkali and can be extracted with cold 0.25 per cent NaOH solution. Those feathers or parts of feathers which contain melanin are more resilient and less subject to wear than the unpigmented feathers. There is, however, no evidence to support the view that the resilience of the feather directly depends only on the quantity of the pigment present. It seems that wherever pigment granules accumulate in different parts of the feather, the quantity of viscous keratinised substance present also increases, and it is this substance which endows the feather with greater resilience.

Electron microscope investigations of feathers have shown that melanin (particularly phaeomelanin) granules are complex secondary structures composed of extremely small primary structures, the so-called primary granules. The secondary granules are freely scattered over the keratinised substrate or lie on a membrane of tonofibrils. This results in an overall effect of various iridescent shades (Philip, Langermalen, and Gralen, 1950; Mattern, 1956; Schmidt and Puska, 1961).

The origin of the pigment cells has long been disputed. Some authors have believed that the melanophores are connective-tissue cells, others have regarded them as epithelial formations. It has even been conceded that they might originate from both sources. A number of authors (Khvatov, 1935, a, b; Dorris, 1936, 1938, 1939; Lopashov, 1945; Nickerson, 1944, 1946; Khvatova, 1948) have assumed that the melanoblasts, which later acquire the capacity to produce pigment, are formed at an early embryonal stage from the cells of the nerve ridge, after closure of the neural tube, that is, from the elements of the so-called ectomesenchyme.

In the resting feather anlage the melanophores lie in the connective-tissue papilla close to the inner surface of the epithelial sheath. During the development of the feather and the proliferation of the papilla (pulpa) the melanophores, or rather their processes, which contain the melanin granules, come into close contact with the epithelial cells.

Melanoblasts are found in the skin and in the feather anlage of all birds, independently of their colouring, even in albinos (Hanson, 1949; Nachtsheim, 1957). *In vitro* culture of tissue from the feather papillae of white-hen races has shown that the papillae contain melanoblasts capable of differentiation and of pigment production in certain conditions (Cock and Cohen 1958; Cohen 1959). At the base of the papilla of each feather follicle there is a 'reserve' of melanoblasts, part of which is transformed into melanocytes during the further development of the feather. This reserve is replenished by cell division and partly by migration of melanoblasts from the surrounding corium.

Each time a new generation of feathers develops, a part of the melanoblasts is used up. Transplantation of embryonal skin—in particular from the wing region (Eastlick, 1938, 1939, a, b)—as well as mutual homo- and hetero-transplantation of coelomic epithelium into the skin of the wing anlage and *vice versa* (Rawles and Willier, 1939; Rawles, 1940 a, b, 1944, 1945) led to similar results. The melanoblasts may preserve their embryonal features for a prolonged period, and do not then form pigment (Ris, 1941; Willier, 1941; Trinkaus, 1952). Only under certain physiological conditions can the melanoblasts be transformed into melanocytes and begin to form pigment granules (Faulkner, 1932; Hays, White, and Sanborn, 1948; Hutt, 1953). If the conditions for this transformation and for the subsequent invasion of the epithelial structures by melanophores are not present, the feather will remain unpigmented, i.e. white. If corium tissue or tissue from the feather pulpa of albino birds is added to tissue cultures of melanoblasts, it will inhibit the differentiation of these cells into melanocytes. Isolated melanocytes, containing melanin, are present in the embryonal skin when the feather anlage is formed. A great number of melanophores lie in the anlage of the developing embryonal feather at the base of the epithelial layer, most frequently in the zone adjoining the pulpa. In many species the melanophores play little or no part in the development of the embryonal-down plumage. There is no essential difference between eumelanin and phaeomelanin as far as the formation of the granules in the melanophores of the definitive feather is concerned. Groups of pigment granules can be seen in the resting anlage of the feather, in its epithelial part, and partly in the papilla. The pigment-containing cells lie mainly at the base of the anlage at matrix level. The melanoblast 'reserve' may be found somewhat more basally. Each of the pigment cells has several processes which fill the spaces between the other epithelial cells. The intercellular spaces in the upper part of the papilla frequently contain pigment granules. In chimaeric formations obtained by the fusion of several feather anlages from birds with different pigmentation, melanin is never deposited in those parts of the 'combined feather' which develop from material derived from albino birds (Danforth, 1937, b; 1939, a, b; Lillie, 1940).

In the first stages of feather development there is a marked increase in the number of differentiated melanophores. Some of them turn into multinuclear (giant) cells (Willier, 1952). It is typical that the activation of the melanophores is always preceded by differentiation of the structural elements of the epithelium. This happens in development of the embryonal-down plumage as well as in formation of the definitive feathers (Hamilton, 1940, a, b; Watterson, 1941, 1942; Willier, 1953). By the time the epithelial cells begin to form regular rows (the future barbs) the processes of the pigment cells begin to grow into the spaces between them.

Thorough study of the structural changes in the shaft of the developing feather, and experiments involving partial separation of the epithelial and connective-tissue elements in the feather anlage, have provided convincing evidence that a certain degree of differentiation in the epithelial part of the young feather is the main factor activating the melanocytes (Weidenreich, 1912; Foulks, 1943; Rawles, 1948; Willier, 1950, 1952).

When the epithelial cells are integrated into the barbs system, conditions are ripe for the invasion of melanoblasts from the 'reserve' at the base of the pulpa, for their transform-ation into melanophores and for activation of melanogenesis. Pigment granules appear and rapidly multiply in the cyto-plasm of the melanophores. Pseudopodia varying in length and number then appear and subsequently elongate to enter the interstitial spaces between the epithelial cells. This infil-tration takes place from the centre of the shaft towards its periphery, mainly between the rows of cells which will form the barbs. Every primary pigment cell begins to branch out as soon as it reaches a certain size, and the ramification be-comes interwoven with similar processes from other cells. The tips of these branches come into direct contact with the cells of the second-order barbs and deposit pigment granules on their surface. The number of epithelial cells containing in-creasing amounts of pigment grows rapidly. The melanin granules deposited at the surface of the epithelial cells enter the deeper layers of the cytoplasm. With subsequent keratini-sation the pigment granules become embedded into the horny substance of the epithelial cells. In the final stages of feather development, the melanophores (having preserved some pig-ment granules in their cytoplasm) die off, undergo phagocy-

tosis, and are partially enclosed between the cells of the desiccated pulpa and the external epithelial sheath.

With completion of the differentiation of the primary barbs
and the barrel, the pigmentation of the larger structural elements takes place in a similar manner. During formation of
the flattened cells of the cortical layer and of the large multi-
angular cells of the medullar layer, a large number of pigment
granules accumulates in these structures. More pigment is
deposited on the external surface of the barbs and of the barrel than on the internal surfaces. The quantity of pigment in
the barrel decreases from the apex towards the base. The
feather shaft is either free of pigment or the cells contain
only isolated melanin granules. The environment and the
physiological state of the bird exert an influence on melanogenesis and the pigmentation of the developing feathers. The
supply of various amino-acids in the diet, particularly tyrosin,
is an important factor in normal melanogenesis (Lloyd-Jones,
1915; Schroeder and Lois, 1955; Klain, Hill, Gray, and Olsen,
1960). The level of tyrosinase activity in the feather anlage
determines the limits of melanin synthesis in the activated
melanocytes (Charles and Rawles, 1940). Formation of the
typical pigmentation in regenerating feathers requires the
presence of vitamin B^1 in the food (Belen'kii, 1941, a). Birds
which are black require large quantities of riboflavin; Hutt
(1953) assumes that this substance is essential for melanin
synthesis. Riboflavin deficiency leads to the death of fledglings, particularly those with a black plumage. Vohra and
Kratzer (1950) observed that phenylalanine deficiency impairs
melanogenesis in turkey-chick vestiture. Exposure of skin
areas covered by regenerating feathers to extreme temperatures may completely suppress the function of the melanocytes
and lead to the formation of depigmented areas in the young
flight feathers (Raspopova and Khvatov, 1935).

Lipochrome pigments

In the presence of lipochromes, i.e. fatty pigments, bird feathers are brightest of all. This bright colouring is the result
of a variety of diffuse pigments referred to by special names:
the yellow pigment (zooxanthin), the red (zoonerythrin-

porphyrin), the blue (ptilopin), the green (zooprasinin or fasi-anoverdin), and others. The so-called lipocyan reaction is typical for lipochromes: if one immerses a feather coloured by long-wave absorption of the spectrum (red or yellow) in concentrated sulphuric acid, the colour will change into one belonging to the short-wave part of the spectrum (blue-green to blue). The brightly fluorescent golden yellow shades of some tropical birds belong in the same category (Driesen, 1953). Bogdanov (1856, 1858 a, b) was the first to study the physical and chemical properties of the lipochromes and to recommend a basic classification. Subsequent studies by other authors, particularly Götz (1925), Desselberger (1929, 1930), Völker (1937-51), and Driesen (1953), have widened our knowledge of the lipochromes, although various questions on the chemical structure of these pigments are still unsolved. It has been shown that the intensity of red or pink pigmentation in the plumage depends directly on the presence of carotenoids in the food (Giersberg and Stadie, 1933; Adlersparre, 1938, 1939; Kritzer, 1943). Unlike the melanins, the lipochromes have little stability when exposed to external influences. Plumage colouring may alter under the influence of external factors outside the moulting period (Meier, 1957; Völker, 1957). Some diets, or unilateral nutrition consisting, for example, mainly of fats, sometimes lead to the complete disappearance of lipochromes from the developing feathers and to their replacement by melanin or another lipochrome (Larionov, 1928; Schereschewsky, 1929). In these instances the colour change may take place during the development of the new feather generation. A colour change in a fully developed feather, by infiltration of a new pigment into the pre-existing structures, is impossible. There are only two bird species in which plumage colouring changes under the influence of external factors and subsequently reverts to the original shade. One is the plantain-eater (*Turacus corythaix*), whose purple-red feathers turn blue when exposed to rain. This is due to the presence of a special pigment, turacin, containing a copper salt the colour of which depends on the moisture content (Church, 1869). On the basis of its chemical structure and its 'sensitivity' to water, turacin can be classified as belonging to a separate group (different from the melanins and lipochromes). Unlike the lipochromes, it is not soluble in fat-solvents, but like these pigments it gives a positive lipocyan reaction. Turacin has been produced synthetically*. The other exception is the Egyptian heron: in this species the yellow pigment in the head feathers undergoes a chemical change when exposed to light, and turns white.

The genesis of the lipochrome pigments has been inadequately studied. Their source and the way they infiltrate into the developing part of the feather are still obscure. It has been established, however, that the formation of these pigments is *not* connected with special pigment cells. It is known that the feather anlage contains droplets of a lipid substance in which the lipochromes are dissolved. Throughout the development of the feather they are formed in various parts of the pulpa. This has been confirmed for the growing feathers of finches, goldfinches, canaries, parrots, and some other birds. Later, the coloured fat droplets are found among the primary accumulations of the epithelial cells which form the barbs. In the first stages of keratinisation the fat droplets disappear from the distal parts of each barb, and the lipochrome is directly adsorbed by the viscous keratin substance; sometimes it is precipitated in the shape of fine particles which later dissolve in the keratin. The colouring of the structural elements with lipochromes takes place in the same order as the deposition of melanins, namely from the periphery of the epithelial cylinder to its centre, or in a centripetal direction. Where great quantities of lipochromes accumulate during structure differentiation, the cell material of the first-order barbs is stimulated to a more intensive growth than that of the second-order barbs. Consequently, the parts of the first-order barbs coloured by lipochromes (or with melanins) are relatively more bulky.

The formation of lipochromes may be induced experimentally even in those birds which under normal conditions have no lipochromes. Rawles (1939) transplanted the skin of white-robin embryos into the base of the pulpa of growing feathers in White-Leghorn chicks. An unstable pink pigment can

---

* Turacin is a copper compound of uroporphyrin III (With, T. K., 1957, *Nature, Lond.*, 179, p. 824).—*Ed.*

frequently be found in feathers coloured with melanin (Shtegman, 1956).

To sum up, it must be emphasised that marked changes in the environment have a more marked influence upon the lipochromes than upon the melanins. Among all the environmental factors, diet is the most important. Deficiency in certain food constituents, particularly those connected with the formation of riboflavin (a substance perhaps required for melanin formation) and also deficiency in carotenoids (which participate in lipochrome formation), leads to inadequate' pigmentation or to colour changes in developing feathers.

STRUCTURAL COLOURS

Structural or optical colouring depends on the physical properties and microscopic structure of certain parts of the feather which have different refractive indices. Feather colouring depends not only on its pigment content but also on various pigment combinations with different structural features. The first attempts to explain bird feather colouring were confined to references to their structural features, since no pigment could be isolated from fully developed feathers. At that time Bogdanov discussed the inconsistency of this concept in a book on the subject (1858, a, b). Subsequent studies yielded adequate explanations of the nature of structural colouring (Goessler, 1938; Frank, 1939; Auber, 1958; Becker, 1959; Raxumova, Lemzhikin, Lebedev, and Pen'kina, 1959; Crawford, Brandt, and Friel, 1960).

White is the simplest of all structural effects. White feathers have no pigment. Their effect can be explained (like the whiteness of snow) by the complete reflection of light by the wall of transparent, air-filled cells in the medullar layer of the barrel and the barbs. As early as 1858 Bogdanov (1858, b) observed that if the cells are arranged in a similar manner, but their walls are not fully transparent, the resulting colour will be of a blue or pale blue shade. The degree of transparency can also be diminished by a layer of rough keratin particles on the feather surface (Schmidt, 1952).

In more recent studies some workers have assumed that the majority of structural colours, and in particular blue, are produced by combinations of the thick pigment layer arranged in one or several rows within the medullar layer; the cell walls are thickened and covered by transparent cells of the cortical layer (Auber and Mason, 1955; Auber, 1957). If the pigment lining in the cells of the medullar layer is absent or poorly developed, and the layer of keratinised cells is sufficiently thick, the resulting colour will be pale blue. If this 'pale blue structure' is combined with the presence of a yellow lipochrome the cortical layer will be green. In other words, a green colour may be produced even in the absence of a green lipochrome. Similarly a violet colour can be produced either by a violet lipochrome (ptilopin) or by a combination of the 'pale-blue structure' with a red lipochrome.

The silky sheen of some feathers is due to the presence of long thin second-order barbs free of hamuli, the mirror-smooth surface of these barbs reflecting the light. A velvety or matt appearance is due to the presence of numerous modified brush-shaped or thorn-shaped barbs arranged in dense parallel rows perpendicular to the feather surface, so that little light is directly reflected. A shiny, metallic, or iridescent colour in the green, blue, or violet shades can be explained by optical interference, the second-order barbs being covered by transparent keratin membranes, which are sometimes arranged in several layers. Optical interference takes place when light is reflected from the outer or inner membrane surfaces. The colour will vary with the thickness and number of transparent membranes, with the angle of light incidence on the feather, and with the optical refraction of the substance constituting the membrane. In iridescent feathers the second-order barbs are wide and flat and lie at right angles to the first-order barbs. Like the blue structural colours, the metallic sheen results from the presence of a pigment lining. Albino bird feathers, therefore, never have a metallic sheen.

Wear and tear, and mechanical erasure of the structural elements on the surface and at the feather tips, lead in time to changes in the colour of the vestiture, even between moults. This applies equally to colouring produced by pigments and to structural effects (Allen, 1896; Anon, 1948; Staples, 1948; Harrison, 1952).

4

FEATHER AND PLUMAGE PATTERNS

The variable distribution of pigments and thin keratin structures produces a feather pattern which is only an individual component within the complex mosaic of the overall plumage pattern. Patterns appear only on those feathers, or their vanes, which are not covered by other feathers. The pattern is visible on the outer feather surface; on the inner surface it is either completely absent or only weakly developed. This is also the case with feathers which provide a single colour for the plumage and in which the pigment is evenly distributed.

Feather patterns differ in their common background and in their additional colouring. Several basic types of pattern can be distinguished, according to the distribution of pigments and structural elements in the vane in relation to the quill. These include a transparent pattern (varying from a single dark stripe in a feather to multiple stripes which give a wavy or striped appearance). and a longitudinal pattern, or a combination of the two. The quill pattern may consist of differently shaped coloured spots (oval, heart-shaped, or lancet-shaped) or they may form a narrow zone along the quill. The pigmented spot may lie near the tip of the feather (terminal spot) or somewhat more basally (pre-apical spot). A narrow coloured zone may form a margin round a vane with a different colour. The individual pattern of homonymous feathers may differ, not only in different species but even in the same individual at different ages. or in birds of the same species but of different sex (Volchanetskii, 1948; Michener, 1953; Goodwin, 1956, 1957; Webbe, 1958; Bowers, 1959).

The nature of the process which leads to pattern formation has frequently been investigated (Agar, 1924; Boetticher, 1950). Environmental conditions and physiological changes, particularly the neurohormonal, exert a marked influence upon the developing feather and upon its pattern. The pattern in a fully developed feather and the degree to which the general pattern of the species is shown reflect the physiological condition of the bird during feather formation and particularly during moult.

Homogenous colouring is the result of similar activity by the melanocytes, or by the diffusion of lipochromes to give an even distribution equidistant from the generative zone of the developing feather. Heterogenous distribution of pigment within the feather is the final result of a very complex process. Intermittent patterns are formed by constant physiological rhythms, established during feather follicle formation. Study of the development of transverse stripes on Plymouth Rock hen feathers shows at once that feathers developing simultaneously in different pteryles are at different pigmentation phases. When a black stripe develops in some feathers, others form white stripes. Moreover, the two halves of the vane of the same feather may form their pigment at variable rhythm, producing an asymmetrical pattern (Gericke, 1958). Montalenti (1934, 1947) compared the development of pattern in feathers from different areas of the bird's body, and found feather follicles in which the rhythm at which the pigment was deposited coincided, but the stripes which formed were of different width, owing to changes in the speed of barb growth. The same author holds that on the whole the pattern is predetermined in the feather anlage. The assumption that the pattern is determined *a priori* in the feather anlage is, however, no substitute for an explanation of the way the pattern is formed. In the same study Montalenti showed that feathers belonging to different generations and developing from the same follicle can change their pattern; changes may also occur owing to hormonal factors. It is obvious that the formation of each given individual pattern is governed by a number of factors, among which the following three are the most important.

1. Periodic activation of the melanocytes.
2. Reactivity of the parts formed in the lower zone of differentiation and in the generative zone of the young feather.
3. The rate at which the young feather barbs grow.

These conditions are all interrelated. For example, experimental alteration of the rate of growth leads to marked changes in the reaction threshold of the developing barbs. It is also clear that regulation of the rhythm of some physiological processes depends on the nervous system.

Barb differentiation, and the later marked elongation, occur in a plane lying perpendicular to the direction in which the shaft grows. In this plane (or, as we have said above, in the annular zone) various parts of the barbs (arranged in a specific order) are differentiated simultaneously. In the dorsal part of the feather quill, at the sides, are formed first-order barb bases and the central sections of adjacent barbs, the apices of the following barbs and in the ventral region. It is easy to understand, therefore, how an even infiltration of melano- phores into the differentiation zone results in the formation of regular transverse pigmented stripes. Local changes in the reaction threshold of the epithelial tissue in certain parts of the young feather result in formation of another pattern. Formation of a differently coloured margin at the edge of the vane can be explained by changes in the reaction thres- hold in the terminal parts of the barbs during formation. It will be recalled that the anlage of the terminal parts of all subsequently developing barbs is confined to a narrow zone in the ventral region of the young shaft (Fraps and Juhn, 1936).

The formation of latticed or spotted patterns such as occur in guinea-fowls is a more complex process. In these cases the periodic character of the accumulation of pigment is extended further to circumscribed areas in the pigmentation zone (Hardest, 1933; Henke, 1935). It is a characteristic feature of complex patterns that melanins, that is, pigments formed by mobile cells, the melanocytes, take part in their formation. The activity of such pigment cells is frequently combined with various changes in feather structure. Diffuse infiltration of lipochromes into the epithelial cylinder only leads to the homogenous dyeing of the barbs. Combination of two differ- ent types of pigmentation with a wide range of structural aberrations produces the highly complex patterns of colibris, birds of paradise, peacocks, and pheasants (Grager, 1925; Dunn and Landauer, 1930; Vevers, 1954; Sager, 1955).

Growth rate is an important factor in certain pattern forma- tions, since any change in growth rate will be reflected in pigment accumulation. For example, in Plymouth Rock hens the transverse black stripes will be much wider than the white stripes in rapidly growing feathers, the opposite being the case in slowly growing feathers. But these rules cannot be applied to all birds. In the brightly coloured races of domestic fowls, for instance, feathers growing at different rates may have identical patterns; and conversely, in some pterylae different patterns may develop in feathers growing at identical speeds. But even in these birds experimental alteration of growth rate will lead to corresponding changes in their usual pattern. The growth rate cannot be regarded as the only factor determining feather pattern.

There is more evidence to support the contention that a special rhythm in the activity of the melanophores plays a leading part in the formation of complex patterns. The studies of Gericke and Platt (1932), Lopashov (1945), and Nickerson (1944, 1946) produced interesting data on periodicity in pigment-cell activity. Pieces of young feathers from Plymouth Rock hens were transplanted into the body cavities or into the anlage of the extremities of very young White Leghorn embryos. Both pigmented and pigment free parts of the feather were used separately for the transplantation. It appeared that in both cases (pieces taken from the black stripes as well as from the white) melanophores emigrated from the transplanted piece. Hence, even the white zones of developing feathers contain melanocytes capable of emigrating into the developing parts of young feathers and of depositing melanin granules when activated. Melanophores taken from the black stripes produced the typical striped pattern after transplantation into a new host. If the growth rate of the young feathers was experimentally accelerated, the pattern became less distinct.

As the melanoblasts and the melanophores derived from them are present in all parts of the developing feathers (though certain areas, nevertheless, remain free of pigmentation), it must be assumed that at certain times the function of the pigment cells is suppressed by the accumulated products of the melanophores themselves, since some time is required for excretion of these products into the bloodstream from the epithelial parts of the developing feather. The intensity of pigment formation by the melanophores is important to the character of the resulting pattern, as well as to the function of the pigment cells themselves. It seems that changes in the physiological correlation between the epithelial and the connective tissue parts of the feather anlage or the shaft are followed by changes in the general pattern of the feather.

The formation of feathers with different patterns in the same follicle provides further evidence against the hypothesis that the pattern in the feather anlage is predetermined. In Plymouth Rock hens abnormally coloured or evenly dyed feathers develop very frequently instead of the usual striped feathers. In these cases newly developing feathers are dyed differently from those of the preceding generation. This fact disproves the idea of an early determination of pattern in the feather follicle. The above phenomena are not caused by hormonal factors, since feathers developing simultaneously from different 'abnormal' follicles can differ from one another. It may still be postulated that these differences are due to local disorders in the innervation of individual feather follicles.

In many bird species regular pattern changes may be observed after each moult, and are the basis of changes connected with age, season and sex (Beebe, 1908; Heinroth, 1910; Henke, 1939; Novikov and Blagodatskaya, 1948, 1950; Harrison, 1948; Harrison and Harrison, 1959, a, b). At certain set times changes will occur in the properties of the feather follicle as a consequence of general physiological changes. In many species the first moult after the young bird has left the nest will produce a new plumage pattern. If the feather anlage is formed before the onset of moult, however, a combined plumage pattern will develop: the upper part of the vane will have the features of the juvenile plumage and the lower part those of the new and final plumage (Kuhn, 1928; Göhringer, 1951).

Formation of the general plumage pattern in birds is a complex process. The chain of physiological changes caused by environmental changes is manifest in plumage colouring and above all in the intensity of pigment distribution in the feathers of both the ventral and dorsal body surfaces. The importance of the plumage pattern for adaptation has been discussed in detail in the works of Charles Darwin (1868) and Severtsov (1939) and also in the summaries by Henke (1937) and Kott (1950).

The general plumage pattern in birds represents a combination of a great number of differently coloured feathers. One might say that each individual feather pattern is subordinate to the general pattern of the whole plumage. In consequence, feathers growing in different parts of the same pteryle may show different pigmentation. A symmetrical distribution of pigment in individual feathers can be observed only in rare cases. The presence of pigments may be confined to any part of the hard vane. Regular arrangement of feathers in different pterylae forms the general plumage pattern characteristic of a given species. The plumage can be dyed evenly or in stripes, speckles, spots or combinations of these. In individual birds the function of the pigment cells can be disturbed to such a degree that the formation and deposition of pigment becomes impossible; albino birds are the result. There are complete and partial albinos. Conversely, increased activity of the chromatophores may produce a homogenous dark pigmentation in individual birds of multicoloured species—the phenomenon of hypermelanism.

During the individual development of a bird, plumage pattern usually becomes more complicated. To some extent this repeats the historical sequence in the development of the plumage pattern in birds: the original one-tone reddish-brown colour was gradually replaced by bright multicoloured patterns (Eldern, 1936; Mashtaller, 1940; Petrov, 1940; Kagelmann, 1951; Kimball, 1952).

There is usually a striking difference in the plumage pigmentation on the ventral and dorsal body surfaces (Carins, 1951; Harrison, 1960). With few exceptions, the plumage on a bird's back is more intense than that of the underside. Regional colour differences develop gradually. There are no such differences in the down plumage of the fledgling—if the down plumage is coloured at all—although in some species there is still a difference between the colouring of the dorsal and the ventral surfaces. In some fledglings a primitive pattern appears on the back, and regional differences in the colouring of the nest plumage in fledglings are also relatively indistinct. The final plumage pattern develops only with the formation of the definitive plumage, which is preceded by one, two, or even three moults. Features characteristic of certain age-groups do not always strictly reflect the actual age of the bird. In some birds of prey, for instance, the definitive plumage is preceded by three plumages which are not changed completely during the moults. In consequence adult birds may still carry feathers of all three preceding plumages.

Some individuals in species with a dimorphous plumage may display disorders in the usual bilaterally symmetrical pattern. Cases of gynandromorphism have been described among gallinaceous and passeriform birds. Here the disorders in the plumage pattern have a precisely bilaterally asymmetric or mosaic character (Ognev and Ognev, 1924; Pezard, Sand, and Caridroit, 1926; Espinasse, 1936; Hutt, 1937; Crew and Munro, 1939; Jerome and Huntsman, 1952). This phenomenon has not yet been explained*. There is no evidence to connect it with any humoral (hormonal) factor. In this context the findings of Lillie (1931) are of interest: this author observed unilateral hypertrophy of one of the cerebral hemispheres in gynandromorphic birds.

In many birds which show sexual differences in the plumage pattern, these differences appear during development of the second contour plumage. Only a few forms (some parrot species) are exceptional, in that the characteristic differences in the plumage already appear in the nestlings. In the overwhelming majority of bird species there are no sexual differences in juvenile plumage colouring: the colouring is paler than that of the adult birds and its shade is similar to that of the female. The different sexes acquire their characteristic vesti- ture only after the first moult. In some cases (domestic spar- row, linnet, starling, and others) changes in the general plumage pattern may take place even between moults, owing to gradual wear and tear of the peripheral parts of the vane. In consequence new parts of the feather, earlier covered over and differently coloured, may become visible and form a new plumage pattern.

The habitat exerts its influence on the general plumage pattern. Variations in the plumage pattern of birds living in different geographical latitudes mainly relate to the distribu- tion of melanin and its derivatives (Serebrovskii, 1925; Gill- ham, 1959; Harrison and Harrison, 1959, a, b; Jollie, 1947). Dement'ev and Larionov rightly assume that exogenous factors exert their influence upon the regulatory systems of the body,

---

* Bilateral gynandromorphism is due to a chromosomal aberration occur- ring before or during the first division of the egg.—*Ed.*

thus bringing about metabolic changes. The character and the intensity of the oxidative processes will change with a number of conditions, especially temperature, nutrition, and exposure to light, and the changes will affect pigment formation. Birds of different species living in identical conditions will have similar plumage. In this context it will be of interest that dimorphous forms of chickens, turkeys, and ducks show an ecliptic (smoothed-out) pattern (Tallent, 1931; Stressmann, 1948; Kimball, 1958).

CHANGE OF PLUMAGE (MOULT)

Feather distribution and growth

The feathers are arranged in a specific order on the bird's body, forming groups similar in shape, structure, and colour, according to the function the group fulfils. Feather orientation on the bird's body follows a common rule whatever the location: the apical ends of the feathers are orientated towards the tail end of the body. Feathers on the left and right side of the body are arranged symmetrically, but the vanes of certain groups (flight feathers) are asymmetric. The feathers are arranged in rows, regularly grouped into well-defined areas, the pterylae, as opposed to areas free of feather follicles, the apteria. Nine basic pterylae are recognised in the plumage of birds (Dement'ev, 1940, b; Shul'pin, 1940; Friant, 1947).

1. The spino-sacral pteryla (*pt. spinalis*).
2. The upper arm bone pteryla (*pt. humeralis*).
3. The abdominal pteryla (*pt. gastrica*).
4. The neck and head pteryla (*pt. capitis*).
5. The wing-pteryla (*pt. alaris*).
6. The thigh pteryla (*pt. femoralis*).
7. The shank pteryla (*pt. cruralis*).
8. The tail pteryla (*pt. caudalis*).
9. The anal pteryla (*pt. ani*).

The names of the pterylae indicate their position.

In contrast to the contour feathers, the down feathers may be found only on some parts of the skin. The apteria extend over symmetrical areas of the skin and eight of these are the largest feathers.

The number of feathers on a bird's body varies to a certain degree according to season and age. There is a direct but not strictly proportional relationship between the total number of feathers and the size of the bird's body: about 1,000 in the colibri, 1,500-2,000 (Wetmore, 1936) in small passeriform birds, 5,000-6,000 in seagulls, 9,000-10,000 in ducks, over 25,000 in swans (Dement'ev, 1940, b; Korelus, 1947; Brodkorb 1951; Wing, 1952).

The feathers in different pterylae vary in size, shape, and structure according to their function, as, for example, do feathers on the trunk and on the wings. The wing feathers are subdivided into flight feathers and covering feathers (*remiges primariae*) attached to the upper extremity of the second finger, and second-order flight feathers (*remiges secundariae*) attached to the ulna. The quill base of these feathers is supported by the wing skeleton; this ensures stability during flight (Fig. 14).

The number of first-order flight feathers varies within a relatively narrow range (from eight to twelve) in different species, whereas the number of second-order flight feathers may vary from six to thirty-seven (Stresemann, 1927). The elongation of second-order flight feathers observed in birds adapted to soaring flight leads to the formation of special 'aft-sails' which frequently cover the bright lateral pattern (Shtegman, 1952). The first-order and second-order flight feathers are numbered from the outer edge of the wing to the trunk. It should be noted that the outermost (first) flight feather is the smallest of all.

Numerous publications have dealt with the way the plumage and structure of flight feathers is organised in relation to the aerodynamic properties of the wings in different birds. In this context mention may be made of the papers by Gladkov and Rustamov (1949), Saunders and Weiss (1950), Shestakova (1956), Oehme (1959), Engelmann (1959), and Borodulina (1960). In these publications the authors describe the arrangement of the flight feathers, the microscopic structure of the surface cells covering the vane, and how the barbs are attached to one another and the feathers to the wings.

The humerus region is covered by the so-called humeral feathers (*remiges tertiariae*); these play only a secondary rôle

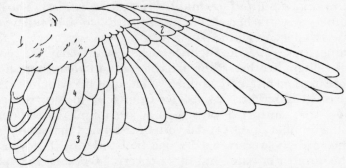

1, Flight primaries; 2, Their coverts; 3, Flight secondaries; 4, Their coverts

Fig. 4. *The distribution of feathers in the main tracts of the pigeon's wing*

in flight. The feathers which cover the first-order and second-order flight feathers (as well as the flight feathers themselves) are of different shape and structure. The former are narrower, elastic, and firmly attached in their deep feather follicles. Both categories of feathers are arranged in rows which cover each other in consecutive order. The contours of the feathers in each upper row cover the fluffy parts and a small proportion of the contour part of the feathers in the row beneath them.

From the lower to the upper rows the size of the feathers gradually diminishes. Each row is set slightly more proximally than the preceding one. In consequence the feathers in each row cover the space between two feathers in the next row, like tiles. In addition, the covering feathers differ according to whether they cover the outer or inner surface of the wing and also according to the row to which they belong. Three rows of particularly large feathers form the basis of the wing. The feathers of the first row, which directly cover the lower part of the flight feathers, are the largest: the *tectrices majores, inferiores,* and *superiores.* These are followed, in consecutive order, by the *tectrices mediae, tectrices minores,* and *tectrices marginales.*

Another group of large feathers, the helm feathers (*rectrices*), have their own outer and inner covering feathers (*tec-*

trices caudales inferiores and *tectrices subcaudales*). The helm feathers are attached through their quills to the caudal vertebrae, which are unified in a single bone (pygostyle). These feathers resemble the flight feathers, particularly the second-order flight feathers, but are different in that they show a more marked bilateral symmetry. The number of helm feathers varies in different bird species from four to fourteen pairs. Most frequently five or six pairs are found, corresponding to the number of the caudal vertebrae unified in a single bone. The feathers are arranged along both sides of the pygostyle. The number of outer and inner covering feathers corresponds to the number of helm feathers. The number of these can be used as a taxonomic index in wild birds and as sign of the race in domestic fowls. The number of helm feather and their arrangement is one of the morphological features which has undergone considerable evolutionary change (Khrapovskii, 1959). The helm-feather shape either remains unchanged over the whole extent of the pteryla or, more frequently, changes in each of the pairs of feathers which line both sides of the pygostyle.

The feathers covering the head, trunk, and posterior extremities are of more or less similar structure. The differences between them usually consist in the size of the feathers themselves and also in the relative size of their contour and fluffy parts respectively, and in some cases in the shape of the feathers.

In different pterylae, and sometimes even within the same pteryla, the anlagen of the definitive feathers form at different times. In chickens, for example, the development of the flight feathers begins in the egg, while the small trunk feathers form only at the age of one or two months (Lektorskii and Kuz'mina, 1936, a; Holmes, 1935; Kotova, 1936; Saunders and Weiss, 1950; Engelmann, 1959).

In pigeons (Voitkevic, 1934 a, 1936 g; Novikov, 1934) the times when feathers form and develop in different pterylae are rather more uniform. In young pigeons feather-shaft development begins within a few days of hatching. The first foci of feather formation can be found on the humerus, on those parts of the wing which are nearer the trunk, and as a narrow strip on the back. Feather formation later extends to the outer surface of the wings and to the other parts of the body, extending towards the tail; the ventral surface of the trunk and the extremities become covered at a later stage. We are therefore justified in saying that there are stages in the morphogenetic processes of bird feather-forming tissues. The centre of the highest activity in feather formation is the dorsal surface, particularly in the region of the shoulder girdle. Feather-formation activity decreases from head to tail and from the dorsal to the ventral surfaces of the trunk and of the extremities. In aquatic birds such as ducks and geese the feathers in the different pterylae develop a considerable time after hatching, and the development is spread over a longer period (Straikh and Svetozarov, 1935 a, b). The larger feathers (flight and helm feathers) develop simultaneously, but the growth of the smaller feathers is delayed and takes place at different times in different pterylae. Compared with other birds, particularly chickens and pigeons, the aquatic birds occupy a special place with regard to the anlage of the feather follicles and the initial stages of feather formation. In addition to the differences in the way the anlage is formed, the feathers also grow differently, at different speeds and for a different period, according to the site of the feather follicles. Feathers of different length grow at different speeds, that is, the absolute growth in bulk of each feather in the unit of time is directly proportional to the final length of the feather. From this point of view the growth of the helm feathers in the peacock is highly instructive (Samuel, 1870).

It has been established that in pigeons the growth in bulk per unit of time decreases with increasing age. The growth of the large and small feathers has been studied in various species. There is a fixed proportion between the size of the feathers and their growth rate: the longer the feathers in a given species, the lower the average relative daily size increase. Larionov and Posigun (1935) compared the development of homonymous flight feathers in chickens and in pigeons, and showed that the feathers grow more rapidly in the latter. The authors came to the conclusion that the feather-growth rate is a species-specific feature. Other authors have come to similar conclusions (Heinroth, 1906; Carlisle, 1925; Martin, 1930; Hurry and Nordskog, 1953).

There are only a few reports on the relative speed of growth in relation to the bird's age and to the season. In older pigeons feathers grow more slowly than in younger birds. In these birds no differences in the growth rate could be observed at different seasons of the year (Berdyshev, 1934; Novikov, 1934). However, according to our own observations (Voitkevich, 1940, c) the feathers covering the second-order flight feathers in pigeons regenerate more rapidly in summer and in autumn than in winter.

Feather growth in different pterylae depends on their individual histogenesis. During growth, particularly in pigeons, two periods must be distinguished: one before the formation of the vane and the other the external differentiation of the structures constituting the vane elements (Voitkevich, 1936, b, d). The latter period is characterised by a more marked increase in bulk per unit of time. In chickens, unlike pigeons, no difference between the growth rates of the feathers on the breast and the back can be observed in the first period, although the feathers on the back continue to grow for a somewhat longer period. In the second period, however, the feathers grow somewhat faster in the pterylae on the anterior surface (Juhn and Fraps, 1934, a, b, c, 1936; Lillie, 1940). This means that differences in the growth rate on some pterylae may occur not throughout the period of development but in certain phases only.

Straikh and Svetozarov (1937, b) studied the growth of various feathers in pigeons, geese, and ducks, using mathematical methods to establish growth constants (Shmal'gausen, 1935). It appeared that within one species feathers of equal size situated in different pterylae grew at the same rate. The differences found between the rates of growth of small feathers in different species could be explained by variations in the general character of growth typical of the species in question (Kaufman, 1936; Voitkevich, 1934, a; Larionov, Kotova, and Shtraikh, 1933; Shtraikh and Svetozarov, 1937, a, b).

Quite different laws govern the development of first-order flight feathers. Novikov (1934) showed that in pigeons juvenile flight feather 10 develops within a much shorter period than the other flight feathers, whereas flight feather 1 grows exceedingly slowly. With flight feathers the rate of growth depends not on their final length but, apparently, on the features of the feather follicles in the area in question.

Within a given pteryla a certain pattern can be observed in the growth of the flight feathers. In chicks, for example, the four innermost first-order flight feathers begin to develop almost simultaneously, and their growth curves are almost identical despite the considerable differences in their final size. The six external flight feathers (1-6) begin to develop later, and their growth curves are similar to each other but different from the curves characterising the growth of the first four feathers (7-10). The difference between the onset of development and the rate of growth observed in these two groups of feathers can be expressed by a gradient, the centre of which lies at feather 7; feathers 8-10 constitute the central axis and feathers 6-1 the lateral. Similar rules apply to the second-order flight feathers. Here the peak of the gradient lies at feather 13 (the feathers are numbered in the same order as the first-order flight feathers). The first-order flight feathers (10-6) grow fastest of all, followed by the first-order flight feather 5 and the second-order flight feathers 13-16, the latter faster than the first-order flight feathers 4-1. The order of the onset and rate of growth of various feathers remains the same, from the juvenile plumage throughout the subsequent definitive feather generations.

Differences in the growth of the large feathers, determined by their position, are maintained during the period of the natural moult as well as after activation of new feather generations by plucking. After artificial plucking the growth curves of first-order flight feathers in pigeons are fully identical with the corresponding curves observed in young birds. Berdyshev (1934) measured growing first-order flight feathers in pigeons and established that the rate of growth slows down from the trunk towards the distal wing tip.

In other words, differences in the onset and rate of growth can be observed not only between feathers belonging to different pterylae but also between feathers within the same pteryla. They are more marked in the larger feathers. From the trunk to the distal tip of the wing the flight-feather growth rate decreases. The differences in the rate of growth observed in feathers in different places do not depend on the bird's age.

Differences between various species are determined by the general rate of growth, in the post-embryonal period, typical of the species in question.

The development of the plumage, the rate of growth, and keratinisation depend on nutrition (Krukenberg, 1882; Koch, 1939; Bel'skii, 1949; Podhradsky, 1953; et al.) The content of nitrogen and of sulphur-containing substances in the diet is of particular importance (Buchtala, 1910; Ackerson, Blish and Mussehe, 1926; Lintzel, Mangold, and Stotz, 1929; Bolliger and Varga, 1960). Some emphasise the importance of simple water-soluble compounds containing potassium, iron, zinc, and other elements (Sauermann, 1889; Höhn, 1955; Gross, 1956; Supplee, Combs, and Blamberg, 1958). It has recently been shown that addition of ground keratin to the diet in the form of 'feather-meal' enhances the fattening of domestic fowl and affects plumage (Lille, Sizemore, and Denton, 1956; Woodin, 1956; Harms and Goff, 1957; Vellky, 1960).

The time, sequence, and duration of the moult

The periodic renewal of the plumage in birds is an important adaptation. With time, feathers wear out and lose their characteristic pattern. Change of plumage is one link in an annual cycle of morphogenetic phenomena. One may speak of the seasonal character of the moult, in the sense that it is connected with certain periods of the year. In young birds, plumage renewal coincides with the completion of their general development; in adult birds it usually occurs immediately after the mating season, seldom much later.

Moults can be divided into the juvenile post-nidal and annual (definitive) moult. The post-nidal moult is the first moult: the contour feathers developed during the nesting period are wholly or partially replaced by the feathers of the adult bird (Marble, 1934; Sutton, 1948; Parkes, 1957). Before the moult, the embryonal down feathers are replaced by the first (juvenile) contour plumage; as said above, however, there are no reasons to regard this exchange as a moult. The annual moult, which usually occurs towards the end of the year, may affect the whole of the plumage or only part. In many birds a partial moult occurs immediately before the mating season, ensuring bright plumage-colouring in the mating season (Riddle, 1931; Rand, 1954, a; Swank, 1955; Selender, 1958). Two moulting cycles (one of which is incomplete) are typical for many birds, particularly for migratory ones. The adaptive character of the annual moult is particularly marked in birds migrating over large distances (Brockhuygen, 1956; Marshall and Serventy, 1956; Kozlova, 1957). Sessile birds usually moult only once a year. In species with two annual moults, the greater part or the whole of the plumage is replaced after the mating season. After a shorter or longer interval, which is particularly short in aquatic birds, the second partial moult takes place. This affects the small rather than the wing feathers. This may be followed by another partial moult in spring. In migrating passeriform birds the partial moult takes place in spring, before their flight from their winter quarters. The swallows are the only exception: they have only one moult which occurs in winter. The moult is most complex in black grouse and partridge, for in them the feathers which develop at different seasons differ not only in colour but also in structure. The white partridge, for example, undergoes four moults a year (Mikheev, 1939; Salomonsen, 1939).

Among earlier investigations on the natural moult of wild birds mention should be made of the studies of Severtsov (1856), Bogdanov (1888), Gerbe (1877), Heinroth (1898, 1931), and Jacobs (1935). Bianki (1911) made one of the first attempts to systematise differences in the character of the moult in different species. Shul'pin (1940) published detailed data on the character and time of the moult in different bird species. These authors reviewed the seasonal renewal and plumage moult systematically, taking into account differences between various age groups, while Dement'ev (1940, a, b) summarised interesting details characterising the annual moult in different bird species.

In some birds of prey such as hawks, falcons, owls, and cranes, the anual moult is frequently not completed within a single year but extends over two years (Miller, 1941; Mayr and Mayr, 1954; Steinbacher, 1955; Piechocki, 1956; Sutter, 1956; Verheyen, 1956, a, b; Schiemenz, 1958; Stresemann, 1958). In adult diurnal birds of prey, a chronic continuous moult frequently takes place (Mebs, 1960). There are also differences between the sexes in the time of onset of the moult. In those species which look after their progeny, the female and the male do not moult simultaneously, so that one of the parents is able to guard the progeny effectively. In ducks, for example, the moult which leads to the replacement of the bright mating plumage by the drab summer plumage begins much earlier in the male than in the female (Stresemann, 1940; Salomonsen, 1949). In the female the moult begins after the hatching of the young birds. In swans this order is reversed: here the female moults first (Boase, 1959). Sexual differences may also become manifest in the character of the moult. In the female quail, the flight feathers are replaced during the brooding and nursing of the young birds, whereas in the male the moult begins as soon as the young birds have become independent. Heinroth (1947) reports that the female rhinoceros-hornbill (*Buceros rhinoceros*), which is entombed in the nest and stays in the dark for several weeks, sheds all her feathers at once in the second brooding period. The males of this species, and non-broody females, have a gradual moult during which they never lose their flight capacity.

The moult of most birds is strictly ordered, feathers from different regions changing to ensure continuous flight capacity and heat regulation. Cases in which the moult leads to the simultaneous shedding of the whole plumage are very rare, but this occurs in penguins and is reminiscent of the shedding of the skin of many reptiles (Eggert, 1935). The large feathers of many aquatic and swamp birds are shed within a short period (Straikh and Svetozarov, 1935, a, b, c; Adamesteanu and Suteanu, 1960); in consequence, they are unable to fly for a certain time. Moulting of this type is undoubtedly adaptative, since in a habitat offering reliable protection against predators the total length of time required for the moult is considerably reduced. A variety of topographical sequences in the moult of various birds has been described in studies by Snigirevskii (1950), Rustamov (1956), Williamson (1957, a, b), Bährmann (1958), Frankk and Epprecht (1959), Stresemann and Stresemann (1960).

In many birds the exchange of the plumage in each pteryla is correlated with the state of the moult in other parts of the body. The feathers are exchanged symmetrically on both sides, that is, homologous feathers are exchanged simultaneously. The fixed order in the plumage exchange shows up best in the moult of the larger feathers. Each group of large feathers (helm feathers, first-order and second-order flight feathers) have their own sequence; the latter, however, differs according to the systematic position of the species in question. It is a basic feature in the moult of the larger feathers that those most essential for flight are renewed in the final phase of the moult; the exchange of the first-order flight feathers, for example, begins from the inner edge of the row. In passeriform and gallinaceous birds, in pigeons, and some others, it is the innermost first-order flight feathers (10) on both wings which are shed first. They are followed at certain intervals by the neighbouring feathers on both wings: 9, 8, 7, and so on (Dwight, 1900, a, b, 1925; Larionov, 1945; Wetherbee, 1951; Werth, 1954; Mewaldt, 1958; Verheyen, 1958; Stresemann, 1959).

In birds of prey the moult begins from a slightly different centre: the first feather to be shed is flight feather 7, followed by 6 and 8; then by 5 and 10, and so on (Dement'ev, 1940, a, b). In aquatic birds, too, the moult proceeds from the inner to the outer edge of the wing, with the only difference that the large feathers are shed within a very short time. The moult of the second-order flight feathers most frequently begins simultaneously from both ends of the row, or there is an initial moult centre for this group of feathers on each wing from which the shedding of the feathers begins, proceeding towards the two edges (Straikh and Svetozarov, 1935, a, b, c). In many groups such as the cuckoos and parrots there is no pattern in the moult of the helm feathers.

After the shedding of each feather within the group of large feathers, a certain period elapses before the next feather is shed. The interval varies for feathers of different groups. It is also different for homonymous pterylae in different species. There are, however, some common rules for feathers arranged in a single row. The next feather is shed after the preceding feather has developed to about one third of its ultimate size. There is a close interrelation between the rate of growth, the duration of the intervals between the shedding of adjacent feathers, and the overall duration of the moult as a whole.

The character, time, and duration of the moult are determined by various factors, and in particular by ecological
conditions. This is clear in domesticated birds, for Larionov
(1945) observed that in hens the moult takes much longer
when the birds begin to lay eggs continuously, and in addition,
the exchange of the second-order flight feathers is considerably
delayed as compared with that of the first-order ones. In
domestic chickens the usual order of the moult in the flight
feathers is frequently disrupted: several feathers are shed
simultaneously instead of one, and similar changes can be
observed in the moult of the helm feathers. During the first
moult a greater degree of individual variation may be observed. The character and the intensity of the moult in domestic pigeons, however, is hardly different from that observed
in wild pigeons (Larionov, 1949).

Owing to the practical requirements of poultry breeding,
the time and the sequence of the moult have been studied
in the greatest detail in chickens, ducks, and geese. The post-
nidal (juvenile) and the annual moults of chickens have been
thoroughly investigated (Rice, Nixon, and Rogers, 1908;
Ackerson, Blish, and Mussehe, 1938; Larionov, Kuz'mina,
and Lektorskii, 1933; Larionov, Kotova, and Straikh, 1933;
Kotova, 1936; Jaap and Grimes, 1956; Himeno and Tanabe,
1957). The order of moult observed in various feather
groups in chicken follows the rules described above with
regard to other domestic species. The authors of studies
in this field do not simply describe the moult, but set
themselves the task of establishing a relationship between the
moult and egg-production. The state of vestiture reflects a
number of features connected with the productivity of domestic birds (Bessarabov, 1937). Larionov and co-workers (1933-
1945) published numerous and extensive studies on the moult
of chicks and adult chickens, describing in detail the stages
of the moult in different groups of feathers. They also developed an objective but simple method for a quantitative assay
of the moult.

As the moult of first-order flight feathers is related to the
moult of the whole plumage, Larionov (1945) was able to show
that the feathers in this group can be used as a basic criterion
for the assay of the moult as a whole. By the time first-order

flight feather 5 or 6 is shed, the moult of the smaller feathers has reached its highest intensity; this is the heat or culmination point of the moult. There is a connection between the overall duration and the chronology of the moult, in that the exchange takes place at a slower rate in birds which moult early than in birds in which the moult sets in later. A similar correlation between the moult of the smaller and the larger feathers has also been demonstrated in domestic pigeons (Bel'skii, 1945; Larionov, 1949; Kobayashi, 1953, a).

In contrast to species in which the moult is a gradual process, other domestic birds, particularly aquatic birds such as ducks and geese, which shed their flight feathers within a short period (Straikh and Svetozarov, 1935, a, b, c), are remarkable in that the moult of the trunk plumage is correlated with the sequence in which the helm feathers are shed. The intensity of the moult increases gradually, and the shedding of the flight feathers begins at a time when about one third of the smaller feathers have been renewed. In ducks this process is completed much more rapidly than in geese. Tugarinov (1941) established that in ducks the moult begins with the replacement of the small plumage feathers, and the shedding of the flight feathers begins only twenty to twenty-five days later. Conversely, in geese and swans the moult begins with the shedding of the flight feathers. During the renewal of the flight feathers the intensity of the moult of the smaller feathers decreases. There is no essential difference between the moult in wild and domestic aquatic birds. The differences which have been observed are confined to the time and onset of moulting and the intensity of the process, but never affect the feather renewal sequence.

These studies, and our own observations on the moult of wild and domestic birds, have confirmed that birds can be divided into two groups according to the manner in which flight-feather moult takes place. In those birds which replace their flight feathers gradually, the moult begins with the innermost first-order flight feather on both wings. Other large feathers (second-order, or the flight or helm feathers) begin to be shed after several first-order flight feathers have been replaced. The moult is complete when the outermost first-order flight feather has been replaced. As above, in each group the moult begins from a well-defined initial centre. Feathers on the trunk, the neck, and the head are also replaced according to a certain sequence, in so far as these areas remain evenly covered during the moult. Moult on the neck and head begins later and is completed within a shorter period than on the trunk. There is a certain correlation between the speed of growth of the larger feathers and their time of moult. The feathers which grow fastest lie in the initial moult centre of the group in question. Moreover, there is a direct relation between the replacement sequence of feathers of different pterylae and the time at which they first appear during embryonal life. This relation has been studied in the greatest detail in chickens.

In birds which undergo a more sudden moult, the replacement of the first-order flight feathers follows the same pattern as in birds where the moult of the flight feathers takes longer. The short time during which exchange of the first-order flight feathers takes place (ten days in domestic ducks, fifteen to twenty days in geese) does not always make it possible to observe the precise sequence of feather replacement. In these birds the moult begins when the two central helm feathers are shed. The moult of smaller feathers runs parallel with the replacement of the helm feathers. The replacement of the smaller feathers begins from the lower surface of the trunk, spreading later to the spine, and running from tail to head. Head and neck moult comes last. In geese, flight-feather moult begins shortly after onset of the general moult; in ducks, however, flight feathers moult during the second phase of the general moult and sometimes even towards the end of the moult. Moult of the whole vesture is completed simultaneously with shedding of the extreme helm feathers (Shtraikh and Svetozarov, 1935, a, b). This is the change sequence in feathers from different groups in two representative types of domestic fowl, which otherwise moult in different ways.

The moult intensity is directly proportional to its total duration. The interval between the shedding of two adjacent first-order flight feathers in birds with a continuous moult may serve as a criterion whereby the moult intensity can be assessed, since a correlation exists between the replacement of these feathers and the moult of the remainder of the plumage. Domestication produces great variations in the time and intensity of the moult. In the main, the process tends to lengthen. Frequently, the moult begins, only to be interrupted, and is then resumed somewhat later, the moult continuing from those pterylae in which it ceased earlier. The interval between moults is sometimes prolonged considerably. It has been observed that as a general rule birds which begin to moult later shed their plumage more intensively than those which moult earlier (Larionov, 1934).

The sequence of feather replacement and the intensity of the process are typical for each species. The quantitative features of the moult are equally manifest in the first post-nidal moult and all subsequent periodical annual moults of the definitive plumage.

There are some features of the juvenile moult which differ from all subsequent moults. The juvenile moult is timed to coincide with changes in the properties of the feather follicles, namely the incapacity to produce definitive feathers different from the juvenile feathers in their shape, colour, and pattern, and differing also according to sex (Lloyd Jones, 1907; Parkes, 1952; Bendell, 1955; Westerskov, 1955; Kipp, 1956; Baird, 1958).

The timing of the moult also varies. In some birds the first moult begins immediately after the growth of the juvenile plumage is completed or even earlier, as in a number of colibris, the majority of passeriform birds, and, among domestic fowl, in chicken and pigeons (Welter, 1955; Takewaki and Mori, 1944; Hazelwood and Gorton, 1954; Wagner, 1955, 1957; Aldrich, 1956; le Febre and Warner, 1959). Other birds have only a partial post-nidal moult.

In many aquatic birds completion of growth coincides with the moulting of the small and helm feathers, but the birds of prey do not moult for the first time until they are a year old. On the whole, however, the moult in small birds lasts a much shorter time than in larger birds. The correlation between the moult and the external conditions is also interesting. Among the fledglings of birds which build their nests on the ground or in grass, the post-nidal moult as a rule coincides with the time at which the general growth of the birds is completed. In birds which build their nests in less accessible places (in trees, on rock faces) the first moult occurs much later. In birds which can hide in water and grass or among bushes, as in ducks, geese, and corncrakes, the flight feathers moult rapidly and simultaneously. Gradual moulting of the wing feathers is typical of birds living in trees, and as a result they never lose their capacity for flight. It is characteristic that some birds, living under harsh climatic conditions, as in some mountainous regions, undergo a sudden moult during which the large feathers are all exchanged almost simultaneously, or in two specific sequences (Popov, 1954, 1956). Such changes are particularly characteristic of passeriform birds, which in normal conditions undergo a gradual moult (Dement'iev, 1940, b; Dubinin, 1947). When wild birds are domesticated, the typical moult pattern frequently becomes disorganised (Mayand, 1944, 1950; Piechocki, 1955).

Local phenomena during feather replacement

In its outward appearance the moulting process is the shedding of the old feathers and the development of the new in their place. The same thing happens when old feathers are pulled out and are replaced by new ones. The disruption of the contact between the base of the shaft of the old feather and the underlying anlage of the next feather generation activates it and initiates its development. This raises the question of the nature of the process which leads to the shedding of the old feathers in a natural moult. Is the growth of the new anlage preceded by this shedding of the old feathers? It would appear, however, that in a natural moult there is no preliminary shedding of feathers, which are pushed out by the anlage of the new growing feather. The development of the anlage begins before the old feather falls from its follicle.

It is well known that the skin and its various derivatives are periodically renewed, not only in birds but also in other classes of vertebrate. In reptiles, closest to the birds phylogenetically, the horny scaly vestiture, a formation homologous with bird plumage, is shed after the new vestiture has formed beneath it (Eggert, 1935). The primary embryonal down feathers of birds are pushed out of the follicles at the tips of the shaft or at the tips of the newly formed vanes of the nidal feathers. Later, after the vane unfolds, the connection between the down feathers and the juvenile plumage is less close.

During seasonal moults also, the old feathers have been seen to be pushed out by the proliferating anlagen of the new feathers. Among the trunk feathers of adult birds during moulting one can always find young shafts, and sometimes even matured feathers with the quills of the old feathers attached to their tips. Sometimes, when moulting birds such as ducks are plucked, the quill of the old feather is pulled out with a young shaft firmly attached to it. The tip of the shaft is so closely connected with an indentation in the base of the old feather that this connection may be observed even when the feather is mechanically pulled. During moulting in penguins, the developing shafts break through the bottom of the quill of the old feather and even penetrate its cavity (Studer, 1873, 1878). This provides a very close link between the two feather generations, one disrupted only after the new feathers appear above the skin surface. If the moment at which feathers are shed in moulting birds is noted, it may be seen that the young feather appears on the skin surface simultaneously with the shedding of the old feather or immediately after it. The link between the base of the old feather and the tip of the new one can also be observed in an experimentally produced moult. All these observations lead to the conclusion that in a natural moult development of the new feather begins before shedding of the old feather (Voitkevich, 1934, a; 1936, a).

Histological studies on chicken skin in a state of artificially induced moult reveal that the link between the apex of the developing anlage and the base of the old feather shaft is indeed preserved within the feather follicle during the whole growth period (Lhvatov, 1935). The old feather is shed before the tip of the new shaft leaves the follicle, or somewhat later, which supports the view that the shedding of the old feathers in moulting birds is caused by the growth of the new feathers. Is the developing feather anlage strong enough to push out the old feather? Experiments carried out by us with the flight feathers of pigeons have shown that the young shaft pushes out not only a feather previously pulled out and put back into place, but even another shaft introduced into the follicle and fixed with clamps to the upper edges of the feather follicle (Voitkevich, 1934, d).

Histological studies of the skin of moulting pigeons have shown that during moult the feather anlage development is preceded by changes in the epithelial wall of the follicles. The upper layers undergo intensive keratinisation and desquamation. If the growth of new feather generations is stimulated artificially outside the moulting period, similar changes may be observed in the follicular wall. The desquamation of the epidermis cells naturally weakens the link between the old feather and the underlying tissues and thus facilitates the sliding of the shaft from the follicle. Keratinisation of the epidermis and cell desquamation during moult take place not only in the feather follicles but also all over the skin surface.

The results obtained during investigation of these local phenomena during the moult are important. Workers studying moult conditions will no longer have to discriminate arbitrarily between two different factors, the one causing shedding of the old feathers and the other the cause of the development of the new feather anlage. The factors which stimulate the periodic development of hitherto resting feather anlages lead indirectly to the shedding of the old plumage.

Analysis of the data on the structural development and moult of the feather has made it possible for us to outline a further sequence of experimental studies on the feather-formation process, allowing for the differences in development between the juvenile and definitive plumage. Feather development will be discussed below in the following order: formation of the anlage; its development and growth; and the differentiation of the feather including its shape, structure, colour, and pattern, with artificially activated feather follicles as well as during the natural seasonal moult.

CHAPTER II

EXPERIMENTAL ANALYSIS OF SOME CONDITIONS NECESSARY FOR THE FORMATION, GROWTH AND DEVELOPMENT OF THE FEATHER

THIS chapter reports the results of studies of certain features in the feather forming tissue which emerge during development. While the general regulation of the body cannot be ignored in any study of local features typical of feather-forming tissue, it has, to a certain extent, to be neglected in this account.

The data on the feather-formation process and the material from which the anlage is formed will be discussed first. Then the relationship between growth and differentiation will be examined, together with an account of the relation between the developing feather and the new anlage, and the interaction between the feather anlages developing in different follicles.

RELATIVE STABILITY OF THE MAIN FEATURES OF THE PLUMAGE

We have emphasised above that feather development, structure, and colouring reflect numerous environmental influences which affect the physiology of the body. It has also been shown, however, that the features which as a whole are characteristic of the plumage of a given species are relatively stable. It seemed appropriate to study the relative rôles played by the inherent properties of the feather-forming tissue on the one hand and of the body as a whole on the other, by factors related to the development of characteristic plumage features.

Experiments with skin transplants of varying orientation in birds of different ages and species could be expected to throw light on these relationships. The orientation of a skin area containing feather follicles being altered, it was to be expected that the way the new feathers were formed would demonstrate the degree to which the position of the feather anlage in relation to the whole body would affect feather formation. Young birds and sexually mature birds were mostly used for the relevant experiments.

In experiments on homing pigeons, the spino-lumbar pteryla (Voitkevich and Novikov, 1936, a) was chosen for transplants. In this pteryla the feathers vary in size; the ones nearer the head are smaller, the size increasing towards the tail. The relation between the contour and the fluffy parts also changes gradually, in favour of the latter. Prior to the experiment the small feathers were plucked out all over the pigeon's trunk. Then a skin flap 5 × 7 cm was cut from the back of each bird. Separated from the underlying tissues, the flap was turned 180 degrees in the same plane—so that the part of the pteryla which had lain in the caudal direction now pointed towards the head—and was fixed in the new position. The transplant did not 'take' completely in all experiments, but it 'took' well in seven pigeons on whose backs a considerable number of feathers developed. Independently of the degree to which the reversed piece of skin 'took', the feathers grew in the direction they would have grown, that is diametrically opposed to those around the transplant. Two months later the feathers were plucked from the anterior, middle, and posterior parts of the skin flap and their length was measured. Both the total length of the vane and that of its contour were measured, and the relative proportions were calculated. The same measurements were repeated much later, after the bird's plumage had been renewed during a natural moult. Feathers fixed in the same position on control birds were used for comparison. It appeared that in the first period after the transplant the relation of the contour part to the total length was much smaller than in the control birds. In other words, the contour failed to develop fully, probably owing to insufficient nutrition. Later, when the metabolic conditions within the transplanted skin flap had improved, the developing feathers were in no way different from those in the control group.

Similar results were obtained in experiments on young White Leghorns, the method used being similar to that used for pigeons. It proved much more difficult, however, to transplant a 7 × 10 cm skin flap successfully. A positive result was obtained in nine out of thirty-two chickens treated. Before the operation the trunk feathers were plucked, to increase skin vascularisation and to activate the feather follicles. Observations were continued for over three years. It emerged that in chickens as in pigeons there were no changes in the size, structure and orientation of the feathers, despite repeated plucking and natural moult. Similar observations had been reported somewhat earlier by Klatt (1917). We should also mention the experiments made by Kozelka (1929). He transplanted various derivatives of the epidermis (skin, comb, spores) into areas where these formations did not usually occur. On the new sites such formations displayed all their earlier properties and retained their capacity to react to hormones. These results on chickens and pigeons enable us to draw the conclusion that moving the pterylae to new areas does not lead to fundamental changes in the properties of developing feathers.

In further experiments on 120 five-day chicks (White Leghorn, Rhode Island Red, and Plymouth Rock), autohomo-transplants and hetero-transplants of relatively large standard areas (3 × 3 cm) from the down-feather covered skin of the back were carried out. In these experiments the transplanted skin flap was turned round. The transplant 'took' on 96 chicks. Later, the plumage developing on the transplant was compared with that of control chicks. On the transplant skin areas the number of developing young feathers varied between 68 and 142. Feathers taken from three arbitrarily chosen zones were measured periodically. The whole experiment lasted three years. The results showed that the feathers which developed on the turned skin flap were different from those normally found in the pterylae in question, both in overall size and in the relative proportions of the contour and the fluffy parts. The difference between the proportions of the contour and the fluffy parts of the feather, typical of the most isolated feathers on the dorsal pterylae (when of normal orientation), was to some extent minimised. Such decreases in the usual topographic differences were particularly marked in the case of transplants from one breed to another; e.g. from Plymouth Rock to White Leghorn hens or *vice versa.*

These results warrant the conclusion that the creation of unusual conditions for feather follicles at an early stage, before the feather anlage begins to develop, results in new properties in subsequent generations of definitive feathers.

The results also show that the properties of the feather-forming tissue can change during the individual life of a bird, and that the formation of their properties does not end at the first stage of post-embryonal life. In young birds, the feather-forming tissue possesses a certain lability in changing conditions, but in adult birds the tissue is more stable. Earlier investigations by other authors seem to confirm this conclusion.

Willier, Rawles, and Hadorn (1930) and Willier and Rawles 1938, a, b, c, 1940) carried out numerous experimental skin transplants in chick embryos of different breeds, to study the properties of the feather-forming tissue during ontogenesis and its ability to produce certain structures and patterns. They found that the basic morphological features in the developing feathers were relatively stable; the new host nevertheless exerted a certain physiological influence upon the transplant.

Novikov (1936, a) has also carried out skin transplants in young Plymouth Rock chicks of different ages. Plumage in these birds develops relatively late. Transplants of skin flaps from the back were not followed by any changes in orientation. If skin was transplanted from adult into young birds there was no change in the time at which the contour feathers began to develop. But, conversely, if skin was transplanted from young chicks into older birds, the influence of the new host became manifest in that the transplanted skin flap became feathered earlier than was usual. Larionov, Kuz'mina, and Lektorskii (1938) carried out cross-transplants of heterologous pterylae in Rhode Island Red and White Leghorn chicks. Skin flaps from the pterylae on the back and on the upper wing were interchanged. It was observed that the feather formation changed to some extent in accordance with the new position of the skin flap, but that the transplant never became completely dominated by the new host.

Danforth (1929, a, b, 1931, 1933) successfully transplanted skin flaps on to chickens of different breeds with different colouring and plumage structure. In many birds parts of the heterogenous feather follicles coalesced in the border zones. These heterogenous feather follicles formed chimeral feathers, the vanes of which showed a mosaic made up of patterns from both partners. This mosaic frequently reappeared in subsequent feather generations, although in some case the chimeral differences in the colouring evened out. Later again, Lillie and Wang (1942, 1943, 1944) similarly produced chimeral feathers. In these experiments separate parts of the feather anlage were transplanted in chickens.

SOURCE OF MATERIAL FOR THE FORMATION OF THE FEATHER ANLAGE

Earlier we have said that the development of each of the numerous feather generations begins with the proliferation of ready-made feather anlagen. The anlage is formed at the moment when growth of the preceding feather is completed. Prior to that moment the anlage cannot be formed, as it would block the supply of nutritional material to its predecessor, which continues growing. Moreover, it was necessary to establish precisely where the new feather anlage material originated; whether it develops from the deeper tissues, in relation to the developing feather, or from the basal parts of the feather already there. It was thought that if a young feather shaft was turned through 180 degrees at the stage before the formation of a new feather anlage, and if continued growth in this new position was achieved, the question of the origins of the material for the new anlage could be solved by observing feather orientation in the next generation. If the new feathers grew in the new changed direction, it would be justifiable to assume that the anlage formed from tissues belonging to the preceding feather above the anlage.

The upper covering second-order flight feathers in pigeons

seemed to be the most promising object of this investigation. These are small feathers with deep follicles, and in consequence the feather shafts are well protected against possible trauma.

Experiment 1. All feathers in the above group were removed. Ten days later the shafts (12-14 mm lengths before the vane begins to unfold) were pulled out as far as the upper part of the follicle. Seventeen shafts were put back into the follicle (seven being first turned 180 degrees on their own axis). Observation showed that six feathers completed their development in the first case, but that in the second case all the rotated feathers perished.

Experiment 2. The covering second-order flight feathers were removed from three birds (Fig. 5). When the newly developing shafts were thirteen days old and the vane was also partially formed, the shafts were pulled out to the upper edge of the follicle. Twenty were pushed back into the original position but ten were first turned through 180 degrees (Fig. 5e). Twenty-five days later, when feather growth was completed, fourteen of the twenty feathers which had been left in an unchanged position were found to be normally developed. Three of the ten feathers which had been turned round had completed growth in the new position.

If one compares these findings with those obtained in the preceding experiment, it will be seen that the rotated shafts can survive when shafts at a somewhat later stage (Experiment 2) are used for the operation. Only feathers already carrying small vanes were, therefore, used for the experiments.

Experiment 3. This was carried out on eight pigeons. Four of sixteen feathers survived after having been pulled out and put back into their original positions. Sixty-eight feathers were turned, of which thirteen continued growth.

Experiment 4. This was carried out a year later, after further improvements in the method. In six birds eleven feathers in series were removed from both wings. Fourteen days later every second feather shaft of the young feathers was pulled out on the left (control) wing and replaced in its original position. The same operation was carried out with the shafts of the right (experimental) wing, the only difference being that the feathers were rotated through 180 degrees before being replaced. The operation was performed on thirty feathers, both among control and experimental feathers. At the end of the experiment twenty-four control and seventeen experimental feathers were found to be fully developed. After development

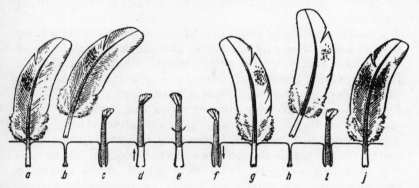

Fig. 5. Diagram of experiments with rotation of the young feathers through 180° and their viability in the rotated state

of the rotated feathers was fully completed and sufficient time had elapsed for the feather anlage of the next generation to be formed, all the experimental and control feathers were removed and the new developing feathers of the next generation were studied. In all cases without exception (a total of thirty-three) the removed rotated feather as well as the non-rotated control feather had been replaced by new feathers in the normal position. It thus appears that the material for the formation of the anlage is newly formed and does not originate from the material used for the growth of the feathers in the preceding generation.

While this conclusion seems adequately supported by these findings, some objections can, nevertheless, be raised. It may, for example, be suggested that the feather anlage did later form from parts of the preceding feather although the material altered its properties under the influence of the underlying tissue, so that the new feathers consequently grew in the original position. This assumption, however, is not consistent with the findings obtained in an earlier study (Voitkevich and Novikov, 1936, a) in which we showed that the size, structure, and direction of growth of the newly formed anlage are stable properties. Another assumption, according to which the anlage could have had time to form in the base of the shaft before the latter was rotated, was disproved by histological investigation of young feathers at the stage of development in question.

Lilley's experiment (1940), in which he dissected the young feather anlage along its main axis, also showed the stability of the local features within each feather follicle. The double feathers which developed after this operation frequently showed no sign of morphological lesion and were identical. Further, it is interesting that in rare cases double or 'twin' feathers can be found (Kuhn, 1953, and Steinbacher, 1954). These feathers show mirror symmetry. These results are no more than the manifestation of a general biological law according to which early stages of development have extensive morphogenetic potential.

THE ROLE OF THE FEATHER FOLLICLE IN THE DEVELOPMENT OF THE FEATHER

The base of the follicle is known to pass directly into the generative zone of the germ and thus to participate in the development of the feather. What is the role of the parts of the feather follicle which form the sac? Pigeon feathers (coverts of the primary flight feathers) were convenient, being experimentally accessible and possessing maximal sized follicles. The barrels from the plucked feathers were cut obliquely to make small tubes, shortened by 3-4 mm compared to the depth of the follicle. The tubes were filled with paraffin and inserted into the follicle. An opening of approximately 2 mm diameter was cut in the wall of the follicle, opposite the lower oblique end of the tube. The developing quill, meeting an obstacle (the tube) left the follicle through this opening and continued to develop outside the follicle walls. Similar feathers within the normal follicles of the other wing served as controls. The experimental and the control quills were examined microscopically to detect any changes. No differences were discovered between the control and the experiment in either the structure of the quill or of the cornified integument covering it. The structural elements began to be formed in both cases at the same time, although the total length of the young feathers was by this time somewhat shorter in the experiment. The growing quill at first deviated by 45-60 degrees from the normal direction, but later assumed an almost normal position. Mature feathers which had been formed outside the follicles were no different in size and structure from the controls.

The walls of the feather follicle play a protective role towards the feather quill and help in anchoring the barrel of the fully formed feather. A characteristic feature in this respect is the change in the depth of the follicles to correspond with the functional load on the feathers of different tracts (Table 1).

Table 1

The size of follicles and the total length of the feathers in various pterylae of the pigeon

Feather pterylae	Total length of feather in mm	Depth of follicle in mm	Ratio of depth of follicle to length of feather, %
Dorsal feathers	36.3	1.6	4.4
Coverts of flight secondaries . . .	69.0	7.4	10.7
Rectrices	128.6	13.0	10.8
Flight secondaries	104.0	12.8	12.3
Flight primaries	168.5	21.1	12.6
Coverts of flight primaries	71.2	18.8	26.4

Table 1 shows that maximal depth of follicles occurs in the case of those feathers which play a vital part in flight—the flight primaries and their coverts.

The latter prevent bending of the flight feathers during wing flap (when considerable pressure is experienced) and ensure proper anchoring of the flight feathers in the wing.

The feathers which cover the trunk, the neck and the head, on the other hand, have relatively small follicles.

CORRELATION BETWEEN
GROWTH AND DIFFERENTIATION

Zonal differentiation of a large mass of intensively proliferating material is a peculiar feature of the development of the feather. In the initial phase the whole rudiment of the feather grows, but soon structural differentiation begins to take place in its apical part, while growth continues in the basal part. The consistent correlation between the rate of differentiation and the formation of new cellular material determines the constant boundary between these two zones. Primary grouping of epithelial cells in the laying-down of the barbs is a sign of the onset of differentiation. The lower boundary of this zone is situated around the circumference of the quill, and is represented structurally by two symmetrical arcuate formations laying down the shaft and those laying-down the barbs. The inter-zone boundary shifts towards the base of the follicle at later stages of development, which is evidently associated with diminished feather growth during this period.

The correlation of growth and differentiation can be investigated by modifying experimentally one of the components of the developmental process. Are the early stages of differentiation connected with accumulation of cellular material, or are they adjusted to a definite time elapsed since the beginning of growth? The intention was either to alter the rate of feather growth or to arrest the growth at various stages of

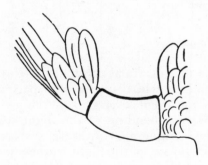

Fig. 6. Diagram of the placing of a collodion cotton dressing on the wing of a pigeon

development. If the rate of formation of the feather structure depends on a definite correlation between the rate of growth and differentiation, then termination of growth should affect the typical course of differentiation.

The test objects were the large flight feathers of the carrier-pigeon. First an attempt was made to arrest their development at the earliest stages, but this proved technically difficult. A method was therefore developed for arresting feather growth at later stages by covering the follicle. After a series of preliminary tests, the following technique was adopted. A collodion cotton dressing was applied to an area of the wing freed from feathers (Fig. 6). Under these conditions the development of the quills could only occur within the follicles. Initially the duration of the experiment was varied. The collodion cotton dressing was removed from the experimental wing after various intervals of time: after four days from the moment of application in the first series (the quill reaching a size equal to half the length of the follicle during this period); after seven days in the second series (the developing feather reaching the surface of the skin); after ten days in the third series (by which time the control feather was showing unfurling of the vane) and finally after thirteen days in the fourth series (being approximately half the time necessary for full development of the feather). Identical feathers developing under normal conditions on the other wing served as controls (Table 2).

Covering the surface of the wing with a collodion cotton dressing for periods of from four to thirteen days did not hinder subsequent restoration of feather growth. The developing quills met no obstacle in the first series of experiments, and their growth therefore differed little from normal. In the second series the apices of the quills were somewhat deformed from contact with the dressing, but growth during the subsequent period was generally normal. When the dressing was removed in the third series, the young quills already had small unfurled vanes at approximately the same stage of differentiation as those on the control wing, although the total length of the quill was less than in the control. This phenomenon was also observed in the fourth series.

The developing vane (on the experimental wings) soon ceased to grow, and its lower part, thinning gradually, turned

Table 2

Growth of feathers, the follicles being covered for various periods of time data in percentages of mean length of normal feathers

Experiment *1*

Days from start of experiment	Series 1		Series 2		Series 3		Series 4	
	Control	Experimental	Control	Experimental	Control	Experimental	Control	Experimental
0	100	100	100	100	100	100	100	100
4	—	Dressing removed	—	—	—	—	—	—
7	1.1	0.2	2.3	Dressing removed	3.8	—	3.6	—
10	17.5	11.7	17.0	8.8	21.6	Dressing removed	21.3	—
13	36.3	30.8	35.1	24.7	41.0	1.1	40.0	Dressing removed
16	55.7	51.2	53.1	40.5	60.1	4.4	57.8	0.9
19	71.9	67.8	70.3	60.6	76.9	18.0	75.2	1.4
22	82.7	75.4	80.3	70.1	87.2	29.1	84.2	12.9
25	93.5	87.7	91.2	86.1	96.3	40.2	95.1	23.3
28	95.1	93.5	95.8	94.0	97.4	52.6	97.4	38.3
31	—	94.4	—	94.7	—	62.4	—	50.0
34	—	96.1	—	96.1	—	72.4	—	62.9
37	—	98.6	—	96.5	—	77.5	—	72.5

into a short shaft connected with the underlying parts of the quill. After some time the horny integument of the quill desquamated and the top of a new vane became unfurled (Figs.7, 8, 9). The section of the vane formed earlier either dropped off or remained attached to the shaft of the feather developing below it. A similar result was obtained in another experiment (Fig. 10).

It must be borne in mind, when considering the figures (Table 2) relating to the two last series, that they do not represent the true picture of the growth of the feathers in the experiment. In fact, the quills measured three and six days after removal of the collodion dressing had the same dimensions. This is because the vanes which began to unfurl by the time of the first measurement had dropped off when the next measurement was made.

Similar results were obtained when the experiment was repeated on adult (two-year) and juvenile (three-month) pigeons.

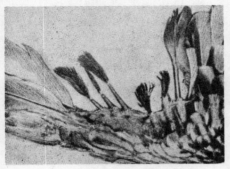

Fig. 7. *Pigeon's wing fifteen days after removal of dressing. Three young quills carry on their apices the vanes of a previous generation of feathers*

Fig. 8. *Wing of the same pigeon as in Fig. 7 but seventeen days after removal of dressing. The vanes have dropped off; the quills of the new generation continue to grow*

Fig. 9. *Wing of the same pigeon as in Fig. 7, twenty-three days after removal of dressing; new vanes of normal form have unfurled from the young quills*

The collodion film remained *in situ* for ten days in both cases, similarly to the third series of preliminary experiments, in which a biphasic development of the vane was observed. The measurements of the growing feathers are given in Table 3.

Fig. 10. Preservation of the connection between the defective vane (in which development had ceased) and the apex of a new normally developing feather

The interruption of differentiation and consequent development of two independent generations of experimental feathers became even clearer. The feather vanes which appeared on the tenth day in Experiment 2 reached a length of 16 mm by the fourteenth day and then dropped off. The underlying quills grew on average to a length of 13 mm by the time of the next measurement. The same occurred in Experiment 3. The wings of one of the birds in this experiment are shown in Fig. 11 (the photograph was taken four days after removal of the collodion dressing); the stage of differentiation is the same in the experimental and the control feathers, although their dimensions are different. The data on the growth of feathers in Experiment 3 are shown graphically in Fig. 12: the white

columns represent the vanes developing immediately on erup-
tion from the follicles, the black columns representing the underlying new quills. When the tops of the white and the black
columns are joined, separately, the resultant lines are parallel.
If the curves are continued below the abscissa, i.e. representing the intrafollicular development of the quill, it becomes
apparent that new feather germs were being laid down at the
base of the follicle at the moment of the unfurling of the vane.
In this way arrest of growth of a young feather entails 'auto-
matic' formation of a new feather germ. The ensuing relationships are shown schematically in Fig. 13. The top part of the

 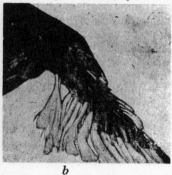

a   *b*

Fig. *11. Growth of flight feathers in the pigeon on
fifteenth day after beginning of activation of the feather
germs:*

*a, on the control wing; b, on the experimental wing four days after
removal of the collodion cotton dressing*

figure relates to a normally developing feather, the relatively
undifferentiated parts enclosed within a horny integument
being shown in black and the unfurled vanes in white. The
lower part of the figure represents schematically the development of the feather when its growth is arrested. The successive
age-changes are shown from left to right. Comparison of
normal and experimental feathers of the same age demonstrates that vanes of the same developmental stage appear in
both at the same time, despite the considerable difference in
the size of the feathers.

It may, however, be questioned whether there are in fact
two generations of feathers or an anomalous development of a

single generation. Support for the presence of two independent generations comes first of all from the parallel growth curves for experimental and control feathers. If the top part of the vane, which is shed, is indeed an independent generation, then the final dimensions of the feathers developing during the second period of development should not differ from the normal control ones. Measurements made with this in view showed that the feathers which developed during the second phase were practically identical with normal ones in terms of length, width, and area of vanes.

Thus, arrest of quill growth occurs when the apertures of the follicles are covered for periods of ten to thirteen days. Differentiation of exactly those parts of the vanes which would have developed under conditions of normal growth continues in these quills. At the same time laying-down and subsequent proliferation of new feather germs take place at the base of the follicles. After removal of the obstacle, parts of the first-generation feathers emerge from the follicles and are shed. New quills, however, continue to grow, subsequently developing into normal feathers. It proved possible to obtain defective vanes of three to five successive generations in the feather follicle by varying the period of time over which the collodion cotton dressing was kept on the wing.

The example of the first abortive generation of feathers provides convincing evidence that the formation of the vane can also occur within the follicle. The onset of differentiation is independent of whether the young quill has reached certain dimensions or not. The period of growth preceding the onset of differentiation of parts of the feather is thus not an essential overall condition for the process of structure formation. Differentiation, which is manifestation of a specific law of feather development, occurs after a definite interval of time after the onset of growth, corresponding to the age of the feather being formed. These phenomena reflect the peculiar nature of the development of such a highly specialised formation as the feather, which differs in the inter-relationship of proliferation and differentiation from other systems of the body (Filatov, 1939).

Table 3

Rate of feather growth, the feather follicles being covered for ten days: measurements in percentages of final length of control feathers

Experiment 2: mature pigeons			Experiment 3: juvenile pigeons		
Days from beginning of experiment	Control	Experimental	Days from beginning of experiment	Control	Experimental
0	100	100	0	100	100
8	13.1	—	8	7.5	—
10	24.6	0.9	11	14.3	0.4
14	47.4	16.7	15	32.0	20.5
17	66.6	13.7	19	56.6	16.2
22	98.9	37.1	24	78.9	47.6
26	97.9	58.7	29	99.5	75.9
30	99.7	77.8	37	106.2	109.9
35	—	91.5	—	—	—
40	—	100.3	—	—	—

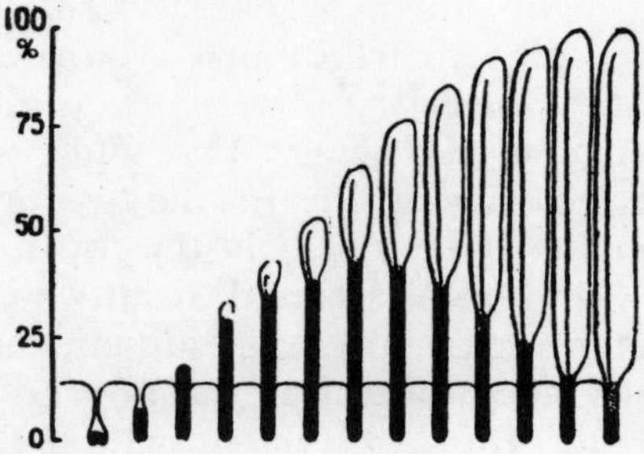

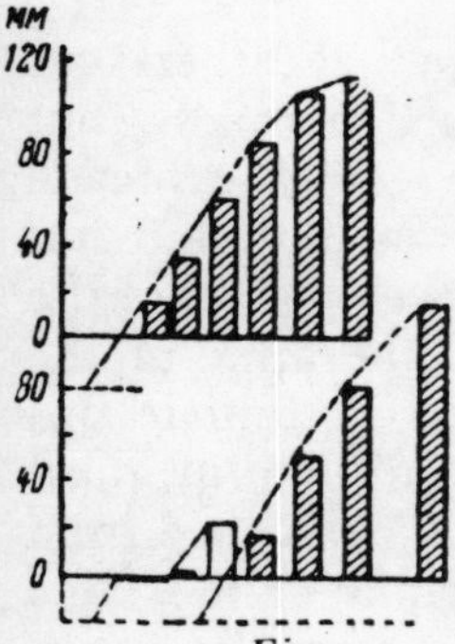

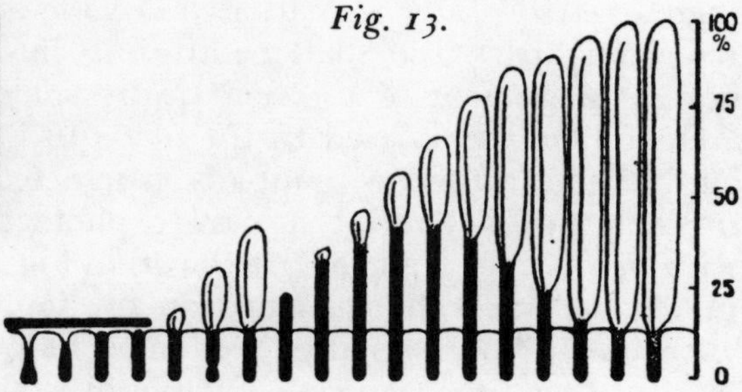

Fig. 12. Diagram illustrating the growth of feathers on the control wing (top) and on the experimental wing (bottom). Abscissa, time from the beginning of feather growth

Fig. 13 Scheme of feather development on the control wing (top) and on the experimental wing (bottom). The live growing part of the feather is shown in black, the vanes in white

TEMPORAL ASPECTS OF STRUCTURE DIFFERENTIATION AND LAYING-DOWN OF NEW FEATHER GERMS

The conclusion that differentiation spreads to the underlying parts of the quill when the rate of growth is slowed down or growth is arrested (Voitkevich, 1936, b) has been confirmed by further experiments in which a supplementary analysis was made of the conditions under which new generations of feathers are formed.

One experiment involved three groups of carrier-pigeons, five birds in each group. Nine consecutive covert feathers over the secondary flight feathers were removed from both wings of each bird; these coverts were similar in size and duration of growth. The new generation of quills which had developed in the pigeons in the first group were cut on the ninth day on both wings at different levels, descending towards the outer edge of the wing. The same operation was performed on twelve-day quills in the second group of pigeons and on eighteen-day quills in the third.

The experimental results were as follows. Feathers cut above a certain level subsequently developed normally, but the removed section was not restored. If the section was made below this level, the growth of the feather was inhibited and then arrested. Later a small area of vane developed from the remaining part, the shaft continuing into the apex of the horny integument of the new quill; out of the follicle this area of vane was carried by the new quill and then dropped off. Normal feathers without any vane defects developed from the new quills. Several successive photographs of the same wing of a Group 1 pigeon are shown in Figs. 14-17. The quills in Fig. 14 were photographed on the fourteenth day of the experiment (five days after section). The quills cut at a high level are seen to have considerably overtaken in growth the three adjacent quills which were sectioned lower down. The latter had stopped growing, and during the two subsequent days produced defective vanes (Fig. 15). The neighbouring quills continued to develop normally. On the eighteenth day the apices of new quills appeared from the follicles, carrying the vanes of the preceding generation of feathers. These were

shed after a certain interval (Fig. 16). The new quills produced vanes on the twenty-third day; these were similar in
shape and structure to those on the normally developing
feathers (Fig. 17). See also the diagrams in Figs. 18 and 19.

Thus, section of a nine-day quill (17 mm long) at a level
above 11 mm does not affect further development except for
the loss of the top 6 mm of the vane or less. In other words, the
length lost is the same as that which would have been lost had
the operation been performed on an existing vane. When the
quill is sectioned at a level below 11 mm, the development of
these feathers is arrested and there is simultaneous formation
of a new feather germ in the generative zone. There are no
physiological connections between the body and the upper
third of the nine-day quill and section of the feather does not
lead to neoplasia. The underlying two thirds of the feather
maintain all the connections with the body's regulatory factors
which ensure the consistent laying down of a new feather.
Consequently, structure differentiation begins before the apex
of the quill reaches the upper edge of the follicle, that is, at
the stage corresponding to the fourth to sixth day of growth.
Additional experiments and microscopic studies showed that
section of six-day and younger quills always led to arrest of
growth of the given generation and development of new
feathers (Voitkevich, 1935, a, 1936, b).

Similar experiments with the feathers of birds in the second
and third groups at later stages of development showed that
the boundary area between the differentiation zone and the
underlying parts of the quill was situated at a lower level.
When eighteen-day quills (mean length 50 mm) were cut,
formation of feather germs was only induced if the section was
no higher than 6 mm from the base of the feather. At later
stages of development section of the quill at lower levels no
longer led to germ formation.

These experiments confirm the earlier morphological
observations, namely that the combination of two spatially
opposed processes—lengthwise growth and differentiation
(spreading from the apex of the quill to its base)—causes the
boundary zone to remain at the same level with respect to the
base of the feather for a considerable time.

Further experiments showed that other kinds of interrup-

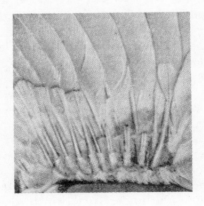

Fig. 14. Fourteen-day quills of feathers (coverts over secondary flight feathers) five days after section at different levels. Six quills on the left continue to develop, although the tops have been cut off; three quills on the right have ceased to develop

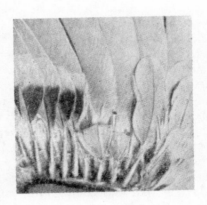

Fig. 15. Wing of the same pigeon as in Fig. 14, two days later; defective vanes have unfurled on the quills which had stopped developing

Fig. 16. Wing of the same pigeon as in Fig. 14, with eighteen-day quills. The apices of three new-generation quills have erupted from the feather follicles

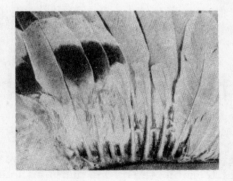

Fig. 17. Wing of the pigeon twenty-eight days after begining of feather growth: six first-generation feathers have developed fully (left), three new feathers continue to develop (right)

tion of the continuity of a quill below a definite level also led
to the arrest of growth of the given feather and laying-down
the germ of a new feather. For example, if a young quill is

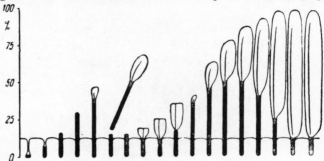

Fig. 18. Diagram of the development of a feather after section
of the quill in the growth zone; a new normal feather is
formed instead of the injured one

cut, pierced, crushed, or simply plucked out, growth is always
arrested and a new feather germ is laid down. This property

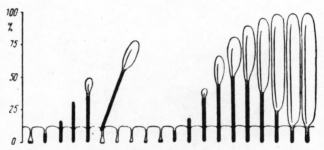

Fig. 19. Diagram of the development of a new feather
after plucking out an immature precursor

of the feather follicle must be regarded as an adaptation phenomenon which enables the bird to maintain a normal feather
covering independently of injury to the living parts of developing feathers.

Further experiments were performed, with the following
variations: the injured feather was either kept in the feather
follicle or removed, and the connection between the injured

feather and the germ being formed was either maintained or interrupted. In a group of pigeons, four consecutive feathers were removed from the middle part of the row of coverts over the secondary flight feathers on both wings. After twelve days the young quills were removed from the left wing and allowed to remain on the right (control) wing. In the other group of birds the quills of the same age were cut at the level of the top edge of the follicles on the one wing and pierced several times at the same level on the other wing.

Growth of the young feathers was arrested as a result of the various injuries (Figs. 8 and 9). There was simultaneous laying down of new feather germs developing under various conditions, namely (1) the young precursor-feather was completely absent; (2) part of the feather remained; (3) all the feather remained, but it was injured below the zone of differentiation. In the last two cases the structural development of the feather did not cease, despite the arrest of growth. Germs of new feathers were laid down and began to develop at the same time. The time of onset of the formation and development of new feathers is determined by the age of the immature quills which are removed or injured. Thus, for example, when the injured or removed quills were twelve days old the new quills reached a length of 12-13 mm on the twelfth day; when the removed quills were eighteen days old, this length was attained on the tenth day. When mature feathers were plucked out the new generation reached the same size on the eighth day. This was determined by the differences in the time of formation of new germs, since the rate of growth of new quills was the same in all cases.

The times of the laying-down of new germs depend on the nature of the injury to the precursor feathers. If the injured quill or part of it remains in the follicle, the new germ, although it is formed from underlying tissues, appears more rapidly if a direct connection with the generative zone of the predecessor is maintained than if the preceding quill is completely removed. Further experiments showed that this phenomenon arose through the stimulating influence of the precursor quill. This accelerated laying down of the germ under the influence of an injured young feather can be maintained in a series of successive generations. If, after similar

7

intervals of time, young quills are removed from some feather follicles and cut in others, these may produce one more generation of feathers over the same total period of time (e.g. after the fifth injury) than those from which the quills were removed (Voitkevich 1935, a, 1936, b).

These findings indicate that injury to the living part of a young feather causes arrest of its growth and induces laying down of a new feather germ. The earlier the infliction of the injury, the longer the time required for the formation of a new germ. When the new germ is formed it does not remain in a quiescent state, as is the case in normal feather development, but continues to develop regardless of the presence or absence above it of the injured precursor feather. The ability of the feather-forming tissue to form a new germ when development is impaired persists through many generations of feathers. This property reflects local peculiarities of the feather follicle, since the development of germs induced in different follicles at a different time retains its rhythm within the limits of one pteryla (Kuhn, 1928, 1932).

A number of authors have carefully analysed the relation of epithelial and connective-tissue components of the feather germ to subsequent structure differentiation, performing delicate exchange transplantations of parts of the germ (Lillie, 1932, 1940, 1942; Lillie and Juhn, 1932, 1938; Wang, 1941, 1943). The overall evidence of these investigations showed that the character, time, and rate of structure differentiation in the feather are determined by its epithelial component. The latter also affects the activity of melanocytes whose pigment forms the final pattern of the feather (Cock and Cohen, 1958; Cohen, 1959).

The dependence of the development of young feathers on general regulatory influences of the body will be discussed in detail below. The present chapter will continue to be concerned with phenomena occurring directly in the feather-forming tissue.

INTERACTION OF
DEVELOPING FEATHERS

The data considered above have dealt with the development of separate feather follicles. However, the development of feathers, both embryologically and after moulting, has a group aspect which suggests the existence of properties appertaining to group development. Such an investigation with respect to plumage appeared interesting in the light of observations made during natural moulting. Thus, for example, the work of Larionov, Berdyshev and Dmitrieva (1933) showed that the change of habit in late-moulting fowls was more rapid. The results of this investigation, however, could not answer the question of whether this rapid shedding of feathers was accompanied by more intensive growth. Moreover, the growth of the feathers was not compared with the intensity of the moulting that is the number of simultaneously growing feathers.

It seemed reasonable to establish the inter-relationships of adjacently growing feathers, because, as already mentioned, the plumage replacement in some pterylae during seasonal moulting always occurs in a definite order. The feather is usually shed while the following one has not yet become fully formed. This does not exclude the possibility of mutual physiological influence of young feathers.

Coverts of the secondary flight feathers were again chosen for the new experiments on feather growth. The experiments on pigeons were varied in two senses: investigation of possible interaction of several simultaneously growing feathers, and the relevant significance of age (stage of development).

Preliminary experiments were performed to find out whether the development of feathers on one wing had any effect on the growth of symmetrically placed feathers on the other wing, taking into account the bilateral nature of the replacement of homologous feathers during moulting. Two covert feathers situated at a distance from each other, were therefore removed from one wing, and at the same time from two to twelve feathers were removed from the other wing. If the feathers on one wing had no effect on the other, a synchronous development could be expected on the other wing. It was found that the development of a different number of feathers on one wing did not affect the rate of development of feathers on the other, from which it was concluded that one of the wings could serve as a control relatively to the other.

The main experiments involved forty-five male pigeons— fifteen series of three birds each. The first part of the experiments was published by Larionov, Voitkevich, and Novikov (1934). The development of the feathers was followed simultaneously on both wings, the left one, with a constant number of simultaneously removed feathers always serving as a control. The symmetrically placed coverts on the right wing were experimental, the number and the time of removal of mature precursors being varied. Simultaneously developing feathers were shown to have a mutual influence on one another by a shift of the development curve towards an earlier time. Within the range of two to twelve feathers, this was the more marked the greater the number of feathers undergoing simultaneous regeneration. The change in feather growth was characteristically confined to its shift in time and was not accompanied by a change in the rate of growth. Consequently, it is the early stage of the development of the feather germ that is the more sensitive to this influence. On receiving certain stimuli, the feather-forming process shifts to an earlier time, maintaining the same chronological order in the course of further development.

The time factor was analysed in a number of other experiments. The experiments were so designed that removal of some mature feathers was separated in time by a certain interval from the removal of others, and the onset of the growth of the germs in some follicles was delayed relative to others by five, ten, fifteen and twenty days. The difference in the times of the onset of growth made it possible to establish an interaction between quills at different stages of their development. In order to ensure closer proximity of these, six feathers were plucked alternately in each series, to be joined later by another six from the interspaces. These experiments again confirmed the existence of interaction. It was found that feathers which began to develop from five to fifteen days earlier stimulated the growth of younger feather germs. This effect was equal to zero if the interval between the onset of development of two consecutive groups exceeded fifteen days.

Thus, the same phenomenon is observed during the growth of young feathers as that seen in the regeneration of tissues and organs in other animals. Over a definite period of time, simultaneously regenerating organs have a mutually stimulating effect on one another (Vorontsova, 1949; Polezhaev, 1950).

In further experiments, attempts were made to isolate the active substances. An extract was made from skin with young quills taken from pigeons; various amounts of the extract were then injected into pigeons in which preliminary growth of feather germs had been induced so that they could serve as detectors. Observations on the growth of the coverts over the secondary flight feathers showed that the extract exerted a stimulating influence and the feathers developed at an earlier time. The degree of such a shift in time depended on the dosage of the extract (for more detail see Voitkevich, 1934c). The likelihood of the formation of biologically active substances in the developing follicles can hardly be disputed. It is sufficient to cite the formation of active substances in the antlers of the deer. Something akin to the non-ossified deer's antlers also occurs in bird skin during the development of plumage. The intensively developing feather quills are massive formations richly supplied with blood. The division of cells and their further transformations, keratinisation, and pigmentation of the structural elements, occurring at a high metabolic level, require the presence of appropriate activators, the formation of some of which is not excluded even within the feather follicle itself. Hinsch (1960) has recently shown a rise in alkaline phosphatase activity during the early period of development of young feather quills.

It is not particularly difficult to obtain a sufficient amount of the raw material for the isolation of the active substances, since a large number of quills can be obtained by preliminary plucking of the whole or a part of a bird's old plumage. The lysate prepared from the skin of pigeons with young developing quills can stimulate regenerative processes under experimental conditions (Voitkevich and Ershtein, 1936).

It has been noted above that the development of a large number of feathers on one wing does not appreciably affect the growth of feathers on the other wing. At the same time, the larger the number of feathers undergoing development in immediate mutual proximity, the greater the stimulation of growth. It may be supposed that the active substances forming in the developing feathers penetrate beyond the limits of the quills and can affect neighbouring feathers within a small distance, according to the permeability of the tissue. The results of supplementary experiments led to some other conclusions. In these experiments the distance between two or four developing feathers was measured, and it was found that the interaction between the regenerating feathers of a given group depended on their number, the distance between them being without appreciable effect. The experiment was then repeated in a somewhat different manner. A feather germ present in all the experiments in the same follicle was selected as a 'detector'; the source of stimulation, the 'inductor', was disposed at various distances from it. The experimental results demonstrated that the effectiveness of the influence did not depend on whether the 'detector' and the group of feathers affecting it were in immediate proximity or at some distance. Nevertheless, the stimulating effect was found to be unequal at the group's outer and inner edges.

Previously the indicator of interaction was always the growth of young feathers which began after the removal of fully formed precursor feathers. The stimulation manifested in a shift of the onset of growth was small, since the feather germs involved were already fully formed. The so-called 'sensitive period' of the formed feather germ probably does not exceed the first day or two of development. Much greater scope for demonstrating a stimulating effect could be achieved if it were possible to include the period of formation of the feather germs.

The results of experiments on the effect, on the laying-down of new germs, of injury to the developing feather were taken into consideration in this connection. Since a certain interval of time is needed for the laying down of the feather germ after injury, the results of interaction could have been expected to be especially appreciable during this period. The basic fact of mutual stimulation of developing feathers was again checked, as a preliminary step, by inducing the growth of normal feathers next to sectioned quills. The stimulation of the laying-down of new feathers was demonstrated so clearly that no special measurements of the growing feathers were necessary. The data of one of the experiments are given by way of illustration.

In a group of pigeons two feathers (coverts over secondary flight feathers) were removed from both wings at two-day intervals: 3 and 4. Two days later, 5 and 6. Two days later still, 7 and 8. After some time both wings showed a stepwise row of six quills of different ages. In the control birds, only two feathers were removed from the wing over the same period of time; ten days after the start of the experiment, all the six young quills on the right wing of the experimental birds were removed simultaneously and cut at the level of the upper edge of the follicles on the left. Young quills were plucked out of the wings of the control pigeons at the same time. It was found that in the control birds, the age difference between the quills existing before they were plucked out was in general preserved, so that the development of the germs being newly laid down was affected. In the experiment, on the other hand, the age differences in the feather follicles at the moment of formation of new germs were levelled out by the interaction of the adjacently situated follicles. The laying-down of feather germs at the site of the younger injured precursor was accelerated, under the influence of neighbouring feathers which had begun developing earlier. The interaction between 'old' and 'young' feather germs was apparent in the effect of the 'old' ones on the young ones, but not in the reverse direction. The remaining part of the preceding quill was also found to have a stimulating effect on the laying down of a new germ. This was seen in particular in that germ laying-down under the influence of six developing quills was accelerated to a more marked degree when the preceding quills were not removed but cut at a certain level (Voitkevich, 1937, c).

The experiments were then repeated, varying the time of removal of mature feathers and the period between the onset of quill growth and section. The results of all the experiments showed that the features characteristic of group development could be better demonstrated when the interaction occurred during the period of artificially induced laying-down of new feather germs (Voitkevich, 1934, c, 1936, a, e).

It was found in the course of the experiments that the stimulating influence of the quills on one another spread unequally towards the outer and the inner edges of the row. These observations were checked in a new series of experiments on pigeons.

On both wings of each bird, nine consecutive feathers (coverts of the secondary flight feathers) were removed. After eleven days, three quills on each wing were cut at the level of the upper edge of the follicle. The position of the sectioned quills was different: on the right wing they were at the end of the distal edge of the row, on the left at the end of the proximal edge. The sectioned feathers were replaced by the laying-down of new feather germs, whose development could be influenced by the neighbouring uninjured and growing feathers (see also scheme in Fig. 20). In the control birds the three homologous sectioned feathers developed in isolation, since the neighbouring six feathers had not been removed (see Table 4).

The data from the controls show that the rate of development of the coverts for the secondary flight feathers does not depend on where in the pteryla they are situated. But if there are normally developing feathers next to the injured quills, the rate of growth of the new quills is altered. Thus, the young

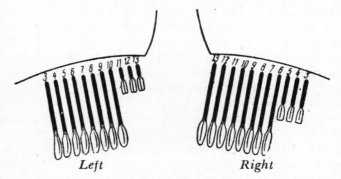

Left   *Right*

Fig. 20. *Diagram of the regeneration of covert feathers of different topography under the influence of a large number of other simultaneously developing feathers. The feathers cut at the level of the upper edge of the follicle were 3, 4, and 5 on the right wing, 11, 12, and 13 on the left wing*

quills on the distal edge of the pteryla developed considerably earlier than those on the proximal edge. Comparison with the control shows that there was generally no shift towards an

Table 4

Growth of new feathers at the site of sectioned ones in the presence of neighbouring developing feathers (data in percentages of final length of feathers)

Days from beginning of experiment	Control		Experimental	
	Right wing, feathers 3, 4, 5	Left wing, feathers 11, 12, 13	Right wing and six distal feathers, feathers 3, 4, 5	Left wing and six proximal feathers, feathers 11, 12, 13
0	100	100	100	100
7	20.4	19.6	21.6	21.7
9	33.9	32.3	33.4	35.0
11	45.5	44.6	47.8	46.8
	Sectioned	Sectioned	Sectioned	Sectioned
18	5.5	4.9	11.4	4.6
21	20.0	22.7	28.2	21.0
24	36.0	38.1	44.8	38.4
29	69.3	70.4	77.4	67.5
34	95.0	98.4	101.9	93.5
39	106.1	105.5	110.4	105.5

earlier development in the case of quills situated proximally to the trunk; they develop simultaneously with feathers not subjected to additional stimulation.

The interaction between simultaneously developing feathers is evidently mediated humorally. Had there been only local influence on the growth of quills, the two variants of the experiments could have been expected to yield similar results. In fact, however, stimulation is or is not present according to the topography of the regenerating feathers.

Further proof of direct action of substances formed in young feathers was obtained by joint culturing of feather quills *in vitro* and by introducing the pulp and the epithelial component of the young quill into the feather follicle during the period of feather-germ regeneration. Actually, the laying-down of feather germs can be stimulated both by allowing the plucked precursor quill to remain in the follicle and by introducing a quill from another pteryla. Stimulation is also effected by leaving a sectioned precursor quill, or part of such a quill, in the follicle. Lillie and Wang (1943) showed that introducing the epithelial parts of the germ into the feather follicle may not only stimulate the development of the quill but also induce the formation of additional feathers. This effect was more marked when the dorsal parts of feather germs were transplanted rather than ventral.

Stimulation of feather growth was also found to occur when neighbouring areas of skin or the walls of the feather follicle were injured (Voitkevich, 1936, a). If the skin on a previously plucked area of the dorsal pteryla is incised, the quills appear earlier around the healing wound than elsewhere.

One of the factors in the design of the above experiments was the fact that observation had shown that a large number of feathers develop at the same time in the course of natural moulting. The consistent regularity of the successive shedding of feathers in individual pterylae is noteworthy in this connection, as is the more rapid replacement of the plumage in late-moulting birds. In both cases mutual interaction of simultaneously growing feathers is presumed. Our experimental results indicate that the mutually stimulating influence of simultaneously growing feathers should be taken into account in explaining the rapid replacement of plumage in late-moulting birds. The successive replacement and growth of adjacently located feathers during moulting can also be regarded as an adaptational feature. It is evident that certain laws in the renewal of the plumage of a moulting bird cannot be explained solely in terms of local processes in the skin.

The results of the experiments reported in this part of the book can be summarised as follows. The two most characteristic features of the plumage of birds are (1) the feather, which is in close physiological connection with the body during its development, but loses this connection on completion of keratinisation, and (2) the constant property of the skin with respect to formation of new feathers, which comes into effect periodically as moulting.

The main properties and features of the feather follicle are associated with the local peculiarities of a given area of feather-forming tissue. A definite type of feather, differing from others in its individual shape, structure, and pattern, is formed in each feather follicle. When a mature bird's pteryla is displaced by transplanting it to an apteric area or that of another pteryla, the change in its orientation and so on does not affect the laying-down and development of feathers typical for the given area. Similar experiments on young birds, however, have shown that with sufficiently prolonged periods of observation it is possible to modify the properties of the feather follicles.

The development of the feather germ occurs either as the result of an impaired connection between it and the quill of the precursor feather, or as a result of the influence of physiological impulses from the body as occurs during moulting. In the developing feather, proliferation and differentiation take place in opposite directions: structural differentiation begins from the apex of the quill, gradually extending to the longitudinally growing parts underneath. The first signs of the formation of structural elements are found after a certain interval from the onset of growth, when the apex of the quill approaches the upper edge of the follicle. Once differentiation begins, it continues at a definite rate regardless of whether the previous development of the young feather was normal or had been arrested. Temporary interruption of the growth of the feather does not stop differentiation or diminish the intensity of this process.

Injury to the living part of a young feather leads to an arrest of growth, when a new germ is laid down at the base of the feather follicle, ensuring subsequent development of a normal feather. The feather-forming tissue has the remarkable property of ensuring the integrity of developing feathers. If a developing feather is not injured, the germ formed at the base of the follicle remains for a long period in a quiescent state. If the new germ is formed after preliminary injury to the immature feather, however, the new feather germ does not enter into a quiescent state, but continues to develop. The follicles form quiescent or developing feather germs according to the state of the precursor feathers.

Besides the individuality of each feather follicle, its morphogenic properties also display a physiological interaction between different follicles. An individual follicle is a small part of a complex system of the feather-forming tissue, but such interaction acquires particular importance for the large mass of developing feathers. Because of this phenomenon, the early stages of development of a mass of feathers are more rapid than the development of a single feather. This effect is enhanced if the inter-follicular interaction occurs not during the period of growth but at the time of the laying-down or regeneration of the feather germs. The stimulating influence increases in direct proportion to the number of simultaneously developing feathers. With non-simultaneously developing feathers, the stimulation is observed in young quills, whereas quills at a later stage of development are not stimulated by activation. Evidently, the successive development of new feathers during natural moulting is reflected in the physiological inter-follicular interaction, which should be taken into consideration when investigating the more general external physiological influences. On some pterylae the mutual influence of the developing feathers does not spread equally in all directions, but has a certain orientation which corresponds with the successive replacement of feathers on the given pteryla during moulting.

CHAPTER III

THE RÔLE OF THE THYROID GLAND IN THE DEVELOPMENT OF PLUMAGE AND IN MOULTING

THE regulatory influence of the nervous system on the development of the body and various morphogenic processes, including the formation of the integument, is mediated not only by direct nerve impulses but also through a series of intermediate links, such as the hormones of the endocrine glands. The essence of the central regulation of metabolism that ensures the formation of plumage in the bird can only be demonstrated if the functional interactions of the nervous system and the endocrine glands are taken into account.

A special place among the hormonal substances belongs to the active principles of the thyroid gland which affect the growth and differentiation of the developing body. The extensive range of the physiological properties of the thyroid hormones is dominated by their effect on the nervous and the vascular systems, on oxidative processes and thermo-regulation, on the metabolism of nitrogen and lipids, water and electrolytes. The stimulating effect of thyroxine and tri-iodothyronine on the activity of cell enzymes, the interaction of ions, and the permeability of various animal membranes has been described (Pitt-Rivers and Tata, 1959). The participation of the thyroid hormones in the regulation of protein and basal metabolism is very important for feather formation. During natural moulting there is a sharp rise in the level of oxidative processes and a stable preservation of a positive nitrogen and sulphur balance, reflecting a high concentration of these elements in the body which are essential for plumage development (Polivanova, 1949).

It has been mentioned, in the introductory chapter, that the initial facts relating to the participation of the thyroid in feather formation were obtained purely empirically. It had been shown that when pigeons and fowls were given large amounts of a dried thyroid preparation (thyroidin) the birds proceeded to moult vigorously. This fact was extrapolated to natural replacement of plumage, but this extrapolation is untenable, since it is not supported by observations on the state of the thyroid in a moulting bird or by sufficiently reliable physiological proofs of the dependence of moulting on the thyroid hormones. The experiments in which artificial moulting was induced by thallium salts (Prawochenski and Slizynski, 1933) should be recalled in this connection. Both in this case and that of the administration of large doses of thyroidin, severe toxic effects on the bird certain to affect the properties of the feather follicles could not be excluded. Actually, no causal physiological relationship between moulting and thallium was claimed as a result of these experiments with thallium salts.

Experimental analysis of the dependence of feather formation on the thyroid gland had therefore to be preceded by an examination of the data on the function of this endocrine organ during the development of the bird and of the formation and replacement of its plumage. It must be mentioned that information on the morphology of the thyroid in birds reported in the publications of individual authors has not yet been collated in the available Soviet and foreign reference books. This is why it has been necessary to summarise to some extent the data on the histophysiology of the avian thyroid, making use both of published material (Studitskii, 1947; Mitskevich, 1957) and of the present author's own observations, made over a period of many years (Voitkevich, 1935, b, 1957).

Our data are based on the anatomical and microscopic investigation of the thyroid glands of the following birds: pigeons, fowls (White Leghorn, Rhode Island Red, Partridge Italians), ducks (Peking, Rouen, Khaki-Campbell, Duclé) turkeys, quails, long-eared and short-eared owls, kestrels, carrion crows, jackdaws, rooks, sparrows, yellowhammers, bull-finches, greenfinches, chaffinches, bramblings, redpolls, sky-larks, starlings, song-thrushes, crossbills, cormorants, white and Dalmatian pelicans, night herons, grey and great white herons. We have investigated the morphology of the thyroid glands of over 850 birds. Some of this material is presented below; no claims are made to an extensive morphological analysis in terms of the comparative-species aspect, since this could form the subject of a special monograph. Basic data on the morphology of the thyroid in birds were essential to establish some structural landmarks which could be used for objective evaluation of its various functional states in connection with feather formation.

The thyroid in birds is a paired organ consisting of two separate lobes. Exceptionally, there may be additional small lobules situated on the common carotid artery. Such accessory formations may develop after extirpation of both main lobes of the thyroid. The size of the thyroid gland alters according to various conditions. It is enlarged in young birds during the period of general growth and development of plumage. The two lobes are usually of almost equal size; in rare cases one lobe may be several times the size of the other.

The shape of the thyroid is either spherical, slightly flattened in the dorso-ventral direction as in Passeriformes, or oval with the long axis in the cranio-caudal direction as in pigeons and fowls. The lobes become elongated with age; for example in the cormorant it becomes spindle-shaped.

The two lobes are situated asymmetrically fairly deep within the upper part of the thoracic cavity. Each lobe usually lies within the apex of the acute angle formed by the jugular vein and the common carotid artery. Species differences, apart from the shape and size of the gland, includes the topography of the lobes, their proximity to one of the above-mentioned blood vessels. In pigeons each lobe lies closer to the jugular vein, often overlying it, and does not come into contact with the carotid artery, so that the thyroid artery is clearly visible. In the Corvidae, on the other hand, each lobe is more closely related to the carotid artery than to the jugular vein.

The thyroid gland is covered by a thin connective-tissue capsule containing fine collagen fibres. The capsule is made up of two independent layers, inner and outer (internal and external capsules). The former envelops the follicular parenchyma of the gland and the latter, which is tougher, serves to fix the lobe of the gland to the walls of the large blood vessels. In small birds such as sparrows the two laminae of the capsule merge, whereas in pigeons, fowls, and ducks they can easily be separated from each other. The right lobe of the thyroid, which in pigeons is somewhat higher than the left, is found on the ventral surface of the right jugular vein. In the Passeriformes the relation of the right lobe of the thyroid to the jugular vein is less marked, the lobe being connected with the lateral-ventral surface of the right carotid artery. The left lobe of the gland is usually situated on the ventral surface of the jugular vein and is also attached to the lateral surface of the carotid artery. In pigeons the common carotid artery is shifted medially as compared with other birds and forms a less acute angle with the jugular vein, so that the gland comes into contact only with the latter.

Blood supply is effected chiefly through the superior thyroid artery, which branches from the carotid artery a little above the thyroid gland. The thyroid artery enters into the thyroid parenchyma through the capsule, giving off a number of branches. In pigeons and fowls the superior thyroid artery approaches the right lobe of the gland near its upper pole and the left near its lower pole or near the middle of the lobe. The inferior thyroid artery, which enters the gland at the lower pole, is less prominent. In Passeriformes the superior thyroid artery leaves the carotid artery near the upper pole of the gland, continues along the lateral or ventral surface of the gland in a caudal direction, and enters the parenchyma nearer the lower pole. This vessel is most prominent in bullfinches. The inferior thyroid artery connects the carotid artery with the dorsal part of the gland.

The number of vessels draining the gland is subject to species variation. In pigeons and fowls there are two or three large veins connecting the gland with the jugular vein. In all the birds investigated the veins leave the dorsal surface of the thyroid, although in pigeons and fowls the vessels appear to come off the lateral surface of the gland. This phenomenon is explained both by pressure on the gland of the surrounding tissues and the close attachment of the gland to the superior thyroid artery.

Among the nerves approaching the thyroid gland the thyroid branch of the vagus is clearly seen passing towards the lower pole, sometimes from the ventral surface but more often from the dorsal. The topography of the vagus in this situation is very similar in birds to that in other vertebrates. It descends between the jugular vein and the carotid artery, in direct contact with the capsule of the thyroid gland. It can be clearly seen on freeing the upper pole of the gland from the capsule and lifting it.

The shape of the gland, its connection with the underlying tissues, and its relative position among neighbouring structures alter with the age of the bird. In young birds the furcula is elastic and is pulled caudally. Their thyroid glands lie somewhat higher in relation to the breastbone than in adults. In mature ducks and rooks the thyroid gland is found deep within the thoracic cavity.

Thyroid glands are anatomically closely associated with the small parathyroid glands, each of whose lobes is a spherical body of a harder consistency than the thyroid. In young birds the parathyroids can easily be recognised by their yellowish colour, which contrasts well with the deep pink colour of the thyroid. In mature birds the parathyroid is more closely bound up with the tissue of the thyroid and is not infrequently included within it. Among the birds investigated by us the parathyroids are most easily found in fowls, larks, and birds of prey.

The microscopic structure of the thyroid glands is very similar in various birds, although there are some slight variations from one species to another. Unlike the mammals, in which the connective-tissue stroma is continuous with the internal capsule, in birds the interfollicular connective tissue is not very marked and follows the course of the blood vessels. The secretory part of the gland is made up of follicles formed by a single-layered epithelium. The size of the follicles changes according to glandular function. The epithelial cells alter their shape and size to a considerable extent during the different phases of the secretory process. The follicular cavities are filled with a homogenous colloidal substance which acts as a

8

depôt of the biologically active hormonal factor. The amount and properties of this reserve colloid alter according to the functional state of the gland.

When the gland becomes more active, the epithelial cells enlarge, vascularisation becomes enhanced, and the interfollicular connective tissue swells. The gland becomes enlarged, sometimes to several times the normal size. Changes in the size of the thyroid according to increased activity are more marked in nestlings than in fledglings.

Attempts to investigate the biological activity of the thyroid gland in birds have mostly been confined to feeding the larvae of *Ambistoma* or frogs with fresh or dried thyroid tissue. Such determination of thyroid activity in glands taken from birds at random phases of their development or functional cycle is quite inadequate for the elucidation of the physiology of the thyroid during the growth of the bird or plumage formation. A method for accurate evaluation of thyroid activity in various animals has been developed (Voitkevich, 1935 b, 1945 e).

A reliable method of determining the histofunctional properties of the thyroid would need to be based on a procedure using objectively determined changes in the microstructure of the thyroid to assess its function. The metamorphosis reaction of the larvae of such amphibia as frogs and toads make it possible to establish the amount and properties of the hormone formed by a thyroid gland of a definite microscopic appearance. Fluctuations in the activity of the gland are known to coincide with changes in the height of follicular epithelium and in the amount and properties of the colloid. By a series of experiments we established a consistent correlation between the structure and function of the gland: the biological activity of the thyroid in the adult animal is directly proportional to the amount of colloid within it and inversely proportional to the height of the follicular epithelium. The concept of a norm for avian thyroid is extremely relative, since various intermediate states lying between diminished and increased function are frequently encountered. Hypofunctional states show characteristically low epithelium and a high content of homogeneous colloid: the effect obtained on testing is directly related to the amount of colloid. High epithelium and a small amount of liquefied colloid are typical for hyperfunctional states. The low biological activity of a functioning thyroid is explained by the fact that its hormonal constituent is being intensively secreted from the gland. Consequently, the concept of the functional thyroid level in the body should not be identified with the notion of the 'biological activity' of thyroid tissue tested on the larvae of amphibia. The more intensely active the thyroid in the body of the bird, the more hormonal substances it forms and secretes, and the lower the effectiveness of such glandular tissue in tests on tadpoles.

The tadpole thyroid tests were carried out according to the following standard procedure. Identical pieces of fresh thyroid gland weighing 1.0 to 0.5 mg each were always used for the transplants, which were introduced into the abdominal cavity of tadpoles through a small incision. Care was taken that the tadpoles in each experiment were uniform. Other series without implantation of glandular tissue served as controls. In the experimental series, clear signs of metamorphosis under laboratory temperature conditions were found four or five days after implanting pieces of thyroid gland. The tadpoles were sacrificed at this stage, in order to establish the length of the body and gut, which undergo consistent shortening during metamorphosis. The figures given in the tables usually represent, in percentages, the difference in these two indices between the control and the experimental tadpoles undergoing metamorphosis (Voitkevich 1935 b, 1945 e, 1957).

Concurrently with such determination of the biological activity of the glands, their microscopic structure is established by making twenty-five measurements, on each section, of the height of the epithelium and the internal diameter of the follicles. The mean dimensions of the follicles and the height of the epithelium thus provide a basis for comparing the state of the thyroid glands in various birds at different functional phases. Judgment of the state of the thyroid glands was thus based on concordant numerical data reflecting the structural aspects of the gland and the activity of the thyroid tissue in a biological test.

This, in brief, describes the fundamentals of our method, which has not yet lost its importance. The extensive use of radioactive iodine for diagnostic purposes in evaluating thyroid function has some technical advantages, but does not exclude the need for data on the microscopic structure of thyroid glands. The use of iodine isotopes makes it possible to judge the nature and intensity of biosynthesis within the thyroid gland. Our biological method, however, gives a fairly accurate idea of the properties of thyroid tissue, with its actual structure in the body as a whole.

THYROID FUNCTION DURING FEATHER FORMATION

Development of juvenile plumage

The avian thyroid gland begins to show signs of differentiation towards the end of the first half of the brooding period. Thus, the particularisation of the main structures in the thyroid gland of chicks begins from the ninth or tenth day of brooding and becomes quite clear on the eleventh day: the first small follicles are formed during the next two days. It is just at this period that the germs of the juvenile plumage are laid down; subsequently they develop non-uniformly on all the pterylae. Bradway (1929) and Benazzi (1929, 1932) first noted significant differences in the micro-structure of the thyroid glands of pigeons and fowls at the moment of hatching. The thyroid of a one-day chick has numerous follicles filled with colloid. At the same time the thyroid of a pigeon is poorly differentiated: only scattered follicles are seen among the epithelial strands. Such a gland only acquires its typical structure at a later date. There are significant differences in the state of the plumage of a newly-hatched pigeon and chick. The latter is not only covered with thick down but also has partially developed feathers, the flight feathers of the juvenile plumage. The pigeon remains covered with sparse down for several days; the quills of the contour feathers begin to develop only from the fourth or fifth day of postembryonic life. There is thus a clearly parallel relationship between thyroid differentiation and the state of the juvenile plumage in chicks and pigeons.

It seemed essential to extend the investigation of this relationship by observing a longer period of development. Chicks continue to grow, and their plumage to develop, over a period of several months (Kotova, 1936; Lektorskii and Kuz'mina, 1936, a). The pigeon grows for 30-35 days and its plumage develops equally intensively. This suggested that the more intensive plumage formation might be associated with more marked structural and functional changes in the thyroid activity of pigeons, as compared with those in fowls.

Simultaneous studies were made of the growth of the plumage and the development of the thyroid in chicks and pigeons, starting with the late stages of the embryonic period. Assuming that conclusions regarding thyroid activity based solely on morphological data would not be exhaustive, we carried out a parallel investigation of the structure and function of the glands (Voitkevich, 1935, b, 1936, h, 1939, b).

White Leghorn eggs were placed in the incubator in such a way that thyroids of embryos and chicks of different ages were available for testing at a given time. Carrier-pigeons were obtained from naturally-hatched eggs. The chick thyroids were investigated from the eleventh day of brooding to the age of two months. In pigeons, the thyroids were taken from the moment of hatching to the time of complete cessation of growth at thirty-five days.

The thyroids from chick embryos were studied microscopically and tested biologically at intervals of one or two days. During the post-embryonic period the intervals between the examinations were longer. Table 5 shows the mean data on the height of the epithelium and the follicular diameter for chick thyroids, and also illustrates the activity of the thyroid tissue in tadpole tests.

The thyroid gland of an eleven-day chick embryo is still poorly differentiated. The epithelial cells are grouped in strands which are transformed into small follicles. When tested, such tissue showed extremely weak activity. After twenty-four hours the small follicles began to show some colloid, which was weakly stained by eosin (Fig. 21). When such glands are implanted into tadpoles, they produce slight but definite stimulation of metamorphosis. A similar result was obtained on implantation of the thyroid from a thirteen-day embryo. The follicular structure became quite distinct on the fourteenth or fifteenth day; the colloid stained well with eosin (Fig. 22) and the activity of the gland rose considerably.

Table 5

Microscopic structure and biological activity of the thyroid gland in chicks of different ages

Age in days		Histological structure		Indices of biological activi	
From the moment of placing the eggs in the incubator	From the moment of hatching	Height of epithelium in μ	Innerdiameter of follicles, in μ	Shortening of the tadpoles' body, per cent	Shortening of the tadpoles gut, per ce
11	–	3.62	4.04	1.5	3.1
12	–	3.54	4.48	0.5	30.0
13	–	3.21	5.26	1.5	30.8
14	–	3.16	6.84	7.6	41.2
16	–	3.04	8.94	12.8	51.6
18	–	3.07	11.24	22.8	58.2
19	–	3.44	13.62	15.4	66.4
21	0	3.88	20.25	15.9	67.4
26	5	5.66	17.90	20.0	69.4
31	10	4.30	14.91	6.8	65.7
51	30	5.64	8.65	9.9	58.6
66	45	4.75	8.64	17.9	68.0
81	60	4.26	26.60	22.6	69.8

The thyroid acquired a typical structure with colloid-rich follicles and showed a high index of metamorphogenic activity before hatching. During the post-embryonic period the chick thyroid passed into a phase of enhanced secretion: the height of the epithelium increased, the hormonal substance was vigorously secreted from the gland, and the colloid within the follicles showed signs of partial resorption (Figs. 23 and 24).

The chick-embryo thyroid thus begins to secrete very early and is already beginning to accumulate the biologically active substance between the eleventh and twelfth days of incubation. By this time the laying-down of the germs of many juvenile feathers of the main pterylae is already nearing completion. Subsequently, when feather growth begins, there is a gradual accumulation of colloid in the gland with an associated rise of the biological activity index, reaching a maximal value at the moment of hatching. During the post-embryonic period of development, the gland no longer undergoes significant changes in activity. The possibility that this may reflect the slow development of plumage cannot be excluded. The reduction of the biological activity of the gland at the age of one month and more reflects the enhanced phase of hormone secretion, which coincides in time with the period of mass growth of feathers on most of the pterylae. (See also Greenwood and Blyth, 1927; Lektorskii and Kuz'mina, 1936, b.)

Let us compare the data obtained for chicks with similar data for young pigeons (Table 6).

Table 6

Microscopic structure and biological activity of the thyroid gland of pigeons of different ages

Age in days		Histological structure		Indices of biological activity	
From start of brooding	From the moment of hatching	Height of epithelium, in μ	Inner dia of follicles, in μ	Shortening of the tadpoles' body, per cent	Shortening of the tadpoles' gut, per cent
18	0	3.7	4.7	0.4	40.7
23	5	6.2	9.1	2.3	53.2
28	10	7.4	17.7	16.2	65.1
33	15	8.0	14.4	5.2	58.2
38	20	6.5	19.9	14.6	62.7
43	25	5.6	26.7	26.0	70.1
53	35	5.7	26.5	26.9	71.3

The thyroid gland of a newly hatched pigeon is poorly differentiated (Fig. 25). Its biological activity is minimal, although the value for the gut resorption in tadpoles reaches 40.7 per cent. This index, and the microstructure of the thyroid of a newly-hatched pigeon, correspond approximately to those of a fourteen-day chick embryo. In subsequent experiments we made a detailed study, at 24-hour intervals, of the thyroid in pigeons from the last day of brooding to the third post-embryonic day. The gland only acquires the typical microscopic structure by the fifth post-embryonic day.

Young pigeons are covered with sparse embryonic down during the first three days after hatching. On the fourth and fifth day quills of contour feathers can be seen through the skin. Consequently the laying-down of contour feathers occurs when the thyroid gland activity is relatively low. The growth of young quills, which begins some time after hatching, coincides with the early phases of secretion by the thyroid gland,

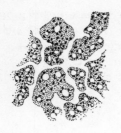

Fig. 21. Thyroid gland of chick embryo on the twelfth day of incubation (× 360)

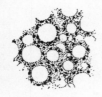

Fig. 23. Thyroid gland of a 24-hour-old chick (× 360)

Fig. 25. Thyroid gland of newly hatched pigeon (× 360)

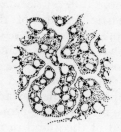

Fig. 22. Thyroid gland of chick embryo on the sixteenth day of incubation (× 360)

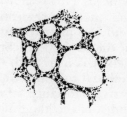

Fig. 24. Thyroid gland of chick ten days after hatching (× 360)

Fig. 26. Thyroid gland of 15-day-old pigeon (× 360)

whose differentiation then becomes very intensive. A characteristic feature of the development of pigeons and other
representatives of nestlings is the almost simultaneous laying-
down and coincident development time of feather germs on
most of the pterylae.

On the fifth and sixth day the tops of the young quills
appear on the surface of the skin. By this time the thyroid
has acquired the typical follicular structure, approximating to
that of the gland in mature birds. Secretion within the gland
increases, and colloid accumulates in the follicles. The index
of biological activity of the gland rises.

By the tenth day of life the webs begin to unfurl on the
feather quills. The thyroid activity at this time is clearly enhanced. This is shown by the height of the epithelial cells and
the intensive resorption of colloid. These changes in the thyroid become particularly pronounced when the development
of the feathers reaches its maximal intensity. The epithelium
height is increased, the follicles are largely emptied, and the
residual colloid is liquefied (Fig. 26). At this stage much of the
active substance is secreted into the body, and the activity
index of the glandular tissue therefore decreases, as compared
with a later period when the feathers cease to grow (30th to
35th day), and the signs of thyroid hyperfunction diminish:
the height of the epithelial cells decreases, colloid is again
accumulated in the follicles, and the indices of biological
activity rise.

To illustrate the parallel course of the intensity of plumage
growth and changes in thyroid function during the development of a young pigeon, the relevant data are shown graphically in Fig. 27. Curve 1 of this graph has been plotted from
the mean data obtained by measuring live growing areas of
the flight feathers during successive stages of growth. Before
the unfurling of the vane, the whole quill was measured, and
afterwards, the part from the base of the vane to the base of
the feather follicle.

When the curve depicting the changes in the dimensions of
the growing part of the feather is compared with that showing
the change in the weight of the thyroid gland and the height
of its epithelium, it can be seen that the two follow a parallel
course. The gland enlarges in accordance with the increased

total mass of growing feather quills. When the intensity of plumage growth declines and differentiation is enhanced, the size of the thyroid and the height of its epithelial cells diminish. The period of maximal proliferation of feather quills coincides in time with maximal thyroid function.

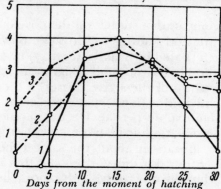

Fig. 27. Change in thyroid activity of the pigeon during the development of juvenile plumage

1, Curve showing the development of the live, growing part of the feather (one division, 7 mm). 2, Change in the weight of the thyroid gland (one division, 10 mg). 3, Height of the epithelium (one division, 2μ)

This parallel relationship suggests that it is reasonable to assume a connection between morphogenesis and thyroid function. A similar conclusion can be drawn from an analysis of the data on chicks. In these, the development of plumage begins even during embryogenesis, though rather slowly. Thyroid differentiation and accumulation of colloid occur early. The curves representing changes in the metamorphogenic activity of the thyroid glands of chicks and young pigeons are shown in Fig. 40. The solid line shows the change in the biological properties of the thyroid in chicks and the broken one that in pigeons. In both cases the period of thyroid differentiation is accompanied by a gradual rise in the index of biological activity. Later, in both cases, there is an increase in thyroid function when the colloid leaves the follicles and the metamorphogenic activity declines. Both in the chicks and the pigeons this phase coincides exactly with the period of the most intensive development of plumage. The more rapidly developing pigeons show these changes to a more marked degree, whereas in the relatively slowly developing chicks the curve of the biological activity of thyroid tissue undergoes smooth changes.

Our earlier comparative studies on the development of the thyroid in nestling and nidifugous birds (Voitkevich, 1935, b, 1936, g, h) were repeated by Studitskii (1947) in a comprehensive investigation. He did not find a significant difference in the time-relationships of the active phases in the two groups, noting signs of thyroid activity in the pigeon as early as the middle of the embryonic period. He further notes that the reaction of embryonic thyroid glands to thyreo-tropic hormone of the pituitary appears at about the same time in the two groups of birds. Studitskii did not test the thyroid tissue for the content of biologically active substances, however, and based his conclusions solely on microscopic data. Taking into account the heterogeneous character of the structure of the developing gland, it is not difficult to see signs of secretory stimulation in individual groups of cells under the influence

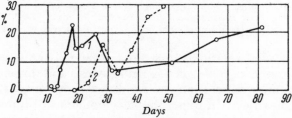

Fig. 28. *Change in the biological activity of the thyroid glands in (1) chicks and (2) pigeons during the period of growth of the bird*

of the pituitary hormone; it does not follow from this, however, that a weakly differentiated gland is able to form hormonal substances in the same quantities as a fully differentiated one. In this respect the observations made by Entin (1936, 1948) on the development of the thyroid in fowls proved to be close to our own.

Similar data are given by Mitskevich (1957) in his monograph. By means of iodine isotopes he showed that the accumulation of the radioactive elements began at approximately the same time in pigeon and chick embryos on the sixth or seventh day of incubation. This does not contradict our data, since the specific function of the secretory cells appears very early. The differences we have noted are quantitative in nature. The differences in the microstructure of the thyroids in the chick and the pigeon on the day of hatching are considerable, as seen from the photomicrographs (Voitkevich, 1935, b, 1936, h) and the illustrations in the above publications by Studitskii and Mitskevich. Characteristically, in order to demonstrate morphogenic activity of the embryonic thyroid glands, Mitskevich had to extend the test to seven days, as against four in our method. Moreover, he did not test the glands from older birds for comparison, which would have demonstrated a significant difference in the activity of the glands during embryonic life and after hatching.

We did not limit our comparative analysis of the thyroid gland only to data on representatives of two species of contrasted character of development. Further studies of the developing thyroid glands included a number of nidifugous birds (ducks, turkeys) and nestlings (rooks, carrion crows, magpies, sparrows). The results were similar to those described for fowls and pigeons. Naturally, the general development of the bird must also be taken into account in analysing the parallel relationship between the intensity of feather formation and the functional changes in the thyroid. Comparison of the data reveals that intensive general growth of the bird usually corresponds to the period preceding final differentiation of the thyroid and its hyperfunctional phase. It of course does not follow from this observation that the thyroid hormone is not essential to those metabolic processes characteristic of a growing body. We wish merely to indicate the peculiar rôle of the thyroid hormone and its considerable involvement in the processes of feather formation. The same conclusion was suggested by our data on the thyroid gland of the cormorant (*Phalacrocorax carbo*).

The material consisted of 188 young birds of both sexes and of various ages. The autopsies on the birds taken directly from the nest were usually so timed as to give ages in days which were multiples of five. In some cases birds at the intermediate stages were used. The initial state was represented by embryos taken five days before hatching. The material was collected until growth was finally completed. The thyroid glands from sexually mature adult birds were used for comparison. Histological preparations were made to measure the height of the epithelium and the internal diameter of the follicles (50 measurements for each lobe of the thyroid using an ocular micrometer). The data obtained are shown in Table 7.

The young cormorants are quite naked when they hatch out from the egg. After some time their skin acquires a bluish-black colour, because of the developing feather follicles. Black down appears on the dorsal surface of the body on the fourth day of life. A day or two later down begins to appear on the ventral surface and only then on the neck and head. Quills of the juvenile contour feathers appear from the feather follicles on the tenth day after hatching. The down covering continues to develop concomitantly with the growth of the contour feathers; this down is then replaced by grey down on most of the pterylae. The juvenile plumage on the main pterylae develops almost simultaneously. The neck and head become covered with small contour feathers considerably later.

There is a definite correlation between the development of feathers of the different tracts (Novikov, 1934). In order to simplify the evaluation of the rate of development of the plumage, therefore, the observations were confined to periodic measurements of the tenth primary flight feather. The growth of the juvenile feathers occurs synchronously with the growth of the bird. By the time general growth is complete, the contour feathers are fully developed. The typical rate of growth of the large flight and steering feathers is preserved even in those young birds which are greatly retarded in their general development or have fasted for some time. The size of the young feather, especially its differentiated vane, is constant for each age. This subsequently made it possible to use the measurements of the tenth flight feather as an index of the growing bird's age.

The weight of the thyroid gland (Table 7) gradually increases during the first thirty days of the bird's life, and then declines a little. The weight of the thyroid in fully-grown

Table 7

Weight and microstructure of the thyroid gland of the cormorant during development

Age, in days	Body weight, in g	Thyroid gland			
		Weight (both lobes)		Height of epithelium, in μ	Diameter of follicles, in μ
		mg	Body weight, per cent		
−5	5	0.6	0.0111	5.22	0
Hatched	41	6.6	0.0110	5.46	7.39
5	234	21.5	0.0092	6.02	16.90
10	551	73.5	0.0115	6.80	23.85
15	10003	124.2	0.0123	8.94	33.74
20	1463	149.4	0.0102	8.30	33.43
25	1702	180.3	0.0106	7.96	34.80
30	1880	217.8	0.0116	7.58	40.39
35	1945	202.1	0.0104	7.51	39.79
40	2040	192.3	0.0094	7.75	39.18
45	2133	153.6	0.0072	7.21	41.11
wo years ♀♀	2147	131.2	0.0061	8.26	41.00
♂♂	2263	149.5	0.0066	7.38	36.24

birds is not significantly different from that in two-year-old mature birds. The thyroid reaches the maximal relative weight in birds ten to fifteen days old, that is during the period after which the rate of general growth diminishes and differentiation, including intensive formation of plumage, is enhanced.

The embryonic thyroid in the cormorant is formed of epithelial strands, individual cells showing signs of secretory activity. Small single follicles containing some colloid can be seen in the thyroid tissue by the time of hatching. During the next ten days there is intensive differentiation of follicular structure. At the end of this period the thyroid has the maximal number of follicles, which, however, are small (Voitkevich, 1944, b).

Later, the development of the thyroid microstructure is associated mainly with increasing height of the epithelium and the size of the follicles, as well as accumulation of colloid. Liquefaction of the colloid, a sign of hypersecretion, begins after the tenth day. The thyroid gland of a fifteen-day-old bird, as compared with the preceding period, shows signs of high functional activity, which remains at approximately the same level over the next ten days. A month after hatching there is a decline in thyroid activity. Comparison of data on its weight and its microstructure shows that there are three phases in the development of the thyroid: the first encompasses the ten days after hatching, during which structure differentiation of the gland is completed and its secretory function becomes enhanced; the second covers the next period, up to the age of 30 days, which corresponds to a relatively high level of thyroid activity with typical signs of hypersecretion; the third extends to the time when the bird's growth is complete, and is characterised by a decline in thyroid function. The relative weight of the thyroid in sexually-mature adult cormorants is approximately half that in the young birds during the period of intensive plumage growth.

These data suggest that in cormorants there are parallel changes in the development of the thyroid gland and the plumage. The intensive growth of the bird towards the end of embryonic life and during the first period after hatching is not accompanied by high thyroid activity. In fact at this time the gland continues to undergo differentiation and the level of its activity is not yet high. A slowing of the rate of general growth coincides in time with the beginning of thyroid hyperfunction. The phase of thyroid hyperactivity is related in time to the period of intensive development of plumage. The bird's growth is completed during the second month of life, when differentiation of the body is also complete. At this time the thyroid has the microstructure characteristic of hypofunction. The glands of young six-week-old birds and those of sexually mature two-year-old birds are very similar in their main features.

The above data may suggest that there is a disparity between the importance of the thyroid hormone in the processes of growth and of differentiation. The bird grows fastest during the period when the level of hormonal activity of the thyroid has not yet reached its maximum. The presence of a certain concentration of thyroid hormone is evidently essential for the general growth of a young bird. The processes of intensive differentiation in the body—the development of plumage being a particular case—occur under conditions of higher thyroid activity.

Development of Definitive Plumage

It has been suggested above that the changes observed in the thyroid of young birds can be related not only to the development of plumage but also to the general growth of the young bird. It seemed interesting to extend the analysis by tracing the relationship between feather formation and thyroid function under conditions excluding body growth, that is to induce mass growth of feathers in a full-grown bird. To achieve this we removed the large wing and tail feathers and the small trunk feathers—except on the upper part of the neck and the head—from adult carrier-pigeons and White Leghorn fowls. Under these conditions the mass growth of new feathers began simultaneously on all the pterylae, the quills appearing on the surface of the skin on the seventh day in the pigeons and on the tenth day in the fowls.

In the first experiment 54 pigeons were subjected to plucking. The thyroid glands were examined at different intervals after removal of the feathers. Feather growth was evaluated as before, by measuring the total length of the young feather and that of its 'living part'. The growth curve for the new contour feathers had much in common with the growth curve for juvenile feathers in young pigeons (see Fig. 27). A series of

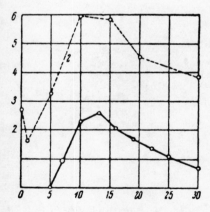

Days after plucking

Fig. 29. Increased thyroid activity in the pigeon during the development of definitive plumage

1, Curve showing the development of the live growing part of the feather (one division, 10 mm). 2, height of thyroid epithelium (one division, 2μ)

additional experiments convinced us that the changes in the
thyroid of the experimental birds described below must be
associated primarily with the massive feather-forming process
and to a lesser degree with such side effects as trauma during
plucking, increased heat loss in the naked bird and so on
(Voitkevich, 1936, c).

Changes in thyroid function can already be observed in the
first few days after plucking, but they increase markedly during the period of development of the new feathers. These
changes, like those in young pigeons, consist of a rapid transition of the thyroid to a state of hyperfunction (Fig. 29). Increased thyroid activity, as judged by the increase in the
height of its cells, runs parallel with the increase in the total
mass of the living part of young feathers. The greatest
'volume' of the feather-forming process corresponds to the
period of thyroid hyperfunction, with its maximal enlargement of the epithelial cells and almost complete evacuation
of colloid from the follicles (Figs. 30, 31, and 32). These data
were confirmed by another experiment in which each bird's
thyroid was not only examined microscopically but also evaluated for activity by biological testing (Table 8).

It can be concluded from the data in Table 8 that the

*Fig. 30. Thyroid gland of con-
trol mature pigeon (× 360)*

*Fig. 31. Thyroid gland of pigeon
ten days after onset of mass
feather growth (× 280)*

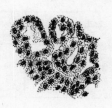 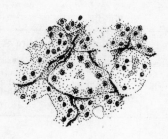

Fig. 32. Thyroid gland of pigeon fifteen days after onset of mass feather growth (× 360)

Fig. 33. Thyroid gland of pigeon in a state of functional thyroid exhaustion after thrice-repeated plucking of immature feathers (× 540)

thyroid gland secretes its hormone at an increasing rate as the plumage develops, and this is reflected in a decrease in the index of biological activity. Towards the end of plumage growth the height of the thyroid epithelium begins to decline, colloid begins to accumulate within the follicles, and the index of the thyroid's biological activity rises. The figures in Table 8 show the fairly good agreement between the data on the structure of the gland and the indices of its activity in the biological test on tadpoles. Taking into account this correlation, the description of the characteristics of the gland's activity in the following pages will be based chiefly on data characterising its microscopic structure (Voitkevich, 1934, a, 1935, b).

In pigeons the artificially induced mass growth of feathers is accompanied by considerable changes in the histology of the thyroid which reflect its state of hyperactivity. The degree of these changes is directly related to the number of simultaneously developing feathers, that is the 'volume' of new growth; regeneration of a few feathers, however, has practically no effect on thyroid function. When a similar artificial development of plumage is induced in fowls the changes in thyroid activity are not as drastic as in the experiments with pigeons.

Table 8

*Microstructure and biological activity of the thyroid glands of mature
pigeons during massive development of feathers*

Time from the moment of plucking in days	Histological structure of the gland		Indices of the biological activity of the gland	
	Height of epithelium, in μ	Inner diameter of the follicles, in μ	Shortening of the body in the tadpoles, per cent	Shortening of the gut in the tadpoles, per cent
2	5.8	18.7	30.5	57.8
5	3.5	36.8	41.1	62.7
7	5.6	16.7	29.2	59.9
12	4.3	19.0	23.1	53.7
15	9.0	19.0	4.9	30.3
17	8.9	8.3	8.1	36.9
32	7.9	21.2	18.7	53.3

Two-year-old White Leghorn hens were used in the new
experiments. The large and small feathers were removed,
except on the head and neck. Autopsies were performed after
definite intervals on batches of four experimental and three
control birds. The times of autopsy were as follows: one
month after plucking, when the feathers are still growing
intensively and the majority of the feathers unfurling their
webs; two months after plucking, when feather growth is completed; and four months after plucking, that is a considerable
interval after the completion of feather growth. The data on
the state of the thyroid in the fowls are shown in Table 9.

During the first two months of observations the thyroid
glands of the control birds showed typically normal features.
The average height of the epithelium was around 4μ, the
follicular diameter a little under 50μ. Towards the end of the
observations there was some increase in the total weight of
the gland and the height of its epithelium, which was evidently associated with the onset of natural moulting.

The experimental fowls did not show such marked changes
in the thyroid during the period of feather growth as did the
pigeons under similar conditions. After thirty days the diameter of the follicles decreased a little, but the height of the
epithelial cells and the weight of the gland showed little

Table 9

Weight and the histological characteristics of the thyroid glands in fowls during mass growth of feathers

Time from the beginning of the experiment, in days	Control			Experimental		
	Weight of one lobe, in mg	Height of the epithelium, in μ	Diameter of the follicles, in μ	Weight of one lobe, in mg	Height of the epithelium, in μ	Diameter of the follicles, in μ
0	49.8	3.9	48.0	49.8	3.9	48.0
30	48.2	4.2	47.0	47.8	3.8	31.3
60	58.2	4.0	49.4	81.0	3.8	51.9
120	63.2	4.7	37.3	61.8	4.3	60.5

change. By the sixtieth day the weight of the thyroid increased; the follicles returned to their initial size, although the height of the epithelium remaining unchanged, and by the end of the period of observation the weight of the gland again diminished.

These data agree to some extent with those for young birds. The thyroid gland of a young pigeon undergoes sharp fluctuations in activity; in the chick the changes are relatively slight. Incidentally, it follows from this that the side effects due to plucking, such as changes in heat loss and so on have no definite significance, since they proved similar for fowls and pigeons.

What might be the responsible factor in the considerable difference in thyroid function observed during artificially induced feather formation in pigeons and in fowls? Plumage growth is known to be more rapid in the pigeons than in the fowls. Larionov and Pozigun (1935) demonstrated that the rate of plumage growth in pigeons was at least double that in fowls. It can, therefore, be supposed that the difference in the reaction of the thyroid gland in fowls and pigeons is connected with the dissimilar intensity of feather formation (Voitkevich, 1938, b, d). However, this is not the only possible explanation. The possibility that the thyroid hormone plays different rôles in the metabolic processes occurring during feather formation in different species cannot be excluded. Moreover, it must be especially borne in mind that the thyroid glands of adult fowls, unlike those of pigeons, have an exceptionally large reserve of colloid within the follicles (Zatvornitskaya and Zimnitskii, 1932).

The data yielded by these comparative studies not only reflect the connection between feather formation and thyroid activity, but also indicate some differences in the degree to which this connection is marked in different kinds of birds.

Plumage replacement (moulting)

The data on the correlation between thyroid activity and feather formation during the period of growth of young birds, and those obtained under conditions of artificially induced mass development of feathers in mature birds, agree well with the data on thyroid activity during natural moulting. It has been noted above that there is no substantial difference between the development of individual feathers outside of moulting periods and the replacement of plumage during moulting; activation of previously quiescent feather germs takes place in both instances. The differences only concern the numbers of simultaneously developing feathers.

Cruickshank (1929) was one of the first to attempt the investigation of the thyroid gland during moulting. He describes data on the weight and structure of the thyroid glands in young fowls with different laying capacities. Moulting was not specially taken into account, since the group of moulting birds included some which were killed between July and September. No appreciable changes were found in the size and structure of the thyroids in these birds. Podhradskii (1935) collected data on the changes in the thyroid of fowls during moulting, noting an increase in the weight of the gland. These authors did not then aim at relating the changes in the thyroid to the feather-forming processes taking place during moulting.

Larionov and his co-workers were the first to make a special study of the thyroid gland during the nesting (juvenile) and annual (definitive) moulting. Larionov, Kuz'mina and Lektorskii (1933) and Larionov (1936, a) showed increased thyroid activity during the replacement of juvenile feathers in chicks aged from forty or fifty to 140 days. This can be judged from the height of the epithelium, which was over 4μ in all the moulting birds and below that figure in the non-moulting ones. Our data on the microstructure and the biological activity of the thyroid glands in chicks during the developmental period have already been mentioned. It has been established that thyroid activity increases with the onset of juvenile moulting. Signs of colloid resorption in the thyroid follicles can be seen in the early stages of moulting (45th day); later there is an intensive release of hormone and a gradual accumulation of colloid within the thyroid follicles.

In another study Larionov (1934) made a histological examination of the thyroids of mature Rhode Island fowls before, during, and after moulting. The height of the thyroid epithelium was found to be 7.4μ during moulting, during the preceding period 4.7μ, and after moulting 5.2μ. Natural replacement of feathers is thus accompanied by increased thyroid activity. The detailed data obtained recently by Tanabe, Himeno, and Nozaki (1957) show activation of thyroid activity during moulting, but without increased uptake of radioactive iodine by the thyroid tissue. Höhn (1949) investigated the thyroid gland in forty wild ducks and found two periods of increased activity, one preceding and coinciding with the onset of autumnal moulting, the other associated with the less intensive partial spring moult.

Seasonal changes in the dimensions of the thyroid in pigeons were first described by Riddle and Fischer (1925). Similar data for a series of wild birds were collected a little later by Haecker (1926).

We had repeatedly observed increased thyroid activity in moulting pigeons: the reserve colloid is resorbed in the follicles and the height of the thyroid epithelium increases to 8 or 9μ as against 4μ in the non-moulting period (Voitkevich, 1934, a, 1936, g). Similar results were later obtained by Elterich (1936), who demonstrated changes in the thyroids of pigeons during the sexual cycle and the subsequent period of moulting.

Observations on wild birds are interesting because their periodic morphogenic processes, including moulting, are sharply delimited in time and are not so much blurred by individual variations as in the domestic species.

Küchler (1935) traced the annual cycle of changes in the

thyroid gland of the robin (*Erithacus rubecula*), the yellow-hammer (*Emberiza citrinella*), and sparrows (*Passer domesticus* and *P. montanus*). He notes three phases in the thyroid activity of these birds: secretion of colloid, its accumulation in the follicles, and expulsion of the modified colloid from the gland. The changes during the third phase are characteristic of natural moulting. Later, Bigalke (1956) obtained similar data on the annual cyclic changes in the thyroid of song birds.

During 1932-1934 we collected from around Moscow the endocrine glands from *Passer domesticus* (150 birds) and *P. montanus* (100 birds) throughout the year and in particular during moulting, as assessed by the number of large feathers shed. In these species the thyroid epithelium is at its lowest during spring and the first half of summer; this index rises from July to January. The increase in the height of the thyroid epithelium coincides with the onset of natural moulting; this state remains throughout the period of plumage replacement. At this time there is resorption of colloid from the follicles, partial vacuolation of the cytoplasm in the thyroid cells, and increased blood supply to the gland (see also Voitkevich and Novikov, 1936, b).

The thyroid glands of small birds, especially the various breeds of sparrow, are still being investigated histologically because of the markedly cyclic character of their endocrine activity (Miller, 1939; Blanchard and Erickson, 1949; Davis and Davis, 1954; Wilson and Farner, 1960). The authors have noted changes associated with moulting in the birds' body weight, fat depôts, and thyroid glands. Oakeson and Lilley (1960) compared thyroid activity in sparrows (382 birds) and found that individual variations were greater among the migrating ones, whereas the index of activity of the thyroid tissue was higher in the resident ones, especially during moulting and in the winter.

To summarise, the feather-forming processes usually coincide with thyroid hyperfunction. The development of the juvenile plumage, its replacement by the definitive plumage, the seasonal moulting of mature birds, and the artificial induction of mass growth of feathers (outside the period of natural moulting) are all characterised by increased thyroid activity (see also the survey by Höhn, 1950). There is a direct correlation between thyroid activity and the intensity of feather formation. The more feathers grow simultaneously, and the more intensive their growth, the greater the changes in the thyroid and the more hormone it produces and secretes into the blood stream. However, direct proof of the dependence of feather formation on the thyroid hormone could only be obtained experimentally. We therefore set up other experiments designed to establish the relationship between the changes in the feather-forming process and changes in thyroid function, namely under conditions of different thyroid hormone content of the body.

PHENOMENA OF FUNCTIONAL EXHAUSTION OF THE AVIAN THYROID

During plumage replacement in the course of natural moulting the avian thyroid passes into a phase of increased activity. This persists during the development of a new generation of feathers. Replacement of plumage can be induced artificially by plucking out the existing feathers. Such activation of the feather follicles can be repeated many times. Development of several feathers has practically no effect on thyroid activity. The relationship between feather formation and thyroid activity could therefore find new confirmation only under experimental conditions ensuring a large 'volume' of feather formation or 'mass development' of feathers.

The capacity of feather-forming tissue for the development of a new generation of feathers is not the same throughout the year. Moulting is preceded by considerable physiological changes in the body, without which feather replacement does not take place. It is reasonable to assume that if the duration of the feather-forming period was extended artificially, the high level of thyroid activity would be maintained. Are the secretory potentialities of the thyroid gland for hormone production sufficient for a single plumage replacement only, or are they appreciably more extensive?

Mass growth of feathers can be prolonged by repeated plucking of mature and immature feathers. This appeared to be a way of prolonging the hyperactive phase of thyroid function. The possibility was not excluded that under such conditions of prolonged activation the thyroid gland would manifest signs of functional exhaustion and the feather-forming tissue would be unable to realise its potential for new growth.

Fifty-two carrier-pigeons were subjected to repeated plucking. Half the experimental birds received daily doses of a dried thyroid preparation. After twelve days the vanes on the new quills became unfurled. At this time some of the birds were sacrificed and their thyroids examined, the rest being subjected to another plucking. Development of new feathers was somewhat delayed, since a certain amount of time was required for the regeneration of the feather germs at the sites of the removed young quills. Sixteen days after the repeat plucking, the feathers of the next generation entered the differentiation phase. At this time the next batch of birds was sacrificed, and the remainder were plucked of their immature plumage for the third time. The birds subjected to thrice-repeated plucking differed in the state of their plumage from those which continued to receive thyroidin throughout similar manipulations. In these the development of feathers on all the pterylae occured normally, and after a month they had well-formed plumage. The state of the birds which did not receive thyroidin was different. In some of the pigeons which had been plucked twice, and in most of those plucked three times, the pterylae of small feathers on the trunk and limbs remained without feathers, no new quills making their appearance. Only the large wing and steering feathers developed; in some birds they were plucked for the fourth time. The large feathers again regenerated, although the rate of their growth was below normal, but small feathers failed to develop as before, so that the trunk and limbs remained naked.

The thyroid glands of the birds which had lost their ability to produce plumage regeneration had a peculiar microstructure, reflecting a state of functional exhaustion. After a single plucking of the young quills the thyroid glands in pigeons showed signs of enhanced activity: enlargement of the epithelial cells, vacuolation, and liquefaction of colloid. Repeated removal of immature plumage was associated with total loss of reserve colloid and manifestations of marked epithelial hypertrophy (Fig. 33). Administration of thyroidin to these young birds restored the ability of the feather follicles to produce new growth, together with a return of the thyroid structure to normal. These results suggest that continuous activation of a number of generations of feathers induced exhaustion of the thyroid and a sharp deficit of thyroid hormone in the body.

The deduction as to the functional exhaustion of the thyroid gland must be considered tentative as yet, since the biological activity of the thyroid and the concentration of the hormone in the body had to be checked under similar experimental conditions.

In a new group of experiments, twenty-four pigeons of the decorative breeds were used. Eighteen of these were plucked, the remaining six serving as controls. The experimental birds constituted three series. The number of successive pluckings corresponded to the ordinal number of the series. The plumage was removed at different times so calculated that at a certain moment there were birds which had been subjected to one, two, and three cycles of plumage regeneration.

All the experimental and the control birds were sacrificed at one time during the period of maximal development of the current generation of feathers. The thyroid glands and the blood of the birds were subjected to biological tests with tadpoles. Small pieces of the gland from birds of each series were then subjected to the usual histological treatment. All the data are shown in Table 10.

The weight of the thyroid in birds subjected to a single

Table 10

Weight, microstructure, and biological activity of the thyroid glands in pigeons

Indices	Control	Experimental series		
		I	II	III
Weight of lobes, in mg	34.0	58.8	76.5	80.3
Structure				
height of epithelium, in μ . . .	3.76	7.55	10.34	11.86
inner diameter of follicles, in μ .	26.4	12.1	5.9	0.8
Activity in the tadpole test				
resorption of tail, per cent . . .	42.0	12.2	5.7	3.4
shortening of gut, per cent . . .	65.6	17.7	6.8	1.2

plucking was almost double that of the control. The thyroid tissue was more dense because of marked vascularisation and hyperplasia. The height of the epithelial cells doubled, the amount of intra-follicular colloid diminished, the colloid was markedly vacuolated. After the second plucking the signs of hyperactivity in the thyroid became even more pronounced. The enlarged and overlapping cells disrupted the usual single-layer arrangement of the follicular walls, and the cavity was no longer present in most of the follicles. The interfollicular connective tissue was hypertrophied and hyperaemic. Such signs of hyperactivity showed practically no increase during the development of the third generation of large feathers. The glands consisted of strands of swollen epithelial cells without signs of follicular structure. Giant prismatic cells with lique-fied cytoplasm became irregularly shaped because of mutual compression.

The biological tests showed that the thyroid glands of the control birds, with their low epithelium, and containing accumulated colloid in the follicles, exhibited strong meta-morphogenic activity (see Table 10).

The thyroid glands of the experimental birds had fewer accumulated active substances and weak metamorphogenic activity. This diminution of thyroid activity was the more pronounced the longer the period of continuous regeneration in the feather-forming tissue (Figs. 34, 35). Following the second plucking there was further depletion of hormone from the thyroid. After the third plucking the glandular tissue was practically inactive. When pieces of such tissue were implanted into tadpoles, their gut (known to be very sensitive to thyroid hormone) showed no signs of resorption, just as did that of the control tadpoles developing without any experimental interference (Fig. 35.j).

The data on the microstructure of the thyroid glands and the results of their biological testing suggests that repeated activation of feather development leads to functional exhaustion of the thyroid within a relatively short time. No hormone is found in the gland, nor is there any in the blood, since the feather germs on the majority of the pterylae no longer have the ability to develop. The results of testing the blood of such experimental birds are shown in Table 11.

Table *11*

Data on the biological activity of the blood of pigeons as tested on tadpoles

Indices	Control	Experimental series		
		I	II	III
Resorption of tail, per cent	−4 5	10.2	3.4	−8.0
Gut shortening per cent	−7.7	21.5	9.8	−8.6

The blood of control pigeons had no appreciable effect on the development of the tadpoles: no acceleration of metamorphosis was observed. The negative sign before some of the figures in the Table shows that the blood contributed to the growth of the tadpoles as a nutrient substance, which does not usually encourage the resorption of larval organs. The blood from pigeons in the first experimental series, tested at the time of maximal development of a large mass of feathers, showed a stimulating effect on tadpole development. The shortening of the gut in the tadpoles in this series amounted to an average of 21·5 per cent. Although this figure is not large, it is quite reliable, taking into account the mass material in our method of testing. Later, after repeated plucking of young quills, the biological activity of the blood proved to be either considerably reduced or absent altogether. How was the stimulating action of the blood of pigeons after a single plucking to be evaluated? Since the histology of the tadpoles' own thyroids showed that accelerated metamorphosis could not be accounted for by their slight activation, the stimulating influence was evidently due to the hormone present in the blood being tested. The thyroid glands of pigeons subjected to a single plucking showed signs of increased hormone release from the gland into the blood. The normal rate of growth of the feather germs, after the first plucking, indicated that the blood contained sufficient hormone to sustain a massive renewal of growth. After thrice repeated plucking, however, no active agent was found in the blood, which explained why

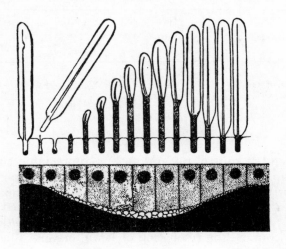

Fig. 34. Diagram of the interdependence of the phases of feather formation and thyroid activity. Increasing mass of the live part of growing feathers is paralleled by enhanced activity of the thyroid epithelium (grey); the amount of colloid (black) within the follicles of the gland declines

the feather germs present in the skin failed to grow (Voitkevich, 1948, b).

The failure of most of the feathers to develop after repeated plucking is thus explained by the functional exhaustion of the thyroid gland. The presence of the thyroid hormone in the body is an essential condition for normal feather formation. The feather follicles of different pterylae are not equally sensitive to the absence of thyroid hormone from the body: the large feathers develop slowly even in the absence of the hormone. The skin of birds subjected to multiple plucking was histologically examined. As already mentioned, during normal

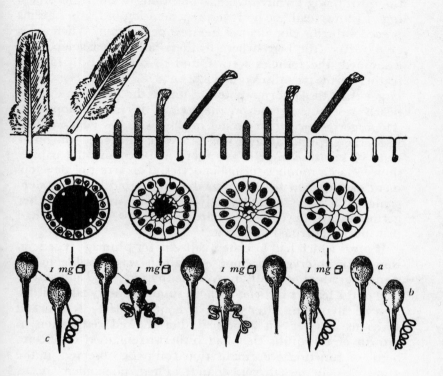

Fig. 35. Diagram of changes in the structure and biological activity of the thyroid gland under conditions of repeated activation of feather-forming tissue

Upper row, thrice-repeated activation of the feather follicles. Middle row, corresponding changes in the microscopic structure of the thyroid glands. Lower row (a) identical tadpoles at the moment of implantation of fragments of glandular tissue; (b) altered tadpoles five days after implantation; (c) control tadpoles (intact). The black spirals denote the gut in tadpoles, which becomes shortened during metamorphosis

feather regeneration the new germ is laid down at the base of the quill being formed. Under conditions of multiple plucking of young feathers, however, regeneration of feather germs precedes the development of the next generation. When areas of skin from the body where feathers failed to develop were examined, the follicles were found to contain fully-formed feather germs (see also Voitkevich, 1938, a). These germs were larger than those normally found under the quills, and more nearly resembled these on the second day of development. These germs, or rather young quills, were less well vascularised, their epithelial layer was somewhat thickened, the outer layer of keratinised cells was more marked, and the papilla showed large numbers of melanocytes. The arrest of development of such new feathers was due to thyroid hormone deficiency. When thyroidin was given to such birds, the feather germs always developed, regardless of how long they had previously remained quiescent.

If birds which had lost their capacity for plumage regeneration were observed for long enough, it was possible to see signs of gradual normalisation of the thyroid gland and activation of the feather follicles without supplementary administration of thyroidin. After about a month, repeatedly plucked birds maintained on a normal diet showed restoration of growth of the quills that had hitherto remained quiescent. Signs of functional normalisation could be observed at the same time in the thyroid glands. These phenomena occur more rapidly if the birds are kept at a high temperature.

A general conclusion which follows from these observations is that feather germs can be laid down when the thyroid hormone is deficient or even absent. The thyroid hormone is, however, essential for the development of feathers.

Similar phenomena were also observed in some birds not subjected to repeated plucking. We plucked pigeons in the autumn after cessation of natural moulting. The new plumage developed normally in most of these birds. Some birds, however, grew only the large feathers, their trunks remaining naked. As in the previous case, histological examination of the skin eighteen days after plucking showed fully formed feather germs, somewhat enlarged as compared with the usual quiescent germs. Their hypertrophied thyroid glands contained no

THE RÔLE OF THE THYROID GLAND

colloid and showed signs similar to those seen in the thyroids of pigeons subjected to repeated plucking. This phenomenon is a particular instance of the manifestations of exhaustion of glandular tissue subjected to prolonged and intensive activity. Pavlov, in his day, pointed out the importance of investigating glandular tissues under conditions of exhaustion and recovery. The phenomenon of functional exhaustion of the thyroid gland which we studied must be taken into account when explaining seasonal periodicity in the activity of endocrine organs.

Thus, deficiency of thyroid hormone, accompanied by a decline in the oxidative processes in the tissues and a drop in the basal metabolic rate of the bird, leads to a loss of proliferative capacity in the feather germs. Under these conditions the feather germ is formed but fails to develop further. This conclusion regarding the differential effect of the thyroid hormone on the different phases of feather development is also confirmed by other facts. In young birds the germs of the nestling feathers are laid down before the differentiation of the thyroid is complete. But development of young feathers is accompanied by increased thyroid activity. Schwarz (1930) described several Plymouth Rock chicks in which the thyroid glands were 'atrophic' (complete absence of follicles). These birds developed naked, with only the flight feathers and the wing vectrices.

To sum up, then, a deficiency or absence of thyroid hormone does not preclude normal development of the large feathers in the wing and tail, or the laying-down of the germs of the small feathers of the body. It is possible that the small amount of hormone either present in the tissues or secreted by the exhausted thyroid gland, and undetected by the usual biological methods, is sufficient to mediate the development of those feathers which play the most vital part in the bird's life. The presence of hormone is an essential condition for the development of feathers on most of the pterylae. This conclusion has already been substantiated by the experimental data described above, but direct evidence furnished by thyroidectomy would make it even more convincing.

THYROIDECTOMY

Ewald and Rockwell (1890) were the first to attempt thy-roidectomy in birds, using adult pigeons as subjects. They described the operative procedure, but it is impossible to tell from their data whether their thyroidectomies were total. Parhon and Parhon (1924) removed the thyroid from goslings, but gave no description of their method. The operation was performed in two stages: one lobe was removed first, the other some days later. Five of the eight operated goslings survived, but only one of these could be presumed to have had a com-plete thyroidectomy. Crew (1927) described one thyroidec-tomised rooster which did not moult for a year after the operation. Greenwood and Blyth (1929) describe thyroid-ectomy on Brown Leghorn chicks of different ages. The gland was in fact totally removed in one or two of the fifteen chicks operated. The method of thyroidectomy in pigeons has been described by Zatvornitskaya and Zimnitskii (1932). Their method does not guarantee complete extirpation, but this they were not attempting, limiting their aim to partial thyroid-ectomy.

The first attempts of a number of workers to master the technique of thyroid extirpation in fowls were unsuccessful. Benoit and Aron (1934) described the condition of thyroidec-tomised mature cocks and drakes. Complete extirpation was achieved in isolated cases only; eleven of the twelve drakes operated showed regeneration of thyroid tissue. Similar data are reported by Parkes and Selye (1937).

Lektorskii and Kuz'mina (1936 b) and Lektorskii (1938) had at their disposal a considerable number of fully thyroidecto-mised birds. They described changes in the growth of twenty-seven thyroidectomised White Leghorn chicks and the development of their plumage. Schooley (1937) mentions thyroidectomised pigeons in his work on hypophyseal changes during the sexual cycle in the pigeon. Lektorskii, in a later work (1940) described changes in plumage colour of nine drakes and three Rouen ducks after removal of thyroid glands. Similar data have been published on several operated Golden Leghorn fowls by Caridroit (1943).

In the above cases, except that of Lektorskii, the authors

had at their disposal only single specimens of thyroidectomised birds, which limited the scope of the necessary observations on the development of plumage and moulting. With an extensive investigation of the correlation between feather formation and the thyroid gland as our goal, we undertook a twelve-year study of thyroidectomised wild and domestic birds of various ages and differing in their taxonomic position. The main experiments were carried out at the Severtsov Institute of Evolutional Morphology of the USSR Academy of Sciences. Some of the operations were performed at the Ornithological Laboratory of the Pavlov Institute of the Physiology and Pathology of Higher Nervous Activity, at Koltushy, and at the Astrakhan State Sanctuary. Thyroidectomy was performed at various times on representatives of the following 30 species of birds:

Alauda arvensis: skylark
Anas platyrhynchos, var. *domestica*: duck (Duclé, Khaki-Campbell, Peking, Rouen)
Ardea cinerea: heron
Asio flammeus: short-eared owl
Asio otus: long-eared owl
Chloris chloris: greenfinch
Coloeus monedula: jackdaw
Columba livia, var. *domestica*: rock dove
Corduelis flammea: redpoll
Corvus corone: carrion crow
Corvus frugilegus: rook
Coturnix coturnix: quail
Egretta alba: great white heron
Emberiza citrinella: yellowhammer
Falco tinnunculus: kestrel
Fringilla coelebs: chaffinch
Fringilla montifringilla: brambling
Gallus gallus, var. *domestica*: fowl (Dungan or *vudzhi*, Partridge Italian, Rhode Island, White Leghorn)
Loxia curvirostra: crossbill
Meleagris galloparo: turkey
Numida meleagris: guinea-hen
Nycticorax nycticorax: night heron

Passer domesticus: house sparrow
Pelecanus crispus: Dalmatian pelican
Pelecanus onocrotalus: white pelican
Phalacrocorax carbo: cormorant
Pica pica: magpie
Pyrrhula pyrrhula: bullfinch
Sturnus vulgaris: starling
Turdus ericetorum: song-thrush

The number of birds operated on totalled over 850. The operations were unsuccessful in redpolls and bullfinches. Total thyroidectomy was achieved in an average of half the birds.

The main procedural factors necessary for successful operation (for details see Voitkevich, 1939, c, 1943, 1944, a, 1945, a; Kabak, 1945) are as follows. Correct and reliable immobilisation of the bird being operated on, and uniform illumination of the operative field, are important. The bird, prepared for operation, is immobilised on a special table. The operation is often performed without anaesthetic.* The feathers covering the neck and part of the chest are plucked from the immobilised bird. The skin is incised in the midline up from the furcula. The crop (when present) is mobilised to give access to the air sacs. These are either incised or pushed aside with a spatula.

After thus exposing the upper part of the thorax it is possible to embark on successive removal of the lobes of the thyroid. When operating on the right side it is essential to exert a maximal pull on the right side of the furcula upwards and to the right. The curved end of the spatula is then placed slightly medially from the upper pole of the gland and is pulled obliquely upwards, moving the crop aside at the same time. Haemorrhage, although slight, is inevitable, and small hard cotton-wool tampons are therefore placed between the blood vessels before the operation, to prevent blood entering the thoracic cavity and reaching the lungs through the incised air sacs. Each lobe of the thyroid is then gradually removed from the external capsule by blunt dissection. During this procedure even slight carelessness can lead to the death of the operated bird.

* In Britain, a licence from the Home Office is required.—*Ed.*

Extirpation of the lobes of the thyroid begins with removal of the air-sac membrane and incision of the capsule of each lobe. For pigeons and small birds this can be done by means of two finely sharpened ophthalmic anatomical forceps, using fine surgical instruments in rare cases only. The wall of the capsule on the ventral side of the gland is carefully picked up with the forceps and pulled upwards, when it is picked up by the second pair of forceps and carefully ruptured. At the same time the capsule is separated by blunt dissection from the underlying parenchyma. Fine scissors have to be used when operating on adult guinea hens, ducks, cormorants, owls, and rooks, because the capsule in these birds is very tough. All the areas of the capsule are then removed. Separation of the capsule towards the jugular vein can only be extended to the point of attachment of the organ to this vessel. In the opposite direction, however, the capsule can be separated freely. With sufficient care the blood vessels supplying the gland can remain absolutely uninjured at this stage of the operation. The operation is easier when there is a layer of fat adjacent to the gland, both in large birds and in adult small birds. In the latter it is easier to shell out the gland from the capsule, except for the dorsal aspect. When the capsule is removed, the gland, which is held by the blood vessels only, contracts and becomes more rounded. In adult birds both the thyroid arteries can be tied next to the right and left lobes of the gland. But we have become convinced that it is not essential to ligature vessels, especially in small birds. This has the advantage of speeding up the operation, which is a very important factor in reducing the risk of mortality.

The thyroid parenchyma must not be squeezed by the forceps, either during separation of the capsule or later during the separation of the gland from the vessels. This rule must be followed for two reasons: first, to avoid excessive bleeding, and secondly (this is the most important consideration) to prevent the very probable risk of leaving *in situ* microscopic fragments of thyroid tissue which can then regenerate. Therefore, since two pairs of forceps are used during the operation, the underlying tissues are held by one pair and the other is introduced underneath the gland. The tissues or vessels between the two compressed forceps are carefully divided by separating the forceps. When vessels are being divided, the forceps should not be opened immediately, so as to prevent thrombosing. Special care must also be exercised in separating the gland from the vagus.

To separate each lobe of the thyroid from the surrounding tissues and vessels, the upper pole of the gland is moved first, and then the rest of the gland by gradual pulling (fowls, ducks, pigeons). Sometimes it is desirable to start the separation of the gland from both poles at once. In birds of prey and passeriforms the two lobes are shelled out successively in a lateral direction.

If no ligatures are applied, the larger vessels connected to the gland, such as the superior thyroid artery, should be separated first; before separating the vessels, their walls should be somewhat compressed by the forceps. If there is bleeding, a tampon is placed on or near the gland so that with suction it is possible to continue the operation. When haemorrhage is severe, large hard tampons are used which are effective even in arresting spurting bleeding from the carotid artery. In the latter eventuality, the operation should be interrupted on that side and removal of the other lobe begun. The interrupted operation can be resumed after from ten to thirty minutes. Longer interruptions are not recommended, since the thrombus formed at the operative site and the tampon become closely bound together, and the haemorrhage can recur with former severity when the tampon is withdrawn.

When both the lobes have been extirpated and bleeding has stopped, all the tampons and blood clots can be carefully removed. If for some reason it was not possible to remove the gland as a whole and it has been taken out piecemeal, the residual small fragments of thyroid tissue are carefully removed and the underlying tissues cauterised with a fine galvano-cautery needle. The upper pole of the parathyroid, formerly adjacent to the lower pole of the thyroid, is also cauterised. Cautery must be applied very carefully, especially in the region of the vagus. The operative area and the incision are then irrigated with physiological solution. Sutures (closely spaced) are applied to the skin only, care being taken not to include the divided walls of the air sac. The skin surface is wiped with ether and covered with collodion.

The thyroidectomy procedures used by other authors cannot be considered satisfactory, because they do not guarantee total removal of the gland. Thus, for example, Greenwood and Blyth (1929) describe two methods of thyroidectomy. In one the thyroid tissue is gradually plucked out after opening the capsule. The authors themselves conclude that this method cannot be successful, since as soon as the thyroid parenchyma is injured troublesome bleeding begins which is difficult to control and makes the operation extremely difficult. Total removal of the thyroid with this technique is obviously possible only in an exceedingly limited number of cases. In the second method the thyroid was pulled away by curved forceps and then quickly severed from the underlying vessels with scissors. This risky method of removal either leaves residual fragments of thyroid tissue or most frequently causes severe damage to the large vessels. A similar method was used by Zatvornitskaya and Zimnitskii (1932): curved forceps were applied between the gland and the vessel and the gland was then torn away from the underlying tissues. These authors encountered many cases of thyroid tissue regeneration. Of ten pigeons subjected to operation, total thyroidectomy was achieved in only two. Whether the gland had been totally removed can only be concluded from careful histological examination of the site from which the thyroid had been extirpated. Simple reopening with visual examination, as carried out by Crew (1927) on a thyroidectomised rooster, is inadequate.

Zatvornitskaya and Zimnitskii recommended that the two lobes of the thyroid be removed separately after an interval of several days. Our observations have demonstrated that two-stage removal of the two lobes is unsatisfactory, for the following reasons: (1) a second skin incision along the line of the old suture often leads to necrosis of considerable areas of skin; (2) a second injury to the recovering air sacs leads to subsequent emphysema; (3) the remaining lobe of the gland undergoes compensatory hypertrophy, which makes the second operation particularly difficult, since thyroid hypertrophy is associated with its hyperfunction, increased vascularity, and hyperaemia. We therefore recommend simultaneous removal of both lobes. In cases of severe haemorrhage the operation can be interrupted for ten to thirty minutes, but it is desirable to remove both lobes completely before suturing.

As mentioned above, extirpation of a hyperactive gland introduces substantial difficulties. Therefore, provided the experimental conditions permit, thyroidin can be administered some days before the operation, when the thyroid rapidly contracts and is no longer hyperaemic.

The bird is transferred from the operating table to a separate cage. Sometimes, when there has been severe blood loss and the bird has been immobilised for a long time, the bird dies after the application of sutures. The best criterion of the success of an operation is the rapidity with which the bird is able to stand up. Post-operative weakness usually disappears after several hours. The next day the birds eat well and are little different from normal.

There are two sorts of post-operative complications. Emphysema occurs frequently, as a consequence of opening the air sacs; this occurs especially frequently in cases of incorrect suturing and repeated incisions. Rarely, emphysema extends to the neck, chest, or trunk from the site of operation. In such cases small incisions must be made in the skin to release the air.

More serious complications are those associated with trauma to the vagus, which in pigeons and fowls leads to paralysis of the crop. The bird at first eats readily, but the crop soon becomes gorged with food, which does not pass on to the stomach, and the bird dies with manifestations of severe cachexia. Trauma to the vagus also causes impairment of the respiratory rhythm, with ensuing asphyxia. With sufficient experience it is possible to avoid trauma to the vagus, but such injuries are fairly common during early operations.

Regeneration of thyroid tissue may also occur after unsuccessful operations. If regeneration occurs in only fifty per cent of the birds, operative success must be rated high. In most cases regenerating tissue can be detected by careful examination of the site of operation. This, however, does not exclude subsequent careful microscopic investigation of the area where the thyroid was present, since in a number of cases regenerating tissue can only be discovered on histological sections. The regenerating tissue is larger than the removed lobe of the thyroid. When regeneration of thyroid tissue takes place, the changes which occur in the body after total thyroidectomy either do not appear or occur some time after the operation and then disappear. Both the size of the residual portions of glandular tissue and its rate of regeneration are significant in terms of the physiological effect on the body as a whole.

Formation of juvenile plumage in connection with the general development of the bird

Among the publications mentioned above, only two give data on the effect of thyroidectomy on young birds. Lektorskii and Kuz'mina (1936, b) operated on chicks aged from a minimum of seventeen days to fifty days. Although in chicks the juvenile flight feathers and the vectrices are laid down and begin to grow during the embryonic period, the authors noted that after thyroidectomy the development of plumage was inhibited. Parhon and Parhon (1924) performed thyroidectomy on goslings over the age of ten days, in which the contour feathers are laid down and develop late. In one gosling in which the thyroidectomy was total and which remained under observation for a month, the down persisted throughout the period.

The most conclusive demonstration of the dependence of the development of plumage on the thyroid gland would be provided only if thyroidectomy were to precede the growth of the feather germs. This could be achieved by thyroidectomy on chick embryos or after hatching in the case of birds in which nestling plumage develops late. Among these are many forms of the nidicolous group and some among the nidifugous water fowl. Over a number of years, we performed thyroidectomies on chicks of various breeds, including the Dungan fowl. Our results were close to those described by Lektorskii and Kuz'mina, and there is no need to discuss them in detail. But since fowls develop their plumage early, they were not a suitable test object for the solution of our problem.

The main bulk of our experiments involved the young of species in which the plumage develops relatively late. These included ducks, in which the details of general growth and plumage development are well known (Shtraikh and Sveto-

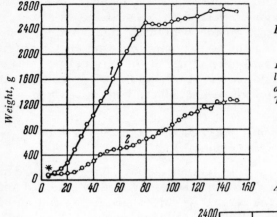

Fig. 36. Growth of ducklings

1, Control. 2, Ducklings thyroidectomised at the age of five days. The asterisk marks the day of operation

Fig. 37. Growth of ducklings

1, Control. 2, Ducklings thyroidectomised at the age of twenty-five days

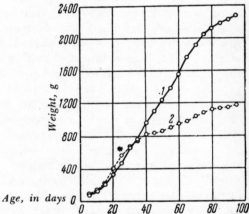

zarov, 1935, b; Kotova, 1936). Most of our experiments were carried out on Peking ducks, but Khaki-Campbell ducklings were also used. In ducks the down begins to be replaced by juvenile feathers only from the age of thirty days, and this process continues over a prolonged period.

The aim was to increase maximally the interval between thyroidectomy and the onset of feather growth, and surgery was therefore performed predominantly on five-day-old ducklings. Subsequently thyroidectomy was also performed on older ducklings, at five-day intervals. Total thyroidectomy was demonstrated by follow-up observations and autopsy in sixteen out of thirty-five operated Peking ducks. The follow-up

*Fig. 38. The effect of thyroid-
ectomy*

*Left, Control duckling aged fifty-
two days. Centre, duckling of the
same age, but thyroidectomised five
days after hatching. Right, normal
five-day duckling for comparison*

*Fig. 39. Duck-
lings aged 70
days*

*Left, two con-
trol birds, Right,
two birds thy-
roidectomised at
the age of five
days*

period for individual birds ranged from three to five months.

Soon after thyroidectomy the ducklings showed retardation
of general growth, which became more marked later (Figs. 36
and 37). The thyroidectomised ducklings remained dwarf
after from three to five months, and their appearance and
behaviour were very similar to those of younger ducklings.
They were sufficiently well nourished, however, judging by
the presence of subcutaneous and internal deposits of fat. The
liver, kidneys, and adrenals were markedly hypertrophied.
The relative weight of the liver and adrenals in thyroidectomised ducklings was four times that in the controls. Skeletal
ossification was retarded, the sternum in a bird four or five
months old remaining as elastic as that in a five-day control
duckling.

The retardation of general growth is inversely proportional
to the age at the time of operation: the earlier the operation,
the greater the retardation of growth. Ducks operated at the

age of seventy days differed little from unoperated controls of the same age (Voitkevich, 1938, f).

If the removal of the thyroid is incomplete, even though only microscopically small fragments of tissue are retained, regeneration of thyroid tissue takes place. In such cases growth is retarded only initially and then begins to recover, but these birds nevertheless do not always reach normal size eventually. The size of regenerated thyroids was always smaller than normal. Prolonged administration of a thyroid preparation, initiated post-operatively, prevented any appreciable deviations from normal development.

The development of plumage in thyroidectomised ducklings is greatly retarded when the thyroid is removed before the onset of the development of juvenile feathers. As in the case of general growth, there is an inverse relationship between the effectiveness of thyroidectomy and the age of the bird at the moment of operation: the sooner the bird is operated on, the greater the retardation of feather development. Thus, ducklings operated on at the age of five days retained their down for a long time, whereas the control birds of the same age acquired contour plumage (Figs. 38 and 39). When such thyroidectomised and control ducklings were compared with each other and also with a normal five-day duckling (the age at which thyroidectomy was performed on the experimental bird) it was seen that the thyroidectomised duckling, although different from its initial state in terms of body size, was very similar in plumage to the five-day bird (Fig. 38). Contour plumage developed in the experimental ducklings at the age of two months. The scapular pterylae and the ventral aspect of the body became clothed in short defective feathers which appeared on the surface of the skin not as quills, but as an already unfurled top of the web in the form of a tassel consisting of a tuft of unravelled barbs. These feathers continued to grow slowly but remained defective (Fig. 40). The primary down remained on the head and neck even longer. The head of three-month-old ducklings was covered simultaneously with down and tufts of juvenile feathers. The rectrices were also defective, and the flight feathers failed to develop altogether when the ducklings were operated on between the ages of five and thirty-five days. Those operated on later showed, besides defective contour feathers, a partial garb of juvenile white down. In ducklings operated on at the age of twenty-five to thirty-five days the scapular and lateral pterylae developed to a degree not very different from similar areas in the control birds; such birds are shown in the foreground of Fig. 41.

Similar results were obtained on ducks of the Khaki-Campbell breed. At an age when the development of plumage in the control ducklings was complete, the thyroidectomised ones were still covered with primary down and sparse defective feathers (Figs. 42, 43). Older birds remained free of contour feathers (Fig. 44).

Normal plumage is formed when thyroidectomy is sub-total, but its development is somewhat delayed compared with that of the control. Flight feathers also develop, but their growth is retarded more than that of the small feathers, the germs of which are laid down earlier in these birds. In general, thyroid-hormone deficiency seriously affects plumage development, but these disturbances are nevertheless relatively less pronounced than the retardation of growth of the bird itself.

The plumage develops normally if thyroidectomised ducklings are given thyroid hormone. In some instances the plumage grows more rapidly than in the control, when the dosage of the hormone preparation is suitable; for example, when the experimental birds were given 400 mg thyroidin each per day their feathers completed their growth earlier than in normal birds.

The experimental results of Kabak and Tal'skaya (1956) obtained on ducklings of the White Peking breed are of interest in connection with the above data. They administered various doses of radioactive iodine to one-day-old ducklings, and showed histologically that the thyroid parenchyma was totally destroyed by doses of 250 and 500 μC I^{131}. This results in severe retardation of the birds' growth, and in inhibition of replacement of down by contour feathers. It is noteworthy that the growth curves shown in Fig. 2 of their paper and in Fig. 36 of the present book representing the growth curve for thyroidectomised ducklings of the same breed coincide precisely. No less interesting is the similarity of the photographs of the two lots of birds in investigations conducted by different

methods and at different times (see Figs. 3 and 5 in the
work referred to, and Figs. 38, 39, and 41 of the present
book).

The experimental results yielded by thyroidectomised
ducklings can be summarised as follows. The thyroid hormone
is essential for the development of contour plumage: in its
absence the feathers either fail to grow altogether or develop
into defective ones. The feathers of some pterylae, which are
laid down earlier, are less affected by thyroidectomy than
feathers which are laid down later. The longer the interval
between the time of operation and the onset of feather growth
on a given pteryla, the more marked is the retardation of
feather development.

These conclusions were further confirmed and refined in
subsequent experiments on a series of various nidicolous birds
which differed in the degree of general differentiation at the
moment of hatching and the rate of postembryonic development. In such birds the development of the germs of juvenile
contour feathers begins after hatching.

Let us consider the experiments on wild birds. The results
given below show the effects of thyroidectomy on the cormorant, the white pelican, and three species of heron.

The technique of thyroidectomy has already been described.
Some of the operated cormorants were reared in the laboratory, the rest were returned to the nest immediately after
operation. The operated birds were placed in large baskets
together with control birds of the same age. A high laboratory temperature, and mutual warming by the birds kept in
the same basket, were essential for survival of the young
cormorants operated on. All the birds were fed every two
hours with freshly cut-up fish. Older birds were fed three or
four times a day. The control and experimental birds did
not feed themselves; the food was introduced artificially by
mouth into the oesophagus. The amount of food was increased
according to the age of the birds.

A number of observations parallel to the laboratory ones
were carried out under natural conditions on birds which
were returned to the nest after operation. Return to the nest
ensured rearing of the thyroidectomised birds under optimal
natural conditions. At first we returned the birds to their own

Fig. 40. Feathers of the scapular pteryla.
Left, from a control duck. Right, from a thyroidectomised duck

Fig. 41. The state of plumage in thyroidectomised Peking
ducks (all the birds aged eighty days)
Centre, control duck; around it, birds operated at different intervals
after hatching

Fig. 42. Khaki-Campbell ducklings aged sixty-five days
Right, control duckling. Left, duckling thyroidectomised at the age of
thirty-five days. Centre, duckling thyroidectomised at the age of
seventeen days

Fig. 43. Control duckling of
the Khaki-Campbell breed aged
seventy days

Fig. 44. Thyroidectomised
Khaki-Campbell duckling aged
seventy days (operation performed five days after hatching)

nests. Later, when we became convinced that cormorants, in
rearing their young, make no distinction between their own
offspring and those of other birds, we returned the thyroidectomised birds to the nests which were best situated for observation. Each nest contained two operated birds and one control bird of the same age. All the birds were ringed. The birds
kept in nests and those reared in the laboratory were periodically weighed every third day. Details were kept of behaviour,
the general habit, and the state of plumage. Despite a number
of difficulties encountered during the return of young operated birds to nests and the making of prolonged observations
under natural conditions, eleven totally thyroidectomised
birds were successfully reared in nests and then taken back to
the laboratory.

We had a total of fifty-six operated birds which survived
for a considerable period post-operatively. Of these, thirty-
three showed various amounts of regenerating thyroid tissue
at autopsy; in twenty-three the thyroidectomy was total. The
operations were performed on birds of different ages, but the
main bulk of the experimental material was made up of birds
operated on from five to ten days after hatching. It was as-

sumed that the effects of thyroidectomy would be more pronounced if the thyroid gland were removed before the onset
of its hyperactivity, that is, before the age of ten days.

The developmental deviations from the normal observed
in thyroidectomised birds reared in the laboratory were approximately the same as those shown by thyroidectomised
birds reared in nests. There were practically no differences
in the development of control birds reared in the laboratory
and in nests. We therefore made no further references to the
conditions of rearing. The effect of thyroidectomy was more
marked in birds operated on five days after hatching. The
older the operated birds, the less the deviation from normal
during the post-operative period; young birds operated on
shortly before cessation of growth showed no discernible differences from the controls.

Table 12 shows the data on the growth of young cormorants
subjected to thyroidectomy at the age of five days. In addition
to the absolute mean data for the experimental and the control
groups, there are also figures for the rate (Cv), the growth
constant (K), and the mean for the period $\left(\dfrac{\Sigma K}{n}\right)$ according
to the familiar formula given by Shmal'gauzen (1935).

The growth of the control birds reared in the laboratory
showed the same periodicity as that of birds kept under natural conditions. The values characterising the energy of growth
were about the same in both environments. The course of
growth was different in the absence of thyroid hormone; the
rate of growth declined immediately after operation, and
the species-characteristic periodicity of growth became less
marked. The difference in weight between the controls and
the birds operated on at the age of five days was greatest at
the end of the period of observation. The mean weight of the
experimental birds was at this time roughly half that of the
controls. Deviation from the normal in birds thyroidectomised
at the age of ten days was already less marked than in those
operated on at the previous stage. Birds operated on twenty
days after hatching showed only slight deviations from normal
growth. When older birds were operated on just before completion of growth there was, as expected, no effect on the
vigour of general growth.

11

Table 12

Body weight, rate and constant of growth of thyroidectomised and control birds

Age, in days from the moment of hatching	Control				Experimental			
	Weight in g	Cv	K	$\frac{\Sigma K}{n}$	Weight in g	Cv	K	$\frac{\Sigma K}{n}$
0	41	1.074	5.906		42	1.114	6.128	
3	120	0.781	5.075	4.749	128	0.530	3.431	
6	262	0.634	4.756		217	0.058	0.436	
9	494	0.383	3.257		230	0.314	2.673	
12	723	0.208	1.974		315	0.357	3.388	
15	890	0.323	3.397		450	0.269	2.827	
18	1230	0.144	1.651		589	0.158	1.819	
21	1420	0.141	1.661		690	0.220	2.752	2.374
24	1635	0.120	1.624	1.909	860	0.182	2.461	
27	1844	0.086	1.250		1032	0.167	2.426	
30	2010	0.060	0.935		1220	0.118	1.830	
33	2135	0.002	0.031	0.570	1373	0.078	1.294	
36	2139	0.027	0.476		1485	0.023	0.408	
39	2200	0.045	0.838		1520	0.035	0.657	0.532
42	2210				1575			

When the thyroidectomised birds were examined at autopsy, large deposits of fat were found within the body cavity and subcutaneously. In the experimental birds the weight of the liver, showing fatty infiltration, was often double the normal. Such disturbances were more pronounced in birds operated on at an early age. These data are important with regard to the nature of development in the absence of the thyroid hormone, since they reflect not only quantitative deviations in growth but also qualitative changes.

Cormorants subjected to thyroidectomy at an early age resembled much younger birds in their outward appearance at the end of the period of observation. The changing phases of behaviour so clearly seen in normal young cormorants were appreciably impaired by thyroidectomy. The experimental birds continued to behave like very young birds for a long time. Such birds, having reached the age of thirty to thirty-five days, continued to produce the characteristic call and to move their heads and take food in the same way as very young normal birds. The signs of aggression typical for normal nearly

fully-grown cormorants did not appear in thyroidectomised
birds of the same age. This suggests that differentiation of the
parts of the central nervous system responsible for the bird's
reflex activity was retarded in the absence of thyroid hormone.

Such birds show significant impairment of plumage development. Birds operated on in down remained naked throughout the remaining period of observation. The only feathers
which showed signs of growth, very delayed, were the flight
feathers, the rectrices, and the scapulars. The feathers which
developed were defective: they were shorter than normal, the
vanes were very narrow, and the growth was slow. The down
gradually wore out and was not replaced (Fig. 45). Birds operated on later showed less marked changes in the development
of contour feathers; these changes were more pronounced
on the dorsal pterylae than on the ventral. The extent to which
the developing feathers were defective was inversely related
to the age at which thyroidectomy was performed. If the
operation preceded the proliferation of feather germs on a
given pteryla, then the feathers usually failed to develop altogether. If they did develop, their size, shape, and structure
were very different from normal. However, if the time of

Fig. 45. Thyroidectomy in the cormorant

Middle, thirty-five-day control cormorant. Right, cormorant of the same
age, thyroidectomised on the fifth day after hatching. Left, a normal
five-day bird, for comparison

operation coincided with the onset of feather development, or even more if their growth preceded it, impairment of further growth and structural development was slight. In cormorants, the head and neck are late in acquiring their plumage. These areas remained featherless in thyroidectomised birds operated on relatively late (from ten to twelve days after hatching).

Since early thyroidectomy was followed by total failure of feather development on the pterylae, it became necessary to determine which phase of the morphogenic process was impaired: the laying-down of the germs, or further development? Histological examination of serial sections of skin showed that fully formed feather germs were present within the follicles, as were young quills with early differentiation of barbs in the apical part. Consequently, the absence of thyroid hormone does not hinder the first phase of feather formation —the laying-down of germs and the onset of their proliferation; but the thyroid hormone is necessary for further development and the whole complex of growth and differentiation of the feathers.

To clarify the extent to which such changes in growth and differentiation were in fact due to experimental absence of thyroid hormone, four birds thyroidectomised at the age of five days were given a preparation of dried thyroid with their food. The daily dose of thyroidin was 200 mg up to the age of ten days and 300 mg for older birds. Parallel observations were made on the development of young birds with postoperative regeneration of thyroid tissue. In the former case, a known high concentration of thyroid hormone was induced artificially in the birds' body; in the latter case the amount of hormone released from the regenerating gland was below normal. The microscopic appearance of the regenerating tissue was usually hyperactive.

Continued administration of a thyroid preparation to thyroidectomised birds quickly restored their growth. Their weight was a little less than that of controls of the same age. The increase in metabolism was so marked that despite voraciousness the birds had no deposits of fat subcutaneously or within the body cavity up to the end of the period of observation (Voitkevich, 1945, c).

The sub-totally thyroidectomised birds showed considerable retardation of growth immediately post-operatively, when the regeneration of residual fragments was only beginning. Later, when the regenerating tissue produced more hormone, the rate of growth of the birds increased. Towards the end of the period of observation the weight and general habit of sub-totally thyroidectomised birds were practically indistinguishable from normal (Fig. 46).

The difference in the hormonal levels attained in the birds of these supplementary series was also reflected in the rate of feather formation. In the presence of excess thyroid hormone feathers of normal shape and structure developed at a more rapid rate than normal. The growth of feather germs was delayed in the partially thyroidectomised birds. The cause was evidently the absence or low concentration of the hormone during the onset of growth. Later both the growth and structural differentiation of the feathers proceeded at the normal rate. These data indicate that with minimal concentrations of the hormone, which are insufficient to ensure a normal rate of growth of the body, the formation of plumage is fully

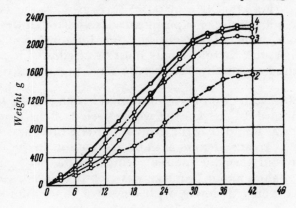

Age, in days after hatching

Fig. 46. Changes in body weight of the cormorant during its development

1, control. 2, Birds thyroidectomised at the age of five days. 3, Birds subjected to continued thyroid administration following thyroidectomy. 4, Birds in whom the thyroidectomy was subtotal and thyroid tissue regeneration took place

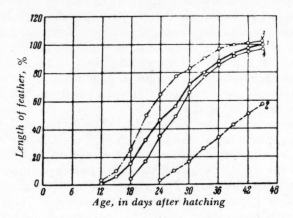

Fig. 47. Growth of the flight feathers during the post-embryonic development of the cormorant

1, Control. 2, Birds thyroidectomised at the age of 5 days. 3, Birds given thyroidin postoperatively (thyroidectomy). 4, Birds with subtotal thyroidectomy and subsequent regeneration of the thyroid gland

recovered (Fig. 47). The material furnished by the last two supplementary series of experiments has shown that the deviations from normal body growth and differentiation of the young bird after thyroidectomy must be attributed to general lack of the hormone rather than to some post-operative side-effects.

Our observations on thyroidectomised young of the Dalmatian pelican did not span the whole period of their development. It was found that the growth of these birds was not retarded to as great an extent as in the cormorant. In the absence of the thyroid hormone the replacement of the black primary down by light contour plumage was greatly delayed. Juvenile feathers developed slowly, with defective vanes (Voitkevich, 1943).

The above finding prompted thyroidectomy on the young of various species of heron at the earliest age suitable for operation. The age in the different series ranged from two to eight days. Operations were performed on a total of eighteen herons, seven great white herons, and fourteen night herons. The young birds were taken from the nests, and underwent thyroidectomy either immediately on reaching the laboratory or from twelve to fifteen hours later. The special topographical features of the thyroid in herons proved to be favourable for operation, since blood loss was minimal (Voitkevich, 1944, a).

Attempts to return the operated birds to nests for rearing, as was done with the cormorants, proved unsuccessful. A few days after their return they were found thrown out of the nests. Whether they died in the nests and were then thrown out, or whether they were rejected by the parents, could not be established. The heron young were therefore reared in the laboratory; they were fed throughout the day with macerated fresh fish and frogs. The gastric contents of adult birds were added to such feeds for the very young birds. The birds were weighed regularly every third day, and notes on their appearance included measurements on a series of feathers.

Our observations on the thyroidectomised young of the heron and the great white heron were limited to from twelve to fifteen days, since the birds did not survive longer and sometimes died even sooner. Death was preceded by such phenomena as ejection of food placed in the beak, progressive general sluggishness, and convulsive extensions of the body and neck. It was impossible to discover whether these phenomena were associated with trauma to the vagus during operation or whether some damage to the parathyroids proved to be critical for these birds. The same thyroidectomy technique was uncomplicated by any side-effects in the vast majority of other species of birds. It was still possible, however, during these brief periods of observation, to note that the operated birds lagged in growth as compared with the controls. The development of plumage was also retarded. This was especially marked on those pterylae where the feather germs were laid down late.

Operations on night herons proved more successful. Of fourteen operated birds three died soon after operation, and thyroid regeneration occurred in seven. Four totally thyroidectomised birds were under observation for a month. These birds were of different ages at the time of operation. This prevented the use of mean data for the indices under consideration, both in the experimental and the control findings. Individual data for birds from different groups were compared.

Table 13 shows the numerical material on the growth of feathers in three birds and on general growth of a control bird, a bird with total thyroidectomy, and one with demonstrable thyroid regeneration.

As Table 13 shows, the birds were of different ages at the time of operation and their weights were also different. Their ages differed by one day. Both thyroidectomised birds were larger than the control one.

Table 13

Body weight and size of feathers during the development of normal and thyroidectomised young of the night heron

Age, in days	Weight, in g			Flight feather 10, mm		
	Control	Total thyroid-ectomy	Subtotal thyroid-ectomy	Control	Total thyroid-ectomy	Subtotal thyroid-ectomy
0	33	56	45	0	'0	0
3	92	138	124	0	0	0
6	176	106	112	2	0	0
9	328	142	195	17	0	0
12	431	229	308	35	3	10
15	516	267	384	52	7	29
18	594	305	452	73	12	51
21	608	332	488	95	20	75
24	704	402	610	113	31	97
27	745	430	667	131	45	116
30	810	486	743	150	58	132
33	817	506	769	158	72	147

Post-operatively, the growth of both birds was noticeably retarded; it then recovered partially but remained slower than that of the control bird. The difference in the growth of the experimental and the control birds persisted throughout the period of observation. The development of those birds in which thyroid regeneration was found at autopsy (data on one of these are shown in Table 13) followed a different course. For six or seven days there was no difference between them and those totally thyroidectomised, the growth being grossly retarded in both cases, but then the weight of the subtotally thyroidectomised bird began to increase at a faster rate, practically catching up the similarly aged control at the age of

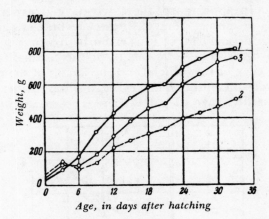

Fig. 48. The growth of young night herons
1, Control. 2, Totally thyroidectomised birds. 3, Subtotally thyroidec-
tomised birds. Asterisk marks time of operation

one month (Fig. 61). The retardation of growth of these
partially thyroidectomised birds immediately after operation
must be associated with the absence or severe deficit of the
thyroid hormone. As the thyroid tissue regenerated and the
hormone began to reach the blood, the bird's rate of growth
increased. Microscopically, the regenerated thyroid glands
showed signs of hyperactivity. Partially thyroidectomised birds
were thus a supplementary control, demonstrating a connection between the rate of general growth and the concentration
of the thyroid hormone in the body of a young bird.

The state of plumage in the thyroidectomised birds was
significant. The difference between the experimental and the
control birds in this respect was more marked towards the end
of the period of investigation. The control birds had normal
plumage, whereas the thyroidectomised ones had underdeveloped feathers on all the pterylae. These defective feathers were
extremely small on the ventral aspect of the body, which remained essentially featherless. The feathers on the dorsal
aspect were a little larger, but still not sufficiently large to
cover the neighbouring apterous areas. The large wing and
tail feathers, which are laid down earlier, developed better
but were nevertheless very different in shape and size from

the normal. In appearance, the thirty-day-old experimental birds closely resembled control birds of a younger age.

The tenth primary flight feather on both wings was measured in all birds. The total length of the feather from the apex to the edge of the follicle, and the length of the developing vane, were measured. The curves showing feather growth indicate that after thyroidectomy there is retardation of longi-

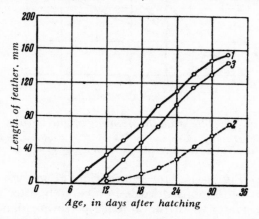

Fig. 49. Growth of flight feathers in the young of the night heron
1, Control. 2, Total thyroidectomy. 3, Subtotal thyroidectomy

tudinal growth of the feather (Fig. 49). In cases of subtotal thyroidectomy there is only temporary retardation with delay of the onset of development. Then, as the thyroid tissue begins to regenerate, the rate of feather growth returns to normal. It follows that the minimal amount of thyroid hormone produced by the regenerating tissue is able to effect this return to normal growth and development of plumage. It is not sufficient, however, to restore the rate of the bird's general growth to normal. It must also be mentioned that when there was a temporary slackening of general growth of the experimental and control birds (21st day) under unfavourable environmental conditions, the rate of feather development was unaffected. Differentiation of feather structure began consistently after a definite interval of time from the onset of growth, although the size of the feather quills in the thyroidectomised birds was considerably smaller than that of those in the controls. It was found that when the total length was the same in experimental and control birds of different ages, the size of the vane differed substantially. For example, on the eighteenth day of development, the tenth flight feather in the control measured 73 mm, the vane being 28 mm; this length was reached in the case of a thyroidectomised bird only on the 33rd day, with the vane measuring 49 mm. At this time (33rd day) the feathers in the control bird had reached their full size and ceased to grow, the length of the homologous feathers in the experimental birds now being only half the normal and the length of the vane only one third of the normal.

Consequently, an adequate concentration of thyroid hormone in the body is essential for normal post-embryonic growth of young night herons. Growth is retarded if this hormone falls to a level below a certain minimum. Plumage, however, develops normally under these conditions. But total absence of thyroid hormone affects the development of plumage more than that of the general growth of the bird.

Our subsequent attempts to achieve total thyroidectomy in such representatives of the nidicolous birds such as pigeons failed in the case of young growing birds. The difficulties were associated with the large size of the crop, high vascularity of the thyroid gland, and fatal effect of even slight haemorrhage. Similar operations on adult pigeons were successful, however, despite a number of technical difficulties.

Experiments on a number of the large members of the passeriforms (rooks, magpies, jackdaws, starlings) yielded results confirming the connection between feather formation and the thyroid mentioned above, and further clarifying some aspects of this connection. The experiments on rooks and magpies were performed together with Vasil'ev at the Ornithological Laboratory at Koltushy (Voitkevich and Vasil'ev, 1939; and Vasil'ev and Voitkevich, 1939).

At this laboratory a method had been developed over a period of years for rearing birds taken from the nest from five to seven days after hatching. Each bird was fed seven or eight times a day. They were fed to complete satiation, that is, until they ceased to open the mouth in response to a repeated low-pitched sound of 'kahr' made over them, which is an unconditioned stimulus of the food reflex in very young rooks. The composition of the feeds was evolved in the light of information collected by opening the stomachs of young and old rooks during feeding; vitamins and mineral components were also added. Post-operatively, if blood loss had been slight, the young birds at first did not differ greatly in behaviour from normal, and accepted food readily. A total of thirty-six rooks were thyroidectomised. Normal birds of corresponding ages, or birds subjected to operation and controlled trauma to the

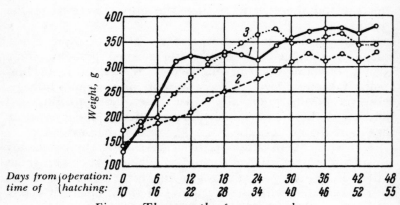

Fig. 50. *The growth of young rooks*

1, Control. 2, Total thyroidectomy at the age of ten days. 3, Subtotal thyroidectomy

thyroid parenchyma, served as controls. A number of comparisons were made using birds which had undergone thyroidectomy with subsequent regeneration of thyroid tissue were used, as well as young rooks which had been castrated and subjected to thymectomy for other purposes and had suffered more general trauma at operation.

The thyroidectomised birds proved less viable than the controls. The poorly feathered thyroidectomised birds died when the air temperature in the laboratory was allowed to drop, whereas the control birds remained well. Altogether, 100 days after operation, two of the thirty-six thyroidectomised birds and sixteen of the twenty control birds were still alive.

The experimental birds showed retarded growth immediately post-operatively as compared with normal and control birds. Figure 50 shows data on the growth of rooks thyroid-ectomised at the age of ten days. A control rook grows during the first twenty days, as shown by the corresponding curve; subsequently (until the 35th day) the bird's weight alters little, the slight increase being due to increasing size of functioning organs associated with the bird's active behaviour. In thyroidectomised birds the rate of growth declines at once after the operation. The period of growth becomes more extended in time. When growth is completed, the birds remain smaller than the controls. The results of thyroidectomy become apparent in a disproportionate growth of individual parts of the body. Particularly noticeable features include a broad and anteriorly somewhat swollen cranium, protuberant 'frog eyes', wide infantile mouth, large and disproportionately protuberant abdomen, loosely wrinkled skin.

Removal of the thyroid to some extent arrests the bird's behaviour at the stage appropriate to the level of development at the time of operation. If the thyroidectomy was subtotal and was followed some time later by regeneration of the gland, growth was retarded only during the initial post-operative period. Later, as thyroid function was restored, the birds reached normal size and did not differ in behaviour from the control birds. When the operation was performed at the age of seventy days it had no effect on the size and general habit of the bird.

The retardation of growth noted above in the case of the experimental rooks was due to the thyroidectomy, since the birds in the control groups developed quite normally. Another confirmation of this conclusion is to be found in the results of the experiment staged under natural conditions. From a nest usually containing three or four nestlings, one was taken and subjected to thyroidectomy and then returned to the nest. Such operations were carried out on birds from eleven nests in the course of two spring seasons. Thyroidectomy was found to cause the same retardation of growth under natural rearing conditions as in the laboratory environment. The most successful experiments in this respect were the last ones performed during the second season, when young rooks operated at the age of three or four days were successfully returned to their nests, to become cretinoid birds which at the age of from twenty-five to thirty days were one third the weight of the control birds.

Retardation of growth in thyroidectomised birds was parallelled by retardation of plumage development. It must be noted that because of reasons mentioned above the birds used in the experiments already had developing feathers on various pterylae. At the time of operation the main pterylae showed feather quills either at the stage preceding the unfurling of the vanes or with partially unfurled vanes. Consequently, the effect of thyroidectomy could manifest itself either on the late stages of growth of some feathers or on the development of those feathers which were the latest to be laid down.

In fact, in thyroidectomised birds the pterylae of the neck, the inferior surface of the wing, the legs, and the back remain featherless. Those feathers whose quills were already there before the operation proceed to develop. The rectrices and the flight feathers, and their coverts, continue to develop after thyroidectomy. However, their rate of growth declines, and so the large feathers in the experimental birds complete their growth from fifteen to twenty-five days later than do those in the controls. These feathers differ from the normal in size, shape, and structure: their vanes are considerably narrower and shorter. The barbs of the vane of large feathers are loosely connected and in small feathers quite disconnected so that the contour part resembles a tassel instead of an elastic laminar vane. The base of the vane of such feathers has no downy part or may show some very much reduced barbs. Similar results were obtained with thyroidectomised magpies and jackdaws. In the case of the latter, the young operated on were returned to the nest.

Next to be considered are the data relating to a fairly large group of experiments on young starlings. Because of their small size, and the loose structure of the thyroid parenchyma and surrounding tissues, operations were often fatal, and even after successful operations, thyroid regeneration could often not be excluded.

But the experiments on starlings were of interest because the rate of development of these birds is even higher than that of other passeriforms used in the previous experiments. On average, a starling is fully grown within eighteen days from hatching. At the moment of hatching, the young are blind, naked, and poorly differentiated. Their weight increases several times over during the first few days. Dark quills of contour feathers become visible under the skin of the dorsal pteryla on the fourth day after hatching, and the feathers then develop very rapidly.

Because of the starling's high rate of development, it was essential, to demonstrate the effects of thyroidectomy, to operate on the birds as early as possible, that is, not later than two or three days after hatching. The difficulties encountered during such operations are evident from the above, and explain the numerous repetitions of our experiments over the years. Of the total of 115 starlings operated on over a period of five years (mostly two or three days old), sixty-four survived. The thyroidectomy was often subtotal, with ensuing regeneration. Total thyroidectomy was achieved in fourteen birds, as demonstrated at the conclusion of the observations. In the early experiments the operated birds were reared in the laboratory. The artificial feeding included components which young starlings receive under natural conditions. In later experiments both the operated and the control birds were returned to their own nests. The experimental and the control birds were weighed and their growing feathers were measured at equal intervals of time. At the end of the growing period the flight feathers in all the birds were cut, and also were tied with a silk thread to the leg, to limit the birds' mobility. This made it possible to continue observations on the young birds for a long time.

Within twenty-four hours there was no effect of surgical trauma on the general condition of the bird, and the injured tissues healed quickly. The weight of five out of the fourteen thyroidectomised birds lagged a little during the period of development but then caught up with the control. The experiments on starlings showed a paradoxical phenomenon which did not fit into the framework of preconceived ideas and so prompted a cautious attitude to the experimental results and numerous repetitions of our experiments under various conditions. Removal of the thyroid in young starlings was found not to inhibit general growth to the same extent as in the case of thyroidectomised chicks and ducklings and the young of the cormorant and the rook. In the isolated instances in which the growth of young starlings did lag after thyroidectomy, the difference was too slight to constitute a retardation of growth. Autopsy on fully developed young birds showed that the thyroidectomised ones had more fat subcutaneously and within the body cavity than the controls. Nevertheless, even taking this factor into consideration, the value reflecting the deviation from the normal rate is smaller in thyroidectomised starlings than that established in experiments on other nidicolous birds such as cormorants, herons, rooks, magpies. The retardation of growth occurring in the absence of thyroid hormone in the latter is less marked than in the nidifugous birds.

The experimental young starlings showed abnormalities of behavioural development. Young starlings are known to react readily to a number of external stimuli, high-pitched sounds in particular. In response to such stimuli the young birds rapidly raise their heads, open their mouths, and emit a loud cry. This reaction, typical of an early stage of development, was retained for a long time by the thyroidectomised birds, when the control ones had already lost it and reacted to these stimuli negatively (timidity). Retarded reflex functions persisted in the young fully-developed birds also.

The plumage in thyroidectomised starlings did not develop equally on different parts of the body. The feather did develop on those pterylae in which the feather germs had been laid down before operation, but the rate of development was lower than in the controls. The vanes of such feathers, the flight feathers and rectrices in particular, were narrow. The feathers of other tracts, laid down later, either developed with defective features such as a very narrow vane with 'decomposed' barbs in the contour part, or failed to develop altogether, the corresponding areas remaining naked. These included the inferior surface of the wings and part of the chest, legs, neck, and head. A small tuft of defective feathers developed on the parietal part of the head.

To summarise our observations it can be stated that the extent to which the thyroid hormone participates in the development of young starlings is different from that of the birds previously investigated. The great vigour of growth in these birds is not determined by the thyroid hormone. At the same time, the differentiation of the body, the behaviour, and the development of the plumage in this breed are governed by the level of thyroid hormone present in the body.

The results of experiments on young thyroidectomised birds showed the thyroid hormone to be essential for the development of juvenile plumage. In its absence the development of feathers is impaired, the more significantly the longer the interval is between thyroidectomy and the onset of feather growth. The feathers whose germs are formed later are affected more seriously than those which are laid down early. When thyroidectomy precedes the proliferation of feather germs, their growth is retarded and considerably extended in time, or they may fail to grow altogether. If thyroidectomy is performed after the feathers of a given tract have begun to develop, their further growth continues with smaller deviations from the normal. The longer the interval between the onset of growth of the feathers and thyroidectomy, the less the degree of impairment of their development and their morphological features.

Ontogenetically, the laying down of feather germs precedes the period of thyroid function and can take place under conditions of total absence of thyroid hormone. The hormone is essential for further development of such germs and feather quills. Under conditions of experimentally induced functional exhaustion of the thyroid gland, new feather germs can be laid down on the trunk pterylae, but they do not proliferate further. The ability of large feathers, already noted, to develop in mature birds with functionally exhausted thyroids does not exist in young thyroidectomised birds.

The flight feathers in a number of birds continued to develop even after thyroidectomy, but this only occurred when the corresponding feather germs had been laid down a long time before operation. In the case of ducks, in which the flight feathers are laid down late, thyroidectomy had an effect both on the flight feathers and on the smaller feathers. Those pterylae on which the germs are laid down later are more affected by thyroidectomy in terms of delayed onset of feather growth, reduction of its rate, defects of vane structure, and so on.

There is a direct relationship between the bird's general

growth and the development of contour plumage, since in rapidly growing birds the juvenile plumage is formed very intensively. Metabolically, the importance of the thyroid hormone with respect to general growth and to feather formation has been found to be unequal. The hormone is necessary for growth to a different degree in different birds: less so in the nidicolous than in the nidifugous birds. The latter grow under conditions of relatively high general differentiation and active involvement with the environment. In nidicolous birds the thyroid hormone was shown to be less important in the metabolic processes underlying the general growth of the bird. But even within this group there are considerable variations in the extent of hormonal control of growth, one extreme being the absence of a discernible dependence of physiological processes associated with growth on the thyroid hormone.

At the same time, no significant species difference has been established in the nature of impairment of feather formation in the absence of thyroid hormone. Thyroidectomised birds of various species show similar deviations from normal plumage formation. The requirements for thyroid hormone are different at different stages of feather formation. More hormone is required as the feather develops. Were the expenditure of energy and the requirements of structural material during the formation of new feathers to be calculated, it would probably be found that these were far from equal during the laying-down of the feather germs, the initial period of quill growth, and the formation of a large mass of structural elements. Laying-down of the germs and their initial growth can occur in the absence of thyroid hormone, but their further development either does not take place or is impaired if the requisite level of metabolism is not attained. The absence of thyroid hormone affects the section of the feather formed during the early part of the developmental period (apex of the vane) less than it does the parts which develop later (downy part of the vane).

The regional differences in feather formation on different pterylae noted in adult birds with functional exhaustion of the thyroid are not observed in young growing birds, evidently because the local properties of the pterylae and the physiological connections with regulatory systems of the body do not arise at once, but undergo a gradual process of establishment in the ontogenesis of the bird and its feather-forming tissue. The formation of the first germs of contour feathers is evidently an important stage in the establishment of regional properties of feather-forming tissue, which later show a certain physiological persistence in the mature birds.

The development of definitive plumage

The development of definitive feathers in adult birds in the absence of thyroid hormone must be considered separately. Observations were made on a series of adult domestic and wild birds. The results yielded by different birds were similar. Let us begin, therefore, by considering the data for thyroidectomised pigeons. By improving the surgical technique, total thyroidectomy was achieved in fourteen pigeons which survived for a long time. The old feathers on small areas of various pterylae were plucked out at different intervals after the operation. It was found that feathers failed to develop on the head, neck, trunk, and legs even when plucking was performed immediately after thyroidectomy. Photographs of pigeons with the back feathers plucked immediately after thyroidectomy are shown in Fig. 51. The back of the experimental bird remained naked during that period when the control pigeon became fully feathered. The germs of small feathers may begin to develop slowly after several months. In several pigeons the feathers in the region of the crop developed only ten months after thyroidectomy, despite the fact that the preceding generation was removed at operation.

Such feathers, retarded in their development after thyroidectomy, differ greatly in size and structure from normal. When thyroidectomy is subtotal and there is regeneration of the gland, the feathers develop normally.

The feather germs, quiescent for a long time, can be activated at any time by giving the bird a thyroid preparation. The size, shape, and structure of the feathers which develop under these conditions of artificial supply of thyroid hormone, do not differ from the normal. It is therefore evident that the absence of small feathers is a reliable index of total thyroidectomy.

Unlike the small feathers, the large flight feathers and rectrices develop abnormally with respect to shape and structure
both in pigeons and in other species. Consequently, the result

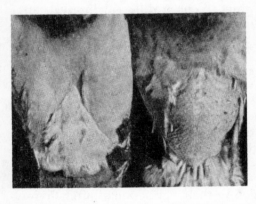

*Fig. 51. The state
of the dorsal pte-
ryla in pigeons
after plucking of
the plumage*

Top, twelve days
after plucking. Bot-
tom, thirty-five days
after plucking. Left,
control pigeon.
Right, thyroidecto-
mised pigeon

of thyroidectomy is the same as that of experiments on functional exhaustion of the thyroid gland. If the analysis of the
latter left some doubt as to the total absence of thyroid hormone from the body, the data for thyroidectomised birds lend
completely convincing support to the conclusion that the
responses of the pterylae to the thyroid hormone are qualitatively different.

Is the thyroid hormone essential for all the phases of the
feather-forming process in mature birds? Serial studies were
made on the effect of thyroidectomy on the laying-down of

the feather germs and the rest of the stages of feather development before and during morphological differentiation. Control observations were made on the development of plumage in thyroidectomised birds given supplementary thyroid preparation.

Our experimental data confirm that the germs of new feathers can be laid down in the absence of thyroid hormone. However, the properties of germs laid down under these conditions are modified. Thus, in normal control pigeons the quills of the flight feathers and rectrices appear from the follicles, on average, seven or eight days after removal of mature precursors. When the feathers are plucked at the time of operation, the quills in thyroidectomised birds appear after nine or ten days. If the feathers are plucked later, the quills appear after fourteen days. Further increase of the interval between the thyroidectomy and plucking-out of old feathers delayed the growth of new ones by from eighteen to twenty days or longer. The same result was obtained when the feather germs were activated from three to fourteen months after operation. The germs of the small feathers proved to be more sensitive to the absence of thyroid hormone. After thyroidectomy their development was delayed by fifty to sixty days.

In the absence of thyroid hormone, not only is the period of quiescence of the feather germs prolonged but also the further rate of growth of the young feathers is altered. The rate of development of primary flight feathers in thyroidectomised and control birds is illustrated in Fig. 52. Comparison of the curves shows that the rate of feather growth in the absence of thyroid hormone (curves 2 and 3) is considerably lower than in the control (curve 1); the feathers in the experimental birds stop growing later. In cases of subtotal thyroidectomy with subsequent regeneration of thyroid tissues, as confirmed later at autopsy, the lag in feather growth was insignificant. The data for the growth of the upper coverts of flight secondaries are shown in Fig. 53; the results are similar to those presented in Fig. 52.

The feathers of homologous pterylae among totally thyroidectomised birds do not grow at the same rate, although before operation no difference in feather growth in the same birds was observed. The reasons for variations in the individual

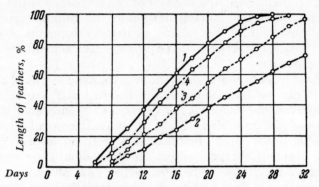

Fig. 52. *Growth of the primary flight feathers in pigeons*
1, Control. 2, 3, Total thyroidectomy. 4, Subtotal thyroidectomy

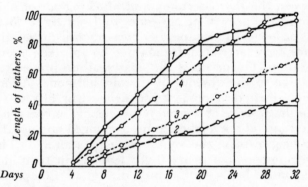

Fig. 53. *Growth of the coverts of secondary flight feathers in pigeons*
1, Control. 2, 3, Total thyroidectomy. 4, Subtotal thyroidectomy

reaction to thyroidectomy need further investigation. It is possible that general physiological changes in the state of the birds, associated with changes in the nervous system and in other endocrine organs, are responsible. Nor can the physiological changes in the feather-forming tissue itself during the pre-moulting and post-moulting periods be disregarded. One way or another, the properties of the pterylae undergo a change. This found particular confirmation in the data yielded by experiments on starlings. One group of starlings was thyroidectomised immediately on arrival in early spring, another, also taken from natural environment, two months later during the reproductive period. The curves in Fig. 54 show that feather growth was retarded to a greater extent in the birds of the first group. We concluded from this that the state of the feather-forming tissue was far from similar during the different periods we had selected.

What then is the relationship between growth and differentiation in the developing feathers of thyroidectomised birds? As already mentioned, the growth of feathers is retarded in such birds. Is there similar retardation in structural differentiation? Both in the experiments described earlier, in which feather growth was retarded artificially, and after thyroidectomy, differentiation of feather structure was found to depend on time and not on the size or mass of the young quill. For example, on the fourteenth day the young flight feather of a normal pigeon reaches a length of 42 mm, the length of the vane being 18 mm. In the thyroidectomised pigeon a vane 18 mm long is found on feathers whose total length is only 27 mm. Another example: in the control, total length of feather 45 mm, vane length 20 mm; in the experimental bird, vane of same length, total length of feather 24.5 mm. Following thyroidectomy, the relationship between the growth and differentiation of the developing feathers is disproportionate. The final length of the feathers, however, is very similar in the normal and the thyroidectomised birds.

The way thyroidectomy affects feather development which has already begun is indicated by the following experiments. The flight feathers and coverts were removed ten days before thyroidectomy in pigeons. By the time of operation the feathers had reached the stage of vane-unfurling. The measurements made on the feathers of control and thyroidectomised birds before and after operation are shown in Figs. 55 and 56. Feather growth was already appreciably affected three or four days after operation. The rate of growth declined and the vanes became narrower. The flight feathers from one control pigeon and from three thyroidectomised birds are shown in Fig. 57. The lower parts of the vanes which had developed after operation become gradually narrower. Sometimes there is a constriction between the parts formed before and after operation, the total length of the feather being increased (the

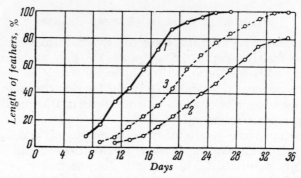

Fig. 54. *Growth of primary flight feathers in starlings*

1, Control. 2, Thyroidectomy performed before moulting prior to onset of 'critical period'. 3, Thyroidectomy performed during the 'critical period'

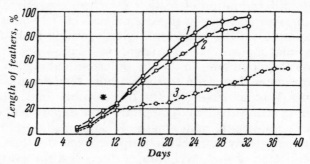

Fig. 55. *Growth of primary flight feathers in pigeons after total thyroidectomy*

1, Control. 2, 3, Experimental; asterisk marks time of operation

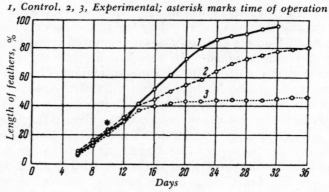

Fig. 56. *Difference in the rate of growth of the coverts of secondary flight feathers in pigeons after total thyroidectomy*

1, Control. 2, 3, Experimental; asterisk marks time of operation

two feathers on the right). The absence of thyroid hormone also affects the developing coverts.

The vane narrows more if the feather develops in the absence of thyroid hormone. Flight feathers 9 and 10 from the two wings of the same bird are shown in Fig. 58. On the right, before operation (normal); in the middle, feathers which developed during ten days before and twenty days after operation; on the left, feathers which began to grow ten days after total thyroidectomy.

The disorders of feather growth and structural differentiation which occur after thyroidectomy can be completely prevented by administration of thyroid hormone. When thyroidectomised birds are given thyroidin the previously naked pterylae become covered with normal feathers. Consequently, the impairment of feather formation observed in thyroidectomised birds is in fact caused by the absence of thyroid hormone.

What is the significance of time in the recovery of normal properties of feather germs or the developing feather? The results of supplementary experiments are relevant. The wing coverts·in thyroidectomised pigeons were removed forty days after operation at various intervals. After this all the birds received thyroidin (100 mg daily for eight days). The feather germs did not develop before the hormone administration. Comparison of the feather-growth curves in Fig. 59 demonstrates that under such treatment development occurs first of all in those follicles from which the feathers of the preceding generation have been plucked a short time before thyroidin administration. The development of the feather germs is long delayed when the interval between removal of the feathers and institution of thyroidin medication has been a long one (twenty days).

The importance of the stage of development of the feather at the moment of thyroid hormone administration was determined in experiments with prior removal of feathers at different times. Thyroidin was given for eight days only (100 mg daily), but the growth of feathers continued to be recorded after this. The results are shown graphically in Figs. 60 and 61. The difference in the time of the onset of growth was not taken into account in plotting the curves. During thyroidin

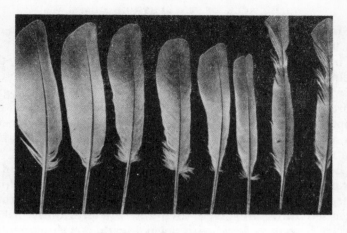

Fig. 57. Primary flight feathers of pigeons

Two feathers on left from normal control pigeon the rest from three thyroidectomised pigeons (thyroidectomy performed ten days after the onset of growth of feather quills)

Fig. 58. Effect of thyroidectomy according to the time of operation

Primary flight feathers of the pigeon. Right, a pair of feathers from a control bird; centre, a pair of feathers which began to develop ten days before thyroidectomy; left, a pair of feathers which grew entirely during the post-thyroidectomy period

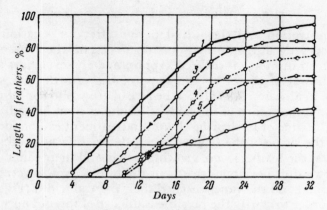

Fig. 59. Growth of the coverts of secondary flight feathers in thyroidectomised pigeons treated with thyroid preparation

1, Control bird. 2, Thyroidectomised bird. 3, 4, 5, Thyroidectomised birds whose feather germs were dormant, before administration of thyroid preparation, for three, fifteen, and twenty days respectively (the times of cessation of thyroidin medication are marked)

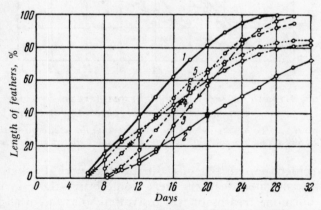

Fig. 60. Growth of primary flight feathers in thyroidectomised pigeons given thyroidin for eight days

1, Control. 2, Total thyroidectomy. 3, Total thyroidectomy and thyroidin administration from the eleventh to the nineteenth day of feather development. 4, Thyroidin administration from the ninth to the seventeenth day. 5, Thyroidin administration from the third to the eleventh day. 6, Thyroidin administration one day before the onset of feather growth

administration and the initial period after its cessation the feathers grew at the normal rate, regardless of when thyroidin administration was instituted. Approximately seven days after withdrawal of thyroidin the slope of the growth curves declined in all cases. The fall in the rate of growth to a minimum reflected the return of the body to a state of complete athyreosis. The time of instituting thyroidin treatment can be judged from the shape of the feather vanes. Before thyroidin administration the feathers were growing slowly and their vanes were narrow; after hormone treatment the rate of growth returned to normal and the vanes reached their natural width (Fig. 62).

In order to clarify the possible influence of thyroid hormone on the final phase of feather development, thyroidin was given

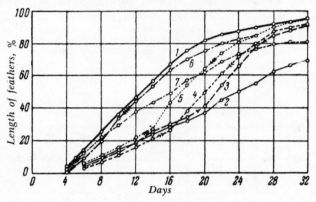

Fig. 61. Growth of secondary flight feathers in thyroidectomised pigeons given thyroid gland preparation for eight days

1, Control. 2, Total thyroidectomy without thyroidin administration. 3-7, Thyroid preparation administration at times designated on the curves

to thyroidectomised pigeons during the period when the specially activated feathers were completing their growth. When hormone treatment was instituted so as to coincide in time with the formation of the lower parts of the feather, particularly the downy part of the vane, the structure of this part developed normally (Fig. 63). As a result of this, the part of the vane already formed became separated by a constriction from that which developed during hormone administration. One such feather is shown in Fig. 63, 5. The upper part of the feather was defective, there were no downy barbs on the lower part of the vane, and beyond that the shaft of the feather passed into the quill. The base of the quill had formed before the administration of thyroidin, but had not been completed. An additional section of the shaft, with barbs normal for the lower part of the vane, and a new quill developed when thyroid hormone was given. The gradient of dependence of feather structure on the hormone was demonstrated by the fact that the formation of the upper parts was less dependent on the thyroid hormone than was that of the lower. This deduction is supported by additional data given later.

The general conclusion based on the material relating to the conditions of development of definitive feathers can be summarised as follows. Definitive feathers can be laid down in the pterylae in the absence of thyroid hormone, but this requires a longer time. Thyroidectomy is followed by the development of structurally abnormal feathers. The degree of defect in such feathers is inversely related to their stage of development at the moment of thyroidectomy. The absence of thyroid hormone affects only the cellular material entering the generative zone of the feather quill at a given moment. The dependence of the feather structures being formed on the hormone alters in an apical-basal direction. The development of feathers whose follicles are situated in different areas of the skin does not depend to an equal degree on the physiological changes in the body produced by thyroid hormone. Thus the development of large feathers is relatively less affected by the hormone. In course of time the feather-forming tissue of thyroidectomised birds undergoes physiological changes as a result of which the feather germs regain the ability to develop, though to a very attenuated extent. The main condition necessary for normal development of feathers is relative continuity of hormonal influences. Thyroidectomy deprives the body of thyroid hormone and creates conditions impossible for normal development of new feathers.

The body can be deprived of thyroid hormone by administering certain sulphur-containing drugs such as sulphonamides and thioureates. We shall not discuss here the various interpretations of the mode of action of these substances (see

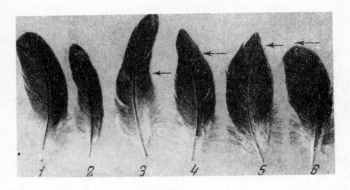

Fig. 62. *Coverts of secondary flight feathers of the same pigeons whose flight feathers were shown in Fig. 60. Experimental conditions the same*

1, Control. 2, Growth after thyroidectomy. 3-6, After thyroidectomy, with administration of thyroidin at different times (institution of treatment marked by arrows)

Fig. 63. *Effect of thyroidin on the late stage of feather development in thyroidectomised pigeons*

1, Control. 2, Total thyroidectomy. 3, 4, 5, Total thyroidectomy with administration of thyroidin during the completion of growth of defective feathers

Voitkevich, 1949, 1957). When these anti-thyroid preparations are given there is a progressive deficit of thyroid hormone in the body, the microscopic appearance of the thyroid gland being similar to that seen in functional exhaustion of the gland. If the preparation is given for a sufficiently long time, the body is deprived of thyroid hormone and a condition of general athyreosis supervenes.

The above data on the changes in feather formation after thyroidectomy may to some extent be in question, because of the possible presence of some thyroid tissue. Such doubts could be excluded by the effect of chemical anti-thyroid preparations. This suggested that it would be desirable to investigate feather formation during administration of more active preparations such as thiouracil and methylthiouracil.

In a series of studies Mitskevich (1947, 1949, 1957) tested the effect of methylthiouracil on the embryos of various birds (fowls, pigeons, thrushes, seagulls). He established that relatively short-term administration of these preparations was sufficient to induce hypertrophy and hyperplasia of the thyroid gland. Such experimental athyreosis led to retardation of the growth and differentiation of the birds and delay in hatching. The embryonic down was underdeveloped. The growth of the flight feathers, which in chicks are known to develop during embryonic life, was also retarded. On the basis of these findings, Mitskevich was disinclined to accept my earlier hypothesis (Voitkevich, 1936) concerning the non-uniform effect of the thyroid hormone on the development of nidicolous and nidifugous birds differing in the nature of their individual development. I had at one time established that the thyroid glands in nidicolous birds differentiated relatively late, at a period when the energy of general growth had already begun to decline. Moreover, I had shown (Voitkevich, 1943, 1944, b, 1945, c) that after total thyroidectomy some rapidly developing birds either showed only slight retardation of growth (cormorants) or no inhibition of growth at all (starlings). Thyroidectomy of young nidifugous birds, on the other hand, was followed by enormous retardation of growth. At the same time the impairment of plumage development under conditions of athyreosis was similar in the two groups of birds. I concluded from this that the thyroid hormone participated to a different extent in the growth of birds of different species.

The experiments with the use of antithyroid preparations were performed on adult White Leghorn fowls and pigeons of a decorative breed. Observations were made on eleven roosters (seven experimental and four controls), four hens (two experimental and two controls) and six pigeons (four experimental and two controls). The experimental birds received thiouracil twice daily for the first fifteen days; the roosters were given 300 mg each time, the hens 200 mg and the pigeons 50 mg. Half the daily dose was placed in a gelatine capsule for each administration and was then introduced via the oesophagus into the crop (Voitkevich and Kostin, 1947).

By the end of the experiment the thyroid glands of the pigeons had enlarged to double the size of the controls, the weight of the two lobes being 88·2 mg as against 42·6 mg in the controls. The microstructure of the glands was greatly altered. The walls of the follicles in the thyroid glands of hens and roosters usually did not collapse, the follicular cavities were of an irregular stellate shape, and there was no colloid (Voitkevich, 1948, a). In the pigeon thyroid glands the emptied follicles showed collapse of the walls, with consequent considerable reduction of the internal diameter. The epithelial cell reaction in the pigeon thyroids was fairly uniform: the height of the epithelium was on average $8·19\mu$ as against $3·83\mu$ in the controls. Unlike this, the reaction in different parts of the follicle in the case of hens, and even more of roosters, was non-uniform: some cells were severely altered, acquiring a prismatic shape (up to 18μ), other cells remained cuboidal or somewhat flattened ($3·4\mu$). The average height of the epithelium for each thyroid lobe was $11·81\mu$ in experimental roosters and $3·04\mu$ in control ones, $7·93\mu$ in experimental hens and $3·25\mu$ in control ones. Comparison of the microstructure of the thyroid glands of hens and pigeons showed that in both cases the thyroid glands were very hyperplastic and completely devoid of colloid, that is they displayed signs similar to the picture of functional exhaustion.

The state of general athyreosis achieved in this way was adequately reflected in the rate of growth and nature of feather development in the experimental birds. The growth of the feather germs was activated by removing fully formed

feathers of the preceding generation. Ten days before administration of the preparation, and then concurrently with its
administration, in each bird there were removed from the
various pterylae two feathers from each of the following tracts:
primary flight feathers, coverts of secondary flight feathers,
feathers of the crop and saddle areas. After another ten days,
two more feathers were plucked from each of the tracts; this
was repeated after twenty and thirty days. Observations were
thus made on feathers whose development had begun under
different conditions. The growing feathers were measured
every other day.

The effect of athyreosis proved to be dissimilar in the case
of feathers from different pterylae and those from the same
pterylae which had begun growing at different intervals after
administration of thiouracil; there were also species differences. The normal rate of feather growth on homologous
pterylae of fowls and pigeons is known to be dissimilar. The
value of the absolute and relative increment of the young
feather per unit time is appreciably greater in pigeons than in
fowls. Correspondingly, the growth of homologous feathers is
achieved in pigeons within a shorter period of time.

The impairment of feather development was more severe in
pigeons than in fowls. The rate of feather growth in the experimental birds was lower than in the controls. When the
onset of germ growth and the administration of thiouracil
coincided in time, the impairment of feather formation only
became apparent in the second period of development. If the
onset of germ growth was preceded by a ten-day course of
thiouracil administration, there was already a considerable
retardation of feather development. If the interval between
thiouracil administration and activation of the feather germs
was increased further, there was no change in the degree of
inhibition of development of the flight feathers and coverts.
Small feathers over the crop and back either failed to appear
altogether under similar conditions or were much retarded in
their development. When thiouracil was stopped, the normal
rate of development of the remaining part of each feather was
restored. If this occurred at a time when a large area of
feathers was developing in the experimental bird there was
additional growth and the final length of the feather was 20-30

13

per cent in excess of normal. The germs of small feathers hitherto dormant began to develop at the normal rate.

The new feathers in the experimental birds had narrowed vanes, the apex of the vane being pointed. The barbules of the contour part of the vanes of small feathers were disconnected because of reduction of hooklets on the barbicels. The downy part of such feathers was much reduced (Figs. 64 and 65).

The effect of thiouracil on plumage development in Brown Leghorns was studied by Domm and Blivaiss (1944, 1946) and Juhn (1944, 1946). The authors noted impairment of feather regeneration similar to that seen after thyroidectomy. Thus, the rate of growth of feathers on the chest and saddle areas in Brown Leghorn roosters fell to one half or one third of that seen in the controls. The normally rounded feathers were replaced by narrow lanceolate ones, and the barbules became disconnected. Under the influence of thiouracil, the characteristic black and brown spotted pattern of the plumage was replaced by a monotone reddish-brown colour. Kabak and Tal'skaya (1956) have shown in experiments on ducks that thioureate reduces the accumulation of radioactive iodine in the thyroid gland, which destroys its parenchyma and thereby prevents thyroid hormone deficit, which in its turn leads to lessening of the impairment of the general growth of birds and formation of their plumage.

The disturbances of the rate of development, shape, and structure of feathers observed during administration of an anti-thyroid substance proved to be identical with those seen earlier after total thyroidectomy, produced either surgically or by radioactive iodine administration, and also under conditions of functional exhaustion of the thyroid gland. In all cases there were similar topographic differences in the reaction of the feather-forming tissue; the germs of large feathers preserved their ability to develop in the absence of thyroid hormone. Small feathers usually failed to develop. Consequently, regardless of the method used to achieve general athyreosis, the changes in the feather-forming process are similar in character.

Fig. 64. Small feathers from the trunk pteryla of the pigeon

1, 2, The lower dorsal area. 3, 4, 5, Area of the crop. 1, 3, feathers from control pigeons; 2, 4, 5, feathers from pigeons given thiouracil

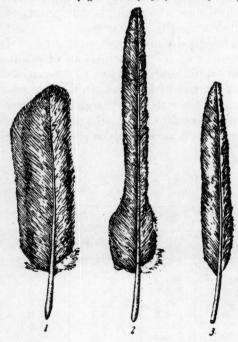

Fig. 65. Homologous flight primaries of the pigeon

1, Feather from a control bird, 2, Feather whose upper part developed during thiouracil administration, the lower part developing normally after withdrawal of thiouracil (the total length of the feather exceeded the normal). 3, Feather which developed entirely during thiouracil administration

The structure and pattern of contour feathers

The changes in the character of the formation and structure of feathers which occur after thyroidectomy are also, indirectly, reflected in their pattern. Thyroidectomy has also been found to have a direct influence on processes associated with altered melanogenesis and deposition of pigment in the structural elements of feathers. In some birds thyroidectomy, like castration, is followed by a change in feather colour. Greenwood and Blyth (1929) reported that in the developing feathers of a single thyroidectomised Brown Leghorn hen the black pigment was replaced by a red one. Similar changes in the pigmentation of plumage in this breed of fowls follow athyreosis induced by thiouracil (Domm and Blivaiss, 1946; Juhn, 1944, 1946). Parkes and Selye (1937) and Lektorskii (1940) have described a diminution of regional differences of feather colour in ducks following thyroidectomy.

We have investigated changes in the shape, structure, and colour of feather both in birds with sex distinctions of plumage colour and in monomorphic ones. Table 14 summarises the data on the change in the size of feathers after thyroidectomy; it shows that whereas the length of the vanes on feathers which had developed under conditions of athyreosis differs little from the normal, the width is almost halved (Fig. 58). The

Table 14

Size of the vanes of flight primaries which developed after thyroidectomy

Species	Length of feather, in mm		Width of feather, in mm	
	Control	Experimental	Control	Experimental
Fowls	147.0	107.4	32.5	17.3
ducks	112.6	116.0	24.0	20.0
pigeons	98.3	89.0	28.3	14.5
crossbills	49.0	46.5	9.7	4.8
chaffinches . . .	51.5	48.0	9.5	5.5
sparrows	50.5	48.4	11.2	6.0
jackdaws	108.0	97.0	27.0	19.0
skylarks	56.0	46.5	14.5	6.3

narrowing of the vane and often a very pointed tip are signs characteristic of thyroidectomy. A similar effect is seen on the feathers of other pterylae. The barbs in the contour part of the vane of large feathers are not so firmly connected as in a normal one; many of the feathers on the trunk of thyroidectomised birds are completely 'decomposed', and the downy part of the vane is much reduced. Experimental fowls and ducks exhibited similar changes in the shape and structure of their feathers.

In hens and roosters the changes in the structure of the body feathers include partial reduction of barbules in the contour and especially the downy part of the vane. The peripheral fringe (free of barbules) which is typical of the upper part of normal feathers in some pterylae becomes the chief structural component in such feathers after thyroidectomy. Sometimes such a fringe is formed on the feathers of those pterylae where it is normally absent. (Fig. 66).

The change in the size of feathers is a result of the under-

Fig. 66. Feathers from the sacral area of the rooster

Left, control. Right, feather with pronounced fringe which developed after thyroidectomy (the firm and downy parts of the vane are missing, the barbs are disconnected)

development of structural elements. Microscopic examination of the structure of feathers from different tracts gave identical results. This is illustrated by the photomicrographs of identical areas of the contour part of the vane of feathers from the upper part of the ventral pteryla. The hooked barbicels which are characteristic processes on the barbules of normal feathers fail to develop in the experimental birds. The structural differences become still more apparent when individual barbs are compared. The microstructural changes undergone by the barbs of the contour part after thyroidectomy are such that their architectonics approach that of down feathers. If thyroid preparations are administered or regeneration of thyroid tissue takes place, the feathers which develop acquire normal structure, shape, and colour. Large feathers show less marked changes in the rate of their growth and less impairment of their structure than the small feathers. Barbicel reduction is not so pronounced, but the vane is less dense than the normal; the shaft is thinner and breaks easily.

The pattern and colour of the large feathers are little affected by thyroidectomy. The metallic sheen on the flight feathers of rooks, for example, is retained. Different pigmentations react differently. Thus, the feathers of those birds whose plumage has a constant monotone melanin pigmentation, remain unchanged after thyroidectomy. Changes do occur, however, if the plumage shows black coloration and other colours too. This can be seen in the case of the grey downy parts of a series of feathers in the magpie; the grey colour disappears in the case of thyroidectomised owls also. The absence of pigment from the lower part of the vane of various feathers is not a consequence of structural underdevelopment. This has been established, in particular, for the plumage of starlings, in which the body feathers on the under parts have non-pigmented white tips; this non-pigmented zone enlarges on each feather after thyroidectomy, forming a white edging along the periphery of the vane.

Birds which have colour distinctions associated with age, seasons, or sex show considerable changes. One such example is the plumage of brightly coloured fowls such as the Italian Partridge. After thyroidectomy the eumelanin-pigmented black feathers in such birds are replaced by brown phaeomelanin-pigmented ones. In particular, this has been demonstrated for the dorsal feathers of fowls with brown watered-silk coloration on the chestnut background of the vane. If new feathers are made to grow by plucking the ventral pteryla or other area in roosters which are then subjected to thyroidectomy, then the upper parts of the feathers, which are the first to develop, are of normal black colour, whereas the lower parts acquire a reddish-brown tint. If thyroidectomy is subtotal, the structural aspects are the first to be altered. Changes in pigmentation occur at deeper levels of hypothyroidism. This is clearly demonstrated by the investigation of the structure and pigmentation of feathers of the intermediate type.

Lipochrome pigmented feathers become much paler after thyroidectomy. For example, in male crossbills the red breast feathers are replaced by pale ocherous yellow ones in the absence of thyroid hormone. Lipochrome pigmentation is known to be distinctly labile and can undergo changes under the influence of other factors such as nutrition and light.

There is little to add to the above in order to describe the changes in the colour and general pattern of plumage in a state of complete athyreosis. Thus, in the Italian Partridge fowls the oval back feathers in the normal female have a partial watered-silk pattern on a dark-brown background. After thyroidectomy lanceolate feathers are formed with a general golden background of the contour part of the vane and only a shaft pattern of brown. Even the flight feathers show a change from the watered-silk pattern to a blurred brown coloration. In roosters, the black rhomboid pattern of the contour part of the feathers on the back and saddle is replaced by a narrow shaft one after thyroidectomy.

There are reasons to believe that such a change in pattern is a specific result of the inhibition of oxidative processes associated with athyreosis. It may be assumed that such changes in the pattern depend on the sex hormones which are known to affect feather formation in fowls which show sexual differences in plumage. Thus it was necessary to verify our conclusions by experiments on birds without sex differences in plumage, but with feathers of a definite pattern. Two breeds of owl (long-eared and short-eared) were therefore subjected to thyroidectomy. The pattern of the feathers in the owls varies on different pterylae from a longitudinal stripe each side of the shaft on the underside of the body, to a definite transverse striation pattern on the dorsal side. Thyroidectomy was performed on one-year-old and young almost fully grown birds.

The weight and outward appearance of the thyroidectomised owls were not very different from normal. Thyroidectomy did not affect the formation of feathers which had begun to form before operation, since some thyroid hormone remained in the body for some time. Feathers which had been laid down later or were induced to grow artificially were different after operation from homologous feathers of the same tracts in normal birds.

Let us consider the patterns of the feathers of just two pterylae which most differ from each other in the normal. The feathers of the lower row of coverts of the flight secondaries of the short-eared owl are shown in Fig. 67. Normally they are yellow with an orange tinge. The downy part is darker than the main background; the top part of the vane is chestnut brown. There are two transverse bands on the vane, and a rhomboid spot at the apex. The feathers from thyroidectomised owls are shorter and lanceolate in shape, the downy part is much reduced, and the distribution of pigment is altered. The main background of the feather becomes paler: the lemon-yellow colour changes gradually to white towards the base of the feather. The pattern is simplified: the chestnut-brown pigment is seen only along the shaft, and peters out towards the base of the vane. In this case the transversely striated pattern of the feathers on the dorsal side of the body becomes similar to the 'shaft-pattern' of the feathers on the ventral side.

The breast feathers from a normal long-eared owl and those which regenerated after thyroidectomy are illustrated in Fig. 68. Small random speckles appeared instead of the fine transverse striations. The chestnut-brown longitudinal band along the shaft became narrower. The development of the feather pattern was observed in two owls in which a fragment of thyroid tissue left behind inadvertently at operation subsequently regenerated. At first, when there was very little hormone, the structure and pattern of the apical part of the feathers developed in the same way as in cases of athyreosis. The lower areas showed a gradual transition to normal structure and pigmentation. The observations on owls prompt the conclusion that after thyroidectomy the main background of feathers becomes paler, the downy part loses pigmentation, and the pattern is simplified. Such changes in the distribution of pigment in the feathers are reversed by the presence of thyroid hormone in the body. Similar results were obtained in a series

Fig. 67. Feathers from the lower row of the coverts of flight secondaries of the short-eared owl
Left, a pair of control feathers. Right, a pair of feathers which developed after thyroidectomy

Fig. 68. Feathers of the pectoral pteryla of the long-eared owl.
Left, a pair of control feathers. Right, a pair of feathers which developed after thyroidectomy

of experiments on young and on sexually mature starlings (Voitkevich, 1940, d, h).

The starling's juvenile garb is of monotone grey with a chestnut-brown tinge. In the definitive plumage black is the predominant colour. The tips (3-4 mm) of the feathers on the back and head are pale brown; on the underparts the top 3-5 mm of the feathers are white. The boundaries between the differently pigmented areas of such feathers are oriented at right angles to the shaft of the feather. The unpigmented tips of the feathers are clearly seen on a newly-shed feather after moulting. Later these tips become gradually worn off and by the mating season the starlings usually have solid black feathers on the ventral side of the body. If thyroidectomy was performed before the onset of natural moulting, the experimental birds did moult, but with some delay. Observations were made on the plumage of such birds.

The garb of the thyroidectomised birds was different from normal. There were changes both in the structure and the pigmentation of the feathers. The barbs were underdeveloped in the feathers of all the tracts. The contour part of the feather became looser. The barbs became shorter and as a result the vanes of the contour and the downy parts were only two-thirds as wide as normal. The partial underdevelopment of structural elements led to a thinning of the vane lamina, especially in the downy part. Microscopic examination revealed that the size and number of the cells forming the barb were reduced. Complete loss of barbules occurred in the peripheral zone of the contour part of the small feathers on the ventral side of the body. A peculiar fringe was thus formed in the peripheral part of the feather, resembling the fringe seen on the neck and saddle feathers of fowls. The narrow lanceolate and elongated feathers drooped on the bird's body, distinguishing such plumage from the normal smooth habit of the normal starling. Barb counts showed that the increased length of the feather was due to an increase in the number of barbs. Thyroidectomy had produced a redistribution of 'building' material.

Thyroidectomy, however, does not prevent the replacement of juvenile pigmentation of feathers by the definitive pigmentation. Changes in the pigmentation of new feathers were roughly similar in nature to those seen in adult birds. Changes

in the distribution of pigment in thyroidectomised birds affect
principally the trunk and neck feathers. The light brown
colour of the dorsal feathers spread to the base of the contour
part of the vanes as a narrow band along the edge of the
feather. This becomes even more apparent in the feathers
on the ventral side. A nonpigmented area, in the form of a
white peripheral border, involved almost the whole of the
contour part of the vane. The ratio of the nonpigmented
area to the total area of the feather in the thyroidectomised
birds remains almost the same as in the normal ones; there
is simply a change in the localisation of the white markings.
The narrow border extends along both sides of the vane for
11-12 mm downwards from the apex of the feather.

As the result of such changes in the structure and pigmentation of the feathers, the garb of thyroidectomised starlings
differed sharply from the usual one. A survey of the collections
in the Moscow State University Zoological Museum showed
us that no such pattern, or any variations close to it, were encountered in nature. We surmise that in the starling the plumage pattern evolved from a longitudinal to a transverse distribution of differently pigmented zones. Reference has been
made above to the data obtained on owls in whose plumage
the transversely striated pattern was replaced by the more
primitive longitudinal pattern after thyroidectomy.

The general conclusion to be drawn from data on the
changes in the structure and pattern of feathers in the absence
of thyroid hormone can be summarised as follows. In the
absence of the hormone all the structural elements of the
feather show underdevelopment. The thickness of the barbs,
the shaft and the barrel is decreased. The hooklets on the
barbicels, which ensure a firm connection of the contour part
of the feathers, are appreciably reduced. In thyroidectomised
birds the firm part of the vane approaches in its structure the
downy part. In most cases the pattern of the feather also alters.
The structural colours do not change very much. The eumelanin pigmentation in birds with seasonal or sex differences in
plumage is often replaced by phaeomelanin pigmentation.
Disturbances in the distribution of pigment lead to changes in
the pattern of the feather. Complicated types of pattern are
replaced by a simpler one, a narrow band along the shaft. The

changes in structure, pigmentation, and pattern which arise with a deficit or absence of thyroid hormone can occur at any stage of development of individual feathers. The 'sensitivity' of the various parts of the feather being formed is found to be non-uniform: the distal parts are more resistant than the proximal. The principle of non-uniformity extends also to the feather follicles in different areas of the body, for the follicles of the large feathers are more resistant than those of the smaller feathers. The pattern of a feather is not determined in the feather germ, but develops during the formation of the young feather (Voitkevich, 1940, c, 1047).

Our data concerning the replacement of a complex pattern of feathers by a more primitive shaft pattern in the absence of thyroid hormone correspond to the observations on plumage pattern in some birds inhabiting different latitudes. There is a direct relationship between simplification of feather pattern and reduction in the intensity of pigmentation. Thus in the eagle owl and pygmy owl the dark transverse bars on the feathers are replaced, on gradual transition from warm to cold climate, by a 'shaft band' or a drop-shaped spot; in other words the pattern becomes more primitive. Changes in the pattern of the feathers should not be associated solely with systematic peculiarities of different species of birds. Such an association becomes all the more difficult when it has been demonstrated that even within the limits of a single species, such as the different breeds of fowls, there is every gradation in dependence of plumage pigmentation on the thyroid hormone. There are as yet no adequate data for making appropriate comparisons between experimental results and changes in the pattern of feathers in the course of historical adaptation of different species to the environment. At the same time it is clear that it may be possible to elucidate the origin of the various types of patterns by taking into account the rôle of the thyroid hormone. In particular, the concept of the so-called 'independent pattern' must be reviewed, since there are no plumage patterns which do not show the effect exerted by the thyroid hormone.

Plumage replacement

Let us now consider the changes in the properties of feather-forming tissue in relation to periodic self regeneration in the absence of thyroid hormone. Schwarz (1930) noted retardation of juvenile moulting in a single hen at his disposal which had been thyroidectomised at the age of seventy-five days. Lektorskii and Kuz'mina (1936, b) observed delay of the first moult in chicks following extirpation of the thyroid gland. When thyroidectomy coincided in time with the onset of natural moulting the latter was not subsequently greatly inhibited. If thyroidectomy preceded the moult, feather regeneration was delayed.

In our experiments on young starlings thyroidectomised soon after hatching, the juvenile moult began with a ten-day delay. At the time when four feathers had been replaced on each wing of the control birds, those operated on had only shed a single inner flight feather. The moulting of small feathers was also retarded. Young pigeons, thyroidectomised at the age of twenty-five days, also experienced a delay in juvenile moulting.

In operated ducklings no juvenile moulting occurred during a five-month period of observation. However, if thyroidectomy was performed much later, for example from ten to fifteen days before the onset of moulting, although the replacement of feathers did begin, it was slow. Clearly, the thyroid hormone is essential for juvenile moulting of young birds. Let us now consider the data on the moulting of mature birds.

Crew (1927), in his report on a case of emphysema in a thyroidectomised adult Campine rooster, noted that the rooster did not moult for a year after operation. Our experiments were performed on Rhode Island and White Leghorn fowls aged eight months and older. Thyroidectomy was carried out on fourteen roosters and eleven hens; it was total in six of each. If the operation was performed five or six months before the onset of natural moulting, feather replacement did not occur. Thus, for example, no moulting was observed in two fowls over a period of thirteen months after operation. If the birds were operated on when moulting had already begun, however, the replacement of feathers was not arrested but was retarded. The successive flight feather was shed after a considerable interval of time, then another one, and then moulting ceased. Feather replacement was resumed after administration of a thyroid preparation.

Svetozarov and Shtraikh (1940, b) performed thyroidectomy on domestic ducks two months before the onset of summer moulting. Observations continued for about a year demonstrated the absence of moulting in the experimental birds. They retained the old very worn vestiture. Feathers shed accidentally through mechanical causes were very slowly replaced by new and defective feathers. Höhn (1949) thyroidectomised three wild ducks two months before the first mating moult and did not observe any appreciable deviations in its subsequent course. He did not check later whether the thyroid tissue had been totally removed.

Thyroidectomised adult carrier-pigeons were kept under observation for from eleven to eighteen months (Voitkevich, 1940, e). Some of the operations were performed after termination of a moult and approximately eight months before the onset of the next one. Three of the experimental pigeons did not moult at all in the course of sixteen months. The replacement of the flight feathers in eleven thyroidectomised pigeons began at almost the same time as the moult of twelve control birds (Fig. 69). Subsequently the difference involved the intensity of the process and the number of feathers replaced.

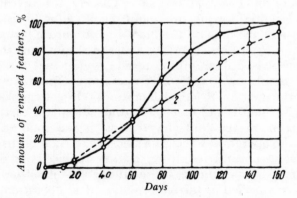

Fig. 69. Moulting of the flight primaries in carrier pigeons
1, Control birds. 2, Thyroidectomised birds

During the first two months the moulting of the primary flight feathers proceeded at the same rate as in the controls. Then the replacement of feathers in the thyroidectomised birds became slower. The moult lag was particularly noticeable on the body and neck pterylae where old feathers persisted for a long time alongside narrow defective new feathers. Only half of the flight secondaries, which begin to moult late, were replaced. Consequently the moult was not completed in birds whose thyroids had been removed. The ability to continue the moult was restored by thyroidin administration.

The results of thyroidectomy on domestic fowls and pigeons indicate that in the absence of the thyroid gland moulting either does not take place or is delayed. The time-relationships between thyroidectomy and the onset of natural moulting are relevant in this respect. Species differences in the sensitivity of the feather-forming tissue to the thyroid hormone are not excluded. Individual differences in the reaction to thyroidectomy can be related to the degree of domestication. The duration and intensity of normal moulting in control domestic birds are known to vary to a considerable extent. This provided the argument in favour of carrying out similar experiments on wild birds. The replacement of plumage in these is more clearly limited in time, is less subject to individual variations, and has a species-characteristic intensity.

These considerations prompted us to experiment on thyroidectomised starlings. A total of fifty-nine starlings were thyroidectomised; of these eighteen died, seventeen later showed signs of thyroid tissue regeneration, and twenty-four were totally thyroidectomised. The controls were made up of eight unoperated starlings and the seventeen whose thyroids regenerated. In order to obtain the maximal interval between the time of operation and the onset of natural moulting, the first group of starlings were thyroidectomised immediately on arrival from winter habitation in early April, the second in early May and the third in June. The twenty-four thyroidectomised starlings made up these groups as follows: twelve birds in the first, five in the second, and seven in the third. The observations on these experimental birds were continued for sixteen months. Curves depicting the course of moulting in starlings from the second and third groups and controls are shown in Fig. 70. The figure does not include the data on the moulting of birds in the first group, because they did not moult at all, either during the moulting period of the controls or later. The birds thyroidectomised later (second group) did moult, but onset was delayed. The regularity of shedding the flight feathers was impaired in some birds: sometimes two or even three flight' feathers were shed from the same wing at once. In the third group of starlings the replacement of feathers began almost simultaneously with the moulting of the controls and then proceeded at a higher rate.

Thus the consequences of thyroidectomy in the same species of birds are different according to the time of operation, especially in relation to seasonal moulting. Moulting does not occur if thyroidectomy is performed a long time before the onset, and it must be mentioned in this connection that no plumage replacement occurred in the three quails we had at our disposal, which had been thyroidectomised a long time before moulting. Moulting does occur, but is delayed, when the interval between the onset and the operation is not less than half the duration of the moulting period. Operations performed just before the onset of seasonal moulting produce slight deviation from the normal, in that the replacement of single feathers is delayed. The arrest or retardation of moult-

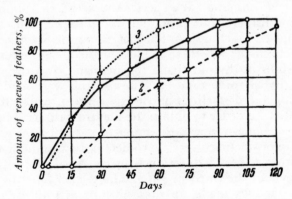

Fig. 70. Moulting of the flight primaries in starlings

1, Control birds. 2, Birds thyroidectomised during the 'critical period'. 3, Birds thyroidectomised immediately before the onset of natural moulting (the birds thyroidectomised a long time before natural moulting are not represented on the graph since they did not moult)

ing in thyroidectomised birds is explained by changes in the properties of the feather germs under conditions of athyreosis. The properties of the feather follicles, particularly the large tracts, are not so greatly altered that they lose the capacity for growth. For example, it was found that in the first group of thyroidectomised starlings, in which no moulting occurred, the development of new feathers was not excluded when large feathers were removed either during natural moulting or at other times, but the onset of quill development and the growth of new feathers were greatly inhibited. This fact also confirms the capacity of the feather germs in non-moulting starlings to proliferate. Consequently, the cause of the absence of moulting involves not only changes in the local properties of feather-forming tissue but also general physiological changes in the body resulting from thyroidectomy.

Further, thyroidectomy performed after moulting has begun produces only a temporary retardation of feather replacement. This is substantiated by supplementary experiments performed on moulting starlings and magpies, which yielded similar results. The mature experimental magpies were one

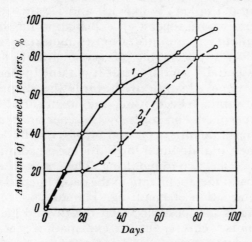

*Fig. 71. Moulting of the flight prima-
ries in magpies*

*1, Control. 2, Thyroidectomised birds (opera-
tion was performed after two flight feathers
had been replaced)*

year old and had been reared in the laboratory (Voitkevich and Vasil'ev, 1939). Thyroidectomy was performed after the onset of moulting, when one flight feather on each wing had been replaced. By counting the number of feathers shed and replaced, it was estimated that the moulting in the experimental birds was delayed by three weeks. It then resumed, but proceeded more slowly and terminated late (Fig. 71). The new feathers were modified and therefore the appearance of the experimental birds which had moulted was different from the controls.

It is particularly noteworthy that those starlings and magpies which had been thyroidectomised a year before during moulting now did not moult at all. The capacity for feather replacement was completely restored only by administration of thyroidin.

We belive that the validity of our data is not compromised in the light of the subsequent and somewhat conflicting results of experiments on the effect of antithyroid substances on the course of experimental moulting. At one time our attempts to arrest the moult of moulting pigeons and fowls by administration of thiouracil failed (Voitkevich and Kostin, 1947). The data considered above suggest an explanation for the ineffectiveness of thiouracil administration to moulting birds with respect to an already-occurring process of natural plumage renewal. An essentially similar result is obtained when the thyroid gland is removed surgically in birds already undergoing moulting. A similar effect, using thioureates, had been observed in experiments on fowls by Galzener and Jull (1946) and Perek and Sulman (1947) and on pigeons by Kobayashi (1952). Further, in individual birds thioureate administration led to some acceleration of moulting. These reports note a decline in the basal metabolic rate in the experimental birds but without a retardation of moulting. The authors' conclusion, that moulting is still possible when the thyroid gland is depressed, of course requires further explanation, since the picture of a thioureate-excited gland does not fit the concept of its depressed state (Voitkevich, 1957).

The results of observations on thyroidectomised birds suggest a connection between seasonal phenomena in the feather-forming tissue and thyroid function. The presence of thyroid hormone in the body is an essential requirement for physiological processes determining the periodic renewal of plumage in birds. The importance of the hormone for these processes is not identical in the periods preceding moulting and during the moult (Voitkevich, 1950, b). The earlier the thyroidectomy, that is the longer the interval between the operation and the onset of natural moulting, the greater the subsequent retardation of feather replacement. Thyroidectomy just before the onset of moulting produces no effect at all on its subsequent course. We conclude from this that the thyroid hormone is involved to different degrees during the various periods of moulting. During the period preceding moulting, the conditions in the feather-forming tissue are such as to realise the developmental potential of the feather germs. Moulting which has begun can continue even in the absence of thyroid hormone. During moulting, the hormone is essential for maintaining these metabolic processes ensuring the formation of new feathers. The thyroid hormone forms one of the links in the chain of processes which prepare the feather follicles for development, but it is not essential for the whole process of moulting.

Consequently, at this stage of the experimental evidence it can already be concluded that the thyroid gland is not the main and certainly not the only factor determining the process of seasonal moulting. Our data indicate that the absence of moulting in thyroidectomised birds is not merely the result of local changes in the properties of feather forming tissue, since the feather germs always retain the capacity for proliferation, but is associated chiefly with general changes which take place in the body when thyroid hormone is deficient or absent.

THE ADMINISTRATION
OF THYROID HORMONE

Experiments on artificial provision of thyroid hormone to compensate for experimentally induced hypothyroidism have already been partially described in the preceding section. As the next step in the investigation of the hormonal dependence of the morphogenic process, it appeared interesting to trace the influence of hyperthyroidism on the formation of feathers.

In this context the particular way hyperthyroidism was produced—whether by stimulation of the subject's own thyroidal gland or by administration of the hormone from without—was of no consequence. The former method was more physiological, but in the light of the problem it had certain disadvantages, such as excluding the possibility of a wide range of variation of the amount of hormone, which is determined by the different functional properties of the thyroid gland in birds of different species. It was therefore preferable to administer a hormone preparation, allowing a wide range of intentional variation in the level of hormone saturation in the body. The use of experimental hyperthyroidism as a sole method of investigation does not give an adequate basis for extrapolating the experimental data to the real relationship between feather formation and the thyroid hormone in the body. It is permissible to use this method only as one of the stages of investigation, not independently but following logically upon the experiments with hypothyroidism and athyreosis. In this sequence, the experiments on induced hyperthyroidism should further the more detailed elucidation of the physiological relations between feather formation and thyroid-gland activity.

Artificial hyperthyroidism was induced by a powdered preparation of dried thyroid gland (thyroidin) given to the birds by mouth in various doses. The state of the bird's thyroid gland itself is noteworthy under conditions of this type of hyperthyroidism. Microscopic examinations and biological testing of thyroid glands, carried out repeatedly on mass material from birds of various species, consistently showed that the gland passed into a state of hyperactivity (Voitkevich, 1935 b; 1936 c, d, e; 1938 c; 1945 e). A great deal of colloid accumulates in the follicles; the epithelium becomes flatter, its cells showing no signs of secretory activity, and the release of hormone into the blood is inhibited. Thyroid tissue in such a state is biologically very active in the well-known test on amphibian larvae. The data yielded by histological studies and biological tests on the thyroid glands of thyroid-treated birds agree in showing that the changes in feather formation which are possible under conditions of artificial hyperthyroidism must be ascribed to the influence of the extrinsic thyroid hormone and not to changes in the function of the birds' own thyroid glands. This must be borne in mind for the explanation of the phenomena described below (see also the review by Mitskevich, 1935).

Development of juvenile and definitive plumage

The development of the already-formed germs of juvenile feathers is stimulated by thyroid hormone. Křiženecký (1926, 1927, 1929, a, b) in experiments on chicks of various breeds showed that the growth of the germs could be stimulated under conditions of hyperthyroidism only in birds of late plumage development (viandoti, Plymouth Rock); in those of early plumage development (Leghorns) the stimulation was either weak or absent. The differences in the time of development of plumage in different sorts of birds depend on the properties of the feather-forming tissue, which is modified during ontogenesis.

Our experiments have demonstrated that the feather germs laid down at different times react differently to changes in the concentration of the thyroid hormone. The feather follicles have been shown to be qualitatively different not only in birds of various breeds or species, but also in different pterylae of the same bird (Voitkevich, 1934, b, 1938, a, 1939, b). Experiments were carried out on young pigeons which had received thyroidin for twelve days starting on the third day of life. It is known that in pigeons the first quills to appear are those on the dorsal and scapular pterylae, the outer surface of the wings and in the region of the tail; the plumage on the thighs, flanks, and the underside of the wing begins to develop some days later. This reference emphasises that the experiments were started when feathers had already begun to develop on some pterylae but not yet on others.

The large feathers which had begun to grow before the administration of thyroidin continued to develop as in the control. The growth of the feathers on the thigh, flank, trunk, and underside of the wings, where the quills develop relatively late, was accelerated. The quills of the young feathers in the experimental birds were 5 to 7 mm longer than in the controls. When the vanes in the latter had not yet unfurled, those in the former already measured 3 to 5 mm in length. Such differences in the effect of hyperthyroidism on the different pterylae must be referred to changes in the properties of the feather follicles during feather development. The late stages of the development of feathers under optimal conditions are very intensive, and excess of thyroid hormone does not affect their growth substantially (Voitkevich, 1936, f).

The stimulating effect of the bird's own thyroid gland on the development of juvenile feathers had been demonstrated experimentally by Novikov (1936, a). He performed reciprocal skin grafts in Plymouth Rock chicks, in which the plumage is known to develop late. When skin was transplanted from a young chick to an older one, the new host was seen to exert an influence on the graft, the feathers on it beginning to develop earlier, which is characteristic of thyroid stimulation. When skin was transplanted from older chicks to younger ones, the plumage development was similar to that in older chicks. This is a further confirmation of an age-linked change in the properties of feather-forming tissue.

Thyroid hormone also exerts a positive influence on the development of feathers in adult birds. Larionov (1934), Larionov and Kuz'mina (1931), Larionov, Voitkevich, and Bel'skii (1934) measured the growing feathers in pigeons and bullfinches and found that the effect of thyroid hormone was to shift the onset of feather development to an earlier time, although further growth occurred at the normal rate. Similar stimulation of feather growth by induced hyperthyroidism was observed in turkeys by Hardesty (1934, 1935) and in fowls by Hosker (1936, a, b). Blivaiss (1946) demonstrated that thyroxin accelerated the regeneration of new feathers both in normal and in thyroidectomised fowls.

Another series of experiments was designed to investigate the effect of thyroid hormone on the formation of feather germs, which, as already shown, can be laid down in its absence. Thyroidin was given to pigeons in which immature feathers of the preceding generation were first plucked in order to induce the growth of feather germs. Young quills were removed from various pterylae on the twelfth day of development. At the same time thyroidin was given to half of the experimental birds (100 mg daily each). The feather germs were being laid down under conditions of hyperthyroidism in one group of birds and under ordinary conditions in the other. The rate of such laying-down was judged from the emergence of quill tips from the follicles. The further growth of the quills was monitored by periodic measurements.

The results of the measurement of the feathers from three different tracts on the sixteenth day after the onset of growth are shown in Table 15.

The length of the quills in the thyroidin-treated birds ex-

Table 15

Dimensions of the feathers in pigeons in a state of hyperthyroidism

Feather tract	Length of feather, mm		Length of feather vane, mm	
	Control	Hyper-thyroid-ism	Control	Hyper-thyroid-ism
Flight	34.7	45.2	7.8	15.8
Flight coverts	21.3	32.0	6.3	13.8
Rectrices	24.2	32.7	3.2	8.5

ceeded that of the controls by twelve to fifteen per cent, whereas the stimulation of the development of already formed germs under similar conditions amounts to only three or four per cent. Consequently, a state of hyperthyroidism stimulates the laying-down of feather germs, i.e. it is achieved in a shorter period of time than normal. Juhn and Barnes (1931) and Danforth (1933, 1937, a, b) demonstrated that feather germs were highly reactive to thyroid hormone. Later Juhn and Harris (1955) showed that the specific effect of thyroxin on the properties of feather germs could also be produced when the hormone was injected locally into the feather follicles.

Further experiments were concerned with the influence of thyroid hormone on the late stages of feather growth. It was found that the development of feathers could only be stimulated when artificially induced hyperthyroidism coincided with or preceded the onset of growth of the feather germs. When thyroidin is given after the onset of feather growth it does not affect the intensive development of plumage in normal birds but greatly stimulates the process in thyroid-ectomised ones.

Consequently, hyperthyroidism alters the rate of feather development only at the earliest stages, with an appropriate shift in the growth curve. Later the tissues of the growing quill alter in such a way that a high metabolic rate does not produce a corresponding acceleration of the differentiation of the feather structure. The reaction of the developing juvenile plumage to an artificially induced state of hyperthyroidism has much in common with the properties of the subsequent definitive feather generations.

The structure, pigmentation, and pattern of the feather

The information on the process of differentiation (i.e. the formation of the structure, pigmentation, and pattern of feathers) under conditions of hyperthyroidism is based on extensive experimental material collected by our predecessors. New feathers which develop in the presence of a high concentration of thyroid hormone are somewhat shorter than normal but have a wider vane. The downy part of such vanes is larger than normal (Zavadovskii, 1923, 1924, a, b, c, 1925; Giacomini, 1924, 1926; Podhradsky, 1926; Kříženecký, 1927; Schwarz, 1930; Gericke, 1934; Hykes, 1934; Prawochenski and Slizynski, 1934; Shtraikh and Svetozarov, 1938; Voitkevich, 1938, d, 1940, c; Lektorskii, 1940; Greenwood and Blith, 1929; *et al.*). Such changes were more pronounced in birds with sexual or seasonal dimorphism. In these birds a single injection of thyroxin leads to the development of elongated primary barbs, which increase the width of the vane in the area then being formed. When very large doses of the preparation are given, such as 20-30 g per fowl, producing signs of general intoxication, the effect on the feathers is as it were inverted, the new feathers being narrower than normal.

We noted a change in the shape of feathers in pigeons, which of course have no sexual distinctions in plumage. It was found that in a state of chronic hyperthyroidism, repeated plucking of immature feathers from the same tracts led to a change in the size and shape of new feathers (Table 16).

The ratio between the main parts of the vane undergo a

change as the size of the feathers diminishes. The downy part increases at the expense of the contour part. The hypertrophy of the downy part of the feathers in fowls given large doses of thyroid preparation has been described by Kříženecký (1927, 1932). Together with the enlargement of the downy part of the vane there is as it were a softening of some of the barbs in the contour part. The angle of inclination of the

Table 16

Length, width, and area of the vanes of control feathers and the third genera-
tion of feathers developing under conditions of chronic hyperthyroidism (mean
figures for one feather)

Feather tract	Length, mm		Width, mm		Area, mm² (measured by planimeter)	
	Control	Experi-mental	Control	Experi-mental	Control	Experi-mental
ight primaries	108.2	89.7	27.2	17.5	2275	1325
ight secondaries	85.7	74.8	25.8	18.2	1695	1085
overts of flight secondaries	67.5	53.0	23.2	18.0	1490	870
ower dorsal area	41.2	20.7	18.3	11.8	590	235
pper dorsal area	27.2	18.3	26.5	10.0	420	135

primary barbs to the shaft of the feather increases in the contour part of the vane. Deformed dichotomous branching of individual barbs is not infrequent; this never occurs in the vanes of feathers under normal conditions. The hooklets on the barbules do not develop properly in a state of hyperthyroidism, thus increasing the looseness of texture of the contour part of the vane. The partial reduction of the hooklets is explained by insufficient nutrition of the parts of the feather which grow rapidly under conditions of induced hyperthyroidism. Under these conditions the processes of 'dissimilation' are known to predominate over those of assimilation; this causes progressive starvation, leading in some cases to death of the bird.

Large doses of thyroidin produce impairment of a series of

vital functions in the experimental birds. Thus Zavadovskii (1925) noted a number of neuropathological phenomena. Further, it was found that the feather depigmentation reaction to large doses of thyroidin was less marked in decerebrate fowls than in normal ones (Bayandurov and Pegel, 1938). Such general changes occurring in the body in a state of artificially induced hyperthyroidism, which are reflected in the formation of feather structure, also affect melanogenesis and pigmentation. When large doses of the hormone are given, the developing feathers show either complete or partial depigmentation (Zavadovskii, 1924, c, 1925, 1927; Zavadovskii and Belkin, 1929; Voitkevich 1936, f, 1938, g; and others). Khvatov (1935), and Raspopova and Khvatov (1935), investigated the structure of the feathers in fowls developing under conditions of hyperthyroidism, and some other experimental modifications, and showed that depigmentation was associated with a number of structural deformities (see also Juhn, 1933, a, b; Juhn and Fraps, 1934, a, b; Lapiner and Radzivon, 1934; Kratzig, 1937). Partial depigmentation of feathers has also been noted in chicks hatched from eggs laid by fowls which had received large doses of thyroid preparation. Khvatov (1935) has made a detailed study of the histogenesis of feather pigmentation and the phenomenon of depigmentation in fowls with hyperthyroidism.

The part played by neural regulation of the activity of the skin chromatophores in the lower vertebrates is well known. There are reasons to believe that the effect of the thyroid hormone on feather pigmentation is mediated by the sympathetic nervous system. According to Vilter (1935) stimulation of the sympathetic nervous system inhibits melanogenesis in all animals subjected to artificial hyperthyroidism and decreases the activity of melanocytes, which leads to depigmentation of epidermal structures. There is, therefore, no basis for accepting Zavadovskii's contention (1924, c) that depigmentation is a specific reaction of the young feather to hyperthyroidism. This phenomenon is more properly regarded as a non-specific result of general pathological changes in the body occurring with marked hyperthyroidism.

When moderate doses of thyroidin are given, depigmentation does not occur; on the contrary, melanin pigmentation is enhanced. Hyperthyroidism induced in birds whose feathers normally have black pigment together with brown coloration (Brown Leghorns, pheasants) leads to an increase in the areas with black pigmentation at the expense of the brown (Zavadovskii and Belkin, 1929; Voitkevich, 1938, g). In drakes with hyperthyroidism, the normal grey watered-silk patterned feathers on the upper part of the ventral pteryla become blackened (Shtraikh and Svetozarov, 1938). Later, Chu (1940), Emmens and Parkes (1940), Juhn (1947, 1954), and Gallien and Pero (1950) made more detailed studies of the phenomenon of hypermelanisation in birds with hyperthyroidism, in experiments on normal, thyroidectomised, or thioureate-treated birds. Melanocyte activity is activated, as are many other cellular elements, when the level of hyperthyroidism is not high. In more recent publications Trinkaus (1948-1953) and Tonutti (1956) have produced convincing data on the positive effect exerted on the differentiation of melanoblasts into melanocytes and their functional activation. Markert (1948) compared the influence of antithyroid substances and thyroxin on the synthesis of melanin and the activity of melanocytes *in vitro*, and demonstrated the specificity of thyroid hormone activity.

Changes in the deposition of pigment on the feather structures being formed determine the changes in the pattern of feathers and plumage. When hyperthyroidism is moderate, phaeomelanin pigmentation is replaced by eumelanin (black) pigmentation. Changes in the pattern of the feathers can be observed in dimorphic breeds of fowls two days after the beginning of experiments with feeding of small doses of thyroid hormone. The threshold of the reaction of separate parts of the feather is related directly to the rate of their growth under normal developmental conditions (Stadie, 1938). With small doses of the hormone, the black pigment only forms narrow bands on both sides of the vane, the width of the black band increasing with the rise, within certain limits, of the thyroid hormone concentration in the body.

The eumelanin pigmentation is also enhanced in those breeds of fowls in which there are no sexual or seasonal differences in plumage colour, such as Plymouth Rock. Hyperthyroidism in these birds leads to the enlargement of the black transverse bands on the feathers. The boundaries of the bands become less definite and the pattern of the feather varies from solid black to blurred barred. A single injection of thyroxin is sufficient to enlarge the width of the black band on the developing feather of the Plymouth Rock fowl (Montalenti, 1934). A large single dose of thyroidin also induces the formation of a solid dark transverse band on the developing feathers of the ventral pteryla in the drake (Shtraikh and Svetozarov, 1938). Similar enhancement of pigmentation has been observed in feathers with lipochromic pigmentations when they develop during a period of experimental moulting induced by thyroxin (Drisen and Völker, 1953).

Whereas athyreosis in dimorphic birds is associated with weakening of plumage pigmentation and obliteration of contrasting differences in the patterns of the dorsal and ventral aspects of the body, hyperpigmentation induced by thyroid hormone is also accompanied by a blurring of regional differences in plumage. It is relevant to recall here some earlier data obtained from experiments on hyperthyroidism in which a change in the pattern of feathers was noted, and tended to be explained in terms of the rejuvenation of the bird or of the induction of feminising manifestations in the plumage of the male (Torrey and Horing, 1922, 1925, a, b; Horing and Torrey, 1923; Cole and Reid, 1924; Cole and Hutt, 1929; Grew, 1925; Champy and Morita, 1928). Later, Larionov (1938, 1939), Mühlbock (1939), Lektorskii (1940), Voitkevich (1940, c), Watterson (1959) and other authors elucidated the nature of regional differences in plumage pattern in terms of more recent data on hormonal induction.

Therefore, when relatively small doses of the hormone are given the changes in the shape and structure of feathers are comparatively slight: the tip of the feather is more rounded, the vane is wider and shorter. If the concentration of the hormone is raised considerably, new feathers are not only smaller but also show reduction of a number of structural elements: the downy part of the feather is hypertrophied with some diminution of the contour part, in which the barbs become partially disconnected. The vane shows depigmentation, predominantly in its apical part. Hypermelanisation is observed when the doses of thyroidin or thyroxin are more physiological: the black melanin displaces the brown phaeomelanin and spreads to those parts of the vane which are normally free of the pigment.

Experimental hyperthyroidism leads to a morphogenic effect opposite to that associated with hypothyroidism and athyreosis. The latter has demonstrated that the physiological processes underlying the initial and the final stages of feather development were not equivalent. Whereas in thyroidectomised birds the lower parts of the feathers are underdeveloped, it is precisely these that develop most vigorously in a state of hyperthyroidism. Whereas athyreosis is accompanied in a number of breeds of fowls by partial or complete replacement of black eumelanin by brown pheomelanin, exactly the reverse phenomenon is observed under conditions of hyperthyroidism, when eumelanin pigmentation is enhanced. The black pigment can be formed in the bird's body only at a definite level of thyroid-hormone concentration.

Plumage renewal

Interesting results were obtained with thyroid feeding in relation to the properties of feather-forming tissue with respect to periodic self-renewal. It has been established that artificial hyperthyroidism causes premature accelerated moulting. The first experiments on artificial hyperthyroidism were carried out by Georgievskii (1896), and by Carlson, Rooks, and Mackie (1912) who noted concomitant changes in the outer garb of mammals and birds. Zavadovskii (1923, 1924, a, b, 1925, 1932), Syrnev (1924), Torrey and Horning (1925), Occhipinti (1927), Křiženecký (1929, a, b), Kuhn (1929), Larionov (1934, 1935, b) and many others investigated hormonally-induced moulting on large numbers of domestic birds. It is not necessary to list all the publications on this subject, since many merely confirm earlier work and make no original contribution. Characteristically, many of these authors, while claiming to explain the causes of natural moulting, furnished no data at all on the factors governing either juvenile or annual replacement of plumage. Larionov and Kuz'mina (1931) were the first to make a comparison between the course and sequence of natural and experimental moulting in pigeons.

Regional differences in the reaction of different pterylae persist during hyperthyroid moulting. In pigeons, the different pterylae and feather follicles react differently to increased concentration of thyroid hormone. The lowest threshold of stimulation is to be found on the pterylae of the breast, back, shoulder, and forearm and the highest on the head, neck, tail, and wings. Similar data have been also obtained for fowls (Larionov and Lektorskii, 1931).

Histological examination of the skin of moulting birds showed that experimental moulting was based on the same underlying phenomena as natural moulting. The dormant already-formed feather germs present at the base of the quills of the old feathers are stimulated to proliferate. Simultaneously, the inner walls of the feather follicles undergo enhanced keratinisation, which leads to loosening of the quills of the old feathers anchored within them (Pakhmurin, 1934). The quills of a new generation of feathers are activated for development and push out their predecessors (Voitkevich, 1934, a, d; Khvatov, 1935). Such phenomena, constituting the local mechanism of plumage replacement in birds, are identical with the sloughing of reptiles (Drzewicki, 1929; Eggert, 1935).

Further investigation of experimental moulting was directed towards finding methods which would enable the production of plumage renewal by physiological means (Rylovnikov, 1934). A parallel study was made of the peculiarities of the reaction of feather-forming tissue under conditions of excessive concentration of thyroid hormone in relation to seasonal, sexual, and species properties of the birds.

Various methods have been used to activate moulting artificially (Zavadovskii, 1925; Martin, 1929, Hutt, 1930). Larionov, Voitkevich, and Novikov (1931, a) compared the effectiveness of chronic and single administration of thyroid preparations. They found that the intensity of experimental moulting in pigeons depended on the mode of administration, the total amount of the preparation being the same in every case. The moult was more pronounced after administration of a single dose of the preparation than after daily administration of small doses equal to the sum of the single doses. When a large single dose was given, evoking more intensive moulting, there was none of that concurrent and considerable general negative reaction of the body which is typical for chronic feeding with small doses of thyroidin. At the end of the experiment the weight of the birds given single doses was practically the same as that of the controls. Other birds, subjected to chronic thyroidin administration, showed considerable loss of weight.

The difference in the effect according to the mode of administration of the thyroid preparation has been explained by experiments on pigeons, which show that the main periods of experimental moulting are not the same with respect to the renewal of the plumage as a whole (Voitkevich and Novikov, 1934). The properties of feather-forming tissue alter at different periods of experimental moulting. The rate and sequence of feather replacement during chronic hyperthyroidism in the course of moulting are the same as those observed with brief treatment before the onset of moulting. This indicates the importance of the latent period during which preliminary physiological processes, essential for the development of the typical reaction, take place in the feather-forming tissue. This gives rise to the conclusion concerning the multi-phase nature of the changes which occur in the bird's body under conditions of experimental hyperthyroidism. Experiments involving artificial hyperthyroidism in birds demonstrate that the feather-forming 'tissue' is a complex system with properties which are subject to change.

The properties of feather-forming tissue

The references cited above show that in order to evoke artificial moulting in the spring, considerably larger doses of thyroid preparation must be given than those which are adequate in the autumn. These differences are evidently determined by the properties of the feather-forming tissue, which undergo a change at different times of the year, in particular according to the time of natural moulting. The importance of the local properties of feather follicles, manifested by the regular alternation of active and dormant periods in the follicles, is well known. If it is assumed that the activity of the germs is induced by thyroid hormone, the absence of feather renewal must be regarded as a result of thyroid-hormone deficiency. If this is the case, then the feather-forming tissue should always have the same reaction to similar sufficiently high concentrations of the hormone. In this case, if the dosage of thyroid preparation is kept the same, one moulting cycle should not have any appreciable effect on the experimental induction of the next one.

Experiments were performed on pigeons (four series of seven birds each). A single dose of thyroidin (3 g and 4·5 g) was given in two of the series. The number of feathers shed was carefully recorded. The pigeons in the other two series did not at first receive any thyroidin. Two months later, when the induced moult had finished in the thyroidin-treated birds, and a certain period of time had elapsed, the birds in all four series were simultaneously given thyroidin in the same doses as before. The data on the moult are given in Table 17.

It follows from a comparison of the figures in Table 17 that the intensity of experimental moulting after repeated thyroid administration declines sharply (to about one half). A similar result was obtained by Raspopova (1934) in experiments on thyroid feeding to geese.

The topography of feather replacement during two consecu-

Table 17

Number of large feathers shed in pigeons after a single and repeated administration of thyroidin

Feather tract	Doses of thyroidin			
	3 g	3 g (repeated)	4·5 g	4·5 g (repeated)
Flight primaries . .	44	16	52	30
Flight secondaries . .	63	19	60	32
Rectrices	60	36	68	29
Total	167	71	180	91

tive moults is of great interest, since such a comparison can
indicate the behaviour of feather follicles which either had
been subjected to a single stimulation or had remained quiescent. It was found that repeated activation of the feather
follicles usually failed when the same dose of thyroid preparation was given again. Moulting after the second administration of thyroidin occurred from those follicles from which
no feathers were shed during the first moult. In the pigeons
of one series, of the thirty-five large feathers replaced during
a repeated moult, only two feathers were renewed in the follicles which had already been activated earlier (Voitkevich,
1934, b). Hence, the ability of the feather germs to develop
under conditions of hyperthyroidism can be modified or nulli-
fied according to the properties of the feather follicles during
a given period of time.

The experiments just described were supplemented by a
different experiment in which the first activation of the
feather germs was produced not by thyroid administration
but by plucking the mature feathers of the preceding generation. It was necessary to stage this experiment in order to
refute the possibility of habituation of the body to thyroidin,
which would to some extent have undermined the earlier conclusion concerning a change in the properties of the feather-
forming tissue itself.

Pigeons in which all the large feathers and most of the small
ones had been plucked were kept for a period of thirty-five
days under the same conditions as other pigeons which were
not plucked. After this period of time both groups of pigeons
were given thyroidin (a single dose of 3 g per bird). The
results are shown in Table 18.

The data in Table 18 suggest that besides the general
physiological changes in the body, local changes in the feather-
forming tissue itself play an important part in moulting (Voitkevich and Novikov, 1934; Voitkevich, 1934, b). Differences
in experimental moulting have been shown in birds of different sex. Larionov and Dmitrieva (1931) demonstrated that
moulting in fowls could be induced in the females with
smaller doses of thyroid preparation than those needed for
the males. The same was shown for pigeons (Larionov, Voitkevich, and Novikov, 1931, a). Equal doses of thyroidin produced

15

Table 18

Experimental moulting of previously renewed and of old plumage in pigeons

Feather tract	Number of old feathers shed	Number of shed feathers among those previously renewed
Flight primaries . . .	15	0
Flight secondaries . . .	17	0
Rectrices	22	0
Total	54	0

more intensive moulting in the females. The threshold of the reaction of feather-forming tissue to the conditions created by a state of hyperthyroidism is higher in the males.

There are also species-specific differences in the reaction of the feather-forming tissue. Induced moulting occurs readily on administration of relatively small doses of thyroidin to pigeons and various gallinaceous birds (fowls, pheasants, pea-cocks, guinea-fowl, grey partridges, quails, and others). The most sensitive to thyroid hormone are the guinea-fowl, which in order to produce moulting needed one third of the dose of thyroidin necessary for fowls. Larger doses are required to induce moulting in water birds (Raspopova, 1930, 1934). Thus, according to Shtraikh and Svetozarov (1935, a, b), the amount of thyroidin needed to induce moulting in geese is one-and-a-half times as great as the dose needed by fowls (correcting for the difference in weight). Ducks are still more resistant to excess of thyroid hormone according to the data obtained by Shtraikh and Svetozarov (1937, a, 1938). Earlier, Milovanov (1934) failed to induce experimental moulting in ducks. His doses were evidently insufficient to reach the threshold of the reaction of feather-forming tissue. The reac-tivity of the feather follicles to excessive concentrations of thyroid hormone is still lower in some passeriforms and birds of prey. A number of members of these orders either do not moult at all in response to excess of thyroid hormone or show only slight moulting of small feathers in response to large or even sub-lethal doses of the hormone (Zavadovskii and Rokhlina, 1926; Janda, 1929; Bralis, 1931).

Thyroid hormone in the body during feather formation

Experimentally-produced hyperthyroidism leads to premature moulting which occurs with greater intensity but in the same sequence as in the normal bird. The character of experimental moulting is doubtless affected by the local properties of the feather-forming tissue. These are different in the feather follicles of different tracts and pterylae, and are also modified by such factors as season, sex, and species.

The question arises whether it may be concluded solely from experiments involving induced hyperthyroidism that the hormone determines the onset of natural plumage renewal. There is no basis for an affirmative answer. We shall later return to the hypotheses concerning the conclusion that thyroid hormone plays a deciding role in the process of moulting. At this stage we shall consider some data on the physiological status of the body during induced hyperthyroidism and during naturally occurring thyroid hyperactivity.

In a series of our experiments the thyroid hormone content of various tissues in the pigeon was determined both in cases of thyroid hyperactivity and of thyroid feeding. In both groups feather-forming processes occurred simultaneously. Secretion by the thyroid gland was stimulated by activating the mass growth of new feathers by plucking out the feathers of the preceding generation. Some of these pigeons, as well as normal ones, were fed thyroidin. The hormone content of the liver and kidneys was determined by means of the tadpole test. Earlier, Zavadovskii and Perel'muter (1926) had shown that the hormone accumulated in the liver, kidneys, other organs, and blood of fowls fed on thyroidin. They estimated the hormone content by transplanting fragments of various organs from the fowls into axolotls, which later developed signs of metamorphosis. We employed similar variants of the test on tadpoles (Voitkevich, 1936, d, f, j, 1938, c). No thyroid hormone can be found in the liver and kidneys of normal pigeons, or at any rate not in such concentration as would affect the metamorphosis of amphibian larvae. On the other hand, large amounts of thyroid hormone accumulate in the liver and kidneys of pigeons given thyroidin. Vigorous metamorphosis occurs when fragments of these organs are implanted into tadpoles. Fragments of the liver and kidneys of pigeons with growing plumage but not treated with thyroidin have no effect on the metamorphosis of tadpoles. Therefore, the thyroid content of the body is far from identical in natural and in experimentally-induced moulting.

The marked difference in the state of the body during thyroid hyperactivity and induced hyperthyroidism indicates that the general physiological background against which feather formation takes place under these conditions is different. It must be mentioned that the doses of thyroid preparation used in our experiments were small compared with those ordinarily used for moult stimulation.

Further experiments were staged to investigate the special features of the distribution and disappearance of the extrinsic hormone. It might have been expected that during feather formation the intensive utilisation of thyroid hormone would entail its more rapid disappearance from the body.

It was from this viewpoint that the experiments on the hormone content of the organs of pigeons of different ages were undertaken. Feather-forming processes are known to be most vigorous at certain periods of the pigeon's general development. Five age-groups were used in the experiments arranged at five-day intervals within the limits of five to thirty days from the time of hatching. The doses of thyroidin were different for each group, in all cases amounting to 0.2 per cent of body weight. The intervals between the administration of the preparation and autopsy varied: eighteen, twenty-four, and forty-eight hours. The tests were performed on fragments of the liver and the kidneys, all of the same weight.

Biological tests showed that the extrinsic hormone disappeared from the tissues (and hence was utilised) more rapidly during those periods when there was mass development of feathers. The most intensive period of feather growth occurs at the age of ten to twenty days. It is in birds of this age that the earliest accumulation of the hormone (after eighteen hours)—and correspondingly its earliest disappearance (after twenty-four to forty-eight hours)—was observed. To exclude the possible objection that the rapid disappearance of thyroxin at a certain age depends not only on feather formation but also on other factors (intensive general growth, transition to independent feeding and active mobility), experiments were carried out on adult pigeons in which the rate of hormone utilisation was studied under conditions of mass feather growth.

Half of the normal and experimental (plucked) pigeons were kept at a high temperature in order to reduce the increased heat loss by the plucked birds. Thyroidin was given in the dose of 2 g per bird. Forty-eight hours after institution of thyroidin the birds were subjected to autopsy and the presence of the hormone in the liver and kidneys was tested, as before.

The tests showed that the hormone content of the organs was higher in the normal pigeons than in those undergoing intensive plumage growth. The liver and kidneys of the latter retained less hormone than those of normal birds. We see in this evidence of its more intensive utilisation during mass feather development. These data give new support to the need for a definite level of thyroid hormone in the body, for the feather-forming process to take place. It does not, of course, follow from this that thyroid hormone is not utilised in the course of other biological and physiological processes. But it is equally clear that feather formation requires large quantities of structural material and energy-producing factors.

Experimental hyperthyroidism differs from the state of the body in which its own thyroid gland is hyperactive, and this must be specially taken into account when extrapolating experimental data to the normal process. The data on the change in the body's saturation with the hormone during a period of feather formation can, therefore, be taken only as an indirect proof of the connection between this process and the thyroid gland.

The experimental data described above and the available published material provide a fairly complete picture of the dependence of feather formation on those metabolic processes whose intensity and character are determined by the thyroid hormone. Such dependence begins during the embryonic period of development and persists throughout the bird's lifetime. The differentiation of the thyroid gland and the onset of proliferative phenomena coincide during the embryological period of development. In the ontogenesis of the bird the first phase of feather formation—the development of the embryonic down and simultaneous laying-down of the feathers of nestling plumage—precede the period of normal thyroid activity. This led to the early conclusion that the presence of thyroid hormone was not essential for the laying-down of the feather germs. Then it was shown that the formation of the germs under experimental conditions and the onset of their proliferation could also be achieved in the absence of thyroid hormone from the body.

Examination of the thyroid glands during the post-embryonic life of birds showed that there was a parallel increase in thyroid activity and the intensity of the feather-forming process. The highest level of thyroid activity coincided with the period of mass growth of young feathers. This is clearly seen when comparisons are made between birds in which the duration and intensity of feather growth are different.

Feather growth, induced artificially or occurring during natural moulting, is accompanied by thyroid hyperactivity. The presence of thyroid hormone in the body is not equally essential for the various stages of feather formation. Formation of the feather germs or their regeneration is not impaired when the hormone is deficient or absent; but it is essential for other stages of feather development. Small feathers do not grow immediately after thyroidectomy; they develop later, showing considerable deviations from the normal. Large feathers, however, do not lose their ability to grow. Differences in the properties of feathers of different tracts were discovered in the course of experimentally-induced hyperthyroidism.

If the concentration of the thyroid hormone is varied, considerable changes in the rate of growth of young feathers become apparent during the early period of development. The growth curve for feathers is therefore shifted to either a later (athyreosis) or an earlier period (hyperthyroidism). The development of the feather structure can, however, be altered at any stage.

The formation of the structure, colour, and pattern of feathers requires a certain metabolic rate which is determined by the thyroid hormone together with other factors affecting metabolism. Absence of the hormone results in underdevelopment of the structural elements; excess leads to partial overdevelopment. As a rule, athyreosis is accompanied by the formation of narrower vanes, partial reduction of barbs, and approximation of the contour part of the vane to the downy one. The distribution of pigment is altered to a marked degree in the feathers of those birds whose plumage shows seasonal or sexual distinctions. In such birds athyreosis is accompanied by partial loss or complete replacement of dark eumelanin by light brown phaeomelanin. The various types of patterns we have observed become simplified, approaching a universal primitive shaft pattern. During hyperthyroidism the opposite is true, the development of the dark melanins being enhanced at the expense of the lighter ones. When there is an excess of the hormone, the sharp increase in catabolic processes leads to an inversion of the hypermelanisation effect and the development of depigmented feathers with defective structure.

Changes in the development, structure, and pattern of feathers occur equally after surgical removal of the thyroid gland and under the influence of anti-thyroid drugs. The changes in the structure and colour of feathers which occur under conditions of athyreosis are completely reversible by compensatory administration of thyroid hormone.

Different species of birds exhibit identical disorders of feather formation in the absence of thyroid hormone. Species differences of general growth and development of birds in a given systematic group also disappear. Differentiation of the body, of which the development of plumage is a particular case, depends more closely on thyroid function than general growth. Retardation of growth under conditions of general athyreosis is relatively greater in the slower-growing breeds. In faster-growing breeds the hormone is, on the contrary, less important. But the hormonal influence on the structure, colour, and pattern of feathers persists to approximately the same degree in both cases.

The regional peculiarities of the reaction of the feather-forming tissue to thyroid hormone manifest themselves gradually in the ontogenesis of the bird. In adult birds the properties of different pterylae are not identical, and these properties show great persistence. During the development of each feather there is a combination of persistent hereditary properties of the feather follicle and great plasticity with respect to hormonal influence. The connection between moulting and general physiological processes stimulated by thyroid hormone has been demonstrated in experiments with total exclusion of the thyroid gland and with excessive concentration of its hormone in the body. In the former case, moulting does not occur; in the latter it can be induced voluntarily at unusual times. The rate of moulting can be either accelerated or retarded.

The activity of the thyroid gland is enhanced during natural renewal of plumage. In birds with species differences in the rate of feather development, the enhancement of thyroid activity is related to the period of mass feather growth. Furthermore, the different seasons of the year during which thyroid activity was excluded were shown to be significant with respect to moulting. Following thyroidectomy performed a long time before the onset of moulting, there is no subsequent renewal of plumage. If the operation is performed later, during the 'critical period', moulting does occur, but with some delay in feather replacement. The retardation of plumage renewal is directly related to the interval between the time of operation and the onset of natural moulting. The capacity for feather renewal is restored at any time by administration of thyroid hormone. The duration of the so-called critical period is different in different birds, and is related both to the properties of the feather-forming tissue and to the metabolic features peculiar to each species.

Premature and accelerated moulting which occurs with artificial hyperthyroidism does not by itself warrant a conclusion regarding the rôle of the bird's own thyroid gland in the periodic renewal of plumage. Experimental hyperthyroidism, induced even by relatively small doses of the preparation, is accompanied by physiological changes in the body which are not observed even at the highest levels of activity of the bird's own thyroid gland. Experiments with artificial hyperthyroidism were designed predominantly not to determine the rôle of the body's regulatory factors but to elucidate the properties of the feather-forming tissue, and in particular to establish the differences in the reaction of this tissue at different stages of feather renewal. The properties of the feather germs before, during, and after moulting are different. The reaction of the feather follicles has been found to be different in birds of different sex and species.

The changes in the properties of the feather-forming tissue which are concerned with preparing it for moulting occur a long time before the first feathers are shed. The hypothesis that the thyroid gland participates in the mediation of moulting sounds rather paradoxical in this connection; in the physiological processes which as a whole determine the onset of moulting, its rôle decreases with the approach of the period of natural feather renewal. If this postulate is carried to its logical conclusion, the significance of the thyroid hormone during the moulting itself should be practically zero. However, the other aspect of the process—formation of a new generation of feathers—must not be overlooked. It is for this mass new growth that a certain metabolic rate is essential, and this rate, together with other factors, is ensured by thyroid hyperactivity.

Without diminishing the significance of the experimental data discussed above, it must be stressed that the final conclusion concerning the rôle of the thyroid hormone in feather formation can only be reached after examining the importance of other hormones in this morphogenic process.

CHAPTER IV

THE RÔLE OF THE SEX GLANDS IN THE FORMATION OF PLUMAGE CHARACTERS

UNLIKE other endocrine glands, the sex glands begin to function at the latest period of development of the young body. Whereas the thyroid and the hypophysis already begin to show signs of secretory activity during the embryonic life of the bird (Studitskii, 1947; Mitskevich and Mamul, 1953), the activity of the sex glands becomes manifest only at a late stage of post-embryonic development (see the review by Larionov, 1940, b, for a more detailed account of the development of the sex glands in birds). This indicates that the influence of the sex hormones on feather formation does not extend to all the stages of ontogenesis, but becomes felt during the formation of definitive plumage.

The study of the rôle of the sex glands in feather formation is connected with the general problem of sex differences in the plumage of birds, the problem of sexual dimorphism. Darwin (1868, 1871) was the first to organise systematically the extensive descriptive material on this subject, and he made a comparative analysis of the various types of plumage, pointing out the independence of the sex differences in plumage from the activity of the sex glands. The nature of the sex differences in the organisation of plumage is directly connected with age and seasonal changes.

In many species of birds the nestling plumage is the same in both sexes, but after the first moult it is replaced by a brighter garb, different in the males and the females. In a number of representatives of the gallinaceous and the anatid birds the changes in the plumage are seasonal and occur periodically in mature birds after moulting. The age, sex and season of the structure and pattern involves the whole plumage but is particularly prominent in certain tracts.

The connection between such plumage characters and sex hormones has been established by numerous experimental studies. The dominant rôle in these has been played by such procedures as castration, transplantation of gonads, and administration of sex hormones. Exchange grafts of skin, individual feather follicles, and parts of the feather germs in birds of different sex have been of supplementary significance. The main experimental data have been obtained on domestic birds (fowls and ducks) which have clear age differences and sex-determined differences in the structure and pattern of plumage. A number of early investigations (Poll, 1909; Pezard, 1912-1928; Goodale, 1914, 1918; Zavadovskii, 1922, 1923) established that the male plumage was potentially an attribute of both sexes in birds. When a rooster, drake, or cock pheasant is castrated, no significant changes are produced in the pattern of its plumage. De-sexed females, however, develop the male type of plumage after moulting. When a castrated rooster or a de-sexed hen undergoes ovarian transplantation, a female type of plumage develops. Similar results are obtained on injection of oestrogens. Analogous observations proving the dependence of the so-called nuptial plumage on gonadal induction are reported by Benoit (1924, 1934), Horowitz (1934), Krizhenetskii (1935), Van Oordt and Junge (1936), and other authors.

It has been found that the female sex hormone played the principal rôle in the genesis of the sex differences in the plumage of the gallinaceous and anatid birds. The formation of the male garb occurs in the absence of sex glands in much the same way as it does in the presence of the male sex hormone in the body. Various details of the hormonal mediation of dimorphic plumage in domestic birds were elucidated more precisely in later experiments with castration and administration of the female sex hormone (Domm, 1927, 1939; Greenwood, 1928; Greenwood and Crew, 1926; Greenwood and Blith, 1931, 1932; Caridroit, 1933).

Such a relationship between plumage dimorphism and gon-

218 THE FEATHERS AND PLUMAGE OF BIRDS

adal activity does not exist in all birds with sex differences in their plumage. Thus, in a number of the passeriforms the development of distinct age and sex differences in plumage does not depend on sex hormones. Khakhlov (1927), Novikov (1936-40), and Keck (1934) showed that castration of dimorphic passeriforms of both sexes (sparrows, bullfinches, crossbills, chaffinches, and others) produced no changes in the structure and colour of new feathers. Equally independent of the influence of sex hormones is plumage with only slight sex differences or plumage completely devoid of such differences. Our experiments on pigeons, starlings, rooks, and jackdaws showed that castration produced no changes in their plumage.

Consequently, there are two groups of birds, with different physiological properties in relation to the formation of plumage pattern and the influence of sex hormones. In one group the development of the plumage pattern depends on the presence of the sex hormone in the body. In the other group the differences in the plumage develop independently of the sex hormones (Nekrasov, 1953; Matthews, 1960).

The first group includes those birds in which normally the absence of sexual differences in plumage is determined by a peculiar reaction of the feather-forming tissue to sex hormone. This concerns the so-called henny-feathering of cocks in some breeds of fowls (Campine and Sebright). After moulting the characteristic normal female plumage is replaced in castrated cocks and de-sexed hens of these breeds by an unusual plumage which can be regarded as male. Trans-sex ovarian and testicular grafts, and transplantation of skin, between usually cock-feathered and henny-feathered birds enabled the breed differences in plumage properties to be related to the reactivity of the feather-forming tissue (Greenwood, 1928; Greenwood and Crew, 1926; Danforth, 1939, b; Watterson, 1959). The feather follicles in castrates form new feathers of the cock type, which are normally absent in these breeds. Thus the feather germs in these birds are able to react equally to oestrogen and to androgen. Normally their feathers are devoid of red pigment, but after castration such a pigment appears in the new feathers. The appearance of the pigment can be suppressed by administration of any sex hormone (Nickerson, 1946, and Willier, 1950).

Finally, there are among the gallinaceous birds those (white partridges) that exhibit seasonal changes in plumage which are not induced by sex hormones. In such cases, castration or injection of sex hormone does not prevent the characteristic seasonal changes in plumage pattern. Novikov (1939, c, d) demonstrated the importance of the thyroid hormone in this process.

Investigation of the development of plumage at different levels of sex hormones in the body showed that the hormonal influence was not equally realised in different species of birds (Novikov, 1946). The properties of feather-forming tissue underwent considerable changes in the process of historical development; the ability to react to the sex hormones has been affected in particular. Therefore, the rôle of sex hormone in the different phases of feather formation should be more effectively investigated in birds belonging to the first group. The brief review of experimental data given below is based on the studies by the authors cited above and our own observations.

DEVELOPMENT OF THE STRUCTURE AND PATTERN OF FEATHERS

The early ontogenic phase of feather formation—the development of embryonic down and the laying-down of the contour feather germs—occurs during the period when no sex hormone is yet formed in the body. In fowls, which mature sexually relatively early, the first signs of gonadal activity, as judged by the development of secondary sex characteristics such as combs and wattles in cockerels, are seen from thirty to forty days after hatching. Therefore the laying-down and to some extent the development of the nestling plumage occur in fowls as in other birds without the influence of the sex glands. The possibility of some effect of the female sex hormone present in the egg yolk being exerted at this time is not excluded (Kopec and Greenwood, 1929). Injection of egg yolk into de-sexed female Brown Leghorns leads to the development of female feathers. This suggests that the unresorbed yolk which persists in the chick after hatching may affect the formation of young feathers. This can explain the causes of some similarity between the monomorphic nestling plumage of young birds of both sexes and the definitive plumage of the mature female of the same species. However, since the amount of sex hormone in the hen egg yolk is small, it is difficult to envisage its being sufficient to affect the whole of the embryonic and part of the post-embryonic development. In the absence of oestrogen, the female characteristics do not develop and the plumage acquires a character approaching that of the male. However, no such changes are observed during the development of the juvenile feathers, although feathers continue to grow after complete resorption of yolk in the young bird.

It is relevant to note further that the nestling plumage and the definitive plumage of the females have only a remote superficial similarity. In the birds of the second group referred to above, in which the character of the plumage does not change with the presence or absence of sex hormone, there are also clear age distinctions in plumage. Let us recall also that the laying-down and the development of contour feathers in de-sexed birds occur approximately at the same times as in normal birds. To avoid misunderstanding of our conclusion that the sex hormones do not affect the early ontogenic phases of the feather-forming process, it must be stated that it refers to the processes of growth and differentiation of the basic structural elements of the feather. It is noteworthy in this connection that in the case of many birds whose plumage develops relatively early, the females as a rule have better-developed feathering than the males (Siegel, Craig, and Mueller, 1957). In some breeds of chicks, moreover, there is a correlation between the nature of plumage colour and the rate of post-embryonic growth of the bird (Collins and Wentworth, 1958).

Replacement of nestling plumage (monomorphic in most forms) by the final plumage, which is different in birds of the two sexes, occurs during the first moult, which is near in time to the onset of gonadal activation (Juhn, Gustavson, and Gallagher, 1932; Kuhn, 1932). This circumstance acquires special significance for the formation of successive generations of feathers, renewed during the annual moults. Therefore the specific effect of sex hormone, under ordinary conditions of the bird's development, can be demonstrated only on definitive feathers and not those of the juvenile plumage. It is possible to produce premature induction of new plumage-colour characters by experimental selection of appropriate doses of sex hormone (Hamilton, 1941; Willier, 1942).

In birds of the first biological group, the effect of sex hormone extends not only to the formation of the structure and pigmentation of feathers, but also to their growth (Champy and Demay, 1933; Champy, 1935; Juhn, 1937, 1938). This was established by comparing the data on the growth of feathers of homologous pterylae in birds of different sex. According to Bel'skii (1936) the male sex hormone, whose morphogenic importance during the formation of feather characterisation is very slight, exerts an inhibitory effect on the growth of large feathers. Conversely, the large feathers of castrated White Leghorns and Rhode Island fowls grow quicker than those non-castrated roosters, and reach a greater length. There are also regional differences in the rate of growth of feathers of different pterylae, which react to sex hormone. In cocks the highest rate of growth belongs to feathers of the posterior part of the ventral pteryla, followed in order of diminishing rate of growth by the feathers of the anterior part of the ventral pteryla, the rump, and the flanks (Juhn, D'Amour, and Gustavson, 1930; Juhn, D'Amour, and Womask, 1930; Juhn, Faulkner, and Gustavson, 1931). These regional differences persist in castrated cocks. No such differentiation of the rate of feather growth occurs in normal hens. When oestrogen is given to castrated birds, the feathers of different tracts develop similarly to those in normal females, that is without appreciable topographical differences.

Differences in the threshold of the reaction have been established for the feathers of different tracts: the highest threshold occurs in feathers with the highest rate of growth, in the posterior part of the ventral pteryla, and a low threshold is characteristic of slow-growing feathers, as on the rump and flank. Different reactivity has also been demonstrated in separate parts of the young feather, which grow at different rates. The peripheral parts of the feather, with their maximal rate of growth, have a higher threshold for the reaction to sex hormone. Those parts of the feather situated nearer the shaft (the bases of the barbs), which have the slowest rate of growth, have a low threshold. The rate of growth of the structural parts of the barb changes in the direction of the feather's main axis. The explanation of the causes underlying the development of a primitive shaft pattern at low concentrations of sex hormone is to be found in these terms. Higher concentrations of the hormone are necessary for the spread of the pigmented zone on the vane. Brief exposure to a large dose of the female sex hormone induces the formation of a narrow transverse bar, female in structure and pigmentation, in the developing feathers of castrated or normal Brown Leghorn cocks (Domm, Juhn, and Gustavson, 1939). Such a bar can be detected on opening the feather quill forty-eight hours after a single injection of oestrogen (Juhn and Gustavson, 1930).

The male plumage possesses characteristically marked distinctions in the size and structure of the feathers on the dorsal and ventral aspects of the body. The dorsal feathers in cocks are lanceolate in shape. A peripheral fringe, formed by the upper parts of barbules carrying underdeveloped barbicels, extends round an appreciable part of the contour part of the vane. The feathers of the ventral area resemble the female type in shape: the vanes are oval and there is no peripheral fringe. Under the influence of the female sex hormone, the rate of growth of the feathers on the dorsal aspect is accelerated to equal the rate of growth of the ventral feathers (Lillie, 1932; Lillie and Juhn, 1932). As a result, oval feathers similar in shape to those on the ventral aspect develop on the dorsal aspect of the body. Such changes do not extend to the feathers of the head and neck.

Regional differences in the size and shape of the feathers are slight in ducks. They occur in flight secondaries and the under-tail feathers. Sex differences in the plumage of ducks involve predominantly pigmentation and to a lesser extent structure. In fowls, on the other hand, hormone-regulated structural characteristics are relatively more prominent than differences in pigmentation. The development of the pigmentation and pattern of feathers does not depend on sex hormone in all of those breeds of fowls which have sex differences in plumage characters. The transverse bars on the feathers of Plymouth Rock fowls do not change after castration or administration of female sex hormone.

The hormonal influence of the gonads is not associated with a definite generation of feathers; it can be detected at all stages of the development of the vane. The effect of the sex hormone is first of all seen in characteristic changes in the pigmentation of feathers and only then, at a higher concentration of the hormone, can changes be observed in the structure and shape of the feathers. When small concentrations of sex hormone are given for a brief period, only pigmentation undergoes a change, without appreciable alteration of structure. In practice, with the concentrations of sex hormone employed experimentally, and also during natural moulting, the specific changes extend both to the pattern and the structure of the feathers. The total characterisation of the sexual type of plumage is not predetermined during the laying-down of the feather germ, but develops according to the conditions during the formation of the young feathers of each generation. Uninterrupted hormonal influence is the main factor in the formation of feathers of a sexual type.

After castration of the male or de-sexing of the female the feather germs and the developing feathers are no different in structure from those of normal cocks, but their ability to proliferate is strongly activated. They can form a typical male type of feather at any time of the year, outside the period of moulting, which is not characteristic of normal males. In dimorphously pigmented breeds the differences in the plumage pattern are related to the reactivity of the feather germ melanoblasts to sex hormone. The latter affects the differentiation of the melanoblasts to pigment cells or melanocytes. Thus, in the Brown Leghorns oestrogen induces the appearance of melanocytes in the feathers of the breast pteryla, which only form granules of a rusty-brown pigment, whereas in the absence of this hormone new melanocytes can produce only black melanin (Willier, 1948, 1953). Similar changes in the reaction of melanophores have also been noted in other tracts, where changes in pigmentation combine with large structural rearrangements in the vanes of the new feathers (dorsal and sacral areas).

The local effect of thyroxin on the developing pigmentation and structure of feathers has already been described. Greenwood and Blyth (1935) made intradermal micro-injections of

16

oestrogen in the region of the breast pteryla of Brown Leghorn cocks. The doses of the hormone were so selected that
they were ineffective when injected in a more generalised way.
It was found that a reddish-brown pigment was formed in the
feathers undergoing regeneration in immediate proximity to
the site of injection, and a black pigment in the more distant
ones. Some feathers had red pigment on one side and black on
the opposite side. Such direct action of the hormone on
melanocyte activity was then confirmed by Hamilton (1940, a).

The evidence of numerous experiments confirms that
melanoblast-differentiation pathways are different in different
birds. The extreme variants in this respect are henny-feathered
breeds in which these cells undergo melanogenic activation by
both sex hormones, although they are generally insensitive to
hormonal induction and independently of it can either form
the pigment (breeds of black fowls) or perish in the feather
papilla at the early stage of melanogenesis without forming
the pigment (White Leghorns and Wyandottes). Transplantation of such melanophores with different physiological properties into the feather germs of other birds does not inhibit their
proper reactivity (Danforth and Foster, 1929; Danforth, 1939,
b, 1944; Espinasse, 1939; Wang, 1948).

The properties of the feather follicles undergo a change
during the ontogenesis of the bird. If the feather germs of a
young bird are activated by plucking, then up to a certain
time the feathers which develop are of the nestling type. Later
the same follicles produce feathers of exclusively definitive
type. If the time of activation of the feather germs is carefully selected, the upper part of the feather will be of the
juvenile type and the lower of the definitive type (Kuhn,
1932). Such a course of development of the definitive plumage characters, which become apparent from a definite
moment in the bird's life, is not associated with a particular
generation of feathers; this reflects the rôle of general physiological changes in the body, and is evidently of neuro-hormonal origin. At the same time, it must be noted that changes
in the properties of feather follicles, and the establishment
of regional differences of sensitivity to sex hormone, occur
asynchronously on the different pterylae. The sex hormone
appears in the body at a certain stage in the bird's general

development; as its concentration increases, there is a successive reaction to it by feather follicles of different localisation with different thresholds of stimulation. This change in the properties of the feather follicles, leading to the formation of feathers of a new type (definitive instead of juvenile) precedes the period of moulting, and it has been observed that the changes in pigmentation of the young feathers overtake the tendency for structural changes to occur in response to the hormonal influence. It would not be an exaggeration to state that of the several thousands of feather follicles within a bird's skin, each has individual features which manifest themselves during their development, particularly in the reaction to sex hormone.

Feather germs and melanocytes are now considered by comparative endocrinologists as peculiar and very sensitive 'receptors' of hormonal influences (Watterson, 1959). The organisation of the feather follicle resembles the embryological beginnings of many organs in which the mesenchymal and epithelial components are present in definite quantitative and spatial relationships. Such complex structures, with extensive structure-forming potentialities, are laid down repeatedly and in large numbers in the skin of the adult bird. During development the highly vascularised dermal papilla is surrounded by a thickened ring or 'collar' of intensively proliferating epithelial cells (see Fig. 3). The melanoblasts localised at the base of the 'collar' and the central connective tissue shaft, which ensures the nutrition of the developing quill, together represent a 'receptor', a peculiar 'recorder' which transmits the hormonal changes taking place in the body to the feather structure being formed. The wavy proliferation of the epithelial cells in the apical edge of the 'collar' form ridge-like protuberances which eventually develop into barbs. The continuous stream of additional cells reaching the base of the 'striation' enlarges these protuberances, which include within them melanoblasts as well. There is a strict quantitative ratio between the melanoblasts and the elongating cells of the barbs. The melanoblasts, which cannot be detected by ordinary microscopic examination until a certain developmental stage, begin to synthesise the pigment, giving rise to the annular pigmented zone of the feather quill.

In this zone, the pigment synthesis in the melanocytes can alter depending on the nature of the hormonal influences, and thus bring about a circular change in the colour of the quill (somewhat as a sock lengthens in knitting on four needles).

Wang (1941, 1943) separated the connective tissue and the epithelial components of the feather germ by microsurgery and made reciprocal transplants between feather follicles of different pterylae. The newly formed composite feathers reacted to sex hormone in accordance with the epithelial component and the properties of the pteryla from which the quills were taken.

The characteristic effect of sex hormone on the morphogenesis of the feather appears in connection with the thyroid hormone. Thyroxin evokes the formation of black pigment and widening of the vane in Brown Leghorns and some pheasants. Reddish-brown pigmentation and narrowing of the vane are typical for a state of athyreosis. The authors of the early investigations tended to see a feminising effect of thyroxin in the structure and pigmentation of the feathers in Brown Leghorns (Torrey and Horning, 1922, 1925, b). The results of thyroidectomy were regarded as signs of masculinisation (Crew, 1927; Schwarz, 1930). Zavadovskii (1928) considered that such conclusions were based on superficial resemblances. The morphogenic rôle of these hormones was differentiated by examining the effect of thyroidectomy on the plumage of birds possessing different reactions to sex hormone (Voitkevich, 1938, g). I concluded that with respect to rate, formation of structure, and final dimensions, the growth of a feather depends chiefly on the thyroid hormone, which creates the background for the development of the mosaic of characteristics induced by the sex hormones. Other authors also reached similar conclusions from the results of the action of oestrogen on thyroidectomised, castrated, and thioureate-treated Brown Leghorns (Fraps, 1938, a, b; Blivaiss, 1947, a, b; Domm, 1948; Trinkaus, 1948, 1953).

A comparison of the periods of natural moulting and the cycles of gonadial activity over a year shows that renewal of plumage does not coincide with the period of greatest sexual activity. During moulting, or before its onset, the sex glands undergo a depression, which is relatively more marked in males than in females. The development of new feathers during natural renewal of plumage usually takes place at minimal concentrations of sex hormone in the body. It is possible that the formation of the male type of plumage, resembling the plumage of castrated birds, is directly related to a low concentration of sex hormone in the body. The results of experiments on artificial activation of feather germs, caused by partial plucking of roosters and drakes during the period of maximal sexual activity, are interesting in this connection. The new feathers acquired the female appearance, that is, the results were the same as those produced by administration of female sex hormone. Similar results followed the transplantation to roosters of large amounts of testicular tissue.

In the light of modern data on the biochemistry of hormones, such results are explained by the fact that biosynthesis of the female and the male sex hormones is closely related. At high concentrations, part of the male sex hormone is transformed into female sex hormone, which determines the development of the female type of feathers. The reaction of the feather-forming tissue to a certain concentration of sex hormone is not the same in birds of different species; for the formation of the female type of feathers, different amounts of sex hormone are required in different birds.

The data considered above prove that it is the female sex hormone, formed both in the ovary and partially in the testis, which induces the development of feathers of a certain shape, pigmentation, and pattern. The specificity of action of the sex hormones is not shared by other steroid hormones. Thus the adrenal cortical hormones have no such action, as has been shown by Hamilton (1940, c) and Watterson (1959).

PLUMAGE RENEWAL

Ornithologists and poultry-breeders are well aware that the annual moult follows the period of high gonadial activity (Ghadbourne, 1897; Groebels, 1928; Dement'ev, 1940, b; Shul'pin, 1940). The periods of seasonal renewal of plumage and reproduction do not coincide. This relationship is consistently preserved in most species of wild birds, although (as already mentioned) in many birds of prey the moult may be prolonged and may partly involve the period of reproduction. Such an overlap of these processes is often observed in birds subjected to domestication.

Investigation of the sexual cycle in birds in connection with natural moulting has established the presence of two periods in gonadial function during the year, one of high activity and one of quiescence. The periodicity of sexual activity is clearly manifest in wild birds and somewhat blurred in domestic ones (Larionov, 1938; Voitkevich and Novikov, 1936, b; Van der Meuhlen, 1939; Moreau, Wilk, and Rowan, 1947; Vaugien, 1948; Kobayashi, 1953, b; Williamson, 1956). Outside the period of reproduction, the sex glands show signs of functional inhibition, reflected in the size of the gonads being smaller than in the period of activity. The generative and secretory function of the sex glands reaches a high level during the spring and partly during the summer. During this period the weight of the testes in the males of many species of wild birds increases 150 to 200 times over as compared to the quiescent period (Voitkevich and Novikov, 1936, b). The microscopic appearance of the gonads at this time indicates high incretory activity (Mori, 1948).

Comparison of the data on the annual changes in the size and activity of the sex glands with the data on the time and character of the moult suggests that the shedding of feathers is adjusted in time to that period when the regressive changes in the sex glands which occur after reproduction are already advanced. Ornithologists know that the onset of moulting may shift depending on the time of change in the activity of the sex glands. Moulting never begins during the period of intensive egg-laying. It may occur earlier if the regression of the sex glands is rapid. On the contrary, in those birds in which, under natural or experimental conditions, a high level of sexual activity persists longer than usual, no moulting occurs at the times which are typical for the species in question (Miyazaki, 1934; Van Oordt and Damste, 1939). Natural moulting can be delayed or slowed down by injection of oestrogens or androgens (Kobayashi, 1954, a; Onishi, Taketomi, Kato, and Miyazono, 1955; Tanabe, Himeno, and Nozaki, 1957). The connection between moulting and sexual activity has been carefully studied in domestic birds (Larionov, Berdyshev, and Dmitrieva, 1933).

Larionov's monograph (1945) gives extensive data on the connection between seasonal moulting and egg-laying in domestic fowls. He showed that the most active phases of the two processes did not coincide. Egg-production drops in the moulting birds; this depression is the greater the more intensive is the subsequent moult. The fall in egg production during moulting is also in some measure related to more general phenomena associated with the unfavourable conditions of the autumn and winter seasons. The temperature factor is known to affect gonadial function in birds (Shtraikh and Svetozarov, 1936; Vasil'ev, 1948). Nevertheless, the degree of depression of sexual activity in hens during this period is always the more marked the more intensive the moult (see also the early findings of Cramer, 1930).

Larionov showed that despite the apparent antagonism between moulting and sexual activity, the two processes were interrelated. Moulting begins earlier and is more intensive after a preceding depression of sexual activity; sexual activity can only be restored after moulting has been completed. It is known in poultry-farming that the weight of eggs increases after the hens have moulted. The completion of moulting coincides with a new phase in ovarian function.

These data seem to me to provide arguments in favour of a common regulation of the two processes and to prove that the concept of the independence of rhythmic events in the feather-forming tissue and the sexual cycle is incorrect. In the most productive birds the moult begins later and occurs at a faster rate. According to Larionov's data, the birds which reach the middle of the moulting period early have a lower annual output of eggs than those in which the first half of the moulting period is later. The rejection of birds and the formation of a brood flock according to the character of the moult is undoubtedly convenient and is based on adequate biological data.

The common regulation of the processes of reproduction and feather formation is reflected in the moulting properties in birds of different sex. Some facts characteristic of the sex differences in the moulting of birds of different sex according to the conditions of nesting have been mentioned above. In domestic fowls males begin to moult before the females. The delay in the moulting of hens may be explained by high ovarian activity. In those breeds of fowls in which the onset of plumage-formation is different, as for example in White Leghorns and Rhode Islands, there is also a subsequent difference in the duration of the moults, but this is true only of the males. The females of the same breeds show little difference in the onset of feathering and the further course of plumage renewal, this being due to the high ovarian productivity.

Sex differences are also noted in experimental moulting induced by large doses of thyroid preparations. Zavadovskii (1927) and Zavadovskii and Lipchina (1928) showed on fowls, and Voitkevich and Novikov (1931, a) on pigeons, that larger doses of thyroidin were needed to induce artificial moulting in the males than in the females. These observations were confirmed in similar investigations by Miletskaya and Lapiner (1934) and Miletskaya, Lapiner, and Damrin (1934). Moreover, the same authors showed that the intensity of artificial thyroidin-induced moulting could be reduced by simultaneous administration of thyroidin and sex hormone. Larionov (1945) demonstrated in experiments on large numbers of fowls that the feather-forming tissue in hens was considerably more sensitive to thyroid hormone than that in cockerels. During experimentally-induced moulting there is at first a sharp drop in egg production, which then rises, often exceeding that of control hens. Mass growth of feathers induced artificially in pigeons by plucking produces—as in thyroid-induced moulting—a depression of gonadial activity, which is more marked initially (Novikov and Larionov, 1936).

Experiments with castration have yielded data relevant to the common regulation of the feather forming process and gonadial activity. Zavadovskii (1922) was the first to observe changes in the onset of moulting in castrated cocks. Bel'skii (1936, a, b, 1938) established on extensive material that castrated fowls experienced continuous renewal of plumage instead of the single annual moult. The moult begins in May or June in normally moulting cocks, whereas those cocks which were castrated in the late autumn began to moult in December. Continuous moulting was also observed in castrated ducks (Shtraikh and Svetozarov, 1937, a, b, c, 1938). The renewal of feathers on the different pterylae in castrated fowls and ducks occurs in the same succession as in non-castrated birds. In fowls it begins with the shedding of the extreme proximal flight primaries, followed in strict succession by the rest of the flight feathers, moving towards the distal edge of the wing. There is a corresponding moult of the small feathers. Moulting in castrated ducks as in normal begins with renewal of the small feathers and the rectrices; after a while there is rapid renewal of flight feathers with continuing moulting of the small feathers. The time and intensity of a single moulting cycle in castrated birds does not differ from the normal. The difference between normal and castrated birds lies in the fact that in the latter another moult begins immediately after completion of the preceding one.

The birds mentioned above in which there is some autonomy from the hormonal influence of the gonads in the development of the structure and pigmentation of feathers, also show differences with respect to the cyclic processes in the feather-forming tissue. When these birds are castrated they do not undergo continuous moulting. After castration there is only some shift of the onset of the annual moult to an earlier date. The extent of this shift depends on the time of operation and is different in birds of different species.

When small passeriforms are castrated they begin to moult approximately thirty days earlier than normal ones (Novikov, 1936, a, e). Our observations on castrated adult male pigeons showed that the moult occurred about forty days earlier than normal (Voitkevich, 1940, e). When young pigeons are castrated before the juvenile moult there is only a slight shift in the times of plumage renewal. Castrated starlings, according to our observations, moult at approximately the same time as normal birds. In these birds, the duration and intensity of moulting, as well as the times of its occurrence, are unaffected by the removal of gonads. The results of castration experiments indicate that the exclusion of the sex glands in birds of one group leads to continuous moulting, whereas in other birds there is some shift in the times of onset of seasonal moulting.

A definite correlation between changes in the weight of the

gonads and of the thyroid gland during the annual cycle has been noted repeatedly in a number of the studies cited above. Riddle (1925) was one of the first to draw attention to the reciprocal relationship between the sizes of these glands in pigeons during the different seasons. Bel'skii (1940) studied the successive changes in the size and microscopic structure of the thyroid glands and the hypophysis in White Leghorn cocks and capons over a period of a year. He showed that enhanced thyroid activity could also be observed during high gonadial activity. The gonads of male and female fowls react differently to extirpation of the thyroid gland (Voitkevich, 1940, f). In a joint study with Larionov we have shown that in female pigeons the increased thyroid activity was adjusted in time to periods of egg-laying. The sex differences in thyroid function correspond to the differences in the general reactivity of male and female pigeons under conditions of thyroid-induced moulting (Voitkevich and Larionov, 1938). Comprehensive material on correlated changes in the endocrine organs in birds has been collected in a more recent survey by Benoit (1950). Thus, a rise in thyroid activity occurs in birds of high sexual productivity not only during plumage renewal but also during active reproductive activity of the gonads.

The interesting phenomenon of continuous moulting in castrated fowls and ducks cannot be explained without taking into account the changes in thyroid function. The exclusion of the thyroid gland can, in its turn, alter the character of the annual cyclic features of gonadial activity. Thus, the thyroid-ectomised starlings which were under our observation for over eighteen months remained permanently in a state of high sexual activity, as judged by the weight and microscopic structure of the testes and the yellow colour of the beak (Voitkevich, 1940, g). Other facts cited above agree in showing that removal of the thyroid gland does not exclude the possibility of the onset of moulting, that the growth of plumage is accompanied by increased thyroid activity, and that the onset of moulting is preceded by depression of gonadial activity. Without at this stage touching on the common mechanism coordinating these events, it must be stated that these inter-relationships are persistently consistent.

The depression of the reproductive and incretory activity

of the gonads during moulting is an obvious fact. This apparently favours the realisation of the proliferative potentialities of the feather-forming tissue. There seems to me to be no need to seek in this a sign of physiological antagonism between the sex and the thyroid hormones, particularly as the latter is essential for ensuring regenerative processes both in the skin and the gonads. The antagonistic factor is known to be produced in the sex gland itself. The sexual cycle of mammals serves as an example of the inhibitory rôle of the corpus luteum hormone, progesterone, with respect to the reproductive and oestrogenic ovarian function. During the period of corpus luteum hyperactivity, the hormonal balance in the body and the state of the other glands may be compared with the phenomena evoked by castration. Fraps (1949) noted that progesterone was present in the blood plasma of fowls which failed to produce eggs. Such facts and hypotheses formed the basis for testing the effect of progesterone on the moulting of birds. A number of studies along these lines have been carried out in recent times.

Shaffner (1954, a, b, 1955) first showed that fowls injected with progesterone ceased to lay eggs and underwent premature moulting. This effect is more pronounced in young fowls. Egg-laying ceases completely two weeks after the beginning of injections and accelerated moulting occurs from about the same time, its intensity being only a little lower than that of thyroxine-induced experimental moulting. The later studies by Adams (1955, 1956), Juhn and Harris (1955, 1956), and Harris and Shaffner (1957) again confirmed this phenomenon and introduced a more detailed account of some of its properties (Kobayashi, 1958). Intradermal injections of various hormones showed that only thyroxine was able to evoke and stimulate the proliferation of dormant feather germs or those activated by preliminary plucking. Progesterone has no such action. Premature moulting under the influence of progesterone also occurs in cocks but not to the same extent as in hens. The physiological interrelationships (and egg-laying) return to the pre-experimental state within twenty-five to thirty days from the last progesterone injection. According to Pino's observations (1955) artificial moulting can also be induced in fowls by injecting 2-amino-5-nitrothiazole.

When all the data discussed in this chapter are considered together, there appears to be a definite physiological relationship between reproductive processes and plumage renewal. Moulting occurs during a period of depressed sexual activity; it can be suppressed by sex hormones or induced again by progesterone. The intensity of moulting is greater the more marked is the depression of the sex glands. This fact could also be interpreted in the converse sense, that is that depression of sexual activity is more profound during intensive moulting. It follows from this that there are no reasons to suggest that the cause of these changes involves any other particular process. These causes are evidently more general in character and are controlled by general physiological regulatory factors. The trophic principle of the adenohypophysis is known to exert a stimulating effect on both thyroid and sex-gland activity. Although the hypophysis is not the only regulator of the morphogenic processes in which we are interested, it is the chief link in the transmission of environmental influences (mediated by the nervous system) to the gonads and the thyroid gland. These phenomena will be considered in the following chapters. But it can be mentioned here that the consistent interrelationship between the reproductive process and plumage renewal became established in the course of historical development. It is undoubtedly adaptive in character, since the body is unable to provide the energy and material for two powerful morphogenic processes at the same time. This has necessitated the presence of centralised coordination.

CHAPTER V

THE PITUITARY (ANTERIOR LOBE) AND FEATHER FORMATION

THE special position of the pituitary in the system of endocrine organs is determined first by its close anatomical and physiological ties with the central nervous system, the mid brain. The adenohypophysis is in direct contact with an outgrowth of the brain forming the highly vascular neurohypophysis. The most massive part of the adenohypophysis—the anterior lobe—is a glandular complex with a number of hormonal functions. The concept of pituitary activity is associated chiefly with its trophic effect on the secretory level of the other endocrine glands.

The thyrotropic effect (influencing the thyroid gland) of the active principle of the anterior lobe of the pituitary has been established experimentally for all classes of vertebrates. Larionov, Voitkevich, and Novikov (1931, b) were the first to obtain the thyrotropic effect on pigeons, observing the characteristic hypertrophy, hyperplasia, and hyperaemia reactions in the thyroid glands of the experimental birds. This effect was later demonstrated in other birds also.

The question of the site of formation of the thyrotropic principle in the adenohypophysis is still under discussion. Precise morphological criteria of the hormonal activity of the pituitary, especially in connection with the phases of the feather-forming process, could be found on a basis of sufficiently clear-cut histofunctional indices. Let us recall how the investigation of the rôle of the thyroid gland in feather formation was greatly facilitated after the discovery of indices which gave an objective evaluation of thyroid activity depending on changes in its fine microscopic structure.

The anterior lobe of the pituitary has been the subject of a great number of microscopic, physiological, and histochemical investigations. The multiplicity of function of this endocrine organ is determined by two main types of secretory cells: basophils and eosinophils. Investigation of the rôle of the pituitary in morphogenic processes cannot be carried out without a concept of the localisation of the main hormones in a concrete cytological substrate. The performance of preliminary experiments was made easier by observations on the microscopic structure of the pituitary in different animals, which demonstrated the unequal distribution of the various secretory cells in this gland (Voitkevich, 1939, d).

Thus, for example, in all the birds we examined the anterior lobe of the pituitary clearly showed two distinct areas, with basophil cells predominantly in the anterior part and eosinophil ones in the posterior part. This peculiarity of the microscopic structure of the pituitary in pigeons had been noted earlier by Zatvornitskaya and Zimnitskii (1932). Zonal differences in the adenohypophysis of fowls were described by Lektorskii (1938). The separate testing of such parts of the anterior lobe of the avian pituitary for hormonal content was complicated by the small size of the organ. It was therefore necessary to make a preliminary study of the pituitaries of large mammals, in which the zonal distribution of the two types of secretory cells is well marked. Such investigation was important, because subsequently bovine pituitaries were used as raw material for the preparation of thyrotropic hormone.

We had shown in a series of studies (Voitkevich, 1937-9) that the tissue of the basophil zone, situated in the central and anterior region of the adenohypophysis, which is easily recognised and can be distinguished microscopically, contained an active principle with biological activity which was different from that of its other part. The hormone formed in the eosinophil cells is able to stimulate the growth of a young animal without exerting any appreciable influence on the function of peripheral endocrine glands. Conversely, the active principle of the basophil cells does not affect growth but stimulates the function of other endocrine organs, includ-

ing the thyroid gland. The conclusion that the pituitary basophils had a thyrotropic action was confirmed for birds as well
by Lektorskii (1938). He also showed that the thyrotropic
properties were the exclusive prerogative of the basophil cells
and were not connected with the topographic peculiarities
of the different parts of the anterior pituitary. The immense
experimental material yielded by numerous investigations of
the histophysiology of the pituitary later made it possible to
differentiate in greater detail the fine cytological distinctions
within the group of the basophil and eosinophil cells. At the
same time additional data were obtained which confirmed
that the thyrotropic hormone was formed in a distinct group
of basophil cells. No references are given here to the appropriate literature because these data are presented very fully
in well-known textbooks on endocrinology.

THE STRUCTURE AND PIGMENTATION
OF FEATHERS

Passing now to the results on the relationship between the
trophic factor of the pituitary and feather development, let
us consider the data on the state of this gland in birds during
plumage renewal. Schooley (1937) and Schooley and Riddle
(1938) have described the anterior pituitary and its cytological
changes during ontogenesis and during the various phases of
the annual cycle in pigeons. Similar data for fowls are given
by Lektorskii (1940) and Bel'skii (1940). Differentiation of
single secretory cells becomes apparent towards the end of the
first half of embryonic development. Studitskii (1947) showed
that in the middle of the embryonic period the pituitary of
the chick embryo can activate the thyroid gland, when transplanted on chorio-allantois, on the eighth to eleventh day of
development. In the pituitary of pigeons the differentiation of
secretory cells begins relatively later. The number of basophils
increases appreciably in the first month after hatching
(Schooley, 1937), during the intensive growth of the juvenile
plumage; the eosinophils undergo differentiation fairly early
and are found in relatively large numbers in the pituitaries
of embryos during the second half of their development.

We investigated the microscopic appearance of the pituitary

in pigeons during repeated artificially induced mass growth of feathers, in other words under conditions of activated hyperactivity of the bird's own thyroid gland. Simultaneous tests were made on tadpoles, using fragments of hypophyseal tissue from experimental and control pigeons (for method see Voitkevich, 1945, e, 1948, b). The data in Table 19 can be interpreted more precisely by comparing them with the data on the state of the thyroid glands of the same birds considered

Table 19

Weight, *microscopic structure, and biological activity of the pituitary in* pigeons (mean data)

Indices	Control	Experimental series		
		I	II	III
Weight in mg	4.6	3.2	6.3	4.8
Number of basophils per field	4.4	3.5	7.5	8.1
Acceleration of tadpole metamorphosis following implantation of pigeon pituitary				
tail resorption, per cent	24.3	118.1	22.4	9.3
gut shortening, per cent	27.6	9.4	27.9	12.5

earlier in Table 10, where the details of experimental conditions are also given.

No significant changes in the structure and activity of the adenohypophysis were seen in pigeons after a single removal of plumage (Series I). Enlargement of the hypophysis was noted after repeated removal of immature feathers (Series II).

The number of basophil cells in the anterior lobe of the pituitary decreases during the initial period of mass growth of feathers. The increased outflow of hormone from the pituitary evidently occurs at the expense of basophil cell destruction as well. Subsequently, when the feather-forming tissue is again activated, the number of basophils in the pituitary exceeds the normal. The changes in the microscopic structure of the basophil cells are in a definite relationship to the total duration of continuous plumage growth. Following a single plucking, the structure of the basophil cells in the pituitaries of pigeons differed little from normal. The cytoplasm of most of the basophils was richly granular. Repeated plucking enhanced the loss of granules by the basophils and partial vacuolation of their cytoplasm; the number of such cells increased, isolated cells showing signs of degeneration with nuclear pycnosis; the remaining basophils showed characteristic loss of granules.

The resuls of tests on amphibian larvae showed that the pituitaries of normal birds had relatively more thyrotropic hormone and produced considerable acceleration of metamorphosis. The implanted pituitary stimulated the thyroid activity of the tadpoles, as established by histological examination of the appropriate part of the tadpoles. The percentage of resorption of the larval organs in the tadpoles in this series was 24·3 and 27·6 relative to the same indices in normally-developing control tadpoles. After a single plucking, the pigeons' pituitaries had less effect on the metamorphosis of tadpoles, the percentage of resorption being 19·4 and 18·1. This reflected the loss of thyrotropic hormone from the pituitary. When another period of mass growth of feathers was induced, the activity of the pituitary in the biological test became a little higher. Such an effect resembles that seen in the hypophysis of thyroidectomised birds (Lektorskii, 1940; Voitkevich, 1946; Voitkevich and Arkhangel'skaya, 1947). In both cases the absence of thyroid hormone is combined with increased thyrotropic hormone content of the pituitary. Thrice-repeated plucking is followed by marked depletion of thyrotropic hormone from the pituitary tissue. During this period the pituitaries of the pigeons show no further changes in the number of basophils, but the cytological changes noted above are in complete agreement with loss of the active principle from the pituitary tissue. It follows from such comparisons that during prolonged artificially-induced mass growth of feathers the influence of the pituitary on the thyroid gland first increases and then declines.

The functional relations between the pituitary and the thyroid during mass feather formation were further interpreted by comparison with the results of blood tests on the experimental birds (for method see Voitkevich, 1948, b). In pigeons in Series I the blood taken during the development of a large mass of feathers affected the metamorphosis of tadpoles. This influence was very slight or practically absent following a repeat activation of the mass growth of feathers

17

(see Table 11). How was the enhanced hormonal activity of the blood in pigeons after a single plucking to be explained? It was doubtless the result of a certain rise in the concentration of the thyroid hormone, since the activation of the tadpoles' own thyroid glands was slight. The thyroid glands of pigeons subjected to a single plucking showed the characteristic signs of increased secretion of hormone; the normal development of feather quills observed at this time indicated that the blood contained sufficient concentration of thyroid hormone to ensure the metabolic rate necessary for growth. After three pluckings, however, no active substances could be detected in the blood. The thyroid glands were at this time in a state of functional exhaustion; this was further confirmed by the absence of feather germ growth.

The nature of the relation between the pituitary and the feather-forming process, and the rôle of the thyroid in this connection were defined more precisely in the following experiments. Pigeons in which functional exhaustion of the thyroid glands (absence of proliferation of feather germs on most pterylae) was produced by frequently repeated removal of immature plumage were subjected to implantation of fragments of the basophil zone of the adenohypophysis of large animals. Over a period of a month these experimental birds still failed to develop their plumage, since their thyroid glands remained in a state of functional exhaustion. The additional stimulation by the hypophyseal thyrotropic hormone was ineffective under these conditions. In parallel experiments, in which the pituitary tissue was introduced into normal birds in the same amounts, there was invariably a characteristic thyrotropic effect—increased thyroid activity and stimulation of the growth of feather germs activated for development (Voitkevich, 1937, a, b). The results of this experiment confirms that the pituitary hormone only affects the thyroid gland by increasing the secretion and outflow of its hormone. The additional stimulation of the thyroid exhausted during a period of hyperactivity, however, proved to be ineffective (Voitkevich, 1937, b).

Perek, Eckstein, and Sobel (1957) made a histochemical examination of the pituitaries from moulting and laying hens. They found contrasting differences in the cytological appearance of the anterior lobe. During moulting there is an increase in the number of basophils with signs of high activity. Eosinophils, on the other hand, are activated during egg-laying. Further experiments, in which young birds were injected with diethylstilboestrol, revealed two types of cell among the basophils: thyrotropic and gonadotropic. The changes in the cytological appearance of the pituitaries of experimental pigeons during plumage renewal, described above, concerned chiefly the thyrotropic ones.

Hypophysectomy in chick embryos thirty-three to thirty-eight hours after the beginning of incubation (Fugo, 1940) leads to retardation of thyroid gland development. The absence of the hypophysis does not preclude the formation of the thyroid gland from the appropriate embryonic structures and accumulation of colloid within its small follicles. In such embryos the primary down plumage evidently develops normally, and the laying-down of the contour feather germs also occurs normally, since it is synchronised with the development of embryonic down.

The way in which hypophysectomy affects the subsequent stages of feather formation was shown by the experiments carried out by Mitchell (1929), Hill and Parkes (1934, 1935, a, b), and Lektorskii (1940). The results of hypophysectomy proved to be identical with the results observed with thyroidectomy. After hypophysectomy the feathers regenerated more slowly than normal and were lanceolate in shape. The fringe of the contour part of the vane, deprived of barbules, developed in the same way as in thyroidectomised fowls. These phenomena are explained by the fact that the thyroids of hypophysectomised birds were in a depressed state: the stretched follicles were filled with homogeneous colloid and the secretory epithelium of the follicles was greatly flattened. When thyroid hormone was given to hypophysectomised birds the feathers which developed were of normal structure and colour. The results concerning the moulting of hypophysectomised birds were doubtful, because the period of observation was not sufficiently prolonged. The data considered above indicate that the pituitary hormone must affect the feather-forming process, exerting its influence through the thyroid gland.

The physiological connection between feather formation

and the pituitary is also confirmed when the thyrotropic hormone level in the body is raised experimentally. Our first experiments in this field, performed thirty years ago, proved unsuccessful. We could not produce significant changes in feather formation in pigeons given an extract of whole fresh adenohypophysis, even when the administration of the preparation was specifically adjusted to a definite period of feather development.

The data we obtained later, during experiments on the localisation of the main hormones within the adenohypophysis, convinced us of the futility of using whole extract (Voitkevich, 1939, d). Since the thyroid-stimulating hormone is formed in the basophil cells of the pituitary (according to the latest data, in the thyrotropic cells), it is natural to assume that in the whole extract the action of the trophic component is weakened by the action of the substances formed within the eosinophils (which we confirmed experimentally). It followed from this that the presumed effect on feather formation could only be demonstrated by separate testing of the hormonal substances from the different cytologically distinct zones of the anterior pituitary.

The experiments were staged on fifteen moulting carrier pigeons, divided into three series of five birds each. In Series I the old feathers on the left wing of each bird were plucked, and this induced the development of two new coverts of flight secondaries. Concurrently, fragments of the anterior pituitary, containing predominantly either basophil or eosinophil cells, were implanted in the pigeons of the other two series. Three days later the homologous feathers on the other wing were removed and new fragments of the pituitary implanted (the fragments implanted each time weighed 200 mg each). Periodic measurements of the developing feathers showed that under the influence of the substance from the basophil zone, feather development was stimulated in a way similar to that demonstrated for treatment with thyroid preparations. We find an explanation for such coincidence of the results in the data characterising the state of the thyroid glands of the same pigeons (Table 20).

As can be seen from Table 20, the hormone formed in the basophil cells of the pituitary does stimulate thyroid activity,

Table 20

Thyroid glands of pigeons after implantation of fragments of the pituitary of different cytological appearance

Series	Weight of both lobes of the pituitary in mg	Height of epithelium μ	Internal diameter of the follicles, μ
Control	29.2	8.4	24.8
eosinophil zone .	30.2	9.9	23.8
basophil zone . .	96.0	14.0	19.4

which in turn affects the growth of feathers. Further experiments with implantation of fragments from different zones of the pituitary to birds of several species did not demonstrate any significant deviations from normal shape, structure, colour, and pattern of feathers, that is the effect was essentially the same as that produced by administration of small doses of thyroid hormone (Voitkevich, 1938, e, 1939, d). The extensive testing of hypophyseal extracts and hormones, for their effect on the structure and pattern of feathers in fowls and pigeons, showed that the peripheral effect was determined by activation of the gonads of the experimental birds (Pompen, Dingemanse, and Kober, 1933). Experiments with young birds revealed that they could undergo precocious sexual maturation accompanied by signs of sexual dimorphism in plumage (Domm, 1931; Domm and Van Dyke, 1932). Placental hormones exert a feminising oestrogen-like effect on the developing feathers of the dimorphous breeds of fowl (Juhn and Gustavson, 1930).

Experimental studies on many species and varieties of birds revealed entirely new types of dependence of the feather-forming process on hormonal influences. Our usual concepts of the morphogenic action of the pituitary is associated with its control of the functional status of the thyroid or the gonads, whose hormones in turn affect the various reproductive structures. Experiments on some species of tropical birds showed additional aspects of hormonal influences. During periods of gonadial quiescence the African weavers have a monomorphic vestiture, which the females retain during the reproductive period, although it is preceded by moulting. The male acquires a vivid black and yellow plumage and his beak becomes black. Castration of the male does not affect the colour of the plumage before or after moulting, but the beak loses its black colour and becomes white, which is the usual colour during the period of sexual quiesence. Injections of sex hormone into castrated and normal males affected only the colour of the beak, without altering the pattern of the plumage. Consequently, in this species the periodic changes in plumage colour did not depend on sex hormones. It was found further that these changes were under the control of the luteinising hormone of the anterior pituitary (Witschi, 1936). This hormone, as well as chorionic gonadotropin, induces the pattern of the nuptial plumage. This influence is exerted directly on the melanophores, by-passing the gonads, since the effect is the same in castrates. In another tropical bird, the bird of paradise, whose pattern is also indifferent to sex hormone, there is a similar physiological interdependence between plumage colour and the luteinising hormone of the pituitary, the latter affecting not only the feather-germ melanophores but also those of the beak (Watterson, 1959).

The beak melanophores have different sensitivity to sex hormones in different birds: this ranges from complete independence to a positive reaction in both sexes. Dependence on androgen is encountered more frequently than dependence on oestrogen, for there is a relationship which is the converse of that shown for the pigment cells of the feather. At the same time, in some species of birds both can react to the thyroid and pituitary hormones (Witschi and Woods, 1936; Novikov, 1936-40; Tucker, 1949).

The above data are also of general biological interest, since they demonstrate the possibility of direct action of the pituitary hormone on morphogenesis, as represented by feather formation.

PLUMAGE RENEWAL

Parallel investigations were made of the effect of the thyrotropic hormone of the pituitary on feather renewal. It had been supposed that the hormonal activation of the thyroid would stimulate moulting which had already begun, or would induce it at an unusual time. Our earlier attempts to obtain such an effect by administration of whole extracts of the adenohypophysis proved unsuccessful, for reasons explained above. We therefore resorted to separate administration of the hormone from different areas of the anterior pituitary and of pure thyrotropic hormone.

When young chicks underwent periodically repeated implantations of fragments from the basophil zone of the pituitary, their juvenile moulting was completed twelve days earlier than that of chicks which received the substance from the eosinophil zone or of control birds (Voitkevich, 1939, a). In our experiments the moulting was accelerated both in adult pigeons and in those birds which received implants from the basophil zone. The total amount (by weight) of feathers shed over a thirty-day period was three times greater than that shed by the pigeons which received the substance from the eosinophil zone or by the controls.

We used the method described by Rowland and Parkes (1934) and Kabak (1945) for the preparation of thyrotropic hormone, isolated either from the whole adenohypophysis or from the basophil zone only. We used fresh or frozen bovine pituitaries taken from the abattoir no later than twenty-four hours after the animal's death. When the whole adenohypophysis was used, the yield of thyrotropic hormone was about twelve per cent of the initial dry weight of the substance, whereas the yield was twenty-one per cent when the substance from the basophil zone was used. A suspension of thyrotropic hormone in $1/50$ N NaOH neutralised with $1/10$ N HCl was used for the injections.

Table 21 gives the results of preliminary tests of the hormone on guinea-pigs (1 ml per day), young ducklings (1 ml per day) and adult starlings (0.5 ml per day). Each time 7.5 mg of the powder was emulsified in 1 ml of liquid.

Comparison of the data in Table 21 shows that birds, like guinea-pigs, are reliable subjects for testing thyrotropic hormone (see also Kabak, 1945).

Our first experiments with administration of pure thyrotropic hormone were performed on adult birds (pigeons and starlings) during the period of their natural moulting. The

Table 21

Mean weight of thyroid glands (in mg) after five injections of thyrotropic hormone

Raw material for the preparation of the hormone	Guinea-pigs	Ducklings	Starlings
Control	16.3	22.3	10.1
Whole anterior lobe	38.7	30.3	20.6
eosinophil zone .	31.2	28.2	17.6
basophil zone . .	52.2	51.1	42.7

daily dose was increased (30 mg dry preparation emulsified in 1 ml fluid). The pigeons were divided into two series: those in which before the experiment one or two flight primaries had been replaced and those in which the number was three or four. Injections of thyrotropic hormone were continued for fourteen days. Five days after starting the injections the rate of moulting rose, but later feather replacement was slowed down. The control birds thus completed their moult before the experimental ones. Similar data were obtained in experiments on starlings (Fig. 72).

The peculiar two-phase action of the pituitary hormone was explained by microscopic examination of the thyroids from the experimental birds. It was found that the pigeons' thyroids which had hypertrophied under the influence of thyrotropic hormone (mean weight of thyroid 162 mg, as against 42 mg in the controls) underwent changes typical for the state of functional exhaustion. This occurred when the thyrotropic hormone exerted its additional effect on the thyroids already hyperactive during the natural moulting. This resulted in a rapid onset of relative athyreosis, which precluded normal feather formation.

Further experiments were performed on adult quails. Since the reasons for the need to experiment on wild birds have already been discussed, we shall not reiterate these, and will pass instead straight to the description of the results. The experiments involved twenty-four birds, divided into three groups.

The first group contained eight quails. Thyrotropic hormone was given to four birds in a dose of 0.5 ml daily for twenty days, the remaining birds in this group serving as controls.

The second group consisted of seven birds, three of which were thyroidectomised. All these birds received the same amounts of thyrotropic hormone for twelve days.

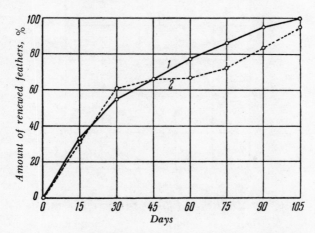

Fig. 72. Moulting of flight primaries in starlings

1, Control. 2, Under the influence of the hypophyseal thyrotropic hormone

The third group included nine normal birds to which we gave the hormone for various periods and also compared the action of the preparations obtained from different zones of the pituitary. Injections were in all cases started a month before the onset of natural moulting.

The experimental birds in the first group showed signs of the beginning of moulting on the fifth to eighth day after the first injection. During the next twenty days these birds had shed from five to seven flight feathers. Feather renewal on other pterylae was no less intensive. The control birds in this group started to moult later, approximately at the time when six or seven flight feathers had been replaced in the experimental birds (Fig. 73). Significantly, in the second group premature moulting occurred only in the normal birds which had received thyrotropic hormone. The thyroidectomised quails did not moult either during the injections or later when the control birds had begun to moult.

The third group of birds showed that in order to induce premature moulting it was sufficient to make three injections of the preparation isolated from the basophil zone. The same

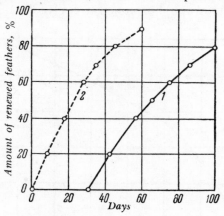

Fig. 73. Moulting of flight primaries in quails

1, Control. 2, Under the influence of the injection of hypophyseal thyrotropic hormone

result could only be obtained after six injections of the preparation obtained from the whole adenohypophysis (Voitkevich, 1940, a). Therefore, the thyrotropic substance formed in the basophil cells of the pituitary can induce premature moulting which occurs as the result of activation of the thyroid.

The peculiar physiological antagonism between the hormones formed within the basophil and the eosinophil cells was demonstrated in our experiments with joint and separate testing of areas of pituitary tissue which had a different microscopic appearance (Voitkevich, 1939). The morphogenic action of the thyrotropic hormone from the basophils was significantly inhibited by the additional administration of the substance from the eosinophil cells. The phases of high eosinophil and basophil activity in the pituitary of fowls are usually, as already mentioned, adjusted to different and mutually excluding morphogenic processes: egg-laying and moulting. The thyrotropic hormone formed in the basophils can also induce premature, accelerated moulting. The lactogenic hormone or prolactin, whose formation is more often associated with the eosinophil cells, inhibits moulting. The latter phenomenon was demonstrated experimentally on moulting pigeons by Kobayashi (1953, c). The author suggested that prolactin lowered the sensitivity of the feather germs to thyroxine. Juhn and Harris (1958) obtained even more telling results in experiments with permanently moulting capons given prolactin. These data agree with the observations on sparrows subjected to extended periods of light (Laws and Farner, 1960). The gonads were not inhibited under the influence of prolactin. Furthermore, their characteristic reaction of hypertrophy in response to prolonged exposure to light was clearly manifest.

The physiological connections between the newly formed plumage and the endocrine organs in birds have features in common with those of reptiles in which the hypophyseal influence activating the thyroid gland and hence epithelial proliferation is very prominent (Noble and Bradley, 1933; Eggert, 1935).

CHAPTER VI

THE RÔLE OF THE NERVOUS SYSTEM IN THE DEVELOPMENT AND RENEWAL OF FEATHERS

MOULTING has evolved in adaptation to environmental conditions. The connection with the environment is mediated by the nervous system which is also involved in the regulation of internal physiological processes.

The rôle of the nervous system in mediating between the environmental conditions and the functional activity of numerous organ systems in the body has been the subject of fundamental research by the Pavlovian school of physiology. Pavlov came to the conclusion that each organ was as it were under triple control. The activity of the organ depended on functional innervation, which either induced or arrested its activity, on vascular innervation, which regulated the supply and outflow of various substances, and finally on trophic innervation (involving, according to modern data, both the somatic and the autonomic nervous systems), which determined the extent of utilisation of substances in each organ in connection with the requirements of the body as a whole.

Numerous studies have been devoted to the rôle of neural connections in the processes of reparative regeneration (see the reviews by Vorontsova, 1949, and Polezhaev, 1950). These investigations proved the trophic influence of the nerves on the regeneration of various tissues and organs. Avian skin, with its highly differentiated derivatives, is not outside the sphere of influence of the nervous system. The published references to the innervation of avian skin and the rôle of neural regulation of feather-forming phenomena indicate the relative scarcity of experimental investigations in this field.

Periodic renewal of plumage is accompanied by considerable structural and physiological changes in the skin. Abundant innervation is clearly seen along the course of the large blood vessels which lie within the deep layers of the dermis (corium). The greatly branching vascular network lies directly underneath the epithelium, ensuring the vascularity of the connective tissue papillae of numerous feather germs. The enormous increase in blood supply during the period of mass feather growth leads to an increase several times over in the weight of the skin with its developing feathers, as compared to skin in its normal state.

Rakhmanov and Voznaya (1932), Dement'ev (1940, b), Troitskii (1948), and Leshchinskaya (1952) describe the innervation of the skin of various birds. The large main nerve trunks enter the various skin areas corresponding to the paired spinal nerves. The nerves pierce the lower layers of the dermis (corium), sending numerous branches under the epidermis. No simple or complex nerve endings were found directly within it. The muscles in the skin are well innervated, especially those muscle bundles which are attached to the base and walls of the feather follicles. Groups of nerve fibres which give off fine branches pierce the connective-tissue part (pulp) of the feather germ. Some of the nerve fibres which approach the feather follicle give off a number of branches which surround the base of the feather follicle. The innervation of different feather follicles is not the same; it is more abundant in the case of the follicles of large feathers. During the development of young feathers, in addition to increased blood supply, there is an intensive in-growing of new nerve fibres into the pulp of the rapidly enlarging feather quill. The highly dynamic organisation of the blood supply and innervation of the feather follicles not only manifests the high degree of trophic provision made for the morphogenic process, but also reflects the possibility of the products of local metabolism affecting the general physiological processes of the body.

Some of the experimental data collected up to now give a general idea of the influence of the nervous system on the development and renewal of feathers. But many aspects of neural regulation of the feather-forming process still remain obscure. For analytical purposes, it is convenient to distinguish between the neural regulation of general physiological processes which are connected with metabolism during the periods of moult, and the neural influences impinging on separate feather follicles with their individual properties.

Let us first consider the indirect evidence for the dependence of feather formation on the nervous system. The first phenomenon which draws attention is the parallel relationship between the seasonal changes in the environment and the annually repeated renewal of plumage which always occurs at the same time. Next there is the strict consistency in the moulting of the feathers on the different pterylae. During natural moulting there is as a rule complete symmetry in the shedding and regeneration of the large feathers on the two sides of the body. In most birds the first flight primaries to be shed are the extreme proximal feathers of the tract, one feather being shed from each wing simultaneously. After a given interval the next pair of feathers is shed. Thus all the feathers on both sides of the body are shed and renewed in strict succession. Such strict synchronisation of plumage renewal on both sides of the body and on the different pterylae, which is characteristic of naturally moulting birds, is preserved when moulting is hormone-activated at unusual times. These phenomena cannot be accounted for solely by general changes in the humoral environment, that is by the appearance of one or other hormone in the body fluids. The rôle of general humoral changes in the body must of course be taken into account for a rational explanation of the nature of moulting; however, such changes do not determine the sequence, the definite gradient in the renewal of feathers, and hence the constant consistently repeated rhythm of moulting on each tract. It is conceivable that the qualitative differences of the feather follicles, their so-called local properties, are reflected not only in the ability to form feathers with individual structure, pigmentation, and pattern, but also in different local reactivity to the influences exerted by the regulatory factors of the body. The psyiological mosaic of the feather-forming tissue's reactions, that is its capacity for regeneration within the feather follicles, is realised during moulting in a definite sequence in small well-innervated areas of the skin.

The weakened anchorage of the feather quill within the follicle also indicates a change in the properties of the feather follicles during moulting. Such anchorage depends, in particular, on the tone of the muscle bundles in the skin which are in contact with the follicular wall. It is known from experience in poultry slaughter that the method of slaughter affects the degree to which the feathers are anchored within the skin and the speed of subsequent plucking of the carcasses. If the birds are slaughtered by passing a blade through the oral cavity and cranium towards the brain stem (Khvatov, 1935), the subsequent removal of feathers is relatively easy. Injury to the medulla and the areas of the brain above it leads to a relaxation of muscle tone in the skin, and evidently to other phenomena which result in loosening of the feathers within the follicles. A change in the anchorage of old feathers in the follicles is also an important factor in the local mechanism of feather shedding during natural moulting. The dormant feather germ is known to have the ability to proliferate at any time, as soon as the old feather above has been removed. If, under the influence of a nerve impulse, the old feather is to some extent loosened within the follicle, favourable conditions are created for the development of the previously dormant feather germ, and consequently for the further extrusion of the loosened old feather.

Further, it is known that various powerful stimuli applied to the nervous system produce a series of peripheral disorders, and in particular lead to functional disturbances in the epidermis. No less well known is the rôle of nervous and psychic traumata in the pathogenesis of thyroid disorders, chiefly of the type of hyperthyroidism. Birds are no exception in this respect. Fright may cause sudden moulting. In such cases it is difficult to decide whether the sudden moult is determined directly by nerve impulses bypassing the thyroid, or acting through it, since the development of new feathers is accompanied by increased thyroid activity regardless of the cause responsible for the moult. At the same time it is obvious that nerve impulses are the primary cause of sudden plumage renewal. Of the studies concerned with 'fright moult', three of the more recent include those by Michener and Michener (1946), Dathe (1955), and Mester and Prünte (1959).

Experimental investigations of the dependence of feather formation on the nervous system were performed either under conditions of interrupted local nervous connections or with extirpation of various areas of the brain. Berdyshev (1934) studied the effect of denervation on the development of feathers in pigeons. Surgery was performed on the nerve trunks passing along the superior and inferior edges of the wing (the radial and median nerves), which innervate the follicles of the flight primaries. An incision was made in the scapular area and the appropriate nerve was exposed; a section of nerve measuring 3 mm was then excised. At various intervals after such an operation the old feathers were removed from both wings. Then the growth of five new flight feathers on the denervated and the control wings of each bird was recorded. New feather growth was shown to be retarded on the denervated wing. This retardation was more marked during the early period of feather development; it was less pronounced later. In Samuel's experiments (1870) and in our own on pigeons, all the nerves on one wing were cut by transecting the axillary plexus. The development of feathers (secondary flight coverts) on both wings was compared in the two birds. In addition to retardation of growth, the feathers on the denervated wing also showed a delay in the shedding of the external cornified sheaths from the young feather quills, accompanied by delay in the unfurling of the vanes. These experiments on local denervation indicate that the nervous system participates in the regulation of feather development. Since denervation alters the rate of development, nerve impulses evidently exert their effect on the trophic requirements of the young feather quills.

The rôle of the central nervous system in feather formation was demonstrated by Bayandurov and Pegel (1935, 1938), Belen'kii (1941, b, 1943), and Belen'kii, Tamarchenko, and Kotov (1943). These workers performed either partial or complete extirpation of the cerebral hemispheres. In birds the most complex forms of nervous activity are known to be associated not with the cortex but with the corpora striata of the hemispheres. In the first of the studies cited above, the size and topography of the excised areas of the cerebral hemispheres were varied. An effect on feather formation was observed only when both hemispheres were totally removed. Such operations are of course accompanied by considerable trophic changes in the whole body, which must be taken into account in investigating any local processes. Bilateral hemispherectomy is regarded by physiologists as very gross intervention, producing far from adequate reactions in the body; at the same time, it was Pavlov who remarked that not a single physiologist concerned with the brain could avoid this method, which, though crude, had none the less yielded many valuable results.

Bayandurov and Pegel (1935, 1938) and Bayandurov (1949) traced the changes in feather formation in fowls and pigeons after total or partial hemispherectomy. Several flight feathers and coverts were plucked at various intervals after decerebration. Their rate of growth was recorded by periodic measurements. Retardation of feather growth was noted in adult pigeons after destruction of the frontal or temporal areas of the cerebral hemispheres. More pronounced disturbances in the development of the structural elements of the vanes were seen after total bilateral hemispherectomy. The experimental birds also increased in weight (artificial feeding). When hemispherectomy was unilateral, feather formation was inhibited on one wing only, contralateral to the extirpated hemisphere. The authors obtained similar data from experiments on adult fowls.

The results obtained in experiments with young birds were different in character. Decerebration of chicks led to retardation of general development and arrest of body growth. The growth of feathers in decerebrate chicks not only was not inhibited but was to some extent accelerated, as compared with intact controls. Bayandurov (1949) explains the different results yielded by experiments on birds of different ages by differences in the metabolism of young and adult decerebrate birds. According to his data, removal of the hemispheres in young and in adult animals produces general trophic changes in the body which are opposite in character. In essence, the difference is that in adult animals the intensity of oxidative

18

processes declines, whereas in young animals, on the contrary, it rises.

Ivanova (1955) carried out a series of experiments in our laboratory on partial decerebration of young pigeons. Investigation of the method was directed especially towards discovering the earliest possible time suitable for removal of the cerebral hemispheres, i.e. long before functional differentiation of the brain and formation of the first conditioned connections. It was found that bilateral hemispherectomy on the day of the hatching of the still completely helpless pigeon did not produce such profound general trophic disturbances, during the subsequent period of development, as those observed by Bayandurov in experiments with chicks. The young pigeon without the hemispheres developed to a normal size.

The effect of the operations varied according to the nestling's stage of development. According to Bel'skii (1945), the nestling period in pigeons consists of three stages. In the first stage, as shown by Ivanova (1955), all the vital functions of the young bird are mediated by the regulatory activity of the lower parts of the brain. The young birds whose cerebral hemispheres had been removed showed only some impairment of the nestling food-reaction to the parent providers, whereas their growth followed its normal course. In the second stage there is already impairment of the neural regulation of vegetative processes and inhibition of the formation of conditioned-reflex connections. The birds' growth at this time lags somewhat behind normal, because of impaired somatic function. The formation and growth of juvenile plumage shows no appreciable deviation from normal. Later the young birds cease to grow, even when they continue to be fed intensively by the parents. Consequently, the neural activity mediated by the cerebral hemispheres is included in the complex of physiological functions of the body only during the second period of nestling development, when it comes to control the further development of the body through both the vegetative and the somatic systems.

When the growth of new feathers was activated in the experimental nestlings by preliminary removal of the precursors, separate large feathers were formed without special deviations from normal; however, when large numbers of feathers were removed, the development of new ones was manifestly retarded. The greatest retardation of feather growth was noted on the dorsal pteryla, which is the earliest to produce feathers. A similar result with respect to feather formation was obtained in young experimental pigeons completing their growth. At this age the two cerebral hemispheres were removed not simultaneously but in a given sequence, after a long interval. Thus, the natural development of plumage, as well as regeneration of individual feathers, can occur normally under altered general trophic conditions in birds deprived of their cerebral hemispheres. Under similar conditions, the growth of a large group of feathers, requiring considerable mobilisation of 'plastic' material, is inhibited.

Belen'kii (1941, b, 1943) studied the influence of partial decerebration on the development of feathers and moulting in pigeons. He observed a number of disorders in the development of feathers in hemispherectomised birds. He pointed out the significance of the nervous system not only in the regulation of the physiological processes associated with feather regeneration, but also in the more general processes of periodic moulting. Following partial decerebration of birds during natural moulting, there is retardation of feather renewal and growth, the same effect being also observed during experimental thyroid-induced moulting. The author explains the latter phenomenon by increased anchoring of the feathers within the follicles. Bayandurov (1949), on the other hand, showed increased sensitivity to thyroid hormone in partially decerebrated pigeons and fowls, leading to an earlier onset of moulting and rapid renewal of plumage in thyroid-fed birds. The conflicting experimental data of the two authors may be accounted for by a possible difference in the age of the experimental birds. At the same time, the evidence provided by these data as a whole indicates that in addition to the direct neural influence on the function of the skin, the cerebral hemispheres regulate the humoral milieu of the body, which ensures the realisation of the feather-forming process. The hemispheres are known to influence the activity of the lower parts of the central nervous system, which are directly involved in the regulation of growth and development.

In fact, the state of the endocrine organs, and in particular the thyroid, undergoes a change after hemispherectomy in birds. Strokina (1939) observed inhibition of thyroid activity in such experimental birds. Belen'kii (1943) considers that removal of the forebrain leads to an inversion of the neural mechanism which regulates thyroid hormone metabolism. Ivanova (1955) established that during the first stage of nestling development the follicles and the colloid substance were formed normally in the hemispherectomised pigeons. During the second stage the regulation of vegetative processes was impaired, with resulting atrophic changes in the thyroid epithelium, destruction of the follicles, and disturbances in the thyroid circulation. These disorders were enhanced during the later stages of development.

Anti-thyroid substances do not produce such a marked reaction in the thyroids of hemispherectomised chicks as they do under normal circumstances (Voitkevich, 1957). When small doses of thiouracil are given to chicks deprived of one cerebral hemisphere, the contralateral lobe of the thyroid shows either no crop reaction or only a slight one. This, in our view, confirms that the thyroid is not only subject to hormonal influences but is also closely connected with neural regulation.

There appears to be no need to review the literature covering the various aspects of neural regulation of the thyroid gland, since this field is outside the scope of the present study. The data considered above were presented with the limited aim of emphasising that the investigation of the complex of conditions essential for feather formation could not be carried out without taking into account the influence of the nervous system on the activity of such endocrine organs as the thyroid gland, the gonads, and the pituitary.

The consistent alternation of reproductive and moulting periods, the cyclic changes in gonadial and thyroid activity, are coordinated by the nervous system in relation to seasonal changes in the environment. The discovery of hypothalamic neurosecretion made it possible to visualise more concretely the pathways mediating the neural regulation of endocrine activity and in particular the rôle of the pituitary as an intermediary between the neural and the hormonal functions, a link transforming the nerve impulse into extensive hormonal influences on the body's tissues. Such a specific rôle of the pituitary was further elucidated by experiments which disclosed a causal relationship between animal reproduction and photoperiodicity in nature.

Nutrition and temperature are among the external factors essential for reproduction and plumage formation (Rowan, 1928; Bissonnette, 1930-33; Larionov, 1938; Kabak and Tereza, 1939; Smetnev, 1944; Polivanova, 1949). These conditions are important for both these biological processes, but they do not determine their rhythmicity. Numerous observations and experimental studies have demonstrated the determining rôle of light in the rhythmicity of reproduction in warm-blooded animals (birds and mammals) (Ivanova, 1736; Rowan, 1936, 1938; Bissonnette, 1933, 1943; Marshall, 1936; Svetozarov and Shtraikh, 1938; Polikarpova, 1940; Voitkevich, 1945, b, d; Belyaev, 1950). There have been several summaries of the factual data in this interesting field, including surveys by Bissonnette (1936), Svetozarov and Shtraikh (1940, a, d, 1941), Larionov (1945), Voitkevich (1948, c), Benoit (1950, 1957) and Farner (1961).

The dependence of animal reproduction on the natural light conditions had long been suspected, from its strictly seasonal nature. The coincidence in the time of reproduction of many warm-blooded animals, as well as the changes in the time of reproduction which occur when animals are moved to different latitudes, suggested the experimental investigation of the interrelationship between biological rhythms and the factor of natural photoperiodism. It was found that artificial prolongation of daily light, imitating the increasing length of daylight in the spring led to premature activation of the sex glands in wild and domestic birds, outside the usual reproductive period. Light deficiency was associated with depression of the sex glands (Kirkpatrick and Leopold, 1952). It was further demonstrated that the effect of light following a pathway consisting of the eyes, the optic nerve, the central part of the optic analyser in the brain, the hypothalamus, the hypophysis, and the sex glands (Benoit, 1937, 1957; Svetozarov and Shtraikh, 1940, 1941). The effect of light on the hypophysis and hence on the gonads is mediated by the nervous system.

In this way the most important endocrine organ, the pituitary, which is anatomically the most isolated from direct influences of the external environment, is the main centre for transforming the light stimuli into broad humoral effects on the body's tissues. The pituitary and the hypothalamic area of the brain are known to be part of a single morphological and functional entity.

In addition to the visceral sympathetic innervation coming from the superior cervical ganglion via the carotid plexus) which regulates the vascular bed of the pituitary, the latter also receives an enormous number of fibres from the neurons of the hypothalamic nuclei, chiefly the supraoptic and the paraventricular (Markelov, 1948). The neurosecretion produced by the neurons of these nuclei 'flows' down these fibres, which form the supraoptic-hypophyseal tract. Part of this secretion becomes modified in the proximal part of the neurohypophysis, and enters numerous capillaries of the special portal system which supplies blood to the anterior lobe of the pituitary. The remaining part of the hypothalamic neurosecretion is deposited in the distal part or posterior lobe of the neurohypophysis, which takes part in the regulation of water and mineral metabolism (see reviews by Tonkikh, 1946; Eskin, 1946, Voitkevich, 1960).

Most of the experimental studies on the hypothalamo-hypophyseal connections have been made on mammals and the lower vertebrates. The number of studies on birds is much smaller, because of the special features of the cranium and the difficulty of access to the hypothalamic area. Transection of the pituitary stalk in drakes leads to ineffectiveness of light stimulation with respect to the pituitary and the gonads (Benoit, 1937). A similar effect was observed when the pituitary stalk, that is the tract for transporting the neurosecretion, was transected in fowls (Wolfson, 1941; Shirley and Naibandov, 1956; Legait, 1956, 1958).

Assenmacher and Benoit (1956) noticed that in the Peking and Rouen breeds of duck the portal veins passing towards the anterior pituitary were not anatomically included in the pituitary stalk, but ran separately. The authors transected the stalk in these drakes, either together with the blood vessels or separately. Light stimulation produced no effect on the gonads in any of the birds with transected blood vessels. When the latter regenerated, or if the stalk only was cut, leaving the blood vessels intact, the stimulating effect of light was clearly manifest. Rupture of the portal vessels after unilateral castration also prevented the compensatory reaction of the remaining testis. These data agree in showing that blood rich in the neurosecretion is the main physiological link between the hypothalamus and the anterior pituitary. The nerve impulse, transformed into a humoral factor, passes by this bridge and is then translated into a hormonal influence upon the gonads. Such an operation results in the atrophy of the posterior pituitary and reduction of secretory cells in the anterior lobe. Histological examination of the other endocrine organs shows that the character of the changes is the same as after hypophysectomy. The thyroid glands shrink, the thyroid parenchyma shows signs of atrophy, and the capacity for assimilating radioactive iodine declines, although not to the levels typical of hypophysectomy. The birds lose weight, egg-laying ceases, and there is atrophy of the ovary, the oviduct, and the accessory structures of the head and retardation of natural moulting.

Imitation of daily light conditions in the laboratory results in stimulation of the gonads in wild and domestic birds, accompanied by rhythmic changes in the level of the basal protein and fat metabolism (Perek and Sulman, 1945; Miller, 1951, 1955; Farner, Newaldt and Irving, 1953; Farner and Wilson, 1957; Farner, 1958). Activation of the hypothalamo-hypophyseal system, together with the characteristic gonadial reaction, is confirmed by microscopic and histochemical examination of the hypothalamic neurosecretory nuclear areas and the hypophysis (Kobayashi and Farner, 1960). Various changes in the hormonal milieu of the organism in turn affect the neurosecretory activity of the hypothalamic nuclei. Thus, Legait (1958) noted that in fowls the mean diameter of the nuclei in the cells of the paraventricular hypothalamic nucleus decreased when thyroid activity was low. The diameter increases in fowls with hyperthyroidism. Characteristically, moulting fowls also have enlarged nuclei in the secretory neurons, which reflects their state of enhanced activity.

In recent times there have been scattered reports on the possibility of partial radioactive injury to individual birds, which is reflected in the state of their plumage. Thus, Harrison and

Harrison (1956) in Britain described the unseasonal appearance of nuptial plumage in the redshank, suggesting that this phenomenon was a consequence of exposure to penetrating radiation which affected the regulatory components of the reproductive process.

Light exerts its activating effect on reproduction when all the links in the chain considered above are intact. The reaction to light is not uniform in birds of different species. A common factor in the effectiveness of light stimulation for all the birds studied is the need for some minimal exposure, below which no gonadial activation takes place. Continuous exposure to lengthened daily light over a long period does not, however, maintain a high level of sexual activity. Under constant light conditions, the egg production of hens shows a tendency towards a gradual decline (Larionov, 1941, b; Byerley, 1957).

When the duration of light is decreased, or a long period of artificial daylight is suddenly replaced by a short one, sexual activity either declines or ceases, and moulting begins. Numerous experiments of this sort on different species of birds gave similar results, indicating that short periods of daily light associated with declining sexual activity are needed for the proliferation of feather germs and renewal of plumage. Sudden transition to darkness after prolonged exposure to lengthened periods of daily light produces vigorous moulting in various birds: fowls and pigeons (Larionov, 1941, a, b, 1955), starlings (Burger, 1941), turkeys (Harger and Parkes, 1957) and ducks (Van Khe-min, 1959). Characteristically, the birds react to shortened periods of daily light, or to being kept in the dark, by moulting only when they have previously been kept for a certain time under conditions of extended daily light (Kobayashi, 1953, d, 1954, b). Prolonged twenty-four hour exposure to light, on the other hand, prolongs natural moulting (Kobayashi and Okubo, 1955). The onset of juvenile moulting can be delayed and the renewal of feathers slowed down by exposing young birds to conditions of extended daily light (Plumart and Mueller, 1954; Moultrie, Muellar, and Payne, 1955).

Consequently, the apparent antagonism between the gonads and the thyroid, between reproduction and moulting, is determined by a single hypothalamo-hypophyseal complex which transforms nerve impulses into hormonal influences. Rhythmic events in the environment, the foremost among them being the solar-light radiation, affect the two morphogenic processes through the mediation of neural regulation.

CONCLUSION

THE experimental data described above provide sufficient evidence for including feather formation in the group of events whose occurence is under hormonal control. The relationship between the inherited properties of parts of the feather-forming tissue and hormonal induction is extremely complex; it is subject to very wide variations, according to the phase of the feather-forming process and the age and species of the bird. Therefore attempts at schematic treatment of the relationship between general regulatory factors of the body and feather formation may distort the essence of the morphogenic process under consideration. Nevertheless, the material presented above concerning the rôle of hormones in the development of feathers and the renewal of plumage permits certain generalisations.

First there is the complex participation of hormones in the metabolic processes which underlie feather formation. This physiological system includes at least three interacting hormones. Of the three main endocrine organs—the thyroid, the gonads, and the anterior pituitary—in the overwhelming majority of birds the two former are the most closely associated with the maintenance of the metabolic level essential for feather formation. When a comparative study of the morphogenic importance of each gland is made, the thyroid occupies the leading position, followed by the gonads. The rôle of the pituitary is different; its trophic principles affect the function of the other endocrine glands, which mediate its influence on metabolism. Analysis of the data on plumage formation during different stages of avian ontogenesis shows a gradual increase in the importance of hormonal influences. A successive change of plumage, differing in its organisation, is characteristic for most birds: primary (embryonic) is followed by nestling (juvenile) and final (definitive) vestiture. The development of each vestiture has three main successive phases: the laying-down of the germs, their proliferation, and the development and renewal of feathers.

The primary embryonic down is formed early in embryonic life, coinciding with the early differentiation of the thyroid gland. Hormonal influence becomes clear during the development of the juvenile vestiture: the laying-down of the germs of this generation of contour feathers occurs simultaneously with the development of embryonic down. When the time of formation of the germs of the juvenile plumage are compared with that of the development of the thyroid in different birds, it becomes clear that the possible influence of its hormones at this period must be minimal. Yet the process of the development of the young feathers requires increased thyroid activity.

Characteristic feathers are formed on each pteryla (for example, the flight feathers and the coverts of the wing), whose attributes reflect the properties of the different feather follicles. Development can occur within each feather follicle if the systematic thyroid hormone level is sufficiently high. In the absence of thyroid hormone, the typical course of development, in terms of both growth and differentiation, is impaired. The relationship between local properties of the feather-forming tissue and hormonal induction is far from identical during the development of various random areas of feather-forming tissue in the same bird. Thus, the physiolocal stability of the follicles of large feathers is higher than that of the small ones. The nestling plumage of a young bird develops before the onset of sexual maturity, that is outside the hormonal influence of the gonads. The structure and pigmentation of the juvenile plumage are formed under the hormonal influence of the thyroid gland.

Other relationships obtain during the development of definitive plumage. At this time the bird's body is greatly enriched by thyroid and sex hormones. The importance of the thyroid hormone for feather formation is generally similar in young and in mature birds. The feather germs of the definitive vestiture, like the juvenile, can be laid down under conditions of hypothyroidism or athyreosis. The presence of thyroid hormone, however, is essential for the growth, differentiation of structure, and formation of pattern of the feathers. The properties of the feather follicles are not constant but undergo changes during the ontogenesis of the bird. The feather follicles which at one time formed juvenile feathers later form definitive ones.

All the birds investigated so far fall into two groups with respect to the dependence of their definitive plumage's main characteristics on sex hormone. The first group consists of those birds (for example fowls, pheasants, ducks) in which the age, sexual and seasonal plumage characteristics are determined by the hormonal influence of the gonads. In these birds the definitive garb, unlike the juvenile, develops under the complex influence of at least two endocrine glands.

The plumage of the birds in the second group may, or may not differ in the two sexes; in these birds the plumage does not alter when the sex hormone level in the body is varied.

Greenwood and Blyth (1929) attempted to explain the connection between the development of plumage characterisation and hormones; as Kříženecký (1935) and other authors did later, using experiments with artificial feeding of thyroid. These authors reached the unwarranted conclusion that the sex-plumage characterisation depended on the functional state of the thyroid, allegedly different in males and in females. Later, Trinkaus (1953) also insisted on this. However, the presence of sexual differences in the activity of the thyroid in birds of different sex was not confirmed by special investigations (Voitkevich and Larionov, 1938). The weakness of the hypothesis put forward by these authors rests in the erroneous interpretation of the early experiments on thyroid administration and thyroidectomy, since it was considered that the female type of plumage developed in the former case and the male type in the latter. Our investigations did not confirm this hypothesis, and showed that thyroidectomised birds developed an entirely new type of plumage. We compared the results of thyroidectomy in birds with markedly distinct plumage characterisation, namely birds with plumage dimorphism dependent on sex hormone, birds with plumage dimorphism independent of sex hormone, and birds without sex distinctions in plumage. In all birds of these three groups the feathers which developed under conditions of athyreosis were identical in structure and very similar in the type of pigmentation. The concepts stated by the authors cited above are thus groundless. Our data suggest that the influence of sex hormone in each feather-forming process is realised only at a definite level of metabolism, which is maintained by the thyroid hormone. All the same, female plumage does not develop in thyroidectomised birds given oestrogen. Large doses of the latter only produce some modification in feather pigmentation (Blivaiss, 1947, a, b). After thyroidectomy, hypophysectomy, and transection of the pituitary stalk, that is, under conditions of hypothyroidism and athyreosis, the feathers which develop are uniform in structure and should be termed the athyreoid type of plumage.

In terms of rate of growth, differentiation of structure, pigmentation, and pattern, the development of feathers depends to a large extent on thyroid hormone. The thyroid hormone, being a powerful factor in stimulating oxidative processes, ensures that level of metabolism at which the specific influence of sex hormone becomes possible. The reaction of melanoblasts to oestrogen alters according to the level of thyroid hormone in the body (Trinkaus, 1953). We thus see that the range of thyroid-hormone influence on feather formation is considerably wider than that of sex hormone. The same relationship between the hormones is seen in the effect of thyroid hormone on the formation of regional peculiarities of plumage in many birds.

The conditions which affect the character of pigment deposition and the properties of different feather follicles must be taken into account in explaining the processes which together determine the plumage pattern in birds of a given species. The pigmentation, pattern, and structure of the feathers differ on different parts of the bird's body. An adaptational difference in the pigmentation and pattern of plumage on the dorsal and ventral aspects of the body is characteristic of most species of birds. What is the relationship between the local properties of feather-forming tissue and hormonal influence in the origin of such regional variation of plumage?

An answer to this question is to be found in the studies of Larionov (1939), Lektorskii (1940), Novikov (1946, 1949) and Voitkevich (1940, c, 1947). Larionov and Lektorskii showed that in Rouen drakes the feathers which developed on the dorsal aspect of the body following thyroidectomy had a pattern which was normally typical for the feathers on the underparts. Whereas normally the feathers on the underparts are of a light 'watered silk' appearance and those on the dorsal side are dark brown, after thyroidectomy the feathers on both sides become the same pale grey colour. The reverse picture is produced by artificial administration of thyroid (Shtraikh and Svetozarov, 1937, a). The feathers on both sides of the body become dark brown, that is, similar to those normally occuring on the dorsal side. Analogous contrasting changes in plumage under conditions of hyperthyroidism and athyreosis were obtained in a dimorphic breed of fowls (Voitkevich, 1938, g). Consequently, in extreme circumstances, such as either the absence of thyroid hormone or conversely an excess of it, the differences in the pigmentation of plumage over the different parts of the body become less marked or disappear altogether. One or other type of pigmentation becomes predominant according to sharp changes in the metabolic rate. It follows from this that the regional distinctions in plumage pattern are not determined solely by the local properties of the feather forming tissue (thresholds of sensitivity) or solely by general changes in metabolism, but are the result of the interaction of both these factors. Under ordinary conditions a given level of metabolism proves to be sufficient to ensure melanocyte activity within the feather follicles of one tract, but insufficient for another.

Such regional properties of different parts of the feather-forming tissue do not become established at once during the formation of the follicles, but develop gradually during the ontogenesis of the bird. They are very slight in nestlings and young birds, reaching a maximum with the onset of sexual maturation.

It is relevant to consider also the data on the nature of the processes underlying the geographical variation of pigmentation associated with the climatic conditions of the environment. Many studies in this field failed to provide a rational explanation of the nature of the processes responsible for such variability, chiefly because the question of its historical origin was considered separately from the development of pigmentation during the individual development of the birds. Dement'ev and Larionov (1944) postulated a hypothesis based on sufficiently solid factual considerations. Variations in pigmentation are known to result from unequal deposition of the basic pigment, melanin. The variety of melanin pigmentation is associated with different oxidation of the basic pigment and dissimilar density of deposition of its granules within the structural elements of the feather. It was discovered that the different phases of oxidation of the basic pigment corresponded to the level of thyroid hormone within the body. The concentration of thyroid hormone is one of the most important conditions for determining the level of oxidative processes, which is relevant to feather formation. For most species of birds a correspondence has been demonstrated between the metabolic level and the intensity of plumage pigmentation; the latter is more vivid in males than in females. The parallel relationship between the geographical characteristics of plumage pigmentation and the environmental temperature is not fortuitous. The intensity of the basic physiological processes is closely connected with the temperature conditions. The character of melanogenesis represents, as it were, an external manifestation of the adaptation of the metabolism and hence the vital functions of the body to definite climatic conditions. The similarity of pigmentation, determined by a definite level of oxidative processes, can be explained in the light of these data.

Two endocrine glands, the thyroid and the gonads, were the ones principally mentioned in connection with the complex nature of the hormonal influences on feather formation. The influence of the pituitary is different in that its hormones exert a regulatory effect on the activity of the thyroid gland and the gonads. At the same time, it would be fitting to recall the individual cases indicating a direct influence of the pituitary hormone on melanocyte activity, such as the experiments on the change in nuptial plumage in the weaver finch (*Pyromelana franciscana*) under the influence of the luteinising hormone of the pituitary (Witshchi, 1936). However, in this case also the pituitary hormone action becomes possible at a certain level of basal metabolism which is ensured by the thyroid hormone.

In summarising the material presented here, the following characteristic becomes apparent: the connection between the physiological processes underlying feather formation with thyroid activity is less variable in various species of birds at different stages of ontogenesis than that with gonadial activity. The dependence of feather formation on the level of metabolism, which is controlled by thyroid hormone, has been established for all the birds investigated so far. In some birds this dependence concerns the rate of feather growth and formation of vane structure, in others the pigmentation and pattern of feathers. This cannot be said of the connection between feather formation and sex glands, which has a more particular nature. It shows all variants, from complete absence of sex-hormone effect on plumage characterisation, to a manifest influence on plumage in birds of both sexes.

A study of the formation of feathers during the various periods of individual development demonstrated the character of the changing relationship between local physiological properties of the feather-forming tissue and general hormonal influences in the body. In other words, during avian ontogenesis the centralised influences coming from the nervous system through the endocrine glands become increasingly important.

A growing rôle of hormonal influence has also been noted during the main stages of development of each feather. The first stage—the laying-down of the feather germ—can occur without any appreciable dependence on hormonal influences. The development from the germ to the mature feather requires certain quantitative relationships in metabolism, determined by the hormones of the endocrine glands. The final stage for each generation of feathers—moulting (which is also the initial phase of development of the new generation) —is only possible as the result of complex hormonal influences. An attempt is made in Fig. 74 to represent schematically the increasing centralised influence on the development of successively renewed plumage and the ontogenesis of an individual feather.

In the development of each feather there is a peculiar combination of stable local inherited properties of the feather follicle and great lability with respect to influences from the dynamic *milieu intérieur* of the body. Feathers retaining the characteristics typical of a given pteryla develop under diverse conditions. When the organism is adequately saturated with thyroid and sex hormones, the feathers which develop should be termed the thyro-sexual type. In the absence of thyroid hormone, only the athyreoid (and consequently also asexual) type of feathers can develop.

The physiological basis of moulting also contains the interaction of feather-forming tissue with more general influences. This can be seen in the successive renewal of feathers on each pteryla, the interaction of adjacent feather follicles, the change in the follicular properties after completed moulting, and so on. It is not only the hormonal influence during feather regeneration that is significant for plumage renewal, but also the physiological relationships which form in the body during the period preceding moulting. Juvenile and definitive moults do not take place in the absence of thyroid hormone, but occur only if thyroidectomy is performed a long time before the onset of natural moulting. Neuro-humoral influences which precede moulting are necessary for those processes which determine the physiological readiness of the feather-forming tissue to allow proliferation of the feather germs. Late removal of the thyroid, however, does not preclude the onset of the next moult, but even so thyroidectomy does have an effect: moulting is delayed and proceeds more slowly. But the successive pattern of plumage renewal remains the same as in the normal.

The hormonal influence of the sex glands becomes as it were superimposed on that general physiological background of metabolism, which is determined by the thyroid hormone. In the period preceding the first juvenile moult there is no influence from the sex glands, since they are not yet active. The definitive moult, by contrast, is preceded by a phase of high gonadial activity. Moulting begins after a decline of the high sex-gland activity, and continues as a rule during a period of its depression. Is this a reflection of an antagonistic relationship between reproduction and moulting? There is

19

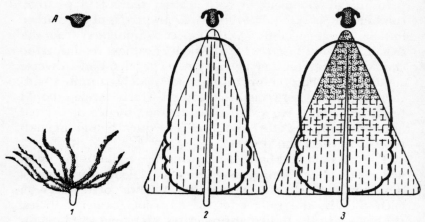

Fig. 74. Diagram illustrating the change in the role of hormonal influence in the development of different plumages and the formation of the parts of an individual feather

Germs of (1) the embryonic, (2) the juvenile, and (3) the definitive generation of feathers. The embryonic feather develops without hormonal influence; the juvenile feather develops at a high systemic level of thyroid hormone (vertical stippling); the definitive feather develops when the activity of sex hormones and pituitary hormone (horizontal stippling and dots) becomes superimposed on the background of thyroid hormone activity. The importance of thyroid hormone is relatively greater for the development of the lower part of the vanes of contour feathers

no experimental evidence to support the view that reproduction and moulting are antagonistic phenomena. Thyroid hormone is essential for both. The level of secretory activity of the thyroid, as of the gonads, depends on influences passing through the pituitary from the hypothalamus and other parts of the central nervous system.

The results of castration proved dissimilar in birds of different biological groups. In many wild birds castration is not followed by changes in the time and rate of moulting. Administration of sex hormones, as shown by Novikov (1947) also produces no change in the time of onset and rate of moulting. In other birds castration leads to a slight shift of moulting to an earlier period. In domestic birds such as fowls and ducks, thoroughly investigated in this respect, after castration the periodic renewal of plumage is replaced by a continuous succession of one moulting cycle after another.

A substantial difference between domestic birds and wild ones is the lengthened sexual cycle and increased sexual productivity in the former, which is connected with appropriate physiological tone in the systems regulating metabolism. Castration is known to be accompanied by a lowering of the tonus of the nervous system. Obviously, this change will be more marked in birds with high sexual productivity. Such birds show very pronounced changes in the pituitary following castration. This, in turn, is reflected in the activity of other endocrine glands which cannot fail to produce repercussions in hormonally-determined processes. Evidently, this may explain the difference in the reaction of feather-forming tissue to castration in different birds.

Experimental castration produces changes in the pituitary which resemble those seen after thyroidectomy. The number of basophils of altered structure increases in the anterior pituitary after castration. The amount of the trophic principle in the pituitary itself and in the humoral milieu of the body increases sharply. This is reflected, in particular, in activation of the thyroid (Bel'skii, 1940). Thyroidectomy in turn is accompanied by similar changes in the structure and activity of the pituitary. The blood of thyroidectomised birds contains more of the pituitary trophic hormone, as manifested by the uninterrupted stimulation of their sex glands (Voitkevich, 1940, g). Such data, and the fact that it is precisely in the basophil cells of the pituitary that those hormones which stimulate the thyroid and the sex glands are localised, led us to conclude that the basophils produce not a series of hormones but a single common trophic substance (Voitkevich, 1939, d, 1957).

The historically determined distribution of secretory function in the pituitary between two types of cells corresponds to the two interrelated aspects of development—growth and differentiation. The hormonal principle formed in the eosinophils is included in the complex of physiological conditions essential for the achievement of growth, whereas the hormonal principle secreted by the basophils is integrated into the hormonal activity of other glands and thus affects the differentiation of the young body. We believe that the adenohypophysis, with its two types of secretory cells, does not form a multiplicity of hormones but only two basic hormonal principles, the derivatives of each of these exhibiting *vis à vis* each other a certain physiological antagonism, as already often mentioned above.

It should be recalled in this connection that the teaching of the trophic function of the nervous system does not require the postulate that each innervated organ has its specific 'determinators' brought by nerve cell dendrites. Equally, there is no evidence for ascribing to each type of secretory cells in the pituitary the formation of a multiplicity of specific hormones. The separate phases of the secretory cycle in the development of each type of secretory cell are of course not identical and this may be reflected also in the multi-stage synthesis of the hormonal principle. The state of the body's *milieu intérieur,* into which the pituitary hormone enters, and its further modifications, cannot be excluded from the chain of conditions which are essential for the realisation of a physiological process.

The reaction of each endocrine organ to a stimulating agent is directly related to the concentration of the hormone in the humoral milieu of the body. If, by way of juxtaposition, one talks about the conditions which determine the level of activity of a gland, it must be admitted that the primary responsible factor is not the trophic hormone of the pituitary but the systemic level of the hormone of the gland concerned. This level is determined by metabolic requirements, the intensity of utilisation of the hormone in the tissues, and the corresponding compensatory stimulation by the pituitary (Voitkevich, 1948, b).

The utilisation of thyroid hormone increases during the period of mass feather formation. The possible lowering of thyroid-hormone concentration is compensated by increased thyroid-gland activity, which usually occurs in the presence of the stimulating agent from the pituitary. Consequently, thyroid-gland activity during the renewal of plumage is not the cause of moulting but a response to the body's increased requirements of thyroid hormone in connection with the development of new feathers. Uninterrupted and prolonged activation of the thyroid gland and the pituitary leads to physiological strain and functional exhaustion of the two glands, which is adequately reflected in the depression of proliferative processes within the feather-forming tissue.

The functional exhaustion of an endocrine organ, in its various gradations, evidently represents a phenomenon whose significance cannot be overlooked in analysing the periodicity of endocrine gland activity and the morphogenic processes associated with it. The activating effect of light on the animal endocrine system is consistent in character; the amount and duration of the stimulating action are of decisive importance for its concrete manifestation. There is a definite twenty-four-hour and seasonal periodicity in the alternation of the phases of light and of darkness in nature. The whole long historical pathway of adaptational modification of the animal world has been closely connected with the natural factor of a regular light régime. Experimental variations of the light conditions, as practised in the laboratory, are accompanied (as already mentioned) by corresponding functional changes in the hypo-thalamus-pituitary-gonads system. The effect of light is also mediated by other endocrine glands. Histological examination of the pituitaries of animals subjected to extended light periods showed stimulation of secretion in the basophil cells. Under these conditions there is activation not only of the gonads but also of the thyroid (Voitkevich, 1944, c, 1945, a, 1950). Novikov and Favorova (1947), by experiments on birds, confirmed that light stimulated the thyrotropic activity of the pituitary. The amount of thyrotropic hormone in the pituitary was found to increase when uninterrupted round-the-clock lighting was used for a short period. The systematic level of the hormone was also high, as judged by the signs of thyroid stimulation. When uninterrupted lighting was continued for a long time although the number of basophil cells increased, their altered structure and the small amount of thyrotropic hormone in the pituitary demonstrated the presence of functional exhaustion. This phenomenon is also confirmed by a state of hypoactivity in the thyroid gland. The functional exhaustion of the basophil cells could presumably be abolished by terminating the continuous stimulation of thyrotrophic activity. When periods of light are made to alternate with darkness, the pituitary activity returns to normal. When darkness is maintained the outflow of the hormone from the pituitary declines and some of it is stored in the basophil cells. Alternation of periods of light and darkness is essential for maintaining a certain relation within the pituitary between the phases of secretion and transfer of the hormone to the blood. The historical adaptation of secretory function occurred against the background of regular alternation of day and night.

The relationship between the length of day and night alters with the seasons of the year and it is not the same in the various latitudes. The seasonal changes in the ratio of daily light to darkness are reflected in the function of the hypothalamo-hypophyseal system. The secretory activity of the hypophysis increases with increasing duration of daily light during the spring. The possibility is not excluded that during maximal daily light under natural conditions, the basophil cells of the animal's pituitary may go through a phase of functional exhaustion. Total exhaustion of the basophil cells cannot occur in temperate latitudes, with their short period of darkness during the summer nights. In the summer-autumn period the ratio of the duration of daily light and darkness is as it were a reverse copy of the ratio during the spring-summer period. Consequently, the same phases of pituitary activity can repeat themselves during different seasons of the year. In many animals the reproductive period precedes the longest day. In nature, renewal of vestitures is adjusted to a certain interval after maximal daily light.

Experiments imitating spring-light conditions showed that activation of sex glands was none the less replaced later by a phase of depression, even under conditions of continuing intensive exposure to light. It is impossible not to associate this phenomenon with depletion of the trophic principle from the body, which is an indication of some functional exhaustion of the pituitary. The gonads can maintain a high level of activity for a prolonged period if there is stimulation by the pituitary hormone. It has been noted above that when the thyrotropic activity of the pituitary is high, sexual activity in monocyclic birds is maintained during the period which is normally one of depression (Voitkevich, 1940, g).

Many species of birds experience two moults per year, of

which one (spring) precedes the reproductive period and the other (autumn) follows it. Larionov (1945) and Novikov (1947) explain the definite sequence of these morphogenic processes by the alternation of thyrotropic and gonadotropic activity of the pituitary. Without furnishing the necessary proofs, Novikov assumes two cycles in the thyrotropic activity of the pituitary (spring and autumn) between which there is increased production of the gonadotropic hormone. We have no reason to agree with this assumption on the basis of the principle of monohormonal activity of the basophil cells of the pituitary. We postulate that the increased thyroid activity which occurs in the spring is an additional factor in the stimulation of gonadial reactivity to the increasing concentration of the pituitary hormone. The functional exhaustion of the pituitary during the period of maximal daily light must also be taken into account in explaining the cyclic periodicity of biological processes. In nature, when the length of daily light decreases the activity of the basophil cells in the pituitary is restored at some stage, and the amount of the trophic hormone becomes sufficient to stimulate thyroid activity anew. The restoration of basophil cell activity requires a certain time under conditions of diminishing daily light during the summer-autumn season. During this period the systemic concentration of the trophic hormone of the pituitary no longer reaches the level which was present during the increasing duration of daily light in the spring and ensured stimulation of the gonads. The temperature of the environment and the intensity of uptake of the thyroid hormone by the tissues are particularly important among the conditions which determine the activation of the thyroid.

The light conditions over the twenty-four hours are the main factor determining normal activity of the pituitary basophils, that is the condition which ensures thyroid activity throughout the year. Thyroid activity does not show the marked seasonal variations characteristic for the gonads of monocyclic birds. There is no reason to believe that the periodicity of plumage renewal depends on the seasonal changes in gonadial activity.

Evidently the adaptation of birds of different groups to environmental conditions differed in character, and this has become reflected in the variations of the nature, times, and intensity of reproduction and moulting. In various species of birds a common physiological mechanism has developed which coordinates reproduction and plumage renewal. The leading rôle in this mechanism belongs to the central nervous system, which receives, integrates, and mediates external stimuli which—in the form of nerve impulses—are transformed in the pituitary into broad humoral influences transmitted further to the tissues through other endocrine organs.

The accumulated experimental material suggests that functional exhaustion of the pituitary explains the physiological adaptations of the body to the successive alternation of periods of light and darkness during the twenty-four hours. Besides the many widely variable external conditions, the daily-light régime is strictly consistent for each season of the year. In the vertebrates the adaptation to this most important environmental factor has been associated with the most crucial link in the regulation of physiological processes—the diencephalic-hypophyseal system.

The cosmic factor—solar radiation—is the main source of energy for various forms of vital activity and is simultaneously the cause of the cyclic aspect in the manifestation of biological functions. The discovery of the causal relationships between seasonal rhythms of light radiation and the cyclic events in the activity of endocrine organs, and the elucidation of the ways in which these connections are realised, explain the protective plumage pigmentation, the seasonal and nuptial garbs, the moulting and sexual cycles, reproduction and seasonal migration of birds. The latter is one of the forms of historical adaptation, whose physiological basis is a curious 'focus' of two cyclically achieved generative processes in the gonads and skin. The characteristic adaptational changes in the activity of the gonads, and the character of moulting in birds which migrate over great distances, have been reinterpreted in the light of experimental studies of morphogenic processes in connection with periodicity in nature (Groebels, 1928; Marshall, 1942, Rowan, 1946; Borekhuysen, 1956; Kozlova, 1957; Wolfson, 1952, 1954, 1959).

The practical management of the feather-forming process must be based on a preliminary study of the physiological substrate of this phenomenon. Moulting in birds is associated with a number of physiological changes in the body, which are reflected in particular in the decline of the highly-active phase of sexual function. The prolonged moulting in domestic birds (six or seven months in fowls) is undoubtedly a negative factor in their productivity (egg-laying). Thus the problem of regulating the periods and rate of moulting is very important for increasing the egg-laying productivity of poultry. The correlation between the character of the moult and egg-laying has long suggested a series of zootechnical indices for bird rejection and for selecting a breeding flock (Kempster, 1925; Vernon, 1926; Marble, 1930; Tikhomirov, 1932; Larionov, 1935, a, b; Kvitko, 1935; Milochenko, Trembelev, and Baitman, 1935). The attempts to regulate moulting by administration of hormonal preparations proved unsuccessful, since the laws of normal moulting were ignored and no account was taken of the conditions required by the body for this process. Clearly, a separate link in a complex physiological chain of events, such as the thyroid hormone, considered in isolation, cannot by itself produce the whole series of processes which underlie natural plumage renewal.

In the early studies devoted to the activation of animal reproduction under the influence of light, there are repeated references to a shift in the onset of moulting corresponding to changes in the periods of reproduction. Light stimulates the development and sexual maturation of young birds, modifying the periods and rate of moulting according to the conditions (Svetozarov and Shtraikh, 1940, a, b; Novikov, Blagodatskaya, and Manzhelei, 1957). In nature, the spring moult occurs during the lengthening but still short daily light; the autumn (principal) moult coincides with the shortening of the daily-light period. The early-moulting birds are more productive in terms of egg-laying; artificial shortening of daily light provokes earlier moulting in late-moulting birds and thus improves their productivity (Moshkov, 1957). Under laboratory conditions ensuring a constant uniform light situation, the characteristic cyclic features of both morphogenic processes become blurred. In domestic fowls, as shown by Larionov (1941, a, b), constant exposure to light (from twelve to fourteen hours of daily light) leads to extension of the moulting period and to sluggishness in its course; under these conditions egg-laying drops sharply. In order to increase egg productivity, the duration of daily light is extended up to twenty-two or even twenty-four hours a day, and is then followed up with a period of darkening. Windowless chicken coops have been found convenient for regulating the sexual cycle of poultry regardless of the season of the year (Pigarev, Kostrikov, and Chavchanidze, 1956; Pigarev and Pokornaya, 1959).

Larionov (1945) has shown that differential illumination of fowls is most effective for increasing annual egg productivity. Thus, a gradual extension of daily light to seventeen or eighteen hours, followed by a sudden reduction of daily light to six hours, leads to very intensive moulting, which is completed in a month to six weeks. As the result of this, the experimental fowls experienced two periods of high egg productivity over eighteen months, separated by a short period of intensive moulting. The total egg productivity of the flock exceeded that of the controls. At present it appears feasible that for each flock of poultry the number of periods of egg-laying and of moulting could be planned for a definite time ahead, with a real promise of increasing the total index of egg productivity. For each period of egg-laying, a gradual increase of illumination to twelve hours and longer is envisaged, and for the moulting period a reduction to from six to eight hours. Thus, over a two-year period Larionov (1957) produced in 100 young Leghorns three periods of egg-laying and three moults at preplanned intervals. The shortening of the total time required for plumage removal led to a considerable increase in the total egg productivity of the experimental flock. Such interventions are successful whether the birds are kept in cages or under free-range conditions (Lehrman, 1959; Hixon, 1960). Such measures are obviously profitable, since the lengthening of daily light is achieved by supplementary electric lighting and the shortening by darkening the hen houses. The effectiveness of these measures has also been confirmed under battery conditions. Similar results are also obtained under controlled daily-light conditions in animal husbandry. Shortening the daily light after a prolonged period of extended illumination leads to premature moulting and more rapid renewal of fur in fur-bearing animals (Belyaev, 1950). Light is therefore not simply one of many factors which stimulate physiological processes, but constitutes the basic environmental condition necessary for the onset and completion of morphogenesis.

Illumination is the leading factor among the numerous conditions essential for the realisation of reproduction and moulting. When other environmental factors are favourable, variation in illumination determines the changes in the character and rate of integumental renewal in warm-blooded animals. In the case of cold-blooded animals, environmental temperature plays an important part as well as light. The experimental material accumulated so far confirms the postulated identity of the neurohumoral mechanism for all the land-inhabiting vertebrates, which underlies periodic renewal of integument and determines its consistent rhythmicality in relation to environmental factors.

REFERENCES

Bayandurov, B. I. (1949), *The trophic function of the brain*, Medgiz.

Bayandurov, B. I. and Pegel, V. A. (1935), 'The trophic function of the brain', *Trudy Tomsk. Med. Inst.*, 2, pp. 185-90.

(1938), 'The effect of hyperthyroidism on the moulting and feather depigmentation of decerebrate fowls', *ibid.*, 10, pp. 66-73.

Belen'kii, N. G. (1941 a), 'The rôle of vitamin B_1 in the regeneration of skin formations in birds', Papers presented at the first session of the Moscow Society of Physiology, Biochemistry and Pharmacology, pp. 21-2, Medgiz.

(1941 b), 'The rôle of the central nervous system in the moulting of birds', *ibid.*, pp. 22-3.

(1943) 'The rôle of the central nervous system in the moulting of birds', Reports 1 and 3, *Zap. Pushkinskoi Zootekhn. Lab.* 24, p. 17.

Belen'kii, N. G., Tamarchenko, M. E. and Kotov, M. I. (1943), 'The rôle of the central nervous system in the moulting of birds', Report 2, *ibid.*, pp. 28-32.

Bel'skii, N. V. (1936 a), 'The effect of castration on growth and plumage renewal in birds', *Trudy Inst. Eksper. Morfogeneza*, 4, pp. 349-68.

(1936 b), 'Gonadal hypertrophy in unilaterally castrated birds', *ibid.*, pp. 369-94.

(1938), 'The sex gland as a factor in the seasonal changes in the pituitary and thyroid glands', *Byul. Eksper. Biol. i Med.*, 6, 6, pp. 710-13.

(1940), 'Seasonal changes in endocrine activity in normal and castrated birds', *Uch. Zap. Mosk. Gos. Univ.*, 43, pp. 261-90.

(1945), 'The relationship between growth and differentiation in the postembryonic development of pigeons', *Dokl. Akad. Nauk SSSR*, 49, 9, pp. 712-14.

(1949), 'Nutrition in birds at various stages of development', *ibid.*, 68, 3, pp. 621-4.

BELYAEV, D. K. (1950), The rôle of light in the regulation of biological rhythms in mammals', *Zh. Obshch. Biol.*, **9**, 1, pp. 39-51.

BERDYSHEV, A. P. (1934), 'Studies on the mechanism of feather formation', *Trudy Inst. Ptitsepromyshlennosti*, **2**, 1, pp. 62-88.

BESSARABOV, V. A. (1937), 'Class selection of breeding flocks of fowls by outward characteristics', *Usp. Zootekhn. Nauk*, **5**, pp. 51-70.

BIANKI, V. L. (1911), *Birds: Columbiforms and Procellariiforms*, first half-vol., St. Petersburg.

BOGDANOV, A. (1856), Note sur le pigment des plumes d'oiseaux, *Bull. Soc. Nat. Moscow*, **29**, pp. 429-62.

 (1858 a), Etudes sur les causes de la coloration des oiseaux, *Rev. Mag. Zool.*, ser. 2, **10**, pp. 180-1.

 (1858 b), *Feather Pigmentation in Birds*, Biological Monograph, Moscow.

 (1888-92), 'Contributions towards the history of scientific and applied studies in zoology and related subjects in Russia (1850-88)', *Trudy Zool. Otdeleniya Obshchestva Lyubitelei Estestvozn., Antropol. i Etnograf.*, **I-IV**.

BORODULINA, T. L. (1960), 'The morphological features of feather anchorage in the bird's wing', *Zool. Zh.*, **39**, 1, pp. 124-35.

BUTURLIN, S. A. and DEMENT'EV, G. P. (1934), *The Birds of the U.S.S.R.*, Moscow.

COTT, H. (1950), *Adaptive Coloration in Animals*.

DARWIN, C. (1868), *Domestic Animals and Cultivated Plants*.

 (1853), *The Origin of Man and Sexual Selection* (in Rus.)

DEMENT'EV, G. P. (1940 a), 'Moulting in hawks', *Zool. Zh.*, **19**, 4, pp. 479-88.

 (1940 b), *A Handbook of Zoology*, **6**, *Birds*, pp. 21-92, Moscow.

DEMENT'EV, G. P. and LARIONOV, V. F. (1944), 'Studies on the pigmentation of vertebrates: (1) The origin of geographical variations of pigmentation', *Zool. Zh.*, **23**, 5, pp. 189-97.

DENISOVA, M. N. (1958), 'The significance of down in nidifugous birds', *Uch. Zap. Mosk. Obl. Ped. Inst.*, **65**, pp. 191-207.

DENFORS, S. (1935), 'Genetic mosaic in the feathers of the domestic fowl', *Trudy Lab. Dinam. Razvitiya*, **10**, pp. 339-44.

DUBININ, B. V. (1947), 'Moulting peculiarities of wing plumage in some passeriformes', *Priroda*, **12**, pp. 60-62.

ENTIN, T. I. (1936), 'The morphogenesis of the avian thyroid gland, *Arkh. Anat., Gistol., Embriol.*, **15**, 1, pp. 104-13.

 (1948), 'The thyroid gland of fowls under normal and experimental conditions', *ibid.*, **28**, 1, pp. 37-65.

ESKIN, I. A. (1946), 'The factors which determine the rhythm of the sexual cycle', *Usp. Sovrem. Biol.*, 22, 3, pp. 319-30.

FILATOV, D. P. (1939), *The comparative morphological direction in the mechanism of development, its object, aim and pathways*, Izd. Akad. Nauk SSSR, Moscow.

GAISINOVICH, A. E. (1961), *K. F. Vol'f and the theory of the development of the body*, Izd. Akad. Nauk SSSR.

GENKE, K. (1937), *The physiology of the garb pattern development in animals*, Biomedzig, Moscow-Leningrad.

GEORGIEVSKII, K. K. (1896), *The action of thyroid preparations on the animal body*, Thesis, St. Petersburg.

GLADKOV, N. A. and RUSTAMOV, A. K. (1949), 'The morphological and functional investigation of the wing plumage in birds (the significance of the proximal flight feathers)', *Zool. Zh.*, 28, 6, pp. 553-60.

HEINROTH, O. (1947), *The Birds*, English ed. by M. Cullen.

IVANOVA, S. A. (1936), 'Seasonal changes in the gonads and the factors which produce them', *Usp. Sovrem. Biol.*, 5, 6, pp. 34-49.

IVANOVA, T. M. (1955), 'The rôle of the cerebral hemispheres in the development of pigeons', *Zh. Obshch. Biol.*, 16, pp. 50, 63.

KABAK, Ya. M. (1945), *Practical textbook on endocrinology*, Sovetskaya Nauka, Moscow.

KABAK, Ya. M. and TAL'SKAYA, I. N. (1956), 'Destruction of the thyroid by internal ionizing radiation (radioactive iodine) and some protective methods (experiments on birds)', *Probl. Endokrinol. i Gormonoterap.*, 2, 2, pp. 3-32.

KABAK, Ya. M. and TEREZA, S. I. (1939), 'The rôle of temperature and light in the regulation of seasonal changes in the reproductive system', *Trudy Lab. Dinam. Razvitiya*, 11, pp. 227-42.

KHAKHLOV, V. A. (1927) (HACHLOW, V. A.), 'Kastrationsversuche an Dompfaffen (*Pyrrhula*)', *Arch. Entwicklungsmech.*, 110, 2, pp. 279-300.

KHOLODKOVSKII, N. A. and SILANT'EV, A. A. (1901), *European Birds*, St. Petersburg.

KHRANOVSKII, P. A. (1959), 'The morphological peculiarities of the structure of the tail and new suggestions concerning the evolution of sexual distinctions in birds', *Zool. Zh.*, 38, 12, pp. 1897-9.

KHVATOV, B. P. (1935 a), 'The mechanism of feather renewal in experimental hyperthyroidism', *Probl. Zootekhn. Endokrinol.*, 1, pp. 307-17.

(1935 b), 'The process of feather pigmentation and depigmentation in hyperthyroidism', *ibid., pp.* 318-27.

KHVATOVA, V. P. (1948), 'The rôle of the melanophores in the pigmentation of epidermal structures', *Trudy Krymsk. Med. Inst.*, 12, pp. 79-82.

KOTOVA, O. D. (1936), 'Plumage development and growth in chicks and ducklings', *Usp. Zootekhn. Nauk*, 2, pp. 475-86.

KOZLOVA, E. V. (1957), 'The relationship between seasonal migrations and periods of moulting in palaearctic wheatears', *Transactions of 2nd Baltic Ornithological conference*, Izd. Akad. Nauk SSSR, pp. 153-8.

KRIZHENETSKII, N. (1935), 'The principles underlying the analysis of the connection between the gonads with sex-linked plumage distinctions in birds', *Trudy Lab. Dinam. Razvitiya*, 10, pp. 117-136.

KÜCHLER, W. (1935), 'The histological changes associated with the secretion and resorption of colloid in the thyroid gland and their significance in the annual cycle of birds', *ibid.*, pp. 151-60.

KVITKO, N. Ya. (1935), 'Investigations of the problems of growth, feeding and rearing of birds', *Trudy Inst. Ptitsepromyshlennosti. Voronezh*, 1, 1, pp. 1-59.

LAPINER, M. N. and RADZIVON, E. N. (1934), 'The comparative effect of thyroxine and dried thyroid on moulting and feather depigmentation in fowls', *Probl. Zootekh. Endokrinol.*, 1, pp. 348-58.

LARIONOV, V. F. (1928), 'The effect of diet on the pigmentation of *Pyrrhula pyrrhula*', *Trudy Lab. Eksper. Biol. Mosk. Zooparka*, 4, pp. 121-6.

—— (1934), 'The rôle of the thyroid in plumage renewal', *Trudy Inst. Ptitsepromyshlennosti*, 2, 1, pp. 40-61.

—— (1935 a), 'An experimental investigation of the relationship between moulting and egg productivity in hens', *Usp. Zootekhn. Nauk*, 1, 3, pp. 469-76.

—— (1935 b), 'The importance of moulting in the fattening of fowls', *ibid.*, pp. 477-87.

—— (1935 c), 'Über die Veränderung der Wachstumsgeschwindigkeit der Feder während der Mauser', *Zool. Anz.*, 111, 7-8, pp. 212-19.

—— (1936 a), 'The biphasic action of the thyroid on the development of chicks', *Trudy Inst. Eksper. Morfogeneza*, 5, pp. 285-301.

—— (1936 b), 'Zur Frage der Bedeutung des Schilddrüsenhormons beim Federwechselprozess', *Biol. General.*, 12, 1, pp. 153-62.

—— (1938), 'The phenomena of hormonal induction in individual development', *Trudy Inst. Eksper. Morfogeneza*, 6, pp. 281-398.

(1939), 'Regional pigmentation and the factors responsible for it', *Dokl. Akad. Nauk SSSR*, **23**, 2, pp. 203-5.

(1940 a), 'The temperature factor and post-embryonic development of birds', *Trudy Inst. Eksper. Morfogeneza*, **7**, pp. 291-305.

(1940 b), *Textbook of Zoology: Birds*, ed. G. P. Dement'ev, **6**, Moscow.

(1941 a), 'Plumage renewal and egg-laying in birds under constant light conditions', *Dokl. Akad. Nauk SSSR*, **30**, 4, pp. 371-3.

(1941 b), 'Shortening of the moulting period in birds by a sharp change in the duration of daily light', *ibid.*, **33**, 3, pp. 227-9.

(1945), 'Plumage renewal and its connection with reproduction in birds', *Uch. Zap. Mosk. Gos. Univ.*, **88**, pp. 1-95.

(1949), 'Comparison of moulting in wild and domestic pigeons', *Okhrana Prirody*, **6**, pp. 58-65.

(1955), 'The influence of light on the moulting of birds', *Byul. Eksper. Biol. i Med.*, **40**, 10, pp. 63-5.

(1957), 'The specific influence of light on reproduction in birds', *Dokl. Akad. Nauk SSSR*, **112**, 4, pp. 779-81.

LARIONOV, V. F., BERDYSHEV, A. P. and DMITRIEVA, E. V. (1933), 'Natural moulting and its connection with egg prductivity in hens', *Trudy Inst. Ptitsepromyshlennosti*, **1**, 3, pp. 1-45.

LARIONOV, V. F. and DMITRIEVA, E. V. (1931), 'Über den Geschlechtsdimorphismus der Hühnermauser bei Schilddrüsenfütterung', *Arch. Geflügel.*, **5**, pp. 102-5.

LARIONOV, V. F., KOTOVA, O. D. and SHTRAIKH, G. G. (1933), 'The juvenile moulting of chicks and internal secretion', Report III, *Trudy Inst. Ptitsepromyshlennosti*, **1**, 3, pp. 55-62.

LARIONOV, V. F. and KUZ'MINA, N. (1931), 'Die innere Sekretion der Schilddrüse und die Dynamik der Gefiederentwicklung bei Tauben: I Federregeneration und Mauser bei der hyperthyreose', *Biol. Ztbl.*, **51**, 3, pp. 81-104.

LARIONOV, V. F., KUZ'MINA, N. and LEKTORSKII, I. N. (1933), 'The juvenile moulting of chicks and internal secretion', I, *Trudy Inst. Eksper. Morfogeneza*, **1**, pp. 46-54.

(1938), 'Skin transplants in Leghorn and Rhode Island chicks', *ibid.*, **6**, pp. 413-25.

LARIONOV, V. F. and LEKTORSKII, I. N. (1931), 'Die Flügelmauser der Hühner bei Schilddrusenfütterung', *Arch. Geflügel.* **5**, pp. 388-93.

LARIONOV, V. F. and POZIGUN, N. F. (1935), 'Changes in the rate of growth during moulting', *Trudy Inst. Eksper. Morfogeneza*, 3, pp. 215-22.

LARIONOV, V. F., VOITKEVICH, A. A. and BEL'SKII, N. V. (1934), 'Plumage regeneration in pigeons under various humoral influences', *ibid.*, pp. 161-7.

LARIONOV, V. F., VOITKEVICH, A. A. and NOVIKOV, B. G. (1931 a), 'Die innere Sekretion der Schilddrüse und die Dynamik der Gefiederentwicklung bei Tauben: IV, Die experimentelle Mauser bei verschiedenartiger Fütterung de Schilddrüsse', *Ztschr. vergl. Physiol.*, 15, 3, pp. 420-30.

(1931 b), 'Der Einfluss der Hypophyse auf die Schilddrüse bei Tauben', *Ztschr. vergl. Physiol.*, 14, 3, pp. 546-56.

(1934), 'The interaction of components in plumage regeneration', *Trudy Inst. Eksper. Morfogeneza*, 2, pp. 151-9.

LEKTORSKII, I. N. (1938), 'The state of the endocrine system in thyroidectomised chicks: (I) The anterior pituitary', *Trudy Inst. Eksper. Morfogeneza Mosk. Gos. Univ.*, 6, pp. 465-83.

(1940), 'The nature of regional differences of pigmentation in the plumage of birds', *Uch. Zap. Mosk. Gos. Univ.*, 43, pp. 243-60.

LEKTORSKII, I. N. and KUZ'MINA, N. A. (1936 a), 'Plumage development and its connection with growth in Leghorn, Rhode Island, and Plymouth Rock fowls', *Trudy Inst. Eksper. Morfogeneza*, 4, pp. 181-8.

(1936 b), 'The role of the thyroid in the development of plumage in chicks', *ibid.*, pp. 259-78.

LESHCHINSKAYA, E. M. (1952), 'Seasonal changes in the skin of mammals', *Zool. Zh.*, 31, 3, pp. 434-42.

LOPASHOV, G. V. (1945), 'The principal mechanism of feather-pattern formation', *Usp. Sovrem. Biol.*, 20, 1, pp. 121-2.

L'VOV, V. (1887), 'A comparative study and description of hair, bristle and spines in mammals and feathers in birds', *Uch. Zap. Mosk. Gos. Univ.*, 4, pp. 1-86.

MARKELEV, G. I. (1948), 'Evolutional vegetology and its problems', *Zh. Obshch. Biol.*, 9, 5, pp. 385-409.

MASHTALLER, G. A. (1940), 'Rudimentary pigmentation in birds', *Dokl. Akad. Nauk SSSR*, 29, 1, pp. 75-8.

(1940), 'Recapitulation phenomena in the development of pigmentation in birds', *ibid.*, 29, 2, pp. 153-6.

MENZBIR, M. A. (1909), *Birds*, St. Petersburg.

MILETSKAYA, S. A. and LAPINER, M. N. (1934), 'The relationship between the male sex hormone and the thyroid hormone', Report I, *Probl. Zootekhn. Eksper. Endokrinol.*, 1, 3, pp. 265-77.

288   THE FEATHERS AND PLUMAGE OF BIRDS

MILETSKAYA, S. A., LAPINER, M. N. and DAMRIN, A. (1934), 'The relationship between the male sex hormone and the thyroid hormone', Report II, *ibid.*, 1, 4, pp. 278-82.

MILOVANOV, F. N. (1934), 'The problem of thyroid administration to ducks', *ibid.*, 3, pp. 217-27.

MILOCHENKO, V. I., TREBELEV, A. M. and BAITMAN, G. G. (1935), *Egg Productivity in 'pereyarka' hens under conditions of artificial illumination*, Sbornik Opytnykh Rabot, (Tomilino) Pishcheprom, Moscow.

MIKHEEV, Z. M. (1939), 'Moulting and changes in the willow grouse (*Lagopus lagopus* L.) of the eastern palearctic', *Sb. Trud. Zool. Muzeya Mosk. Gos. Univ.*, 5, pp. 65-108.

MITSKEVICH, M. S. (1935), 'The role of hormones in the body's growth', *Sb. Rost Zhivotnykh* [Symposium *Animal Growth*], pp. 209-80, Biomedgiz.

(1947), 'Impaired development of the chick embryo as a result of the depression of embryonic thyroid activity by methylthiouracil', *Dokl. Akad. Nauk SSSR*, 58, 4, pp. 693-6.

(1949), 'Blocking of thyroid activity by methylthiouracil in the embryos of some birds', *Dokl. Akad. Nauk SSSR*, 69, 2, pp. 277-80.

(1957), *The endocrine glands in the embryonic development of birds and mammals*, Izd. Akad. Nauk SSSR.

MITSKEVICH, M. S. and MAMUL, Ya. V. (1953), 'Determination of the onset of thyroid activity in avian and mammalian embryos by means of radioactive iodine', *Dokl. Akad. Nauk SSSR*, 88, 4, pp. 733-6.

MOSHKOV, E. A. (1957), 'The dependence of egg productivity on the times of moulting in breeding turkeys with additional illumination', *Ptitsevodstvo*, 9, pp. 42-3.

NEKRASOV, A. D. (1953), 'A survey of the history of sexual selection from Darwin to the present time', in *C. Darwin, The origin of man and sexual selection*, (collected works, Russian translation, Vol. 5) Izd. Akad. Nauk SSSR, Moscow, pp. 77-118.

NIKITINA, R. V. (1955), *Adaptive peculiarities of the downy garb in some insectivorous birds*, Author's abstract of thesis, Moscow.

NOVIKOV, B. G. (1934), 'The laws of plumage development in pigeons', *Zool. Zh.*, 13, 2, pp. 235-49.

(1936 a), 'Skin transplants at various ages in Plymouth Rock chicks', *Trudy Inst. Eksper. Morfogeneza*, 4, pp. 219-27.

(1936 b), 'An analysis of sex-linked dimorphism in the passeriformes', Report I, *ibid.*, pp. 349-67.

(1936 c), 'An analysis of sex-linked dimorphism in the passeriform birds', Report II, *ibid.*, 5, pp. 359-72.

(1936 d), 'An analysis of the sex-linked dimorphism in the passeriform birds', Report III, *ibid.*, pp. 373-80.

(1936 e), 'An analysis of sex-linked dimorphism in the passeriformes', Report IV, *ibid.*, pp. 381-97.

(1938), 'An analysis of sex-linked dimorphism in the passeriformes', Report V, *ibid.*, 6, pp. 485-93.

(1939 a), 'The development of dimorphic characterisation in *Dryobates major*', *Dokl. Akad. Nauk SSSR*, 25, 6, pp. 548-9.

(1939 b), 'Gonadal control over the development of sexual characteristics', *ibid.*, pp. 550-53.

(1939 c), 'The mechanism of seasonal metamorphosis', *ibid.*, pp. 554-6.

(1939 d), 'Sexual hormone and sexual characteristics in *Perdix perdix* L.', *Izv. Akad. Nauk SSSR, Ser. Biol.* 3, pp. 422-44.

(1940), *The mechanism of the development of sexual characteristics in birds in connection with the evolution of sexual dimorphism*, author's abstract of thesis, Moscow.

(1946), 'Intracellular determination of dimorphism in the plumage pigmentation of *Passer domesticus* L', *Dokl. Akad. Nauk SSSR*, 52, 5, pp. 457-60.

(1947), 'An experimental study of periodicity in plumage renewal in birds', *Nauk. Zap. Kiiv. Derzh. Univ. im. T. G. Shevchenka*, 6, 1, pp. 229-54.

(1949), 'The regional sensitivity of plumage to hormones and its experimental investigation', *Trudy Inst. Zool., Akad. Nauk SSSR*, 2, pp. 3-11.

NOVIKOV, B. G. and BLAGODATSKAYA, G. I. (1948), 'The mechanism of the development of protective seasonal pigmentation', *Dokl. Akad. Nauk SSSR*, 41, 3, pp. 577-80.

(1950), 'The development of seasonal garb in polar animals', *Trudy Biol.-Grunt. Fak. Kiiv. Derzh. Univ. im. T. G. Shevchenka*, 5, pp. 147-68.

NOVIKOV, B. G., BLAGODATSKAYA, G. I. and MANZHELEI, V. U. (1957), 'The rearing of water-fowl during different seasons of the year', *Ptitsevodstvo*, 4, pp. 9-11.

NOVIKOV, B. G. and FAVOROVA, L. (1947), 'The effect of light on the thyrotropic activity of the pituitary in birds', *Dokl. Akad. Nauk SSSR*, 58, 4, pp. 693-6.

NOVIKOV, B. G. and LARIONOV, V. F. (1936), 'Changes in the sex gland during experimental moulting of pigeons', *Trudy Inst. Eksper. Morfogeneza*, 4, pp. 317-29.

290 THE FEATHERS AND PLUMAGE OF BIRDS

2

OGNEV, I. F. and OGNEV, S. I. (1925), 'A case of gynandromorphism in the common bullfinch', *Zool. Zh.*, 4, pp. 17-19.

PAKHMURIN, K. K. (1934), 'The dynamics of feather loosening and the onset of moulting in thyroid-fed fowls', *Probl. Zootekh. Eksper. Endokrinol*, 1, 2, pp. 209-16.

PAVLOV, I. P. (1949), 'Trophic Innervation', *Selected Writings*, pp. 67-72, Gosizdat, Moscow.

PEREDEL'SKII, A. A. (1941), 'The mechanisms of the development of skin derivatives in vertebrates', *Dokl. Akad. Nauk SSSR*, 32, 3, pp. 224-6.

PETROV, S. G. (1940), 'Parallel changes in feather pigmentation in different breeds of domestic fowls', *ibid.*, 29, 7, pp. 487-90.

PIGAREV, N. A., KOSTRIKOVA, L. A. and CHAVCHANIDZE, V. I. (1956), 'Special features of moulting in laying hens kept in cages', *Trudy Vses. Inst. Ptitsepromyshlennosti*, 6, pp. 132-7.

PIGAREV, N. V. and POKORNAYA, O. A. (1959), 'A new method of illuminating fowls which stimulates egg-laying', *Ptitsevodstvo*, 7, pp. 17-19.

POLEZHAEV, L. V. (1950), 'A method of organ regeneration in animals', *Usp. Sovrem. Biol.*, 30, 2(5), pp. 258-70.

POLIKARPOVA, E. F. (1940), 'The influence of external factors on the development of the gonad in the sparrow', *Dokl. Akad. Nauk SSSR*, 26, 1, pp. 112-15.

POLIVANOVA, T. M. (1949), 'Protein feeding of laying hens during moulting', *Trudy Inst. Ptitsevodstvo*, 20, pp. 120-211.

POPOV, A. V. (1954), 'Peculiarities of moulting of birds in mountainous regions', *Dokl. Tadzh. Filiala Akad. Nauk SSSR*, 21, pp. 135-8.

—— (1956), 'Data on the moulting of birds in mountainous regions', *Dokl. Tadzh. Filiala Akad. Nauk SSSR*, 16, pp. 89-92.

PRIKLONSKII, S. G. (1958), 'The downy garb of the young of the Lesser Great Eagle from observations carried out at the Okskii Sanctuary', *Trudy Okskogo Gos. Zapovednika*, 2, pp. 177-8.

RAKHMANOV, A. V. and VOZNAYA, V. N. (1932), 'Patho-anatomical investigation of chicks subjected to ultra-violet irradiation: the normal skin of chicks', *Zh. Elektr. S.-Kh.*, 7, pp. 23-30.

RASPOPOVA, N. A. (1930), 'The influence of the thyroid gland and thyroxine on the shedding and structure of feathers in geese', *Mediko-Biol. Zh.*, 7, pp. 47-52.

—— (1934), 'The effect of hyperthyroidism on repeated moulting in geese', *Probl. Zootekhn. Endokrinol.*, 1, pp. 158-70.

RASPOPOVA, N. A. and KHVATOV, B. P. (1935), 'The effect of different temperature factors on feather pigmentation in fowls', *ibid.*, pp. 328-34.

RAZUMOVA, L. L., LEMAZHIKHIN, B. K., LEBEDEV, L. A. and PEN'KINA, V. S. (1959), 'The differences observed in radiographic investigation of the keratin contained in the feathers of birds', *Dokl. Akad. Nauk SSSR*, 128, 1, pp. 186-9.

RUSTAMOV, A. K. (1956), *Zool. Zh.*, 35, 8, pp. 1262-4.

RYLOVNIKOV, M. P. (1934), 'The effect of the thyroid gland on the plumage of birds and its theoretical and practical significance', *Priroda*, 5, pp. 632-4.

SEVERTSOV, N. A. (1856), *Periodic phenomena in the life of the animals, birds and reptiles of the Voronezh Province*, Moscow.

SEVERTSOV, A. N. (1939), *The Morphological Laws of Evolution*, Moscow.

SEREBROVSKII, P. V. (1925), '*The role of climate in the evolution of birds*', *Byul. Mosk. Obshchestva Ispytatelei Prirody*, 34, pp. 375-415.

SHESTAKOVA, G. S. (1953), 'An analysis of the structural differences of the surface of the wings in the Laridae', *ibid.*, 32, 4, pp. 672-6.

(1956), 'The mechanics of birds' flight', *ibid.*, 35, 7, pp. 1043-50.

SHMAL'GAUZEN, I. I. (1935), 'The definition of the main concepts of growth and the methods of its investigation', Sb. *Rost Zhivotnykh*, pp. 8-60, Biomedgiz.

SHTEGMAN, B. K. (1952), 'The functional importance of the elongated proximal flight feathers in the wings of some birds', *Trudy Leningr. Obshch. Estestvo-Ispyt.*, 71, 1, pp. 30-311.

SHTRAIKH, G. and SVETOZAROV, E. (1935 a), 'Natural moulting in water-fowl: I The moulting of geese', *Trudy Inst. Ptitsepromyshlennosti*, 2, 3-4, pp. 3-33.

(1935 b), 'Natural moulting in water-fowl: II The moulting of ducks', *ibid.*, pp. 34-61.

(1935 c), 'A method of collecting feathers and down based on natural moulting', *ibid.*, pp. 62-96.

(1936), 'The importance of temperature and sex hormone in the moulting of birds', *Dokl. Akad. Nauk SSSR*, 13, 2, pp. 153-6.

(1937 a), 'The morphogenic rôle of the thyroid gland in the feather-forming process', *ibid.*, 14, 5, pp. 411-26.

(1937 b), 'The factors which determine the process of plumage renewal', *Izv. Akad. Nauk SSSR (Ser. Biol.)*, 3, pp. 533-58.

(1937 c), (STREICH, G. u. SWETOSAROV, E.), 'Über die Schnelligkeit des Federwachstrums', *Zool. Jahrb.*, 57, 3, pp. 235-74.

(1938), 'The morphogenic rôle of the thyroid gland in the

feather-forming process', *Trudy Inst. Eksper. Morfogeneza*, **6**, pp. 441-9.

SHUL'PIN, L. M. (1940), *Ornithology*, Izd. Leningradskogo Gosudarstvennogo Universiteta.

SMETNEV, S. I. (1944), 'The control of egg productivity in hens by the method of all-year-round management of the flock', *Trudy Selsko-Khoz. Akad. im. K. A. Timiryazeva*, **26**, pp. 5-54.

SNIGIREVSKII, S. I. (1950), 'The moulting of the Tetraonidae family, order Galliformes, in *Symposium dedicated to the memory of Academician Sushkin*, Izd. Akad. Nauk SSSR, pp. 215-36.

STEGMAN, B. (1956), 'Über die herkunft des flüchtigen rosenroten federpigments', *J. Ornithol.*, **97**, **2**, pp. 204-5.

STROKINA, O. S. (1939), Histostructural changes in the thyroid gland of animals subjected to cerebral hemispherectomy', *Trudy Tomsk. Med. Inst.*, **11**, pp. 151-7.

STUDITSKII, A. N. (1947), *The endocrine correlations of the embryology of the higher vertebrates*, Izd. Akad. Nauk SSSR.

SVETOZAROV, E. and SHTRAIKH, G. (1938), 'Light and the periodicity of morphogenic proceses in birds', *Dokl. Akad. Nauk SSSR*, **20**, **4**, pp. 327-31.

⸺ (1939), 'Comparative morphology of the feather in poultry', *Izv. Akad. Nauk SSSR (Ser. Biol.)*, **5**, pp. 800-22.

⸺ (1940 a), 'The importance of light for general growth and sexual maturation in birds', *Uch. Zap. Mosk. Gos. Univ.*, **43**, pp. 261-90.

⸺ (1940 b), 'The hormonal mechanism of moulting in birds', *ibid.*, **27**, pp. 392-6.

⸺ (1940 c), 'The importance of light in the sexual development of birds', *ibid.*, pp. 397-400.

⸺ (1940 d), 'Light and sexual periodicity in animals', *Usp. Sovrem. Biol.*, **12**, **1**, pp. 25-51.

⸺ (1941), 'The extrinsic and intrinsic factors in sexual periodicity', *ibid.*, **14**, **1**, pp. 1-29.

SYRNEV, P. Ya. (1924), 'The effect of feeding thyroid to fowls', *Kazansk. Med. Zh.*, **6**, pp. 17-28.

TIKHOMIROV, B. M. (1932), 'A new principle of judging strong and weak chicks', *Sov. Plitsevodstvo*, **7**, pp. 37-9.

TONKIKH, A. V. (1946), 'New data on the physiology of the pituitary', *Usp. Sovrem. Biol.*, **21**, **3**, pp. 305-22.

TROITSKII, I. A. (1948), *The physiology and hygiene of the skin of farm animals*, Sel'khozgiz. Moscow.

TUGARINOV, A. Ya. (1932), *The Birds of the USSR: Ducks, geese, and swans*, Izd. Akad. Nauk SSSR, Leningrad.

(1941), *Fauna of the USSR: Birds, Vol. I, The Lamellirostres*, Leningrad.

VAN KHE-MIN (1959), 'A method of forced moulting in Peking ducks', *Ptitsevodstvo*, 4, pp. 25-7.

VASIL'EV, G. A. (1948), 'New aspects in the theory of the thermo-regulatory rôle of nuptial behaviour in male birds', *Okhrana Prirody*, 5, pp. 40-7.

VASIL'EV, Yu. A. and VOITKEVICH, A. A. (1939), 'The development and behaviour of young thyroidectomised rooks', *Dokl. Akad. Nauk SSSR*, 22, 6, pp. 377-82.

VOITKEVICH, A. A. (1934 a), 'The state of the endocrine system during plumage development', *Trudy Inst. Eksper. Morfogeneza*, 2, pp. 169-88.

(1934 b), 'The internal secretion of the thyroid gland and the course of development of plumage in pigeons: VI, Changes in the properties of pterylae after moulting', *ibid.*, pp. 195-200.

(1934 c), 'The interaction of various components in the re-generation of plumage', *Biol. Zh.*, 11, 1, pp. 30-40.

(1934 d), 'The rôle of the feather follicle in the developing feather', *Zool. Zh.*, 13, 2, pp. 250-7.

(1935 a), 'The activation of feather germs during their forma-tion', *Dokl. Akad. Nauk SSSR*, 3, 9, pp. 425-8.

(1935 b), 'Some laws of the development of the thyroid in the higher vertebrates', *Trudy Inst. Eksper. Morfogeneza*, 3, pp. 169-214.

(1936 a), 'The influence of regenerative processes in the skin on the rate of feather development', *ibid.*, 4, pp. 239-44.

(1936 b), 'The relationship between growth and differentia-tion in the course of feather development', *ibid.*, pp. 245-57.

(1936 c), 'The structure and biological activity of the mam-malian and avian thyroid at various temperatures', *ibid.*, pp. 279-90.

(1936 d), 'Demonstration of the presence of thyroxine in the tissues of thyroid-fed pigeons by the tadpole method', *ibid.*, pp. 311-15.

(1936 e), 'The source of material for the formation of feather germs', *ibid.*, 5, pp. 265-84.

(1936 f), 'Experiments on thyroid administration to young pigeons', *ibid.*, pp. 303-13.

(1936 g), 'An analysis of the rôle of the thyroid gland in plumage development', *ibid.*, pp. 315-29.

(1936 h), 'Studies on the development of the avian thyroid', *ibid.*, pp. 343-57.

(1936 i), 'The presence of thyroxine in the organs of pigeons during artificial hyperthyroidism and hyperactivity of the bird's own thyroid gland', *Fiziol. Zh. SSSR*, **21**, 4, pp. 605-11.

(1937 a), 'The influence of the anterior pituitary on the thyroid and on feather formation in pigeons', *Dokl. Akad. Nauk SSSR*, **17**, 3, pp. 157-60.

(1937 b), 'The mechanism of the effect of the basophil elements of the anterior pituitary on the plumage of birds', *ibid.*, **7**, pp. 439-40.

(1937 c), 'The rôle of the humoral milieu and tissue permeability in physiological regeneration', *Zool. Zh.*, **26**, 1, pp. 47-54.

(1938 a), 'The connection between the laying-down and growth of feathers and thyroid activity', *Trudy Inst. Eksper. Morfogeneza*, **6**, pp. 426-34.

(1938 b), 'The state of the thyroid gland during feather formation in adult fowls', *ibid.*, pp. 435-40.

(1938 c), 'The presence of thyroxine in the organs of pigeons subjected to thyroid administration at various ages', *ibid.*, pp. 457-64.

(1938 d), 'The role of the thyroid hormone in feather formation in fowls and pigeons', *Dokl. Akad. Nauk SSSR*, **19**, 6-7, pp. 553-6.

(1938 e), 'The effect of the substances from the different zones of the anterior pituitary on chicks', *ibid.*, **20**, 7-8, pp. 637-40.

(1938 f), 'The effect of thyroidectomy on the development of ducklings', *ibid.*, **21**, 4, pp. 402-4.

(1938 g), 'Are the changes in the structure and shape cf the feather following thyroidectomy a sign of its masculinisation?', *ibid.*, **7**, pp. 357-60.

(1939 a), 'The influence of the substances from the various zones of the anterior pituitary on the development of chicks', *Fiziol. Zh. SSSR*, **26**, 6, pp. 340-9.

(1939 b), 'The biological activity of the thyroid glands of pigeons subjected to thyroid administration at different ages', *ibid.*, **27**, 1, pp. 101-7.

(1939 c), 'The method of thyroidectomy performed on birds', *Izv. Akad. Nauk SSSR*, (*Ser. Biol.*), **3**, pp. 469-83.

(1939 d), 'Investigation of the morphogenic rôle of the pituitary in connection with the localisation of the principal hormones in the anterior lobe', *ibid.*, **5**, pp. 720-40.

(1940 a), 'The effect of the pituitary on plumage renewal in birds', *Dokl. Akad. Nauk SSSR*, **26**, 4, pp. 414-16.

(1940 b), 'The differences within the thyroid gland at different periods of moulting in birds', *ibid.*, 5, pp. 519-21.

(1940 c), 'The special features of hormonal determination in feather development', *ibid.*, 7, pp. 721-4.

(1940 d), 'The hormonal determination of the feather pattern in *Asio flammeus* L. and *Asio otus* L.', *ibid.*, 27, 2, pp. 134-7.

(1940 e), 'Moulting in thyroidectomised and castrated pigeons', *ibid.*, 3, pp. 287-90.

(1940 f), 'Sexual distinctions in the gonadal activity of thyroidectomised fowls', *ibid.*, 7, pp. 737-9.

(1940 g), 'The dependence of seasonal periodicity in gonadal changes on the thyroid in *Sturnus vulgaris*', *ibid.*, pp. 740-4.

(1940 h), 'The hormonal control of plumage characterisation in *Sturnus vulgaris*', *ibid.*, 29, 1, pp. 68-71.

(1943), 'The growth and differentiation of thyroidectomised young of *Phalacrocorax carbo* L. and *Pelecanus onocratalus* L.', *Byul. Eksper. Biol. i Med.*, 16, 2, pp. 21-4.

(1944 a), 'Experience in the thyroidectomy of the heron birds', *ibid.*, 17, 7-8, Nos. 1-2, pp. 73-6.

(1944 b), 'The development of the thyroid in the cormorant', *Dokl. Akad. Nauk SSSR*, 44, 2, pp. 69-92.

(1944 c), 'The effect of light on the thyrotropic activity of the anterior pituitary', *ibid.*, 45, 8, pp. 377-80.

(1944 d), 'The dependence of thyroid activity on the light-activated pituitary', *ibid.*, 9, pp. 416-20.

(1945 a), 'The effect of thyroidectomy on the growth and differentiation of *Sturnus vulgaris*', *ibid.*, 46, 8, pp. 368-72.

(1945 b), 'Photo-stimulation of the sexual cycle in *Sciurus vulgaris*', *ibid.*, 47, 1, pp. 75-6.

(1945 c), 'The rôle of the thyroid hormone in the growth and differentiation of *Phalacrocorax carbo* L.', *Izv. Akad. Nauk SSSR (Ser. Biol.)*, 1, pp. 23-54.

(1945 d), 'The importance of the light regime for the thyrotropic activity of the pituitary', *ibid.*, 4, pp. 385-95.

(1945 e), 'The biological activity of the thyroid and the anterior pituitary', *Fiziol. Zh. SSSR*, 31, 5-6, pp. 332-47.

(1946), 'Post-thyroidectomy change in the amount of thyrotropic hormone in the pituitary', *Izv. Akad. Nauk SSSR (Ser. Biol.)*, 1, pp. 117-34.

(1948 a), 'The peculiarities of the reaction of the avian thyroid and pituitary to thioureate', *Vestn. Akad. Nauk Kaz. SSR*, 8(41), pp. 46-53.

(1948 b), 'The principles of humoral regulation of post-embryonic morphogenesis: 1, The dependence of thyroid and pituitary activity on the regenerative processes in the body', *Zh. Obshch. Biol.*, 7, 1, pp. 13-30.

(1948 c), 'Light and the endocrine system', *Priroda*, 2, pp. 34-39.

(1950), 'The rôle of the light factor in the trophic function of the basophil elements of the anterior pituitary', *Nauchn. Izv. Kazakh. Med. Inst.*, 9, pp. 77-96.

(1957), *The antithyroid activity of sulphonamides and thioureates*, Medgiz.

(1960), 'Neurosecretion and the Endocrine Organs', in symposium, *Sovrem. Vopr. Endokrinol.*, Medgiz.

Voitkevich, A. A. and Arkhangel'skaya, N. (1947), 'Changes in the thyrotropic activity of the avian pituitary after castration and thyroidectomy', *Dokl. Akad. Nauk SSSR*, 57, 9, pp. 971-5.

Voitkevich, A. A. and Epshtein, A. S. (1936), 'The morphogenic action of pteryolsate', *Probl. Endokrinol.*, 5, pp. 26-33.

Voitkevich, A. A. and Kostin, I. A. (1947), 'Reaction of the feather-forming tissue to changes in thyroid activity produced by thiouracil administration', *Byul. Eksper. Biol. i Med.*, 24, 9, pp. 161-4.

Voitkevich, A. A. and Larionov, V. F. (1938), 'Sexual dimorphism in the structure and biological activity of the thyroid in pigeons', *Trudy Inst. Eksper. Morfogeneza*, 6, pp. 451-6.

Voitkevich, A. A. and Novikov, B. G. (1934), 'The internal secretion of the thyroid gland and the course of plumage development in pigeons: V, The significance of the various periods in experimental moulting', *ibid.*, 2, pp. 189-94.

(1936 a), 'Skin autotransplants in pigeons', *ibid.*, 4, pp. 209-218.

(1936 b), 'Seasonal changes in some endocrine organs and moulting in *Passer domesticus* L.', *ibid.*, 5, pp. 331-41.

Voitkevich, A. A. and Vasil'ev, Yu. A. (1939), 'Further data on the effect of thyroidectomy on the nidifugous birds', *ibid.*, 25, 4, pp. 338-41.

Volchanetskii, I. B. (1948), 'Transformation of the pigmentation and pattern of plumage in woodpeckers', *Okhrana Prirody*, 5, pp. 54-65.

Vorontsova, M. A. (1949), *Organ regeneration in animals*, Sovetskaya Nauka, Moscow.

Zatvornitskaya, Z. A. and Zimnitskii, V. S. (1932), 'The thyroid gland under experimental conditions', *Arkh. Anat., Gistol., Embriol.*, 11, pp. 114-26.

(1932), 'The avian pituitary in the light of experimental data', *ibid.*, pp. 127-34.

ZAVADOVSKII, B. M. (1923), 'The effect of thyroid feeding on fowls', *Zap. Univ. im. Sverdlova*, 1, pp. 1-20.

(1924 a), 'Hyperthyroidism in fowls', *ibid.*, 2, pp. 175-85.

(1924 b), 'The effect of single doses of thyroid on fowls', *Fiziol. Zh.*, 7, pp. 256-65.

(1924 c), 'The effect of thyroxine on moulting and feather pigmentation in fowls', *ibid.*, pp. 266-70.

(1925), 'A new group of morphogenic functions of the thyroid gland', *Vestn. Endokrinol.*, 1, 2, pp. 91-113.

(1927), 'The inter-relationship of the thyroid and sex glands in the fowl', *Zh. Eksper. Biol. i Med.*, 5, pp. 344-71.

(1932), *Internal secretion in the service of poultry farming*, Moscow.

ZAVADOVSKII, B. M. and LIPCHINA, P. A. (1928), 'Further data on the relationship between the sex glands and the thyroid', *Zh. Eksper. Biol. i Med.*, 9, pp. 477-91.

ZAVADOVSKII, B. M. and PEREL'MUTER, Ts. M. (1926), 'The fate of thyroxine in the blood and tissues of fowls fed on thyroid', *ibid.*, pp. 35-48.

ZAVADOVSKII, B. M. and ROKHLINA, M. L. (1926), 'The effect of experimental hyperthyroidism on various species of birds', *ibid.*, 4, pp. 28-34.

ZAVADOVSKII, M. M. (1922), *Sex and the Development of its Characteristics*, Moscow.

(1928), 'Does the age-linked dimorphism in birds depend on the sex gland?', *Trudy Lab. Eksper. Biol. Mosk. Zooparka*, 4, pp. 74-82.

(1929), 'The rôle of the thyroid gland in determining sexual dimorphism in birds', *ibid.*, 5, pp. 143-52.

(1933), 'Some laws of the humoral interaction of the organs and tissues of the developing body', *Usp. Sovrem. Biol.*, 2, pp. 86-103.

ZAVADOVSKII, M. M. and BELKIN, R. I. (1929), 'The effect of thyroid preparations on the pigmentation and shape of feathers in normal and castrated pheasants', *Trudy Lab. Eksper. Biol. Mosk. Zooparka*, 5, pp. 121-40.

ACKERSON, C. W., BLISH, M. J. and MUSSEHE, F. E. (1926), 'The endogenous nitrogen of hens as affected by moulting', *Poultry Sci.*, 5, 1, pp. 153-5.

(1928), 'The rate of wing moult of hens', *Poultry Sci.*, 7, 4, pp. 177-80.

ADAMESTEANU, I. and SUTEANU, E. (1960), 'Feather-picking inducts', *Monatsh. Veterinaermed.* 15, pp. 56-57.

ADAMS, J. L. (1955), 'Progesterone-induced unseasonable moult in single comb White Leghorn pullets', *Poultry Sci.*, 34, 3, pp. 702-7.

(1956), 'A comparison of different methods of progesterone administration to the fowl in affecting egg production and moult', *Poultry Sci.*, 35, 2, pp. 323-6.

ADLERSPARRE, A. (1938), 'Einiges über Pigmentstoffwechsel und andere Farbenmodifikationen bei Gefangenschaftsmilieu', *Ornithol. Monatsber.*, 46, pp. 1-5.

(1939), 'Über das Verhalten zweier Pyromelana-Arten bei karotinoidreicher und karotinoidarmer', *Kost. J. Ornithol.* 87, pp. 24-7.

AERBY, C. (1885), 'Die Herkunft des Pigments im Epithelium', *Zbl. Med. Wiss.*, 23, 2, pp. 273-5.

AGAR, W. E. (1924), 'Experiments with certain plumage colour and pattern factors in poultry', *J. Genet.*, 14, 2, pp. 265-72.

ALDRICH, E. C. (1956), 'Pterylography and moult of the Allen humming-bird', *Condor*, 58, 2, pp. 121-33.

ALLEN, J. A. (1896), 'Alleged changes of colour in the feathers of birds without moulting', *Bull. Am. Museum Nat. Hist.*, 8, 3, pp. 13-44.

ANON (1948), 'Change of colour in plumage without a moult', *Avicult. Mag.*, 54, pp. 80-89.

ASSENMACHER, J. and BENOIT, J. (1956), 'Nouvelles recherches sur les relations entre la neurosécrétion hypothalamique, le systeme portail hypophysaire et l'activité gonadotrope de la préhypophyse', *Compt. Rend. Acad. Sci. Paris*, 242, pp. 2986-8.

AUBER, L. (1955), 'Cortex and medulla of bird-feathers', *Nature*, 176, 4495, pp. 1,218-19.

(1957), 'The structure producing non-iridescent blue colour in bird feathers', *Proc. Zool. Soc.*, London, 129, 4, pp. 455-486.

(1958), 'Magenta colour in feathers: parallelism', *ibid.*, 100, 4, pp. 571-81.

AUBER, L. and APPLEYARD, H. M. (1951), 'Surface cells of feather barbs', *Nature*, 168, 4278, pp. 736-7.

(1955), 'The structure of the feathers in Chlorophanes and Iridiphanes (Coeredidae)', *ibid.*, 97, 2, pp. 252-8.

AUBER, L. and MASON, M. V. (1955), 'Structurally coloured pattern marks on the inner webs of flight feathers', *ibid.*, 97, 2, pp. 259-265.

BÄHRMANN, U. (1958), 'Zur Mauser einiger Rabenvögel', *Vogelwelt*, 79, 5, pp. 129-35.

BAIRD, J. (1958), 'The postjuvenal moult of the male brown-headed cowbird, (Molothrus ater)', *Bird-Band.*, 29, 4, pp. 224-8.

BECKER, R. (1959), 'Die Strukturanalyse der Gefiederfolgen von Meganodius freycinet und ihre Beziehung zu der Nestlingsdune der Hühnervögel', *Rev. Suisse Zool.*, 66, 3, pp. 411-527.

BEEBE, C. W. (1908), 'Preliminary report on an investigation of the seasonal changes of colour in birds', *Am. Naturalist*, 43, pp. 17-20.

BENAZZI, M. (1929), 'Contributo alla istofisiologia della ghiandola tiroide', *Arch. Ital. Anat. Embriol.*, 27, pp. 296-322.

—— (1932), 'Appunti sulla istifisiologia della ghiandola tiroide embrionale', *ibid.*, 30, pp. 452-68.

BENDELL, F. (1955), 'Age, moult and weight characteristics of blue grouse', *Condor*, 57, 6, pp. 354-61.

BENOIT, J. (1924), 'Action de la castration sur le plumage chez le coq domestique', *Compt. Rend. Soc. Biol.*, 90, pp. 450-53.

—— (1934), 'Activation sexuelle obtenue chez le canard par l'éclairement artificiel pendant la periode du repos génital', *Compt. Rend. Acad. Sci.*, 199, pp. 1671-3.

—— (1937), 'Facteurs externes et de l'activité sexuelle. II Étude du méchanisme de la stimulation par la lumiere de l'activité testiculaire chez le canard domestique. Rôle de l'hypophyse', *Bull. Biol. France et Belgique*, 71, pp. 393-437.

—— (1950), 'Les glandes endocrine', in *Traité de Zoologie*, 15, pp. 290-334, Paris.

—— (1957), 'Radiation lumineuse et activité sexuelle du canard', *Rev. Suisse Zool.*, 64, pp. 577-87.

BENOIT, J. and ARON, M. (1934), 'Sur le conditionnement hormonique du dévelopement test, culaire chez les oiseaux: resultat de la thyroidectomie chez le coq et le canard', *Compt. Rend. Soc. Biol.*, 116, pp. 221-3.

BIEDERMANN, W. (1926-8), 'Vergleichende Physiologie des Integuments der Wirbeltiere, I-IV', *Ergeb. Biol.*, 1-4, pp. 1-342, 388-525, 360-680.

BIGALKE, R. C. (1956), *Über die zyklischen Veränderungen der Schilddrüse und des Körpergewichtes bei einigen Singvögel im Jahresablauf*, Doct. Dissert., Goethe Univ., Frankfurt am Main, 270.

BISSONNETTE, T. H. (1930), 'Studies on the sexual cycle in birds', *Am. J. Anat.*, 45, 2, pp. 289-302.

(1931 a), 'Studies on the sexual cycle in birds, IV', *J. Exptl. Zool.*, 58, 2, pp. 281-313.

(1931 b), 'Studies on the sexual cycle in birds, V', *Physiol. Zool.*, 4, 4, pp. 542-74.

(1933), 'Light and sexual cycles in starlings and ferrets', *Quart. Rev. Biol.*, 8, pp. 201-8.

(1936), 'Sexual photoperiodicity', *Quart. Rev. Biol.*, 11, 2, pp. 371-86.

(1937), 'Photoperiodicity in birds', *Wilson Bull.*, 49, pp. 241-270.

(1943), 'Some studies on photoperiodicity in animals', *Trans. N.Y. Acad. Sci.*, 5, 2, pp. 43-57.

BISSONNETTE, T. H. and CHAPNICK, M. H. (1930), 'Studies on sexual cycle in birds II', *Am. J. Anat.*, 45, 2, pp. 307-31.

BLANCHARD, B. D. and ERIKSON, M. (1949), 'The cycle in the Gambel sparrow', *Univ. Calif. Publ. Zool.*, 47, pp. 255-318.

BLIVAISS, B. B. (1946), 'Feather growth rates in thyroidectomised hens following administration of thyroxin', *Proc. Soc. Exptl. Biol. Med.*, 63, 1, pp. 98-100.

(1947 a), 'Interrelations of thyroid and gonad in the development of plumage and other sex characters in brown Leghorn rooster', *Physiol. Zool.*, 20, 1, pp. 67-107.

(1947 b), 'Development of secondary sexual characters in thyroidectomised brown Leghorn hens', *J. Exptl. Zool.*, 104, 2, pp. 267-309.

BOASE, H., 'Notes on the display nesting and moult of the mute swan', *Brit. Birds*, 52, 4, pp. 114-23.

BOETTICHER, H. (1950), 'Etwas über die Gefiederfärbung und Zeichnung der Spechte', *Zool. Anz.*, 145, 2, pp. 280-97.

BOLLIGER, A. and VARGA, D. (1960), 'Cholestanöl in avian plumage', *Australian J. Exptl. Biol. Med. Sci.*, 38, pp. 265-9.

BONG, C. J. (1913), 'On a case of unilateral development of secondary male characters in a pheasant', *J. Genet.*, 3, 2, pp. 205-216.

BOWERS, D. E. (1959), 'A study of variation in feather pigments of the wren', *Condor*, 61, 1, pp. 38-45.

BRADWAY, W. (1929), 'The morphogenesis of the thyroid follicles of the chick', *Anat. Record*, 42, 1, pp. 157-67.

BRALIS, A. (1931), 'L'influence de l'hyperthyroidisation experimental sur le plumage des oiseaux carnivores', *Acta Biol. (Stockholm)*, 2, 1, pp. 23-25.

BRODKORB, P. (1951), 'The number of feathers in some birds', *Quart. J. Florida Acad. Sci.*, 12, 4, pp. 241-5.

BROCKHUYSEN, G. J. (1956), 'Moult adaptation in relation to long-distance migration', *Nature*, 178, 4531, pp. 489-90.

BRUGE, H. (1956), 'Le plumage des oiseaux', *Naturalistes belges*, 37, 5-6, pp. 89-104.

BUCHTALA, H. (1910), 'Über den Schwefel und Cystingehalt der Keratine von Geflügelarten', *Z. Physik. Chem.*, 69, pp. 310-313.

BURGER, J. W. (1941), 'Experimental modification of the plumage cycle of the male European starling (*Sturnus vulgaris*)', *Bird-Band.*, 12, pp. 27-9.

BYERLY, T. (1957), 'Light and egg production', *Poultry Sci.*, 36, 3, pp. 465-9.

CARIDROIT, F. (1933), 'Dimorphisme sexuel des remiges secondaires dans la race de canards *Khaki Campbell*', *Compt. Rend. Soc. Biol.*, 113, pp. 236-8.

    (1943), 'Effect of total thyroidectomy on crest and plumage of golden Leghorn rooster', *Compt. Rend. Soc. Biol.*, 137, pp. 163-164.

CARIDROIT, F. and REGNIER, V. (1934), 'Conditionnement de la forme et de la pigmentation des remiges secondaires de la cane de Rouen', *Compt. Rend. Soc. Biol.*, 115, pp. 371-2.

CARINS, I. M. (1951), 'Induction of regional specificity in feather structure', *Anat. Record*, 111, pp. 36-7.

CHARLES, D. R. and RAWLES, M. E. (1940), 'Tyrosinase in feather germs', *Proc. Soc. Exptl. Biol. Med.*, 43, 1, pp. 55-8.

CARLISLE, G. (1925), 'Some observations on the base-pennulum ratio and angural ratio of barbules of the primaries in various groups of birds', *ibid.*, 12, 1, pp. 1-4.

CARLSON, A. I., ROOKS, J. R. and MACKIE, J. F. (1912), 'Attempt to produce experimental hyperthyroidism in mammals and birds', *Am. J. Physiol.*, 30, 1, pp. 129-59.

CHADBOURNE, A. P. (1897), 'The spring plumage of the bobolink with remarks on colour change and moulting', *Auk*, 14, 2, pp. 16-19.

CHAMPY, C. (1935), 'Recherches sur l'action des glandes génitales sur le plumage des oiseaux', *Arch. Anat. Microscop. Morphol. Exptl.*, 31, pp. 146-270.

CHAMPY, C. and DEMAY, M. (1933), 'Étude du mécanisme de l'influence de la chalone ovarienne sur les plumes', *Compt. Rend. Soc. Biol.*, 112, pp. 865-70.

CHAMPY, C. and MORITA, J. (1928), 'Détermination thyroiden de la poussée du plumage adulte chez les poulets', *Compt. Rend. Soc. Biol.*, 99, pp. 1116-18.

CHANDLER, A. (1916), 'A study of the structure of feathers with reference to their taxonomic significance', *Univ. Calif. Publ. Zool.*, 13, 11, pp. 238-49.

CHU, J. P. (1940), 'The endocrine system and plumage types: III Further experiments on the relation between the thyroid gland and plumage patterns in domestic fowls and ducks', *J. Genet.*, 39, 4, pp. 493-501.

CHURCH, A. H. (1869), 'Turacin: a remarkable animal pigment containing copper', *Nature*, 48, pp. 209-11.

CLEMENT, C. (1876), 'Note sur la structure microscopique des plumes', *Bull. Soc. Zool. France,* 1, pp. 63-5.

COCK, A. G. and COHEN, J. (1958), 'The melanoblast reservoir available to feather papillae', *J. Embryol. Exptl. Morphol.*, 6, 4, pp. 530-45.

COHEN, J. (1959), 'The pigment cell system in the Light Sussex fowl', *J. Embryol. Exptl. Morphol.*, 7, 3, pp. 361-74.

COLE, L. J. and HUTT, F. B. (1929), 'Further experiments on feeding thyroid to fowls', *Poultry Sci.*, 7, 1, pp. 60-6.

COLE, L. J. and REID, D. H. (1924), 'The effect of feeding thyroid on the plumage of the fowl', *J. Agr. Res.*, 29, pp. 285-7.

COLLINS, W. M. and WENTWORTH, H. (1958), 'Influence of plumage colour on hatching ratio and growth rate in chickens', *Poultry Sci.*, 37, 1, pp. 69-77.

COTT, H. B. (1940), *Adaptive coloration in animals,* London.

CRAMER, A. (1930), 'Wie man die Legatätigkeit während der Vollmauser erhält', *Deut. Landwirtsch. Geflügel,* 9, pp. 1099-1102.

CRAWFORD, G., BRANDT, W. and FRIEL, D. D. (1960), 'Iridescent colours of hummingbird feathers', *J. Opt. Soc. Am.*, 50, 10, pp. 1005-16.

CREW, F. A. E. (1925), 'Rejuvenation of the aged fowl through thyroid medication', *Proc. Roy. Soc. Edinburgh*, 45, pt. 3, 21, pp. 252-60.

(1927), 'Die Wirkung der Schilddrüssenektomie am hennengefiederten Hahn', *Arch. Geflügel.*, 1, pp. 237-9.

CREW, F. A. and MUNRO, S. (1939), 'Lateral asymmetry in the fowl', *Proc. World's Poultry Congr. Exposition, 7th,* pp. 66-9.

CRUICKSHANK, E. M. (1929), 'Observations on the iodine content of the thyroid and ovary of the fowl during the growth, laying and moulting period', *Biochem. J.*, 23, pp. 1044-9.

DANFORTH, C. H. (1929 a), 'The effect of foreign skin on feather pattern in the common fowl (*Gallus domesticus*)', *Arch. Ent-wicklungsmech.*, 115, 2, pp. 242-52.

(1929 b), 'Genetic and metabolic sex-differences: the manifestation of a sex-linked trait following skin transplantation', *J. Heredity*, 20, 7, pp. 319-22.

(1931), 'Persistence of contrasex skin grafts in the fowl', *Verhandl. 2 internat. Kongr. Sexforsch.*, pp. 171-2.

(1933), 'Genetic factors in the response of feather follicles to thyroxin and theelin', *J. Exptl. Zool.*, 65, pp. 183-98.

(1937 a), 'An experimental study of plumage in Reeves pheasants', *J. Exptl. Zool.*, 77, 1, pp. 1-12.

(1937 b), 'Pigment cells in heterogenous feathers', *Anat. Record*, 68, 4, pp. 461-8.

(1939 a), 'Direct control of avian colour pattern by the pigmentoblasts', *J. Heredity*, 30, 2, pp. 133-76.

(1939 b), 'The interrelation of genetic and endocrine factors in sex', in *Sex Internal Secretions*, pp. 328-50, Baltimore.

(1944), 'Relation of the follicular hormone to feather form and pattern in the fowl', *Yale J. Biol. Med.*, 17, pp. 13-18.

DANFORTH, C. H. and FOSTER, F. (1927), 'Skin transplantation as means of analysing factors in production and growth of feather', *Proc. Soc. Exptl. Biol. Med.*, 25, 2, pp. 75-7.

(1929), 'Skin transplantation as a means of studying genetic and endocrine factors in the fowl', *J. Exptl. Zool.*, 52, 3, pp. 443-470.

DATHE, H. (1955), 'Über die Schreckmauser', *J. Ornithol.*, 96, 1, pp. 5-14.

DAVIS, H. B. (1889), 'Die Entwicklung der Feder und Beziehungen zu anderen Integumentgebilden', *Morphol. Jahrb.*, 15, 5, pp. 560-645.

DAVIS, J. and DAVIS, B. S. (1954), 'The annual gonad and thyroid cycle of the English Sparrow in southern California', *Condor*, 56, 5, pp. 328-45.

DESSELBERGER, H. (1929), 'Über die Bildung des Lipochroms der Vogelfeder', *Ornithol. Monatsber.*, 37, pp. 97-101.

(1930), 'Über das Lipochrom der Vogelfeder', *J. Ornithol.*, 78, pp. 328-76.

DOMM, L. V. (1927), 'New experiments on ovariotomy and the problem of sex inversion in the fowl', *J. Exptl. Zool.*, 48, 1, pp. 31-173.

(1931), 'Precocious development of sexual characters in the fowl by homeoplastic hypophyseal implants: I The male; II The female', *Proc. Soc. Exptl. Biol. Med.*, 29, pp. 308-12.

(1939), 'Modification on sex and secondary sexual characters in birds', in *Sex and Internal Secretion,* pp. 227-327, Baltimore.

(1948), 'Plumage and other sex characters in thiouracil treated Brown Leghorn fowl', *Am. J. Anat.,* 82, 2, pp. 167-201.

DOMM, L. V. and BLIVAISS, B. B. (1944), 'Modifications in feather pattern and growth rate following administration of thiouracil in Brown Leghorn fowl', *Proc. Soc. Exptl. Biol. Med.,* 57, 3, pp. 367-8.

(1946), 'Modification in feather pattern and growth rate following thiouracil medication in the domestic fowl', *Anat. Record,* 94, 1, pp. 68-9.

DOMM, L. V., JUHN, M. and GUSTAVSON, R. G. (1939), 'Plumage test in birds', in *Sex and Internal Secretions,* pp. 328-56, Baltimore.

DOMM, L. V. and VAN DYKE, H. B. (1932), 'Precocious development of sexual characters in the fowl by daily injection of hehin: I The male; II The female', *Proc. Soc. Exptl. Biol. Med.,* 30, 1, pp. 349-53.

DORRIS, F. (1936), 'Differentiation of pigment cells in tissue cultures of chick neural crest', *Proc. Soc. Exptl. Biol. Med.,* 34, pp. 448-9.

(1938), 'The production of pigment in vitro by chick neural crest', *Arch. Entwicklungsmech.,* 138, 3, pp. 323-34.

(1939), 'The production of pigment by chick neural crest in grafts to the 3-day limb bud', *J. Exptl. Zool.,* 80, 3, pp. 315-345.

DORST, J. (1950), 'La coloration du plumage chez les oiseaux', *Sci. Bologna,* 85, pp. 311-15.

(1951), 'Contribution a l'étude du plumage des Trogonides', *Bull. Museum, Hist. Nat.,* 22, 2, pp. 639-99.

DRIESEN, H. H. (1953), 'Über die Einwanderung diffuser Pigmente in die Federanlage', *Z. Zellforsch.,* 39, 2, pp. 121-51.

(1955), 'Vogelfedern unter dem Mikroskop', *Mikrokosmos,* 44, 9, pp. 196-202.

DRIESEN, H. H. and VÖLKER, O. (1953), 'Die diffusen Federpigmente des Wellensittichs (*Melopsittacus undulatus*) bei Thyroxine-Mauser', *Naturwiss.,* 40, 2, pp. 61-2.

DRZEWICKI, I. (1929), 'Über den einfluss der Schilddrüsen extirpation auf die Zauneidechse', *Arch. Enwicklungsmech.,* 114, 2, pp. 155-76.

DUNN, L. C. and LANDAUER, W. (1930), 'Studies on the plumage of silver spangle fowl: I, the expression of the spangled pattern during growth', *Bull. Storrs. Agr. Exptl. Stat.,* 163, pp. 12-16.

DWIGHT, J. (1900 a), 'The plumages and moults of the indigo bunting (*Passerina cyanea*)', *Science*, 11, pp. 627-30.

(1900 b), 'The sequence of plumages and moult of the passerine birds of New York', *Ann. N.Y. Acad. Sci.*, 13, 1, pp. 73-360.

(1925), 'The gulls (Laridae) of the world: their plumages, moults, variations, relationships and distribution', *Bull. Am. Museum Nat. Hist.*, 52, pp. 28-32.

EASTLICK, H. L. (1938), 'A study of pigmentation in the chick embryo by means of limb bud transplantation', *Genetics*, 24, 1, pp. 98-9.

(1939 a), 'The pigment-forming capacity of the blastoderm of Barred Plymouth Rock embryos as shown by transplants to White Leghorn hosts', *Anat. Record*, 73, 2, (Suppl.), pp. 64-5.

(1939 b), 'The point of origin of the melanophores in chick embryos as shown by means of limb bud transplants', *J. Exptl. Zool.*, 82, 2, pp. 131-58.

EGGERT, B. (1935), 'Zur Morphologie und Physiologie der Eidechsen-Schilddrüse', *Z. Wiss. Zool.*, 147, 2, pp. 205-62.

ELDERN, G. (1936), 'Über die Ziechnung der Vogelfedern (auf Grund von Melaninfärbung) und die Phylogenie der Fesermuster', *Jena Z. Naturwiss.*, 70, 5, pp. 399-428.

ELTERICH, C. F. (1936), 'Über zyklische Veränderungen der Schilddrüse in den einzelnen Geschlechtsphasen der Tauben', *Endokrine*, 18, pp. 31-7.

EMMENS, C. W. and PARKES, A. S. (1940), 'The endocrine system and plumage types: II The effects of thyroxin injections to normal caponised and thyroidectomised caponised birds', *J. Genet.*, 39, 4, pp. 485-92.

ENGELMANN, C. (1959), 'Über die Befiederung des Flügels beim Hühnerküken', *Arch. Geflugel. und Kleintierkunde*, 8, 8, pp. 243-52.

ESPINASSE, P. G. (1936), 'Bilateral gynadromorphism in feathers', *Nature*, 138, pp. 645-6.

(1939), 'The developmental anatomy of the Brown Leghorn breast feather and its reactions to oestrone', *Proc. Zool. Soc. London*, 109, pp. 247-88.

EWALD, I. and ROCKWELL, D. (1890), 'Extirpation der Thyroidea an Tauben', *Pflüger Arch.*, 47, 4-5, pp. 160-70.

FARNER, D. S. (1958), 'Photoperiodism in animals with special reference to avian testicular cycles', *Photobiol. Proc. 19th Ann. Biol. Colloquim*, Oregon, pp. 17-29.

(1961), 'Comparative physiology: photoperiodicity', *Ann. Rev. Physiol.*, 23, pp. 71-96.

FARNER, D. S., NEWALDT, L. R. and IRVING, S. D. (1953), 'The role of darkness and light in the photoperiodic response of the testes of white-crowned sparrows', *Biol. Bull.*, 105, 5, pp. 434-41.

FARNER, D. S. and WILSON, A. C. (1957), 'A quantitative examination of testicular growth in the white-crowned sparrow', *Biol. Bull.*, 113, 3, pp. 254-67.

FATIO, V. (1866), 'Des diverses modification dans les formes et la coloration des plumes', *Mem. Soc. Phys. Hist. Nat. Genève*, 18, 2, pp. 249-308.

FAULKNER, G. H. (1932), 'Observations on physiological factors influencing the genetic coloration of fowl plumage', *Arch. Entwicklungsmech.*, 26, 6, pp. 663-73.

FEHRINGER, O. (1912), 'Untersuchungen über die Anordnungsverhältnisse der Vogelfedern, insbesondere der Fadenfedern', *Zool. Jahrb. Abt. System.*, 133, pp. 32-8.

FISCHER, H. and HILGER, J. (1924), 'Zur Kenntnis der natürlichen Porphurine: VIII Über das Vorkommen von Uroporphurin (als Cu-Salz: Turacin) bei Turacos', *Z. Physiol. Chem.*, 138, pp. 54-60.

FOULKS, J. G. (1943), 'An analysis of the source of melanophores in regenerating feathers', *Physiol. Zool.*, 16, 3, pp. 352-80.

FRANCK, D. and EPPRECHT, W. (1959), 'Zur Kopfgefiedermauser der Lachmöwe (*Larus ridibundus* L.) im Frünjahr', *Ornithol. Beobacht*, 56, 4, pp. 101-9.

FRANK, F. (1939), 'Die Färbung der Vogelfeder durch Pigment und Struktur', *J. Ornithol.*,

FRAPS, R. M. (1938 a), 'Effects of thyroxin and female hormone on one phase of saddle feather development', *Proc. Soc. Exptl. Biol. Med.*, 38, 2, pp. 201-5.

(1938 b), 'Differential gradient functions in the feather germ', *Physiol. Zool.*, 1, 2, pp. 187-201.

(1949), 'Progesterone in blood plasm of cock and nonovulating hens', *Science*, 109, 2837, pp. 493-4.

FRAPS, R. M. and JUHN, M. (1936), 'Developmental analysis in plumage: II Plumage configuration and the mechanism of feather development', *Physiol. Zool.*, 9, 3, pp. 319-75.

FRIANT, M. (1947), 'Le développment de la ptérylose, au cours de l'ontogenie, chez les passeriformes', *Bull. Soc. Zool. France*, 72, pp. 114-17.

FRIELING, H. (1936 a), 'Die federn', in *Kleintier und Pelztier*, 12, 2, pp. 1-6, Leipzig.

(1936 b), 'Das Federkleid', in *Kleintier und Pelztier*, 12, 4, pp. 1-74, Leipzig.

FUGO, N. M. (1940), 'Effects of hypophysectomy in the chick embryo', *J. Exptl. Zool.*, 85, 3, pp. 271-91.

GADOW, H. (1882), 'On the colour of feathers as affected by their structure', *Proc. Zool. Soc. London*, 11, pp. 409-21.

GALLIEN, L. and PERO, R. (1950), 'Effects du thiouracil sur le plumages des poussins de la race Faverolles saumonée', *Compt. Rend. Acad. Sci.*, 228, pp. 866-7.

GERBE, Z. (1877), 'Sur les plumes du vol et leur mue', *Bull. Soc. Zool. France*, 2, pp. 44-9.

GERICKE, A. M. (1934), 'The thyroid and other endocrine glands in relation with plumage colour in fowls', *S. African J. Sci.*, 31, 4, pp. 415-24.

—— (1958), 'Lateral asymmetry in plumage colour and crest in geese', *World's Poultry Sci. J.*, 14, 1, pp. 16-20.

GERICKE, A. M. and PLATT, C. S. (1932), 'Feather development in barred Plymouth Rock chicks', *Bull. New Jersey Agr. Exptl. Stat.*, 543, pp. 29-34.

GIACOMINI, E. (1924), *Colour changes in plumage of poultry after thyroid administration*, Rept. 2nd World's Poultry Congr., pp. 45-7.

—— (1926), 'Le recenti ricerche sperimentali intorno all'influenza della tiroide sullo sviluppo sulla muta, sul colorito é sulla struttura del piummagio. degli uccelli', *Bull. Soc. Ital. Biol. Sperim.*, 1, 5, pp. 449-56.

GIERSBERG, H. (1923), 'Zur Entstehung der Vogeleifärbung', *Biol. Zbl.*, 43, 2, pp. 167-8.

GIERSBERG, H. and STADIE, R. (1933), 'Zur Enstehung der gelben und roten Gefiederfarben der Vögel', *Z. Vergleich. Physiol.*, 18, 6, pp. 696-708.

GILLHAM, E. H. (1959), 'Variation of plumage colorations in the pochard *Aythya ferina* (Linnaeus) and the tufted duck *Aythya fuligula* (Linnaeus)', *Bull. Brit. Ornithol. Club*, 79, 5, pp. 87-8.

GLASEWALD, F. K. (1926), 'Zur Frage der Übergänge zwischen dunklen und hellen Melaninen', *J. Ornithol.*, 64, 3, pp. 241-54.

GLAZENER, F. W. and JULL, M. A. (1946), 'Effect of thiouracil on naturally occuring moult in the hen', *Poultry Sci.*, 25, 3, pp. 533-5.

GOESSLER, E. (1938), 'Untersuchungen über die Entwicklung und Entstehung von Gefiederaberrationen', *Arch. Klaus-Stift.*, 13, 6, pp. 495-666.

GOFF, R. A. (1949), 'Development of the mesodermal constituents of feather germs in chick embryos', *J. Morphol.*, 85, 3, pp. 443-74.

GÖHRINGER, R. (1951), 'Vergleichende Untersuchungen über das Juvenil- und Adultkleid nei der Amsel (*Turadus merula*) und beim Star (*Sturnus vulgaris*)', *Rev. Suisse Zool.*, **58**, 3, pp. 279-358.

GOODALE, H. D. (1914), 'A feminised cockerel', *J. Exptl. Zool.*, **20**, 5, pp. 421-30.

(1918), 'Feminised male birds', *J. Genet.*, 3, pp. 17-26.

GOODWIN, D. (1956), 'Note on the plumages of the firethroat *Luscinia pectardens* (David)', *Bull. Brit. Ornithol. Club*, **76**, 5, pp. 74-5.

(1957), 'Note on the immature plumages of *Oenanthe monacha* (Temminck),' *Bull. Brit. Ornithol. Club*, **77**, 2, pp. 17-18.

GÖRNITZ, K. (1923), 'Versuch einer Klassifikation der Häufigsten Federfärbungen', *J. Ornithol.*, **71**, 4, pp. 342-54.

GÖTZ, W. H. (1925), 'Über die Pigmentfarben der Vogelfedern', *Verhandl. ornithol. Ges. Bayerns*, **16**, 3-4, pp. 193-225.

GRAGER, R. (1925), *Die Eigentümlichkeiten des Federkleides bei dem Haushuhn, Truthuhn, Rebhuhn, Fasan und der Taube*, Inang. Diss., Berlin.

GREENWOOD, A. W. (1928), 'Studies on the relation of gonadic structure to plumage characterisation in the domestic fowl: 4 Gonad cross-transplantation in Leghorn and Campine', *Proc. Roy. Soc. London, Ser. B*, **103**, pp. 73-85.

GREENWOOD, A. W. and BLYTH, J. S. (1927), 'Thyroid gland and plumage in chickens', *Nature*, **20**, 3022, pp. 174-5.

(1929), 'An experimental analysis of the plumage of the Leghorn fowl', *Proc. Roy. Soc.*, **49**, IV, 25, pp. 315-55.

(1931), 'A significant modification of feather type induced by injections of female hormone (oestrin) to capons', *Vet. J.*, **87**, pp. 42-7.

(1932), 'Reversal of the secondary sexual characters in the fowl: a castrated Brown Leghorn male which assumed female characters', *J. Genet.*, **26**, 2, pp. 199-213.

(1935), 'Variation in plumage responses of Brown Leghorn capons to oestrone: II. Intradermal injection', *Proc. Roy. Soc. London, Sect. B*, **118**, 1, pp. 122-32.

GREENWOOD, A. W. and CREW, F. A. E. (1926), 'Studies on the relation of gonadic structure to plumage characterisation in domestic fowl: 1 Hennyfeathering in an ovariectomised hen with active testis grafts', *Proc. Roy. Soc. London, Ser. B*, **99**, pp. 232-6.

GREITE, W. (1931), 'Über Bildung und Lagerung der Melanine in der Vogelfeder', *Zool. Anz.*, **96**, 1, 2, pp. 41-9.

(1934), 'Die Strukturbildung der Vogelfeder und ihre Pigmentierung durch Melanine', Z. Wiss. Zool., 145, 3, pp. 283-336.

GROEBELS, F. (1928), 'Zur Physiologie des Vogelzuges', Verhandl. ornithol. Ges. Bayerns, 18, 1, pp. 44-74.

(1932-36), Der Vogel, Vols. I-II: Bau und Funktion, Lebenserschenung, Einpassung, Berlin.

GROODY, T. C. and GROODY, M. E. (1942), 'Feather depigmentation and pantothenic acid deficiency in chick', Science, 95, pp. 655-6.

GROSS, R. (1956), 'Water-soluble compounds (non-keratins) associated with the plumage of the pigeon (Columba livia)', Australian J. Exptl. Biol. Med. Sci., 34, 1, pp. 65-9.

HAECKER, V. (1890), 'Über die Farbe der Vogelfedern', Arch. Mikroskop. Anat., 35, 1, pp. 68-87.

(1926), 'Über pahreszeitliche Veränderungen und klimatisch bedingte Verschiedenheiten der Vogelschilddrüse', Schweiz. Med. Wochschr., 15, pp. 337-41.

HAMILTON, H. L. (1940 a), 'Direct influence of hormones on melanophore differentiation in birds', Anat. Record, 78, pp. 120-2.

(1940 b), 'A study of the physiological properties of melanophores with special reference to their role in feather coloration', Anat. Record, 78, 2, pp. 525-47.

(1940 c), 'Influence of sex hormones and desoxycorticosterone on melanophore differentiation in birds', Proc. Soc. Exptl. Biol. Med., 45, pp. 571-3.

(1941), 'Influence of adrenal and sex hormones of the differentiation of melanophores in the chick', J. Exptl. Zool., 88, pp. 275-305.

HANSON, H. C. (1949), 'Notes on white spotting and other plumage variation in geese', Auk, 66, pp. 164-71.

HARDISTY, M. (1933), 'The feather of the guinea-fowl and a mathematical theory of individual feather patterns', J. Exptl. Zool., 66, 1, pp. 53-86.

(1934), 'The effect of thyroxin injections upon the feather of the guinea-fowl', Anat. Record, 60, pp. 55-6.

(1935), 'The effect of thyroxin injections the feather of the guinea-fowl', J. Exptl. Zool., 74, 4, pp. 389-419.

HARMS, R. M. and GOFF, O. E. (1957), 'Feather-meal in hen nutrition', Poultry Sci., 36, 2, pp. 358-61.

HARPER, J. A. and PARKES, J. E. (1957), 'Changes in seasonal egg production of turkeys induced through controlled light exposure and forced moulting', Poultry Sci., 36, pp. 967-73.

HARRIS, P. C. and SHAFFNER, C. S. (1957), 'Effect of seasonal and thyroidal activity on the moult response to progesterone in chickens', *Poultry Sci.*, **36**, 6, pp. 1186-93.

HARRISON, C. J. O. (1960), 'Signal plumage and phylogenic relationship in some doves', *Bull. Brit. Ornithol. Club.*, **80**, 8, pp. 134-40.

HARRISON, J. G. (1948), 'The breeding plumage of some western palearctic wading birds', *ibid.*, **90**, pp. 72-6.

—— (1952), 'Further as to colour change without a moult: subtractive change in the feather as a physiological process, and some remarks on its mechanism', *Bull. Brit. Ornithol. Club*, **72**, 1, pp. 6-18.

HARRISON, J. M. and HARRISON, J. G. (1956), 'Abnormal seasonal assumption of spring plumage in the redshank (*Tringa totanus* Linnaeus) in association with possible radioactive contamination', *Bull. Brit. Ornithol. Club*, **76**, 4, pp. 60-1.

—— (1959 a), 'Plumage variants in drake gadwall', *Bull. Brit. Ornithol. Club*, **79**, 5, pp. 78-9.

—— (1959 b), 'Evolutionary significance of certain plumage sequences in northern shoveler', *Bull. Brit. Ornithol. Club*, **79**, 8, pp. 135-42.

HAUSMAN, L. A. (1924), 'Bird migration and plumage succession', *Am. Naturalist*, **58**, 654, pp. 87-91.

HAYS, F. A. (1957), 'Egg production and reproduction in yearling hens that lacked the normal rest period associated with the first annual moult', *Poultry Sci.*, **36**, 3, pp. 510-12.

HAYS, F. A., WHITE, C. H. and SANBORN, R. (1948), 'Density of feather pigment in Rhode Island Reds', *Am. Naturalist*, **82**, pp. 107-17.

HAZELWOOD, A. and GORTON, E. (1954), 'Subtractive moult or differential abrasion in *Turdus erictorum*', *Bull. Brit. Ornithol. Club*, **74**, pp. 8-9.

HEINROTH, O. (1889), 'Verlauf der Schwingen- und Schwanzmauser der Vögel', *Sitzber. Ges. Nat. Freunde, Berlin*, **1**, pp. 95-118.

—— (1906), 'Beobachtungen über die Schnelligkeit des Federwachstum', *Ornithol. Monatsber.*, **14**, pp. 114-15.

—— (1910), *Beiträge zur Biologie namentlich Ecologie und Psychologie der Anatiden*, Ber. 5th Intern. Ornithol. Congr., pp. 582-702, Berlin.

—— (1931), *Die Mauser*, Proc. 7th Intern. Ornithol. Congr., pp. 173-85, Amsterdam.

HENKE, K. (1935), *Entwicklung und Bau tierischer Zeichnungsmuster*, Leipzig.

(1939), 'Die rhythmischen Musterbildungen und die Bedingungen der Saisondimorphismus bei der Flankenfeder der männlichen Stockente', *Biol. Zbl.*, 59, 5, pp. 459-89.

HILL, R, T. and PARKES, A. S. (1934), 'Hypophysectomy of birds: III Effect on gonads, accessory organs and head furnishings', *Proc. Roy. Soc. London, Ser. B*, 116, pp. 221-6.

(1935 a), Hypophysectomy of birds: IV Plumage changes in hypophysectomised fowls', *Proc. Roy. Soc. London, Ser. B*, 117, pp. 202-9.

(1935 b), 'Hypophysectomy of birds: V Effect of replacement therapy on the gonads, accessory organs and secondary sexual characters of hypophysectomised fowls', *Proc. Roy. Soc. London, Ser. B*, 117, pp. 210-15.

HIMENO, K. and TANABE, Y. (1957), 'Mechanism of moulting in the hen', *Poultry Sci.*, 36, 4, pp. 835-42.

HINSCH, G. W. (1960), 'Alkaline phosphatase of the developing down feather', *Develop. Biol.*, 2, 1, pp. 21-41.

HIXON, F. M. (1960), 'A study of moult and egg production in *Gallus domesticus* as affected by light, heat and different methods of breeding', *Dissertation Abstr.*, 21, 3, pp. 433.

HÖHN, E. O. (1949), 'Seasonal changes in the thyroid gland and effects of thyroidectomy in the mallard in relation to moult', *Am. J. Physiol.*, 158, 3, pp. 337-9.

(1950), 'Physiology of the thyroid gland in birds: a review', *ibid.*, 92, pp. 464-73.

(1955), 'Evidence for iron staining as the cause of rusty discoloration of normally white feathers in anserine birds', *Auk*, 72, 4, p. 414.

HOLMES, A. (1935), 'The pattern and symmetry of adult plumage units in relation to the order and locus of origin of the embryonic feather papillae', *Am. J. Anat.*, 56, 3, pp. 513-36.

HORNING, B. and TORREY, H. B. (1923), 'Effect of thyroid feeding on the colour and form of the feathers of fowls', *Anat. Record*, 24, pp. 395-9.

HOROWITZ, R. (1934), 'Über morphologische Folgen der Kastration bei Hähnen', *Biol. Generalis (Wien)*, 10, 4, pp. 569-92.

HOSKER, A. (1935), 'Moulting and replacement of feathers', *Nature*, 135, pp. 150-1.

(1936a), 'Regeneration of feathers after thyroid feeding', *J. Exptl. Biol.*, 13, pp. 344-51.

(1936 b), 'Studies on the epidermal structures of birds', *Phil. Trans. Roy. Soc. London, Ser. B.*, 226, 1, pp. 143-88.

HUNTSMAN, C. M., JEROME, F. N. and SNYDER, E. S. (1959), 'The relationship between plumage colour phenotypes and the presence of black melanin in the abdomen of broiler chickens', *Poultry Sci.*, 38, 5, pp. 878-81.

HURRY, H. and NORDSKOG, A. W. (1953), 'A genetic analysis of chick feathering and its influence on growth rate', *Poultry Sci.*, 32, 1, pp. 18-25.

HUTT, F. B. (1930), 'A note on the effects of different doses of thyroid on the fowl', *J. Exptl. Biol.*, 7, 1, pp. 1-6.

(1937), 'Gynandromorphism in the fowl', *Poultry Sci.*, 16, 2, pp. 354-5.

(1953), 'Genetic control of pigmentation in the fowl', in *Pigment Cell Growth*, pp. 29-40, Acad. Press, N.Y.

HUTT, F. B. and LONG, J. (1950), 'Sunsuit; a mutation reducing plumage in the fowl', *J. Heredity*, 41, 5, pp. 145-50.

HYKES, O. V. (1934), 'Influence du produit perfusion de la grande thyroide sur le plumage', *Compt. Rend. Soc. Biol. Paris*, 117, pp. 160-63.

INGRAM, C. (1953), 'How a bird moults', *Country Life*, 14, pp. 284-285.

JAAP, R. G. (1955), 'Shank colour and barred plumage in Columbian coloured chickens', *Poultry Sci.*, 34, 2, pp. 389-95.

JAAP, R. G. and GRIMES, J. F. (1956), 'Growth rate and plumage colour in chickens', *Poultry Sci.*, 36, 6, pp. 1264-9.

JACOBS, W. (1935), 'Über die Mauser bei den Vögeln', *Sitzber. Ges. Morphol. Physiol.*, 44, 1-6, pp. 33-8.

JANDA, V. (1929), 'Recherches sur l'influence de l'hyperthyroidisme artificiel sur le plumage chez certains Corvides', *Biol. Listy*, 14, pp. 1-11.

JEROME, F. N. and HUNTSMAN, C. M. (1952), 'Gynandromorphism and mosaicism in the domestic fowl', *Poultry Sci.*, 31, 5, pp. 921-922.

JOLLIE, M. (1947), 'Plumage changes in the golden eagle', *Auk*, 64, pp. 549-76.

JUHN, M. (1933 a), 'A case of spontaneous pigment loss in the Brown Leghorn capon and the plumage reaction to thyroxine', *Endocrinology*, 17, 1, pp. 88-92.

(1933 b), 'Individual feather succession in the hybrid capon', *Proc. Soc. Exptl. Biol. Med.*, 30, 6, pp. 1264-6.

(1937), 'Growth rates of successive feathers from single follicles in the juvenile Brown Leghorn', *Proc. Soc. Exptl. Biol. Med.*, 36, pp. 777-80.

(1938), 'Emergence orders and growth rates in the juvenile plumages of the Brown Leghorn', *J. Exptl. Zool.*, 77, pp. 467-9.

(1944), 'Effect of thiouracil on the plumage of the Brown Leghorn capon', *Endocrinology*, 35, 3, pp. 277-9.

(1946), 'Effect of thiouracil on the juvenile plumages of Brown Leghorn fowl', *Endocrinology*, 39, 1, pp. 14-22.

(1947), 'The effect of thiouracil on feather pigment determination in hybrid fowl', *J. Heredity*, 38, 2, pp. 113-16.

(1954), 'On the two-fold source of pattern in plumage in the fowl, with examples from the hybrid', *J. Exptl. Zool.*, 126, 4, pp. 473-95.

JUHN, M. and BARNES, B. O. (1931), 'The feather germ as indicator for thyroid preparations', *Am. J. Physiol.*, 98, 4, pp. 463-6.

JUHN, M., D'AMOUR, F. E. and GUSTAVSON, R. G. (1930), 'The plumage and oviduct response to the female hormone in fowls', *Endocrinology*, 14, 4, pp. 349-54.

JUHN, M., D'AMOUR, F. E. and WOMACK, E. B. (1930), 'The effect of simultaneous injections of the female and male hormones in capons', *Am. Physiol.*, 95, pp. 641-9.

JUHN, M., FAULKNER, G. H. and GUSTAVSON, R. G. (1930), 'Feathers as indicators of concentration of female hormone in the blood', *Proc. Soc. Exptl. Biol. Med.*, 27, pp. 1078-80.

(1931), 'The correlation of rates of growth and hormone threshold in the feathers of fowls', *J. Exptl. Zool.*, 58, 1, pp. 69-111.

JUHN, M. and FRAPS, R. M. (1934 a), 'Pattern analysis in plumage: I Curve of barb growth', *Proc. Soc. Exptl. Biol. Med.*, 31, 6, pp. 1181-3.

(1934 b), 'Pattern analysis in plumage: II Methods of definitive feather analysis', *Proc. Soc. Exptl. Biol. Med.*, 31, 6, pp. 1183-5.

(1934 c), 'Pattern analysis in plumage: III Action of thyroxine in high concentration', *Proc. Soc. Exptl. Biol. Med.*, 31, 6, pp. 1185-7.

(1934 d), 'Pattern analysis in plumage: IV Order of asymmetry in the breast tracts', *Proc. Soc. Exptl. Biol. Med.*, 31, 6, pp. 1187-90.

(1936), 'Developmental analysis in plumage: I The individual feather', *Physiol. Zool.*, 9, 3, pp. 293-317.

JUHN, M. and GUSTAVSON, R. D. (1930), 'A forty-eight hour test for the female hormone with capon feathers as indicator', *Proc. Soc. Exptl. Biol. Med.*, 27, 4, pp. 747-8.

(1930), 'The production of female genital subsidiary characters and plumage sex characters by injection of human placental hormone in fowls', *J. Exptl. Zool.*, 56, 1, pp. 31-50.

JUHN, M., GUSTAVSON, R. G. and GALLAGHER, T. F. (1932), 'The factor of age with reference to reactivity to sex hormones in fowl', *J. Exptl. Zool.*, 64, 2, pp. 133-85.

JUHN, M. and HARRIS, P. (1955), 'Local effects on the feather papilla of thyroxine and of progesterone', *Proc. Soc. Exptl. Biol. Med.*, 90, 1, pp. 202-4.

(1956), 'Responses in moult and lay of fowl to progestins and gonadotrophins', *Proc. Soc. Exptl. Biol. Med.*, 92, 4, pp. 709-11.

(1958), 'Moult of capon feathering with prolactin', *Proc. Soc. Exptl. Biol. Med.*, 98, 3, pp. 669-72.

JUHRE, F. (1959), *Das Rassengeflügel*, I-IV, Berlin.

KAGELMANN, G. (1951), 'Studien über Farbfelderung, Zeichnung und Färbung der Wild- und Hausenten', *Zool. Jahrb. (Zool.)*, 62, 5, pp. 513-630.

KAUFMANN, L. (1936), 'Rate of feathering in chickens, its inheritance and correlation with certain characters of fullgrown greenleg fowl', *Mem. Inst. Nat. Polon. Econom. Rurale Pulawy*, 16, 1, pp. 205-22.

KAWAMURA, T. (1933), 'Über die Pigmentbildung in der Erstlingsfeder von Coturnix coturnix japonica Temminck et Schlegel', *J. Sci., Hiroshima Univ. Ser. B-1*, 2, pp. 171-91.

KECK, W. N. (1934), 'The control of the secondary sex characters in the English sparrow *Passer domesticus*', *J. Exptl. Zool.*, 67, 3, pp. 315-47.

KELSO, L. (1952), 'Some fundamentals of the feather: IV', *Biol. Leafl.*, 63, pp. 1-5.

KEMPSTER, H. L. (1925), 'Time of moult as an index to productivity of hens', *Missouri Univ. Agr. Expt. Stat. Bull.*, 2, pp. 228-230.

KIMBALL, E. (1952), 'Wild-type plumage pattern in the fowl', *J. Heredity*, 43, 1, pp. 129-32.

(1958), 'Eclipse plumage in *Gallus*', *Poultry Sci.*, 37, 3, pp. 733-4.

KIPP, F. A. (1956), 'Progressive Merkmale des Jugendkleides ben den Spechten', *J. Ornithol.*, 97, 4, pp. 403-10.

KIRKPATRICK, C. M. and LEOPOLD, A. C. (1952), 'The rôle of darkness in sexual activity of quail', *Science*, 116, pp. 280-281.

KLAIN, G. J., HILL, D. C. GRAY, J. A. and OLSEN, E. M. (1960), 'Observations on the influence of dietary protein level and amino acid balance on pigmentation in the feathers of chick', *Poultry Sci.*, 39, 1, pp. 25-9.

KLATT, B. (1917), 'Transplantation der Haube beim Hauben-huhn', *Sitzber. Ges. Nat. Freunde, Berlin,* 5-6, pp. 412-15.

KLEE, R. (1886), 'Bau und Entwicklung der Federn', *Hallesche Z. Natur.,* 59, 2, pp. 110-56.

KLEIN, B. M. (1949), 'Eine Pfauenfeder unter dem Mikroskop', *Mikrokosmos,* 39, pp. 66-9.

KNIESCHE, G. (1914), Über die Farben der Vogelfedern: I Die grünfärbung auf grundlage der Blaustruktur', *Zool. Jahrb., Abt. Anat.,* 38, 3, pp. 329-56.

KOBAYASHI, H. (1952), 'Studies on moulting in the pigeon: V Oxygen consumption of the brooding and of the thiourea-treated pigeon', *Annotationes Zool. Japon,* 25, 6, pp. 371-6.

(1953 a), 'Studies on moulting in the pigeon: III Observations on normal process of moulting', *Japan J. Zool.,* 11, 1, pp. 1-9.

(1953 b), 'Studies on moulting in the pigeon: IV Moulting in relation to reproductive activity', *ibid.,* pp. 11-20.

(1953 b), 'Studies on moulting in the pigeon: VII Inhibitory effect of lactogen on moulting', *ibid.,* pp. 21-6.

(1953 c), 'Acceleration of moulting in the canary by reducing the daily-light period', *Annotationes Zool. Japon,* 26, 2, pp. 156-161.

(1954 a), 'Studies on moulting in the pigeon: VIII Effects of sex steroids on moulting and thyroid gland', *ibid.,* 27, 1, pp. 22-6.

(1954 b), 'Failure of reduction of daily-light period to induce moulting in the canary during the period between the end of September and the middle of May', *ibid.,* 2, pp. 63-70.

(1958), 'On the induction of moult in birds by 17-oxyproges-terone-17-carbonate', *Endocrinology,* 63, 4, pp. 420-30.

KOBAYASHI, H. and FARNER, D. S. (1960), 'The effect of photo-periodic stimulation on phosphatase activity in the hypothalamo-hypophyseal system of the white-crowned sparrow', *Z. Zell-forsch.,* 53, 1, pp. 1-24.

KOBAYASHI, H. and OKUBO, K. (1955), 'Prolongation of moulting period in canary by long days', *Science,* 121, 3140, pp. 338-9.

KOCH, E. L. (1939), 'Zur Frage der Beeinflussbarkeit der Gefieder-farben der Vögel', *Z. Wiss. Zool.,* 152, 1, pp. 27-82.

KOLLIKER, A. (1887), 'Über die Entstehung des Pigments in den Oberhautgebilden', *Z. Wiss. Zool.,* 45, 4, pp. 713-20.

KOPEC, S. and GREENWOOD, A. W. (1929), 'The effect of yolk injections on plumage in ovariotomised fowl', *Arch. Entwick-lungsmech.,* 121, pp. 87-94.

KORELUS, J. (1947), 'Study of bird's plumage with special consideration of number and weight of their feathers', *Vestn. Cespol. Zool. Spalner. Praze*, 11, pp. 218-34.

KOZELKA, A. W. (1929), 'Integumental grafting in the domestic fowl: transplants of combs, spurs and feathers in the study of sex-dimorphism', *J. Heredity*, 20, 1, pp. 2-14.

KRÄTZIG, H. (1937 a), 'Untersuchungen zur Frage der Struktur und farbveränderungen bei künstlicher (Thyroxin) Mauser', *Zool. Anz.*, 118, 1, pp. 65-78.

— (1937 b), 'Histologische Untersuchungen zur Frage der Struktur und Farbveränderungen an Fefern nach künstlicher (Thyroxin) Mauser', *Arch. Entwicklungsmech.*, 131, 1, pp. 86-150.

KRITZLER, H. (1943), 'Carotenoids in the display and eclipse plumage of bishop birds', *Physiol. Zool.*, 16, 3, pp. 241-55.

KRIZENECKY, J. (1926), 'Über den Einfluss der Schilddrüse und der Thymus auf Entwicklung des Gefieder bei den Hühnerkücken', *Arch. Entwicklungsmech.*, 107, 6, pp. 583-604.

— (1927), 'Importance du thymus et du corpsthyroide pour la régénération du plumage', *Compt. Rend. Soc. Biol.*, 96, pp. 1427-9.

— (1929 a), 'Importance of the thyroid in the feathering in pigeons', *Vestn. Cesk. Akad. Zemedel.*, 5, 6.

— (1929 b), 'Die Bedeutung der Schilddrüse bei der Befriederung der Tauben', *Mitt. Landwirtsch. Acad. Brno*, 5, 1, pp. 34-461.

— (1932), *Einfluss der inneren Secretion bei landwirtschaftlichen Nutztieren: E. Mangold's Handb. d. Ernähr. Stoffwechs landb. Nutztieren*, IV.

KRUKENBERG, C. F. W. (1882), 'Die Federfarbstoffe der Psittaciden', *Vergl. Physiol. Studien, Heidelberg*, 2 Reihe, 2 Abt., 29, pp. 36-42.

KÜCHLER, W. (1935), 'Jahreszyklische Veränderungen im histologischen Bau der Vogelschilddrüse', *J. Ornithol.*, 83, 5, pp. 414-61.

KUHN, O. (1928), 'Zur Entwicklungsphysiologie der Feder', *Nachr. Ges. Wiss. Gottingen, Math.-Physik.*, 4, pp. 233-40.

— (1929), 'Über die Mauserreaktion der Vögel nach Schilddrüsenfütterung', *Züchtungskunde*, 4, pp. 521-8.

— (1932), 'Entwicklungsphysiologische Untersuchungen an der Vögelfeder', *Arch. Entwicklungsmech.*, 127, 3, pp. 456-541.

— (1953), 'Zwillingsfedern bei Haustauben', *Zool. Anz.*, 151, 2, pp. 147-56.

LAWS, D. F. and FARNER, D. S. (1960), 'Prolactin and the photo-periodic testicular response to white-crowned sparrows', *Endo-crinology*, **67**, 2, pp. 279-81.

LE FEBRE, E. A. and WARNER, D. W. (1959), 'Moults, plumages and age groups in *Piranga bidentata* in Mexico', *Auk*, **76**, 2, pp. 208-217.

LEGAIT, H. (1956), 'Les voies efférentes des noyaux neurosecré-toires hypothalamiques chez les oiseaux', *Compt. Rend. Soc. Biol.*, **150**, 6.

— (1958), 'Étude caryometrique des élements cellulaire du sys-tème hypothalamo-neurohypophysaire au cours d'états d'hyper-et hypothyroidie chez la poule Rhode Island', *Compt. Rend. Soc. Biol.*, **152**, 5, pp. 825-7.

LEHRMAN, D. S. (1959), 'Breeding biology and physiology: hor-monal responses to sexual stimuli in birds', *ibid.*, **101**, 3-4, pp. 478-98.

LILLIE, F. B. (1931), 'Bilateral gynandromorphism and lateral hemihypertrophy in birds', *Science*, **74**, pp. 387-90.

— (1932), 'The physiology of feather pattern', *Wilson Bull.*, **44**, 3, pp. 193-211.

— (1940), 'Physiology of development of the feather: III Growth of the mesodermal constituents and blood circulation in the pulp', *Physiol. Zool.*, **13**, 2, pp. 143-75.

— (1942), 'On the development of feathers', *Biol. Rev.*, **17**, 3, pp. 247-66.

LILLIE, F. R. and JUHN, M. (1932), 'The physiology of develop-ment of feathers: I Growth-rate and pattern in the individual feather', *Physiol. Zool.*, **5**, 2, pp. 124-84.

— (1938), 'Physiology of development of the feather: II General principles of development with special reference to the after-feather', *Physiol. Zool.*, **11**, 5, pp. 434-48.

LILLIE, F. R., SIZEMORE, J. R. and DENTON, C. A. (1956), 'Feather-meal in chick nutrition', *Poultry Sci.*, **35**, 2, pp. 316-18.

LILLIE, F. R. and WANG, H. (1940 a), 'Physiology of development of the feathers: IV The diurnal curve of growth in Brown Leghorn fowl', *Proc. Nat. Acad. Sci. Wash.*, **26**, 1, pp. 67-85.

— (1940 b), 'Experiments on the morphogenesis of the feather', *Anat. Record*, **78**, 4, pp. 129-30.

— (1941), 'Physiology of development of the feather: V Experi-mental morphogenesis', *Physiol. Zool.*, **14**, 1, pp. 103-35.

— (1942), 'The production and analysis of feather-chimaerae in fowl', *Anat. Record Suppl.*, **84**, 1, pp. 77-82.

(1943), 'Physiology of development of the feather: VI The production and analysis of feather-chimaerae in the fowl', *Physiol. Zool.*, **16**, 1, pp. 1-21.

(1944), 'Physiology of development of the feather: VII An experimental study of injection', *Physiol. Zool.*, **17**, 2, pp. 1-30.

LINTZEL, W., MANGOLD, E. and STOTZ, H. (1929), Über den Stickstoff und Schwefelumsatz mausernder Hühner', *Arch. Geflugel.* **3**, 3, pp. 193-207.

LLOYD-JONES, O. (1907), 'The development of nesting feathers', *Lab. Bull. Oberlin Coll.*, **13**, pp. 3-18.

(1915), 'Studies on inheritance in pigeons: II A microscopical and chemical study of the feather pigments', *J. Exptl. Zool.*, **18**, 3, pp. 453-95.

MARBLE, D. R. (1930), 'The moulting factor in judging fowls for egg production', *Bull. Cornell Univ. Agr. Exptl. Stat.*, **503**, pp. 22-7.

(1934), 'Relation of juvenile plumage to growth and sexual maturity', *Poultry Sci.*, **13**, 1, pp. 195-201.

MARKERT, C. L. (1948), 'The effect of thyroxine and antithyroid compounds on the synthesis of pigment granules in chick melanoblasts cultured in vitro', *Physiol. Zool.*, **21**, 4, pp. 309-27.

MARSHALL, F. H. (1936), 'Sexual periodicity and the causes which determinate it', *Cron. Lect. Philos. Trans. Ser. B.*, **226**.

MARSHALL, F. H. A. (1942), 'Exteroceptive factors in sexual periodicity', *Biol. Rev.*, **17**, 1, pp. 68-90.

MARSHALL, A. J. and SERVENTY, D. L. (1956), 'Moult adaptation in relation to long-distance migration in petrels', *Nature*, **177**, 4516, pp. 943.

MARTIN, J. H. (1929), 'Effect of excessive dosage of thyroid on the domestic fowl', *Biol. Bull. Marine Biol. Lab., Woods Hole*, **56**, pp. 357-70.

(1930), 'Rate of feather growth in barred Plymouth Rock chicks', *Poultry Sci.*, **8**, 1, pp. 161-83.

MASON, H. S. (1948), 'The chemistry of melanin: III Mechanism of the oxidation of dehydroxyphenilalanine by tyrosine', *J. Biol. Chem.*, **172**, 2, pp. 183-99.

MATTERN, I. (1956), 'Zur Histologie und Histochemie der lipochromatischen Federn einiger Gotingiden (Schmuskvögel)', *Z. Zellforsch. und Mikroscop. Anat.*, **45**, 1, pp. 96-136.

MATTHEWS, L. H. (1960), 'Integumentary sex characters in vertebrates', *Mem. Soc. Endocrinol.*, **7**, pp. 134-43.

MAYAND, N. (1944), 'Études sur les plumages et les mues: II Les mues anormales', *Bull. Soc. Zool., France*, **69**, 2, pp. 141-4.

(1950), 'Nouvelles precisions sur la mue des Procellariens', *Alauda*, 18, pp. 222-3.

MAYR, E. and MAYR, M. (1954), 'The tail moult of small owls', *Auk*, 71, 3, pp. 172-8.

MEBS, T. (1960), 'Untersuchungen über den Rhythmus der Schwingen- und Schwanzmauser bei groben Falken', *J. Ornithol.*, 101, 1-2, pp. 175-94.

MEIER, G. (1957), 'Über experimentelle Rotfärbung des Gefieders beim Fichtenkreussenabel (*Loxia curvirostra*)', *Gefied. Welt*, 81, 7, pp. 122-4.

MESTER, H. and PRÜNTE, W. (1959), 'Bemerkungen über die Schreckmauser', *Vogelwelt*, 80, 6, pp. 179-80.

MEWALDT, L. R. (1958), 'Pterylography and natural and experimentally induced moult in Clark's nutcracker', *Condor*, 60, 3, pp. 165-87.

MICHENER, H. and MICHENER, J. R. (1946), 'Loss of feathers at times other than the normal moult', *Condor*, 48, 3, pp. 283-4.

MICHENER, J. R. (1953), 'Moult and variations in plumage pattern of mocking-birds at Pasadena, California', *Condor*, 55, 4, pp. 75-89.

MILLER, A. H. (1951), 'Further evidence on the refractory period in the reproductive cycle of the golden-crowned sparrow, *Zonotrichia coronata*', *Auk*, 68, pp. 380-83.

MILLER, A. M. (1941), 'The significance of moult cankers among the secondary remiges in the falconiforms', *Condor*, 43, 2, pp. 113-15.

(1955), 'The expression of innate reproductive rhythm under conditions of winter lighting', *Auk*, 82, 4, pp. 260-4.

MILLER, D. S. (1939), 'A study of the physiology of the sparrow thyroid', *J. Exptl. Zool.*, 80, 3, pp. 259-81.

MILLER, L. (1937), 'Further studies of the tropical hawk *Harpagus*', *Condor*, 39, 3, pp. 219-21.

MITCHELL, J. B. (1929), 'Experimental studies of the bird's hypophysis: effects of hypophysectomy in the Brown Leghorn fowl', *Physiol. Zool.*, 2, 3, pp. 411-37.

MIYAZAKI, H. (1934), 'On the relation of the daily-light period to the sexual maturity and to the moulting of *Losterops palpebrosa japonica*', *Sci. Rept. Tohoku Univ. Fourth Ser. Biol.*, 9, pp. 183-203.

MONTALENTI, G. (1934), 'A physiological analysis of the barred pattern in Plymouth Rock feathers', *J. Exptl. Zool.*, 69, 2, pp. 269-345.

(1947), 'Physiology of pattern formation in male and female

feathers of barred Plymouth Rock fowl', *Nature,* 159, 4052, pp. 886-7.

MOREAU, R. E., WILK, A. L. and ROWAN, W. (1947), 'The moult and gonad cycles of three species of birds at five degrees of the equator', *Proc. Zool. Soc. London,* 117, 3, pp. 345-64.

MORI, H. (1948), 'Moulting of pigeons in relation to reproductive cycle', *Zool. Mag. Tokyo,* 58, 1, pp. 36-7.

MOULTRIE, F., MUELLER, C. D. and PAYNE, L. F. (1955), 'Moulting and growth of individual feathers in turkeys exposed to 10 or 24 hours of daily light', *Poultry Sci.,* 34, 2, pp. 383-8.

MÜHLBOCK, O. (1939), 'Versuche über die hormonale Beeinflussung der Federfarbe bei rebhuhnfärbigen Leghorn-Hähnen', *Acta Brev. Neerl.,* 9, 2, pp. 264-6.

NACHTSHEIM, H. (1957), 'Pigmentierte Federn beim weissen Leghorn: ein Gutachten', *Züchtungskunde,* 29, 7, pp. 285-8.

NICKERSON, M. (1944), 'An experimental analysis of barred pattern formation in feathers', *J. Exptl. Zool.,* 95, 3, pp. 361-97.

   (1946), 'Conditions modifying the expression of silver in the Silver Campine fowl', *Physiol. Zool.,* 19, 1, pp. 77-83.

NOBLE, G. K. and BRADLEY, H. T. (1933), 'The relation of the thyroid and the hypophysis to the moulting process in the lizard *Hemidactylus brookii*', *Biol. Bull.,* 64, 3, pp. 289-98.

OAKESON, B. B. and LILLEY, B. R. (1960), 'Annual cycle of thyroid histology in two races of white-crowned sparrow', *Anat. Record Suppl.,* 136, 1, pp. 41-57.

OEHME, H. (1959), 'Untersuchungen über Flug und Flügelbau von Kleinvögeln', *J. Ornithol.,* 100, 4, pp. 363-96.

OCCHIPINTHI, P. (1927), 'Effetti della somministrasione di trioide e di timo in fringillidi e in fasiandi', *Arch. Ital. Anat. Embriol.,* 24, 2, pp. 122-9.

ONISHI, N., TAKETOMI, M., KATO, G. and MIYAZONO, Y. (1955), 'Studies on feathering in the fowl: III Effect of injection of estrogen and thyroxine on the moult of primary feathers', *Japan J. Zootech. Sci.,* 26, pp. 1-28.

PARHON, G. I. and PARHON, C. (1924), 'Contribution a l'étude des suites de la thyroidectomie chez les jeunes oiseaux: ses effects sur la croissance et le developpement du plumage: infantilisme thyroiden experimental', *Compt. Rend. Soc. Biol.,* 91, pp. 765-6.

PARKES, K. C. (1952), 'Post-juvenal wing moult in the bobolink', *Wilson Bull.,* 64, 2, pp. 161-2.

PARKES, K. S. (1957), 'The juvenile plumages of the finch genera *Atlapetes and Pipilo*', *Auk,* 74, 4, pp. 499-502.

PARKES, A. S. and SELYE, H. (1937), 'The endocrine system and plumage types: I Some effects of hypothyroidism', *J. Genetics*, 34, 3, pp. 297-306.

PAYNE, L. F. (1947), 'Frequency of the tail wing moult in turkeys', *Poultry Sci.*, 26, 1, pp. 52-60.

PEREK, M., ECKSTEIN, B. and SOBEL, H. (1957), 'Histological observations on the anterior lobe of the pituitary gland in moulting and laying hens', *Poultry Sci.*, 36, 5, pp. 954-8.

PEREK, M. and SULMAN, F. (1945), 'The basal metabolic rate in moulting and laying hens', *Endocrinology*, 36, 3, pp. 240-4.

PESKA, W. (1927), 'Über die Blutgefässentwicklung in den Federkeimen der vögel', *Bull. Internat. Acad. Polon. Sci. Lettres, Cl. Sci. Math. Natur., Ser. B.*, 1, pp. 827-33.

PEZARD, A. (1912), 'Sur la détermination des caractères sexuels chez les Gallinaces: greffe de testicule et castration postpuberale', *Compt. Rend. Acad. Sci.*, 154, pp. 1183-6.

(1915), 'Transformation expérimentale des caractères sexuels secondaires chez les Gallinaces', *ibid.*, 160, pp. 260-3.

(1918), 'Le conditionement physiologique des caractères sexuels secondaires chez les oiseaux', *Bull. Biol. France Belgique*, 55, pp. 1-176.

(1922 a), 'La loi du tout ou rien et le gynandromorphisme chez les oiseaux', *Physiol. Path. Gen.*, 20, pp. 495-508.

(1922 b), 'Notion du seuil differentiel et explication humorale du gynandromorphisme des oiseaux bipartis', *Compt. Rend. Acad. Sci.*, 174, pp. 1573-4.

(1925), 'Le déterminisme des caractères sexuels secondaires chez les Gallinaces', *Rev. Gen. Sci.*, 36, 1, pp. 23-31.

(1927), 'Le déterminisme endocrinien du comportement psycho-sexuel chez les Gallinaces', *Année Psychol.*, 27, 1, pp. 42-49.

(1928), 'Die Bestimmung der Geschlectsfunktion bei den Hühnern', *Ergeb. Physiol.*, 27, 4, pp. 552-656.

PEZARD, A., SAND, K. and CARIDROIT, F. (1926), 'La bipartition longitudinale de la plume: faits nouveaux concernant le gynandromorphisme élementaire', *Compt. Rend Soc. Biol.*, 94, 6, pp. 1074-7.

PFEFFER, R. V. (1952), 'Untersuchungen zur Morphologie und Entwicklung der Fadenfedern', *Zool. Jahrb. Abt. Anat. Ontog.*, 72, 1, pp. 67-100.

PHILIP, D., LANGERMALEN, G. and CRALEN, N. (1950), 'Surface structure of feathers from the white domestic fowl', *Nature*, 166, pp. 1070-71.

PIECHOCKI, R. (1955), 'Über Verhalten, Mauser und Umfärbung einer gekäfigten Steppenweih (*Circus macrourus*)', *J. Ornithol.*, 96, 3, pp. 327-36.

(1956), 'Über die Mauser eines gekäfigten Turmfalken (*Falco-tinnunculus*)', *J. Ornithol.*, 97, 3, pp. 301-9.

PINO, J. A. (1955), 'Forced moulting interruption of egg-laying in White Leghorn hens by the use of euhepeptin (2-amino-5-nitro-thiazole)', *Poultry Sci.*, 34, 3, pp. 540-43.

PITT-RIVERS, R. and TATA, J. R. (1959), *The Thyroid Hormones*, Pergamon Press, London, N.Y.

PLUMART, P. E. and MUELLER, C. D. (1954), 'Effect of sex-linked early feathering on the plumage from 6-12 weeks of age', *Poultry Sci.*, 33, 4, pp. 715-21.

PODHRADSKY, J. (1926), 'Der Einfluss des Hyperthyreoidismus auf Wachstum und Pigmentierung des Gefieders bei ausgewachsenen Hühnern', *Arch. Entwicklungsmech.*, 107, 3, pp. 407-22.

(1935), 'Die Veränderung der inkretorischen Drüsen und einiger innerer Organe bei der Legeleistung', *Z. Tierzuchtung*, 33, 1, pp. 77-103.

(1953), 'Der Einfluss des Milieus auf Entwicklung der Intergumentfarben der Taube', *Biologia, Bratislava*, 8, pp. 109-32.

POLL, H. (1909), 'Zur Lehre von den Sekundären Geschlechtscharacteren', *Sitzber. Ges. Nat. Freunde, Berlin*, 6, pp. 36-42.

POMPEN, A. W. K., DINGEMANSE, M. E. and KOBER, S. (1933), 'Gonadotrope Wirkung bei jungen Vögeln', *Acta Neerl. Physiol.*, 2, pp. 159-60.

POST, H. (1894), 'Über normale und pathologische Pigmentierung der Oberhautbilde', *Arch. Pathol. Anat. Physiol.*, 135, 4, pp. 479-513.

PRAWOCHENSKI, R. and SLIZYNSKI, B. (1933), 'Influence of thallium salts and thyroid preparation upon the plumage of ducks', *Nature*, 132, pp. 482-3.

(1934), 'Influence of thyroid preparations on the plumage of birds', *Nature*, 133, pp. 950-1.

RABL, H. (1894), 'Über die Entwicklung des Pigmentes in der Dunenfeder des Hühnchens', *Cbl. Physiol.*, 8, pp. 256-8.

RAND, A. L. (1954 a), 'Immature females with adult male plumage characters', *Auk*, 71, pp. 474-5.

(1954 b), 'Notes of downy plumages of Loons (*Gaviidae*)', *Canad. Field-Naturalist*, 68, 1, pp. 13-15.

RAWLES, M. E. (1939), 'The production of robin pigment in White Leghorn feathers by grafts of embryonic robin tissue', *J. Genet.*, 38, 6, pp. 517-32.

(1940 a), 'The pigment-forming potency of early chick blastoderms', *Proc. Nat. Acad. Sci. Wash.*, **26**, 2, pp. 86-94.

(1940 b), 'The development of melanophores from embryonic mouse tissues grown in the coelom of chick embryos', *Proc. Nat. Acad. Sci. Wash.*, **26**, 5, pp. 673-80.

(1944), 'The migration of melanoblasts after hatching into pigment-free skin grafts of the common fowl'. *Physiol. Zool.*, **17**, 2, pp. 167-83.

(1945), 'Behaviour of melanoblasts derived from the coelomic lining in interbreed grafts of wing skin', *Physiol. Zool.*, **18**, 1, pp. 1-16.

(1948), 'Origin of melanophores and their role in development of colour patterns in vertebrates', *Physiol. Rev.*, **28**, 3, pp. 383-408.

(1955), 'Skin and its derivates', in *Analysis of Development*, Sect. 7, pp. 499-519, Philadelphia and London.

RAWLES, M. E. and WILLIER, B. H. (1939), 'The localization of pigment-producing potency in presomite chick blastodermus', *Anat. Record*, **73**, 1, pp. 43-4.

RICE, J. E., NIXON, C. and ROGERS, C. A. (1908), 'The moulting of fowls', *Bull. Cornell Univ. Agr. Exptl. Stat.*, **258**, pp. 12-19.

RIDDLE, O. (1907), 'A study of fundamental bars in feathers', *Biol. Bull., Woods Hole*, **12**, 2, pp. 165-7.

(1908 a), 'The cause of the production of down and other down-like structures in the plumages of birds', *Biol. Bull.*, **14**, 3, pp. 163-76.

(1908 b), 'The genesis of fault bars in feathers and the cause of alterations of light and dark fundamental bars', *Biol Bull., Woods Hole*, **14**, 3, pp. 328-71.

(1925), 'Studies on the physiology of reproduction in birds: XX Reciprocal size changes of gonads and thyroids in relation to season in pigeon', *Am. J. Physiol.*, **73**, 1, pp. 5-16.

(1931), 'Season of origin as a determiner of age at which birds become sexually mature', *Am. J. Physiol.*, **97**, 5, pp. 581-7.

RIDDLE, O. and FISCHER, W. S. (1925), 'Seasonal variations of thyroid size in pigeons', *Am. J. Physiol.*, **72**, 5, pp. 464-87.

RIS, H. (1941), 'An experimental study on the origin of melanophores in birds', *Physiol. Zool.*, **14**, 1, pp. 48-66.

ROWAN, W. (1928), 'Reproductive rhythm in birds', *Nature*, **122**, pp. 11-12.

(1936), 'On photoperiodism, reproductive periodicity and the annual migration of birds and certain fishes', *Proc. Soc. Nat. Hist., Boston*, **38**, 1, pp. 147-89.

(1938), 'Light and seasonal reproduction in animals', *Biol. Rev.*, 13, 4, pp. 374-402.

(1946), 'Experiments in bird migration', *Trans. Roy. Soc. Canada, Ser. 3*, 40, pp. 123-35.

ROWLAND, I. W. and PARKES, A. S. (1934), 'Quantitative study of the thyrotrophic activity of anterior pituitary extracts', *Biochem. J.*, 28, 6, pp. 1829-43.

SAGER, E. (1955), 'Morphologische Analyse der Musterbildung beim Pfauenrad', *Rev. Suisse Zool., Geneva*, 62, 1, pp. 25-127.

SALOMONSEN, F. (1939), Moults and sequence of plumages in the rock ptarmigan (*Lagopus mutus* Mont.), Copenhagen.

(1949), 'Some notes on the moult of the long-tailed duck', *Avicult. Mag. London*, 55, pp. 59-62.

SAMUEL, S. (1870), 'Die regeneration'. *Virchow's Arch.*, 50, 3, pp. 323-54.

SARASIN, F. (1934), 'Über Färbungsgesetze des Vögelgefieders', *Rev. Suisse Zool., Geneva*, 41, 2, pp. 177-96.

SAUERMANN, C. (1889), 'Über die wirkung organischer Farbstoffe auf das Gefieder der Vögel bei stomachaler Darreichung', *Arch. Anat. Physiol., Physiol. Abt.*, pp. 543-9.

SAUNDERS, I. W. (1950), 'An analysis of the spatial distribution, tract specificity and orientation of feather germs in the humoral tract of the chick wing', *Anat. Record*, 108, 1, pp. 32-3.

SAUNDERS, I. W. and WEISS, P. (1950), 'Effects of removal on the origin and distribution of feather germs in the wing of the chick embryo', *Anat. Record*, 108, 1, pp. 93-4.

SCHERESCHEWSKY, H. (1929), 'Einige Beiträge zum Problem der Verfärbung des Gefieders beim Gimpel', *Arch. Entwicklungsmech.*, 115, 2, pp. 110-53.

SCHIEMENZ, H. (1958), 'Zur Mauser des Kleingefieders beim Hühnerhabicht (*Accipiter gentilis* L.)', *J. Ornithol.*, 99, 1, pp. 59-66.

SCHMIDT, W. J. (1952), 'Wie entstehen die Schillerfarben der Federn', *Naturwiss.*, 39, 14, pp. 313-18.

SCHMIDT, W. and RUSKA, H. (1961), 'Elektronenmikroskopische untersuchung der Pigmentgranula in den Schillernden Federstrahlen der Taube *Columba trocaz* H.', *Z. Zellforsch.*, 55, 3, pp. 379-88.

SCHOOLEY, J. P. (1937), 'Pituitary cytology in pigeons', *Cold Spring Harbor Symp. Quant. Biol.*, 5, pp. 115-19.

SCHOOLEY, J. P. and RIDDLE, O. (1939), 'The morphological basis of pituitary function in pigeons', *Am. J. Anat.*, 62, 3, pp. 313-51.

SCHROEDER, W. A. and LOIS, M. K. (1955), 'The amino-acid composition of certain morphologically distinct parts of white feathers and of goose feather barbs and goose down', *J. Am. Chem. Soc.*, 77, pp. 1901-1906.

SCHULTZ, W. (1916), 'Schwarzfärbung weisser Haare durch Rasur und dei Entwicklungsmechanik der Farben von Haaren und Federn: II und III', *Arch. Entwicklungsmech.*, 42, 2-3, pp. 141-67, 222-42.

SCHWARZ, E. (1930), 'Pigmentierung, form und Wachstum der Feder des Haushuhns in Abhängigkeit voi der Thyreoideafunktion', *Arch. Entwicklungsmech.*, 123, 1, pp. 1-38.

SELANDER, R. K. (1958), 'Age determination and moult in the boat-tailed grackle', *Condor*, 60, 6, pp. 355-76.

SHAFFNER, C. S. (1954 a), 'Feather papilla stimulation by progesterone', *Science*, 120, 3113, pp. 345-6.

(1954 b), 'Progesterone-induced moult', *Poultry Sci.*, 33, 5, pp. 1079-80.

(1955), 'Progesterone-induced moult', *ibid.*, 34, 4, pp. 840-2.

SHIRLEY, H. V., JR. and NALBANDOV, A. V. (1956), 'Effects of transecting hypophyseal stalks in laying hens', *Endocrinology*, 58, 6, pp. 694-700.

SICK, H. (1937), 'Morphologisch-fuktionelle Untersuchungen über die Feinstruktur der Vögelfeder', *J. Ornithol.*, 85, 2-3, pp. 206-372.

SIEGEL, P. S., CRAIG, J. V. and MUELLER, C. D. (1957), 'Heritabilities, sex differences and phenotypic correlations for sex feathering characteristics', *Poultry Sci.*, 36, 3, pp. 621-8.

SMYTH, J. R., PORTER, J. W. and BOHREN, B. B. (1951), 'A study of pigment from red, brown and buff feathers and hair', *Physiol. Zool.*, 24, 3, pp. 205-16.

SPÖTTEL, W. (1914), 'Die Färbung der Vögelfedern: II Die Färbung der *Columba livia* nebst Beobachtungen über die mechanischen Bauverhältnisse der Vögelfeder', *Zool. Jahrb. Abt. Anat. Ontog.*, 38, 4, pp. 357-426.

STADIE, R. (1938), 'Ein Beitrag zur hormonalen Beeinflussung der Gefiederfarben', *Z. Wiss. Zool.*, 151, 4, pp. 445-66.

STAPLES, C. P. (1948), 'Further as to colour change without a moult', *Bull. Brit. Ornithol. Club*, 68, 2, pp. 80-88.

STEFANESCU, C., BALASESCU, M. and SEVERIN, V. (1961), *Avicultura, II*, Bucharest.

STEINBACHER, J. (1931), 'Eumelanin und Phäomelanin in der Vögelfeder', *Ornithol. Monatsber.*, 39, pp. 2-10.

(1954), 'Eine Zwillingsfeder', *Natur. Volk*, 84, pp. 301-5.

(1955), 'Über die Schwanzmauser der Eulen (Strigidae) und

Nachtschwalben (Carnimulgidae)', *Senckenbergiana Biol.*, **36**, 3-4, pp. 235-40.

STRESEMANN, E. (1927), 'Aves', in *Kükental-Krumbachs Handbuch der Zoologie*, **7**, part 2.

   (1940), 'Zeitpunkt und Verlauf der Mauser bei einigen Entenarten', *J. Ornithol.*, **88**, 3, pp. 288-333.

STRESEMANN, E. and STRESEMANN, V. (1960), 'Die handschwingen-mauser der Tagraubvögel', *J. Ornithol.*, **101**, 4, pp. 373-403.

STRESEMANN, V. (1948), 'Eclipse plumage and nuptial plumage in the old squaw, or long-tailed duck', *Avicult. Mag., London*, **54**, pp. 188-94.

   (1958), 'Sind die Falconidae ihrer Mauserweise nach eine einheitliche gruppe?', *J. Ornithol.*, **99**, 1, pp. 81-8.

   (1959), 'The wing moult and systematic position of the genus *Gampsonyx*', *Auk*, **76**, 3, pp. 269-80.

STRONG, R. M. (1902 a), 'The development of colour in the definite feather', *Bull. Museum Comp. Zool.*, **40**, 3, pp. 147-85.

   (1902 b), 'A case of abnormal plumage', *Biol. Bull. Woods Hole*, **3**, pp. 289-94.

   (1915), 'Further observations of the origin of melanin pigments', *Anat. Record*, **9**, 1, pp. 52-3.

   (1917), 'Some observations on the origin of melanin pigment in the feather germ from the Plymouth Rock and Brown Leghorn fowl', *Anat. Record*, **13**, 2, pp. 97-108.

STUDER, T. (1873), 'Die Entwicklung der Federn', *Inang. Diss. Philos. Fakult. Bern*, **29**.

   (1878), 'Beiträge zur Entwicklungsgeschichte der Feder', *Z. Wiss. Zool.*, **30**, 4, pp. 421-36.

SULMAN, F. and PEREL, M. (1947), Influence of thiouracil on the basal metabolic rate and on moulting in hens', *Endocrinology*, **41**, 6, pp. 514-17.

SUPPLEE, W. C., COMBS, G. F. and BLAMBERG, D. L. (1958), 'Zinc and potassium effects on bone formation, feathering and growth of poults', *Poultry Sci.*, **37**, 1, pp. 63-67.

SUTTER, E. (1956), 'Zur Flügel- und Schwanzmauser des Turm-falken (*Falco tinnunculus*)', *Ornitol. Beobacht.*, **53**, 3, pp. 172-83.

SUTTON, G. M. (1948), 'The juvenile plumage of the eastern warbling vireo (*Vireo gilvus gilvus*)', *Occasion. Pap. Museum Zool. Univ. Michigan*, **511**, pp. 1-5.

SWANK, W. G. (1955), 'Feather moult as an ageing technique for mourning doves', *J. Wildlife Manag.*, **19**, 3, pp. 412-14.

TAKEWAKI, K. and MORI, H. (1944), 'Mechanism of moulting in

the canary', *J. Fac. Sci. Univ. Tokyo, Sect. IV*, 6, pp. 547-75.

TALLENT, V. K. (1931), 'Eclipse plumage in the mallard', *Nature*, 128, pp. 672-3.

TANABE, Y., HIMENO, K. and NOZAKI, H. (1957), 'Thyroid and ovarian function in relation to moulting in the hen', *Endocrinology*, 61, 6, pp. 661-6.

TONUTTI, E. (1956), 'Hormone und örtliche Reizbeantwortung', *Verhandl. Deut. Ges. Inn. Med.*, 62, pp. 177-92, Kongress.

TORREY, H. B. and HORNING, B. (1922), 'Hen-feathering induced in the male fowl by feeding thyroid', *Proc. Soc. Exptl. Biol. Med.*, 19, pp. 275-9.

(1925 a), 'The effect of thyroid feeding on the moulting process and feather structure of the domestic fowl', *Biol. Bull.*, 49, 3, pp. 275-87.

(1925 b), 'Thyroid feeding and secondary sex characters in Rhode Island Red chicks', *Biol. Bull., Woods Hole*, 49, 4, pp. 365-74.

TRINKAUS, J. P. (1948), 'Factors concerned in the response of melanoblasts to estrogen in the Brown Leghorn', *J. Exptl. Zool.*, 109, 2, pp. 135-70.

(1950), 'The role of thyroid hormone in melanoblast differentiation in the Brown Leghorn', *J. Exptl. Zool.*, 113, 2, pp. 149-77.

(1952), 'The embryonic character of the melanoblast', *Anat. Record*, 112, 2, Suppl., pp. 398-9.

(1953) 'Estrogen, thyroid hormone and the differentiation of pigment cells in the Brown Leghorn', in *Pigment-Cell Growth*, pp. 73-89, Acad. Press, N. Y.

TUCKER, B. W. (1949), 'Remarks on a seasonal colour change in the bill and legs of herons', *Brit. Birds, London*, 42, 1, pp. 46-50.

VAN DER MEUHLEN, J. B. (1939), 'Hormonal regulation of moult and ovulation', *Proc. World's Poultry Congr. Exposition, 7th*, pp. 109-12.

VAN OORDT, G. J. and DÄMSTE, P. (1939), 'Experimental modification of the sexual cycle and moult of the greenfinch', *Acta Brevia Neerl.*, 9, 5, pp. 140-43.

VAN OORDT, G. J. and JUNGE, G. C. A. (1936), 'Die hormonale wirkung der gonaden auf Sommer-und Frachtkleid', *Arch. Entwicklungsmech.*, 131, 1, pp. 112-21.

VAUGIEN, L. (1948), 'Sur le cycle saisonnier des gonades chez les oiseaux passeriformes', *Compt. Rend. Acad. Sci.*, 226, pp. 353-4.

VELLKY, I. (1960), 'Acid hydrolysate prepared from feathers in the nitrition of ducts', *Vet. Casopis*, 9, pp. 560-66.

VERHEYEN, R. (1956 a), 'Note sur la mue alaire et caudale chez les engoulevents (Caprimulgidae)', *Gerfaut*, 46, 1, pp. 35-40.

(1956 b), 'La mue de la queue chez les hiboux et les chouettes (Striges)', *ibid.*, 2, pp. 121-5.

(1958), 'A propos de la mue des remiges primaires', *ibid.*, 48, 2, pp. 101-14.

VERNON, W. M. (1926), 'Effect of moult on egg production', *Ann. Rep. Agr. Exptl. Stat. Iowa*, 10, pp. 25-6.

VERVERS, H. G. (1954), 'The experimental analysis of feather pattern in the Amherst Pheasant, *Chrysolophus amherstiae*', *Trans. Zool. Soc. London*, 28, pp. 304-48.

VILTER, V. (1935), 'La formation de la plume et son méchanisme histologique', *Bull. Assoc. Anat.*, Nancy, 36-37, pp. 1-93.

VOHRA, P. and KRATZER, F. H. (1959), 'The effect of phenylalanine deficiency on the growth and feather pigmentation of turkey poults', *Poultry Sci.*, 38, 4, pp. 902-6.

VÖLKER, O. (1937), 'Über fluoreszierende, gelbe Federpigmente bei Papageien, eine Klasse von Federfarbstoffen', *J. Ornithol.*, 85, 2, pp. 136-46.

(1938), 'Porphyrin in Vögelfedern', *J. Ornithol.*, 86, 4, pp. 436-56.

(1940), 'Zur Frage der gelben Feder-Fluoreszenzen', *Ornithol. Monatsber.*, 48, 2, pp. 182-5.

(1944), 'Die Abhängigkeit der Lipochrombildung bei Vögeln von pflanzlichen Carotinoiden', *J. Ornithol.*, 83, 5, pp. 439-50.

(1951 a), 'Die Isolierung eines gelben une eines roten Lipochroms aus Vogelfedern', *J. Ornithol.*, 93, 1, pp. 20-26.

(1951 b), 'Die Identifizierung eines roten Lipochroms aus Vogelfedern', *Verhandl. Deut. Zool. Ges.*, 50, pp. 142-5.

(1957), 'Die experimentelle Rotfärbung des Gefieders beim Fichtenkreuzschnabel' (*Loxia curvirostra*)', *J. Ornithol.*, 98, 2, pp. 210-14.

WAGNER, H. O. (1955), 'The moult of humming-birds', *Auk*, 72, 4, pp. 286-91.

(1957), 'The moulting periods of Mexican humming-birds', *ibid.*, 74, 2, pp. 251-7.

WANG, H. (1941), 'The role of ectoderm and mesoderm in the determination of the characters of regenerating feathers in fowl', *Anat. Record*, 81, 4, pp. 40-1.

(1943), 'The morphogenetic functions of the epidermal and dermal components of the papilla in feather regeneration', *Physiol. Zool.*, 16, 3, pp. 325-50.

(1948), 'Modulation of tract specificity by estrogenic hormone in experimentally produced feather-chimaere of Brown Leghorn capons', *J. Exptl. Zool.*, **109**, 4, pp. 451-501.

WATTERSON, R. L. (1938), 'On the production of feather colour pattern by mesodermal grafts between Barred Plymouth Rock and White Leghorn chick embryos', *Anat. Record*, **70**, 4, Suppl. 2, pp. 100-1.

—— (1941), 'The development history of melanophores in wing skin and feather germs of the Barred Plymouth Rock embryo', *ibid.*, **79**, Suppl. 2, pp. 61-62.

—— (1959), 'Endocrines in development ontogeny of selected hormone-dependent receptors of feather papillae and pigment cells', in *Endocrines in Development*, pp. 84-91, Univ. Chicago Press.

WEBBE, R. (1958), 'Brent geese *Branta bernicla* L. in Denmark and the colour problem', *Dansk. Ornithol. Foren. Tuddsskr.*, **52**, 1, pp. 41-7.

WELTER, W. A. (1936), 'Feather arrangement development and moult of the long-billed marsh wren', *Wilson Bull.*, **48**, 3, pp. 256-69.

WEIDENREICH, F. (1912), 'Die Lokalization des Pigmentes und ihre Bedeutung in Ontogenie und Phylogenie der wirbeltierre', *Z. Morphol. Anthropol., Sonderheft*, **2**, 1, pp. 59-140.

WERTH, I. (1954), 'The moulting of primaries by the common curlew (*Numenius a. arquata*)', *Naturalist*, **851**, pp. 151-2.

WESTERSKOV, K. (1955), 'Notes on the post-juvenile moult and first winter plumage in the pheasant', *Brit. Birds*, **48**, 7, pp. 308-11.

WETHERBEE, O. P. (1951), 'Moult of remiges and retrices in immature song sparrows', *Bird-Band.*, **22**, 1, pp. 82-3.

—— (1957), 'Natal plumages and downy pteryloses of passerine birds of North America', *Bull. Am. Museum Nat. Hist.*, **113**, 5, pp. 345-436.

WETMORE, A. (1936), 'The number of contour feathers in passeriform and related birds', *Auk*, **53**, 3, pp. 159-69.

WILLIAMSON, F. S. L. (1956), 'The moult and testis cycles of the anna humming-bird', *Condor*, **58**, 5, pp. 342-66.

WILLIAMSON, K. (1957 a), 'Post-breeding moult of crossbills', *Scot. Naturalist*, **69**, 3, pp. 190-2.

—— (1957 b), 'The annual post-nuptial moult in the wheatear (*Oennanthe oennanthe*)', *Bird-Band.*, **28**, 3, pp. 129-35.

WILLIER, B. H. (1941), 'An analysis of feather colour pattern produced by grafting melanophores during embryonic development', *Am. Naturalist*, **75**, 2, pp. 136-46.

(1942), 'Hormonal control of embryonic differentiation in birds', *Cold Spring Harbor Symp. Quant. Biol.*, 10, pp. 135-44.

(1948), 'Hormonal regulation of feather pigmentation in the fowl', *Spec. Publ. N. Y. Acad. Sci.*, 4, pp. 321-40.

(1950), 'Specialization in the response of pigment cells to sex hormones as exemplified in the fowl', *Arch. Anat. Microscop. Morphol. Exptl.*, 39, 3, pp. 451-66.

(1952), 'Cells, feathers and colours', *Bios*, 23, 2, pp. 109-25.

(1953), 'Basic mechanisms in the differentiation of pigment cells', *J. Embryol. Exptl. Morphol.*, 1, 2, pp. 297-9.

WILLIER, B. H. and RAWLES, M. E. (1938 a), 'Factors controlling feather development of skin grafts made between chick embryos of different breeds', *Anat. Record*, 70, 3, pp. 81-2.

(1938 b), 'Skin transplants between embryos of different breeds of fowl', *Biol Bull., Woods Hole*, 75, pp. 340-1.

(1938 c), 'Feather characterization as studied in host-graft combinations between chick embryos of different breeds', *Proc. Nat. Acad. Sci., Wash.*, 24, 4, pp. 446-52.

(1940), 'The control of feather colour pattern by melanophores grafted from one embryo to another of a different breed of fowl', *Physiol. Zool.*, 13, 2, pp. 177-201.

(1944), 'Melanophores control of the sexual dimorphism of feather pigmentation pattern in the barred Plymouth Rock fowl', *Yale J. Biol. Med.*, 17, 2, pp. 319-40.

WILLIER, B. H., RAWLES, M. E. and HADORN, E. (1937), 'Skin transplants between embryos of different breeds of fowl', *Proc. Nat. Acad. Sci. Wash.*, 23, 4, pp. 542-6.

WILSON, A. C. and FARNER, D. S. (1960), 'The annual cycle of thyroid activity in white-crowned sparrows of eastern Washington', *Condor*, 62, 6, pp. 414-25.

WING, L. W. (1952), 'Number of contour feathers on a cowbird, *Molothrusater*', *Auk*, 69, 1, pp. 90-1.

WITSCHI, E. (1936), 'Effect of gonadotropic and estrogenic hormones on regenerating feathers of weaver finches (*Pyromelana franciscana*)', *Proc. Soc. Exptl. Biol. Med.*, 35, 2, pp. 287-96.

WITSCHI, E. and WOODS, R. P. (1936), 'The bill of the sparrow as an indicator for the male sex hormone', *J. Exptl. Zool.*, 78, 3, pp. 445-55.

WOLFSON, A. (1941), 'Light versus activity in the regulation of the sexual cycles of birds: the role of the hypothalmus', *Condor*, 43, 2, pp. 125-36.

(1952), 'Day-length, migration and breeding cycles in birds', *Sci. Monthly*, 74, pp. 191-200.

(1954), 'Production of repeated gonadal, fat and moult cycles within one year in the junco and white-crowned sparrow by manipulation of day length', *J. Exptl. Zool.*, 125, 2, pp. 353-76.

(1959), 'Role of light and darkness in regulation of refractory period in gonadal and fat cycles of migratory birds', *Physiol. Zool.*, 32, 3, pp. 160-76.

WOODIN, A. M. (1956), 'Structure and composition of soluble feather keratin', *Biochem. J.*, 63, 4, pp. 576-81.

INDEX

Adenohypophysis, 235–44
aftershaft, 6
aft-sails, 40
albino, 37
anlage, 5, 9, 11, 55, 61–4

Barbs, 6
barrel, 5
bird of paradise, 34
birds of prey, 47, 49
blastema, 9
brown leghorn, 128, 176, 219, 224, 226

Calamus, 5
carotenoids, 28
cassowary, 6
castration, 218, 223, 230, 244, 272
chaffinch, 178
chimera, 61
coccygeal gland, 8
colibri, 34
contour feather, 5, 178
cormorant, 107, 108, 110, 131, 140–148, 173
cornification, 2
cortical layer, 6
corvid, 93, 107
coverts, 41
crossbill, 178
crow, 107
cuckoo, 49
cuticula, 6

Definitive feather, 5
    plumage, 111–19, 161–77, 195–8
development, of feather, 10–21, 57–61, 66–73, 74–90, 213, 219–27, 252, 270
    of plumage, 46, 88, 98–116, 203–205, 259

differentiation, 66–74
down, 5, 7
duck, 11, 48, 51, 94, 95, 128, 131, 135–40, 178, 187–8, 216, 222, 231, 245, 260, 266
dungan (fowl), 21, 135

Egg-production, 229, 261, 262
emphysema, 134

Fasianoverdin, 28
feather, anlage, 5, 9, 11, 55, 61–4
    contour, 5, 178
    development, 10–21, 57–61, 66–73, 74–90, 213, 219–27, 252
    differentiation, 66–74
    down, 5, 7
    follicle, 9, 64–5, 88, 98
    growth, 45, 54, 57–61, 66–73, 74–90, 111, 119, 174, 205, 221–3
    helm, 41
    microscopic structure, 5
    papilla, 9
    pattern, 32, 34, 178, 198, 213, 219–26
    permanent (definitive), 5
    primary, 2, 40
    sheath, 10
    structure, 5, 178, 198, 219–27, 237–44
filoplumae, 5, 8
fledgling, 37
follicle, 9, 64–5, 88, 98
fowl, 42, 50, 94, 107, 115, 128, 133, 134, 178, 181, 187, 208, 222, 224, 229, 237, 240–43, 255, 260, 266–8

Gallinaceous birds, 49, 208, 216
gonadial hormone, 216–27, 266
guineafowl, 131, 208